MC

KU-211-771

WARHORSE

Warhorse

Cavalry in Ancient Warfare

Philip Sidnell

hambledon
continuum

Hambledon Continuum is an imprint of Continuum Books

Continuum UK
The Tower Building
11 York Road
London, SE1 7NX

Continuum US
80 Maiden Lane
Suite 704
New York, NY 10038

www.continuumbooks.com

First published 2006

British Library Cataloguing-in-Publication Data
A catalogue record for this book is available from the British Library.

ISBN 1 85285 374 3

Typeset by Carnegie Publishing, Lancaster.
Printed and bound by MPG Books, Bodmin, Cornwall

Contents

To my wonderful wife, Kerry, and adored son, Alexander:
'Nothing else matters'.

Acknowledgements

I should start by thanking Tony Morris and Martin Sheppard of Hambledon for taking a chance on a first time author and for always swallowing my promises of imminent delivery with a suitably large pinch of salt. Good luck Martin in your next venture. Latterly, Ben Hayes of Continuum was an absolute trooper and, with Anya Wilson, did a great job of pulling it all together in the closing stages.

For sharing their professional historical opinions on various points I am grateful to Jim Bradbury, Peter Connolly, Adrian Goldsworthy, and Ann Hyland and, for sharing their practical experience, Heath Pye, Roger Chalk and Faris.

Special gratitude is also due to James Opie of Book Club Associates for encouraging his new assistant, as I then was, to do more than just talk about his ideas for a book, and for introducing me to a suitable publisher. Other colleagues deserve thanks for their support, but in line for special praise are former BCAers J.P. Hunting and Andrew McClellan, for constructive criticism, and Abigail Mitchell for the generous loan of her laptop computer, which allowed me to make productive use of my daily commute. Thanks too to Clive 'Sten gun' Burroughs, my train buddy, who provided a valuable mobile IT service for the aforementioned laptop, and to David Constant of Constant Designs who developed the initial concept for the jacket.

A deeper level of gratitude is owed to my late father for igniting, in the few short years I knew him, a lasting interest in military history. My first castle and reenacting the Battle of Cynoscephelae on the hearth with my toy soldiers will always be among my most cherished memories. My mother and all my family have been encouraging but my sisters Cathy and Lucy and my nieces Maria and Chloe have been particularly helpful with equestrian aspects, as have their horses, Midnight Express, Merlin, Finn and Arthur.

Among my friends, Nick and Ed have cheerfully put up with more of my cavalry-related monologues than most and provided a useful and knowledgeable sounding board for various ideas. Richard Raycraft has been a bigger influence than he realises, for it was he that rekindled my interest in military history when it was in danger of waning in my teenage years. Professor Philip Sabin and Doctor Jan Willem Honig honed it to a new level of intensity with some wonderfully enjoyable lectures in the War Studies Department of King's College London. They also guided me through the dissertation that proved the genesis of this book.

Last, but by no means least, special thanks must go to my wife and soulmate, Kerry, for patience above and beyond the call of marriage, and to my son Alexander.

Introduction

What situation in military history could match a cavalry charge for sheer drama? From an early stage in the recorded history of human conflict, the thunder of approaching hooves struck fear into the hearts of the men who stood, or, very often, failed to stand in their path. Cavalry often proved decisive in ancient battles, yet most books on ancient warfare concentrate overwhelmingly on the infantry. This book aims to go some way to redressing the balance.

The historian Polybius, writing in the second century BC, concluded from his study of events in the previous century that it was better to enter battle with twice as much cavalry as the enemy and only half as much infantry than it was to be equal in both. Yet modern writers have often dismissed their role in battle as an irrelevance, even suggesting they served little purpose other than to display the wealth of horse-owning aristocrats. Although this function was indeed important, it is the argument of this book that they were used because they were the key to victory. The greatest generals of the ancient world such as Julius Caesar, Hannibal and, above all, Alexander would not have won their most famous victories without a proper appreciation of the battle-winning potential of cavalry.

The focus is deliberately on the shock or heavy cavalry role, since this is the most controversial and lies at the heart of the misconception that cavalry were of severely limited value on the battlefields of the period, particularly in contrast to the medieval period. It is virtually impossible to read a book on ancient warfare without finding some mention of the stirrup, which was not introduced until after the generally accepted close of that period. This is due to a widely held belief, popularized in the 1960s, that the stirrup made mounted shock combat viable for the first time. Even many of those who note the most obvious contrary classical examples, such as Alexander's cavalry, feel obliged to warn against exaggerating their effectiveness in light of their lack of stirrups. Ready acceptance of this view has allowed a general picture to emerge of the ancient horseman being limited to ancillary roles. In this view, they might undertake important scouting missions or harassing raids on campaign, but once battle was joined, they were relegated to carrying messages and, at best, to some relatively ineffectual skirmishing while the infantry did the real fighting. This book argues that there is plenty of clear evidence in ancient sources that this is simply not true. Effective, decisive, shock combat was not an invention of the Middle Ages.

Warhorse does not claim to be a comprehensive survey of all cavalry in all places across the period covered. It deals predominantly with the Greek (including Macedonian) and Roman worlds, although the many peoples they fought against are also considered. This bias is shared with most books on ancient warfare. This was largely dictated by the availability of sources but in any case it serves to show that it is not necessary to seek out the hitherto unknown chronicle of some obscure and forgotten tribe to find examples of the potent potential of cavalry being realized on ancient battlefields. It is precisely the fact that the classical world is so well trodden by historians that makes it such a travesty that full praise of its horsemen has remained unsung.

This book is based, overwhelmingly and deliberately, upon those ancient sources for which translations are readily available. All authors build on and are influenced by the work of others. Rather than rely on a synthesis of modern works, however, my main aim has been to go back to the relevant ancient sources, albeit in translation, and present the evidence that I found there in a manner which is accessible and enjoyable not only to classicists but to the general reader. My interpretations of some ancient battles may be at odds with those of other authors, but I hope it will be clear that they are based firmly on the contemporary evidence viewed without a preconception about the limitations of ancient horsemen.

It was originally intended to carry the story right through the medieval period, to take in the apogee of the knight in shining armour, which is such a familiar figure in popular imagination. Had space allowed it, this would have had the advantage of allowing greater comparison and contrast to be drawn between the two periods. Instead it ends with the battle of Hastings. The choice of 1066 was not entirely arbitrary. Apart from providing a dramatic finale, the Battle of Hastings has been presented by more than one author as proof of a supposed tactical revolution that had recently rendered heavy cavalry, Norman knights in this case, capable of winning a decisive victory through shock action. By the time you read my interpretation of the battle the preceding chapters will, hopefully, have persuaded you that nothing happened at Hastings that would have surprised a general of a millennium or more earlier.

Even if one includes the accounts of Afghan Northern Alliance fighters charging Taliban positions on horseback in the early twenty-first century, the history of cavalry since Hastings is less than one thousand years. The period covered in this book is twice as long. The greater part of the story of cavalry, glorious and tragic in equal measure, but always exciting, has too often been unnecessarily neglected.

Most of all I have tried to write the kind of book I would enjoy reading. The subject combines my two enduring passions: military history and horses. The raw appeal inherent in the subject of warriors charging into battle on horseback, swords and lances in hand, is sufficient justification for writing this book. If the reader finds in it half the interest and enjoyment the subject has given me, then it has succeeded in its main aim.

1

Origins

The horse in its natural state is not particularly warlike and tends to avoid danger where it can, but to the people of the Near and Middle East, which to the authors of the Bible was virtually the whole known world, the horse came to be almost purpose-built for war. Indeed, the earliest surviving representations of domesticated horses show them being used to pull chariots in the armies of the great biblical civilizations: Babylon, Egypt, Assyria and the Hittites. While this is the usual place to start any history of the horse in warfare, the peoples of the region were aware that the horse came from elsewhere. Many centuries later the travelling Greek writer, Herodotus, recorded an echo of this folk memory, relating how the prophetic importance of a strange event in the old Hittite lands of Lycia, now part of Turkey, turned on the fact that 'horses were beasts of war and not native to the country'.[1]

In the late 1960s archaeologists, excavating villages of the so-called Sredni Stog Culture in southern Ukraine, found numerous remains of horses. Examination of the bones and analysis of the age at death suggested that these horses had been used for their meat, either hunted in the wild or herded, and would have provided about 50 per cent of the inhabitants' meat intake. One, however, was different. The skull and some other bones of a stallion (stallions are distinguished by developed 'canine' teeth) were found in what appeared to be a ritual burial at the village of Dereivka. Not only did the teeth show the distinctive marks of wear from a bit, but curved pieces of antler which could be interpreted as the cheek-pieces of a bit were found with it. Replicas of these, tested with a rawhide mouthpiece, proved perfectly functional.[2] This is the earliest unequivocal evidence of a domesticated horse and it is dated, as securely as such things can be, to around 4000 BC.

It had long been assumed, on the basis of the copious archaeological evidence from the Fertile Crescent, that horses were first used militarily for pulling chariots rather than riding; this was said to be because they were then too small and weak to be ridden. The Dereivka stallion, however, was champing at his bit half a millennium earlier than the oldest known wheel. Clearly, horses were ridden before they were used to pull chariots. What is more, the ritualistic nature of the Dereivka burial suggested to archaeologists that the horse had already risen to a position of high status beyond that of a mere working animal.[3] The horse's military potential may already have been being exploited in raids on neighbouring tribes.

The Dereivka finds indicated that the vast majority of the horses would have fallen in the range of 12.2 to 14 hands high, while the Dereivka stallion was approximately 14.1hh.[4] This range matches that of such modern breeds as the New Forest, Fell, Icelandic and Fjord, all of which are popular riding animals. This may be a good point at which to clarify something about horses and ponies and size.

There is a lot of confusion about the difference between horses and ponies; even horse owners sometimes state with absolute confidence that they have a different number of ribs and vertebrae. This is not so, as they are one and the same species, *equus caballus*. Certain breeds of horses are, however, designated as ponies, so all ponies are horses but not all horses are ponies. The criterion is not just size, but the relative lengths of back to legs, ponies being relatively shorter in the legs. It is not, as is widely believed, just a question of height. The tiny Falabella, averaging only 7.2 hands high, is a miniature horse, not a pony.

Modern readers, used to seeing long-legged Thoroughbreds performing at the races, and raised on the image of monstrous medieval chargers, may have trouble imagining how these much smaller animals could be of military use. Speed may be largely a function of leg length but weight-carrying ability does not correspond proportionately with height. Likewise, toughness and endurance, also vital requirements in a war horse, bear no relation to size whatsoever. Consider the following extracts from a work published in 1900 by Sir Walter Galbey advocating the use of *smaller* horses for the British cavalry:

> Granting that the saying, 'a good big horse is better than a good little one', is in the main correct, we have to consider that the merits which go to make a useful horse for campaigning are infinitely more common in small horses than big ones.
>
> All the experiences of campaigners, explorers and travellers goes to prove that small compact animals between 13.2 and 14.2 hands high are those on which reliance can be placed for hard and continuous work on scant and innutritious food.[5]

To support this view, Sir Walter goes on to quote the experiences of the traveller Captain Burnaby, whose locally purchased Kirghiz pony 'about 14 hands in height was as fresh as possible after his march of seventeen miles. In spite of the weight on his back – quite twenty stone – he had never shown the least sign of fatigue'.[6] And this was in the particularly bad Central Asian winter of 1876/77. Another example cited is the more telling because it involves a large group of similar animals. In 1870, 210 horses made a forced march in 'Russian Tartary' in temperatures of up to 117° Fahrenheit, covering 266 miles in six days. At the finish only twelve were reported 'sick' and all of these were cases with sore backs caused by ill-fitting saddles. Of course none of this proves that the Dereivka horse was equally useful as a mount, but it demonstrates that there is no reason why it should not have been.[7]

The evidence of Dereivka makes it clear that the origins of the domesticated horse are to be found out on the Eurasian steppe. The domestication of the horse allowed the people of Dereivka and there-abouts to range deeper into the steppe in search of game, or to avoid enemies, and gave them a great advantage in mobility over rival tribes. In time it completely transformed life in this region and certain tribes developed a highly specialised semi-nomadic lifestyle that was almost completely dependent upon the horse. It is likely that such tribes developed the techniques of mounted warfare from an early stage.

Unfortunately, archaeological evidence in the steppe region is scarce for this early period and, as these early horse tamers left no literature of their own, we cannot pick up their story until they appear in writings of much later peoples. The earliest people from around this area to be known to us by name are the Cimmerians, who were driven out of their homeland by their northern neighbours the Scythians in the early seventh century BC. The Cimmerians, and the Scythians even more, who made their appearance as fierce mounted warriors, are widely believed to have been the inspiration for the mythical centaurs, half man and half horse. The study of cavalry should really start with these riders, but by the time they appear in the historical record others had already developed cavalry via the chariot and left written and pictorial evidence to prove it.

Although the new skills of horse domestication may have spread rapidly across the steppe, it was many centuries before they reached the farming and urban societies to the south. The earliest remains from the Mesopotamian cities date from around 2000 BC or a little later.[8] There are a few remains from Anatolia that have been dated to 3000 BC, but these may represent a first attempt at introduction there that failed.[9] They may even be evidence of an armed incursion from the steppe. They do not reappear in the archaeological record in Anatolia until around 2000 BC. In any case, by the early centuries of the second millennium BC the horse was established in Mesopotamia, Syria and Palestine.

These horses must have arrived via the Caucasus Mountains and Armenia, which accounts for the Babylonians knowing the horse as the 'ass of the mountains', despite its steppe origins. According to genetic analysis, all modern domestic horses are almost certainly descended from the very first domestic herd – if not that of Dereivka, then very probably one not far removed from it in space or time.[10] Domesticated horses must have been exported by whatever means, either by trade, theft or conquest, and all later herds bred from these. Once it was thought that domestication of wild horses was achieved in more than one place, and for centuries equestrian experts attempted to trace the various modern breeds from distinct prehistoric ancestors. The effort put into explaining equestrian diversity by assuming at least four types of primeval horse – a hot-blooded desert horse to spawn the Arab, a heavily built forest dweller siring the 'cold-blooded' breeds of northern Europe, and others – seems to have been wasted.[11] Genetic science has also finally laid to rest the once common belief that Przewalski's horse represents the natural unaltered state of the horse as it appeared before domestication, revealing it instead as a distinct species.

All the evidence suggests that, south of the Caucasus, horses were used almost exclusively to pull vehicles rather than being ridden. The conventional reason for this, that the horses were too puny to be ridden, can no longer be accepted as we now know they were being ridden out on the steppe. Was the chariot seen as a superior weapon system to horse and rider? If so, it is hard to see why chariotry was eventually abandoned in favour of true cavalry. Those chariots that lingered into the period covered by narrative histories performed consistently badly against, or alongside, cavalry. The answer may well have more to do with the fact that learning to ride is a difficult, time-consuming and often painful process. It is not infrequently fatal. Modern tutors can draw on thousands of years of accumulated experience, not proceeding completely by trial and error. An analogy can be drawn with the adoption of the earliest firearms. These were inferior in almost every respect to the longbow they replaced, but anyone could use one with minimal instruction, whereas the longbow had to be practised daily from childhood for its potential to be realized.

The first individuals in the Middle East to buy or capture horses may have tried to imitate the riding skills of the northern steppe dwellers, probably with predictable results in terms of broken bones. Unlike the first riders at Dereivka, these southerners had long since been using wheeled carts pulled by oxen and asses, and had even used heavy ass-drawn wagons in battle. It is not difficult to see how the idea of modifying the cart for use by the horse was seized upon as a less painful course of action. Had the people of Dereivka had this option when they first domesticated the horse, they too might have gone down this technological route, although they would have found driving less useful than riding for their everyday hunting and herding.

The horse nomads of the steppe had perfected their riding skills over centuries through constant use. Driving horses harnessed to a cart or chariot, while far from being easy or danger free, takes less time to learn and is far less likely to result in serious injury. A rider has to coordinate both hand and subtle leg instructions, or 'aids', to the horse while also keeping his balance as the horse moves under him; the charioteer had only to deal with his hands and balancing must have been much simpler. Compared to a rider without stirrups, a chariot driver with his weight firmly planted on his feet can exert much more pull on the reins to execute an emergency stop, if he finds his horses are running away with him; and if that fails he can bail out with less distance to fall. Also, only one of the chariot's crew (most commonly two men, but sometimes more) had to learn to control the horses, and he could concentrate on that alone, while his passenger or passengers gave their full attention to using their weapons. A rider of course had to manage the horse and his weapons simultaneously.

The chariot seems to have been developed in areas where the horse arrived after the wheel, and where the pattern of agriculture and economy meant that using horses was not all that their daily lives required of the inhabitants, which was almost true of the horse nomads. Logic suggests that the chariot was adopted first on the marginal farmlands between the steppe and the densely settled river valleys of the Middle East, where contact with both cultures gave access to the wheel and to the nomads' horses. The area south of the passes through the Caucasus Mountains is the likely site. Chariot-owning peoples then used their new weapon to expand into the areas occupied by the established urban cultures: the Hurrians, for example, moved westwards into Anatolia to establish themselves over the Hittites; and into Syria, further south, to establish the kingdom known as Mitanni. Where they did not conquer, they posed enough of a threat that existing states were forced to adopt the new technology. There is now evidence to suggest that the horse had been introduced into Egypt before the subjugation of that country by the chariot-driving Hyksos, which was complete by around 1700 BC.[12] The horse-drawn chariot had by then become the dominant character-istic of warfare everywhere between the Sahara and the steppe, as it was for the next thousand years.[13]

Use of the chariot also spread around the Aegean coast to Greece, where the culture of the Mycenaean period was heavily influenced by the Middle Eastern states, and throughout Celtic western Europe as far as the British Isles. Britain was one of the last strongholds of the chariot, Julius Caesar encountering them during his invasions in 55 and 54 BC.

In each of these societies chariot warriors became an elite who could devote much of their time to hunting or training for war. Horses were relatively rare and very expensive, as was the chariot and other equip-ment associated with them, so ownership of them became both a sign and a privilege of nobility. In many of these great early civilizations, including Egypt, Babylon, Assyria and Mycenaean Greece, the state intervened and provided the necessary resources and effort required to build and maintain large chariot forces. At the battle of Kadesh in 1294 BC, the Hittites may have fielded as many as two and a half thousand chariots against the Egyptians' two thousand.

Horses were traded on a large scale and studs set up. The production of chariots, weapons and armour also became a major industry. High-ranking officials were appointed to administer the king's stables and ensure the supply of chariots and horses. Surviving letters from kings and pharaohs to one another often include requests or demands for horses. Around 1345 BC, Kikkuli wrote the oldest surviving manual on the training of horses; although from Mittani, he was in the employ of the Hittite king Suppiluliumas I. His tough training regime demanded a high standard of stamina and culminated in fast drives in excess of fifty miles. There is evidence of selective breeding of horses, which seems, to judge from various remains from Egypt and Anatolia, to have resulted in some increase in size. The most recent assessment of the evidence concludes that the horses of these and other regions were in the range of 14.1 to 15 hands.[14] The emergence of distinct regional breeds also began.

The many artefacts and pictorial representations show us in some detail how chariots were constructed and their crews equipped. Inscrip-tions have revealed much about the numbers involved, and the vast infrastructure required to support them, and a little about unit sizes.

Unfortunately, most inscriptions are administrative records or the propaganda of victory monuments and we lack good narrative accounts of battles that would allow us to examine closely the way they actually fought.

Just as the development of cavalry was later characterized by divergence into heavy and light types, so was chariot design. The light type, typified by Egyptian examples, was pulled by two horses, weighed under one hundred pounds and had a crew of two; the driver and an archer. This type was best used as a mobile missile platform, keeping its distance while showering the enemy with arrows. The heavier type was more solidly constructed and carried three or four men, the additional warriors being a combination of shield-bearers and spearmen. Hittite chariot crews appear to have been armed entirely with shields and spears from early on, which suggests these were expected to get in close to the enemy. Heavy chariot development culminated in the robustly built Assyrian vehicles drawn by four armoured horses and carrying a crew of four armoured men. The crew included at least one archer, but spears, shields and swords were also carried. The two types represent the same search for compromise between speed and mobility, on the one hand, and protection and close quarters fighting power, on the other, which later became a perennial feature of cavalry warfare.

It is easier to imagine the tactical role of the light archer chariot than of the heavier type. A very useful weapon system against an all-infantry army, it could simply be driven to within bowshot of the enemy, swarming around his flanks and rear if the terrain allowed enough room, and shooting at him. It is usually shown in action with the horses galloping, but against a slow-moving or stationary enemy it may well have stopped to allow accurate shooting. As the enemy tried to approach, the charioteer would drive away while the archer continued to fire. When they had opened up a safe distance again, he could pull up, allowing the archer to loose off a few more carefully aimed shots. Such chariots had to operate in a spaced-out line, or in small groups, so that there was enough room for each to turn and withdraw at speed without running foul of each other. The smallest tactical unit in Egyptian use was apparently of ten chariots, a handy size for rapid advances and retreats. A large force of chariots using skirmishing tactics could inflict morale-sapping casualties and sow disorder in the enemy ranks. There may even have been occasions when this alone was enough to make the frustrated opposing army withdraw or even collapse into panic-stricken flight.

At first sight, it is hard to imagine how a chariot force using only these tactics could be dealt with, and indeed armies based on ridden cavalry using similar tactics, including the Huns and Mongols, were later among the most feared armies in history. But such tactics had their limitations: conditions were rarely ideal and few enemies were passive. Skirmishing tactics required plenty of space and time to be effective; space to keep a safe distance and time for the mental and physical attrition of the casualties to become critical for the enemy. Against infantry in close order and equipped with good shields, even if they didn't have body armour, the rate of casualties inflicted would actually be quite slow, and if the infantry were well disciplined they were sometimes able to put up with it for hours on end. The safer the distance maintained by the chariots, the less effective their fire. If they ventured in close to make sure their shots took their toll, they risked being rushed by the enemy before they could turn to withdraw, as chariots need a lot more space to turn in than single horses. The faster they moved, the larger the turning circle; the slower the speed, the more vulnerable to being caught. If their opponents kept them on the move, skirmishing chariots were rendered less effective, forcing them repeatedly to fall back. This might eventually trap them against a river or rough ground where they could finally be attacked. Even if it didn't achieve this it would have rendered their fire less accurate and effective while their supply of arrows steadily depleted and their horses grew fatigued with constant advances and retreats.

The enemy might also include foot archers or slingers. If the chariot archers were to achieve anything at all they had to stay within missile range (slings were comparable to ancient bows in range and hitting power) where they and their horses would be vulnerable.[15] Although both crew and horses were sometimes armoured, and each chariot carried a greater supply of arrows than any one foot archer, the foot archers had the advantage of being able to aim with their feet planted firmly on the ground. Operating in closer formation than the chariots, they could return a much greater density of fire over a given area.

Finally, of course, the enemy might have chariots of their own. If so, light chariots would find themselves using up time, their arrows and their horses' energy in a stand-off with the opposing chariots. The infantry battle, in the meantime, might have been won or lost before anything had been achieved by the chariots. We can understand the need for a chariot force to be able to drive the enemy machines away quickly so they cannot direct their long-range fire onto our infantry, and so that the enemy infantry is in turn quickly exposed to this treatment. As a result, chariot forces developed that were trained and equipped to close rapidly with their opposite numbers to reach a rapid decision.* Here at last we come back to the question of chariot shock combat.

Rather than stand and waste time with long-range sniping, a chariot force could also try to rush the enemy and defeat them at close quarters. This was the fundamental attraction of mounted shock action, whether in chariots or on horseback: it offered the prospect of a quick decision and the ability to sweep an enemy off his chosen ground. Imagine the charioteers had advanced into bow range of the enemy and the onboard archers had started to loose off their first shots. If the enemy chariots came on fast and did not look like stopping, what were their choices? They could turn and flee, in which case they needed to make a decision quickly, unless they wanted to be overtaken while the drivers were still trying to turn the horses. Even if they did manage to run it was difficult, if not impossible, for the archers to keep up an effective fire behind them; and if the enemy pursued them at all closely they might never get the opportunity to stop and turn to fight again without once more risking being overwhelmed while turning or still disorganised. Moreover, they would have been driven off from whatever position in their army's array they had been holding, exposing the flank of their own infantry to attack. Alternatively, chariots could meet the enemy charge. If they had been skirmishing, they were probably more spread out (to allow turning space) than the enemy, who was already prepared to charge, so those meeting the main point of the enemy's attack would be outnumbered as well as less able to offer mutual support in the

---

* There is a parallel with the introduction of aircraft in the First World War. They were first employed to help defeat the enemy infantry by directing long-range artillery fire onto them. But airmen increasingly found themselves being obstructed in this role by enemy airmen, at first in an improvised way. Opposing aircraft would come across each other while performing their spotting or observation missions and attack each other with pistols and rifles, all the while using up time and fuel and without achieving their initial purpose. It soon became clear that the best way to stop the enemy spotters fulfilling their crucial role was to send up specialised aircraft to destroy them or drive them from the skies. This led to the development of machines designed primarily for the destruction of their own kind, being more robust and well-armed for a dogfight. Alongside the 'scouts' there were now 'fighter', 'hunter' or 'pursuit' squadrons. Likewise, back in the second millennium BC there must have been chariot 'dog fights'.

ensuing 'dog fight'. In the mêlée there were obvious advantages for the force that had the most men armed for close-in fighting; not that the bow was completely useless, but it is impossible to reload a bow while someone is stabbing at you with a spear.

The actual mechanics of what happened when chariots engaged in shock combat is more difficult to imagine than the skirmishing action. What actually happened when one line of chariots tried to charge at another, or at a unit of infantry? How could the warriors, even if spear-armed, actually get at each other with the length of the horses in front of them unless the enemy had already allowed the chariot to enter their ranks? How could the horses be made to ride into the mass of an opposing unit? Similar questions are fundamental to the story of heavy cavalry and are a recurring theme in what follows, where surviving accounts of riders in battle can help us answer them with some confidence.

Much of what applied to shock cavalry must have applied to chariots too. One of the fundamental assumptions that dominates any detailed discussion of horse-borne warfare is the simple fact that horses, being intelligent animals, cannot be made to run into a solid object. This observation has led many to conclude that the glorious charge that culminates in two bodies of steeds colliding at speed is nothing more than a product of artistic imagination and poetic licence. The pacific instincts of horses can, however, be overstated. Life in a hierarchical herd involves biting, kicking and barging other horses. If the situation demands it, hooves, and teeth to a lesser extent, can also be turned on predators with lethal effect, although flight is the preferred option. Domesticated horses can also be trained to do many things that go against every instinct, jumping through hoops of fire or even through hoops of opaque paper (the latter being more difficult). They can be made to push against objects to move them as police horses learn to do as part of their crowd control training. Still, it remains generally true that horses will not run nose first into things. So how could one line of chariots charge into another?

When such was attempted, one of three things must have happened. First, it is possible that the two sides stopped short, either because the horses baulked or the charioteer, equally naturally, quailed at the thought of the impending collision and reined them in. In this case any fighting in the centre of the line must have been done over two sets of intervening horses with bows and or javelins, or perhaps by some crewmen dismounting and fighting between the chariots, perhaps immobilising the enemy by cutting the enemy's traces.* This would have resulted in a stand-off along most of the opposing lines, while those on the ends attempted to outflank the enemy.

The second possibility requires us to realize that the advancing line of chariots did not constitute a single solid object. Even when closing ranks for a charge it is unlikely that a line of chariots advanced wheel to wheel, for to do so over anything less than a perfectly smooth surface would have resulted in collisions, maimed horses and overturned chariots. As the two groups of chariots came together, some chariots on each side would have found gaps in the enemy line into which to drive. It is even possible that both sides, because both sought to come to blows, adjusted by tacit mutual consent to allow the two lines to interpenetrate in this way. As they passed alongside each other, the chariot crews could then take a tilt at each other, rather as in jousting. We know this sort of thing happened between cavalry forces during the Napoleonic Wars as we have eyewitness accounts such as this one from an officer of the British 13th Light Dragoons at the battle of Campo Mayor in 1811:

> The crash was tremendous, both parties passed each other, and some short distance in the rear of the enemy, the 13th came about; the enemy did the same, and a second charge took place with equal violence, when the conflict became personal with the sabre.[16]

Another witness of the same incident said the dragoons 'rode through' the French 'again, and again a third time, when the enemy's cavalry went off in confusion'.[17]

If one force had bigger gaps in it than the other, perhaps because it was charged while in open order for skirmishing, it would be at a disadvantage. Quite apart from the psychological factors, more of them would find themselves attacked on both sides simultaneously if the enemy were able to pass through the gaps in twos or threes. Casualties to drivers or horses, or even the inclination to finish off an enemy hand to hand, might make some chariots stop alongside each other and engage in a mêlée on the line of meeting. Most of them probably kept moving and passed right through to the rear, before turning to

---

* Despite their obvious vulnerability in a static fight, it was probably rare for horses to be deliberately injured in close combat (rather than by indiscriminate showers of arrows). Such was their value that capture would be a much better option, besides which they are hard to kill quickly close up without the risk of being kicked or crushed by the dying horse.

come back for another pass. Here, the side that was fastest to turn and regroup for another rush would have had a big advantage. The third possible outcome, and this may well have been the most common result, was that one side turned and fled before any contact was made. This was most likely if one side was more spread out (each driver in the line of the enemy charge feeling more isolated and outnumbered), or if one side had fewer warriors or crews that were less well equipped for such close combat.

The psychological aspect becomes even more critical when contemplating how chariots might attack infantry formations. A densely packed group of infantry more closely approaches a solid object than an opposing line of chariots and is more daunting to charging horses, not to mention to charioteers – especially if they are carrying shields and spears. Unless the infantry had already begun to break formation, opening up paths for the chariots to drive into, it must have been very difficult for the chariots to press home a charge.

Of course the mental state of the infantry was also vital. It is hard now to imagine what it must have been like to face such a charge. The terrifying aspect and deafening noise of a line of chariots bearing down out of a cloud of dust must have been unnerving. A determined rush at the infantry might itself be sufficient to cause the footmen to panic and their formation to break up, as each man sought to get out of the way of the contraptions rumbling recklessly towards them. The terror projected by such an attack, and its chances of success, would be multiplied if it came from the flanks or rear. With enemy ranks already starting to fall apart even before contact was even made, chariots could more easily get in amongst them and bring their weapons to bear.

Chariots are often depicted careering victoriously over a layer of fallen foot soldiers and an Assyrian inscription describes the wheels of chariots 'bespattered with blood and filth'.[18] In reality, chariots would have had great trouble physically going over such obstacles at any sort of speed without risking flipping over, but the fact that they could wreak great slaughter among an infantry force whose nerve and discipline had failed need not be doubted. As was the case throughout the rest of the horse's military history, 'shock' combat should be thought of mainly as the psychological trauma of being ridden at by a mass of heavy animals, rather than the physical impact of colliding bodies or weapons.

Some chariot crews wore heavy and expensive armour. This typically consisted of a helmet and a coat of scale armour (called a *girpisu* and *sariam* respectively in Mitanni, and variants thereof in neighbouring states). Such armour was made up of many metal scales (bronze in this period), laced to each other and to a fabric backing so that they over-lapped like the scales of a snake. The most complete ones reached to mid calf and had elbow-length sleeves, contained a thousand scales and weighed over 24 kilograms; others reached only to the waist.[19]

In Mycenaean Greece, a different style of armour, made up of large shaped sheets of bronze, was used circa 1300 BC. A more or less com-plete specimen, known as the Dendra panoply, is an extreme example of a charioteer's armour and could not have been worn by anyone who had to ride or walk around much.

Heavy armour was generally a characteristic of shock cavalry that intended to close with the enemy, cavalry relying upon missile weap-ons tending to be more lightly armoured. Nevertheless, even the crews of light two-man chariots, where the only offensive weapon was the bow, are sometimes depicted wearing scale body armour. The reason behind this was that armour required a trade-off between balance and protection. For a charioteer, balance was not too much of a problem and so the more protection the better, being as helpful in warding off enemy arrows and sling stones as blows from hand weapons. By con-trast, for a horseman balance and ease of movement was much more of an issue, so the trade-off only really became worthwhile when he was intending to indulge in shock combat where such protection was obviously a massive benefit. One of the benefits that stirrups would bring much later was that they made it easier to shift weight and correct balance, compensating for, or allowing, the top-heaviness of heavier body armour. There was also the issue of the weight carried by the horse. Although horses were strong enough to be ridden, any animal can pull much more weight than it can carry (that was the whole point of the wheel). Increasing the weight of the rider starts to have a detrimental effect on a ridden horse's speed and endurance sooner than on a driven one.

In many Near Eastern armies the horses themselves might also be armoured with trappers that covered their chests, shoulders, backs and flanks, just as modern horse rugs do. These could be of thick felt or hair and called a *parashshamu*, with a neckpiece, or *milu*, of the same material; or these could be of scale, when it was called a *sariam* as for human armour. Most early ridden cavalry horses, however, were not armoured, horse armour gradually becoming more common again over the course of several centuries. Horses in heavy work can overheat eas-ily, and in severe cases this can lead them to 'tie up', becoming effectively paralysed, and even leading to their death. That expensive horses were exposed to this risk by the addition of armour suggests they were expected to be right in the thick of battle. The burden of armour would have reduced the horse's endurance. It was therefore more useful to units called upon for one or two short, but potentially decisive, charges than those used in the continuous manoeuvring of skirmishing.

The transition from chariots to true cavalry was a gradual and uneven one. Occasional depictions of ridden horses have survived from early in the second millennium BC, but most seem to represent single messengers or scouts, ill-equipped for combat, or charioteers fleeing on team horses cut loose from wrecked chariots. Written references can be ambiguous as some of the terms equivalent to 'horsemen' may refer to chariot crews. It seems, however, that by the late second millennium BC units of cavalry may have been making their appearance on Middle Eastern battlegrounds. A twelfth century BC plaque from Ugarit in Syria may be the earliest depiction of an organized unit of horsemen, although only one is definitely armed.

The transition is easiest to follow in Assyria from the ninth century BC, due to the surviving record of relief carvings and inscriptions. Assyria had by then become the dominant power in the region, the Hittites and Egyptians having been severely weakened by migrations and invasions of the 'Sea Peoples'. Over the next two centuries a succession of aggressive Assyrian kings carved out the largest empire yet seen, at its height incorporating all of Mesopotamia, Syria, Palestine and Egypt. Although the Assyrians are often credited with being the first to field an organized cavalry force, what can be seen in the surviving evidence may well be a response to developments in the regions beyond their expanding borders.

Urartu, modern Armenia, was a regular target of Assyrian campaigns in which many horses were taken in the form of booty or as tribute payments. Urartu was in direct contact with the steppe peoples to the north and it seems likely that this region was the conduit for the adoption of cavalry in the Middle East, as it had been for the initial introduction of the domesticated horse. An inscription of Menua of Urartu (810–785 BC) lists his forces for one expedition as 1600 chariots and 9174 cavalry.[20] Even if the numbers are inflated, the ratio of cavalry to chariots indicates that conversion was well advanced.

The development of Assyrian cavalry was heavily influenced by their charioteering experience and traditions. Bas-relief sculptures from the palace of Asurnasipal II show riders working in pairs, one armed with a bow and the other with a spear. Most strikingly, while the archer concentrates on shooting, his partner holds his reins for him, continuing the specialization of archer and driver. Both horses and riders are unarmoured. One of the key advantages of this type of unit over chariots was that they were better able to cope with rough terrain, an advantage that would have become immediately obvious in the rugged terrain of Armenia. At least as significantly, they were cheaper as the chariot, which required a lot of skilled labour, was not required.

Asurnasipal II's riders still had a lot to learn from their neighbours, however, as they are shown sitting well towards the rump of the horse. This not only makes good balance and control difficult but risks bruising the horse's vulnerable kidneys. The rearward seat had been used on donkeys and asses because it is the only position on them that is not akin to riding a bread knife, but trying to transfer the same method to horses must have retarded Assyrian riding prowess. It may cause wonder that correct riding techniques took so long to develop, but let us not forget they didn't have approved riding schools and manuals to go by. It was only in the nineteenth century, after all, that Federico Caprilli (1868–1907) popularized the practice of leaning forward over jumps in western Europe, something now so widely accepted as the correct technique that it seems mere common sense.

By the reign of Tiglath Pileser III (745–27 BC), Assyrian reliefs show us horsemen armed only with long thrusting spears, maybe seven feet long, and swords. Some are armoured with helmets and sleeveless scale vests that come only to the hips, allowing the riders to bend freely at the waist. These may be the first confirmed heavy cavalry, for their one-spear armament was obviously only of use in close combat, while their body armour was an unnecessary encumbrance and expense for mere scouts or messengers. Significantly, although they are still depicted in pairs, which may be merely artistic convention, they are all managing their own horses and sitting much further forward, just behind the horse's withers.

Cavalry did not suddenly replace chariots in Assyrian armies; chariots were still used alongside them until Assyria's destruction. The fact that chariots continued to be used may seem surprising to the modern mind used to thinking in terms of linear technological evolution, with each technology being rapidly replaced in turn by a superior one. It may be significant that these last Assyrian chariots were of the heavy, four-horsed type with four armoured crewmen, which may indicate that the shock role was the last to be taken over by cavalry. Here chariots may have retained some advantage due to their imposing bulk and noise, which would have increased their psychological impact on the target.

Probably more significant in the slow disappearance of chariots was the fact that they were symbols of prestige and had been the most obvious distinguishing feature of an elite for a thousand years. They were almost certainly at the centre of a web of tradition, custom and value that would not be quickly thrown away, even if they were being out-performed in a purely military sense. That the prestige value of chariots was greater than that of the ridden horse is demonstrated by the fact that they continued in use as transport for kings and generals long after all their other battlefield roles had been usurped by ridden horses. No doubt ancient grandees felt the chariot more befitting to their dignity, just as modern ones are more often seen in chauffeured limousines or staff cars than walking or bicycling.

When Sargon II launched a campaign against Urartu in 714 BC, the terrain was so rough that the chariots were the first sent home, while the king continued with the infantry and cavalry. The king's chariot was retained, however, even though it had to be dismantled and carried in places. Eventually the weary Assyrians found Rusash's Urartian army, also containing both cavalry and chariots, deployed for battle across their path, ready to fall upon them as they straggled along in column. Caught at a massive disadvantage and with no time to deploy, Sargon in his lone chariot seized the initiative and led the vanguard of cavalry in a pre-emptive attack.

> The unhappy troops of Assur [Assyria] who had marched by a distant route, were moaning and exhausted ... I did not look back, I did not use the greater part of my troops, I did not raise my eyes. With my chariot alone and with the cavalry who march at my side, who never leave my side in a hostile and unfriendly land ... like a mighty javelin I fell upon Rusash [21]

The Urartians broke and fled with heavy casualties inflicted upon infantry archers and spearmen as well as their cavalry: 'his destruction I accomplished, I routed him ... His warriors who bore the bow and the lance before his feet, the confidence of his army, I slaughtered. His cavalry in my hands I took and I broke his battle-line'.[22] Rusash and the chariots meanwhile took refuge in their camp, but when Sargon brought up archers and javelinmen, the Urartian king abandoned his chariot and fled on horseback.

The account is from an inscribed tablet bearing a letter from Sargon II to the Assyrian god, Assur, presumably intended as an offering of thanks for the victory. While not as detailed as might be wished, it does at least demonstrate that one of the fundamental principles of the use of shock cavalry (which presumably applied also to heavy chariots) had been grasped by some. Because the physical and psychological impact of cavalry upon an enemy is multiplied by speed, and because horses make vulnerable targets when stationary, it was one of the fundamental principles of cavalry tactics up to the early twentieth century that cavalry should always attack rather than wait to receive an attack. The author of this advice from a typical nineteenth-century tactical manual would certainly have approved of Sargon.

> Its action is confined to shock action. Hence it should always attack; at the moment of doing which it should attain its maximum speed. As it is powerless at the halt, it should, to defend itself, always advance to the attack.[23]

Moreover, Sargon's cavalry were not merely protecting themselves. By using their speed to fall upon the enemy before they had time to formulate a response, Sargon was able to wrest the initiative and save his army from disaster.

As Assyria expanded its borders, direct contact with nomadic riders increased. In the same year as Rusash's defeat by Sargon, Urartu lost part of its territory to the Cimmerians, who had already moved through the Caucasus and overrun large parts of Anatolia. The Cimmerians had been driven off their pastures on the southern steppes around Dereivka by the Scythians. Through the early part of the seventh century BC, large numbers of Scythians also rode southward off the plains, seeking new pastures, plunder or perhaps adventure and employment as mercenaries. It is of these warriors that the biblical prophet Jeremiah was warning when he declared:

> Behold, a people shall come from the north, and a great nation, and many kings shall be raised up from the coast of the earth. They shall hold the bow and the lance: they are cruel, and will not shew mercy: their voice shall roar like the sea, and they shall ride upon horses, every one put in array, like a man to battle, against thee, O daughter of Babylon.[24]

By the 670s BC the Scythians had obliterated the Cimmerians as an identifiable people, completed the destruction of Urartu and become such a threat to Assyria that Essahardon bought the alliance of the Scythian ruler, Partatua, with the hand of his daughter in marriage. For a while this alliance shored up the failing Assyrians. Partatua's son and heir, Madyas, Essahardon's son-in-law, even led a Scythian host against Egypt. The Egyptians only managed to save themselves from devastation by payment of a large sum of money. When the Medes, from what is now western Iran, rebelled, defeated the Assyrians in battle and besieged the capital, Nineveh, Madyas's Scythians crushed them and saved the city.

The Scythians went on to conquer Media and, according to Herodotus, ruled there for twenty-six years. The period of Scythian dominance may be the root of the reputation for equestrian excellence that the Medes later enjoyed. It seems the Medes had already been using some cavalry, although the instigator of their rebellion was said to have been the first to reorganize their warriors into proper units of spearmen, archers and cavalry, which had previously 'been all mixed up in a mob', again according to Herodotus.[25] A generation of close interaction with the Scythians taught them much about horsemanship and cavalry warfare and it was for their cavalry that they were later renowned.

In 614 BC the Scythians, with their Median vassals in tow, turned on their former allies and destroyed Nineveh and the Assyrian empire. Two years later, the Median leader, Cyaxares, lured the Scythian leaders to a banquet, killed them and rebelled. Deprived of leadership, the bulk of the Scythians returned north, trekking back over the Caucasus Mountains to their old homeland.

The Scythian armies that swept into the Near East fought predominantly as mounted archers, or horse archers as they are usually referred to. Typically they utilized the same hit and run tactics of the light archer chariots already described, only even more elusively due to cavalry's greater suitability for rapid changes of direction. It would be all too easy to conclude from their apparently easy domination of the Near East that such light cavalry enjoyed a clear superiority and that the Scythians had need of nothing else. Such an impression might be reinforced by the fact that the composite-bow-armed horseman remained the characteristic weapon system of steppe-dwelling races for a further twenty-five centuries. The Median and then Persian armies that dominated the whole of the region, after the Scythians were driven out, indeed relied heavily on bow-armed cavalry, but the influence was not all one way. Some Scythians had always carried hand-to-hand weapons, spears and axes, as well as the bow, and when they returned to the north they took with them something that would further enhance their potential for shock action: Assyrian scale armour and the knowledge of how to make it.

Scythian tombs on the steppe have yielded a wealth of artefacts. Most date from the period after their return from the south and many of them contain scale armour. While most Scythian warriors continued to be lightly equipped and to depend mainly on the bow, it is clear that those who had the option, that is the wealthier ones, fought as heavy cavalry, well protected by heavy armour. Although they too possessed bows, they also carried swords, spears and a type of axe called a *sagaris*. Surviving examples of the latter are well adapted for punching through armour. The spears found in tombs were initially identified as short javelins, it only being realized later that they were so long, over ten feet, that they had been broken in half to fit into the tombs. Such long spears could only have been used in shock combat.

The Scythians' influence on cavalry warfare did not end when they passed back over the Caucasus. Fighting mostly as horse archers, their prowess as light cavalry is beyond question, but their contribution to the development of heavy cavalry has received less attention. It was the combination of the swarms of horse archers with smaller numbers of heavily armoured cavalry made up of the nobility that was to prove so potent to their many opponents over the ensuing centuries, allowing these horse herders to defy the might of great 'civilized' empires.

When the Persian Cyrus the Great had overthrown the Medes, formerly the Persians' overlords, and had quickly conquered all of the former Assyrian empire and Anatolia, he turned his attention to the Massagetae, one of many Scythian offshoots. According to Herodotus, this hitherto invincible conqueror enjoyed some early success through the use of a ruse. But his first pitched battle with them soon followed when Cyrus ignored the warning of Tomyris, queen of the Massagetae, that if he continued his bloodthirsty aggression she would show him 'more blood than you can drink for all your gluttony'. The battle began with a prolonged exchange of archery, but a decision was only reached when the opposing forces closed to slug it out in a fierce mêlée in which neither side was prepared to retreat, the Massagetae fighting with spear and *sagaris*. The day ended with Tomyris immersing Cyrus's severed head in a skin full of blood and declaring: 'see now, I fulfil my threat: you have your fill of blood'.[26]

Similarly, when Cyrus's successor, Darius I, invaded Scythian territory to the west of the Black Sea, around 514 BC, the initial Scythian response was simply to pack up their wagons and move away, refusing to give battle. This application on a strategic scale of the evasive tactics of the horse archer avoided defeat at the hands of the far more numerous Persians, but it could not decisively defeat them. The retreating Scythians started to run out of space as the neighbouring tribes refused to aid them or let them pass. Insulted by continued Persian suggestions that they were afraid and that they should acknowledge Persian mastery, they adopted more aggressive, confrontational tactics. The Scythian cavalry started to attack the Persian cavalry patrols and vanguard. 'On every occasion', wrote Herodotus, 'the Scythian cavalry proved superior to the Persian', sending them galloping back to the protection of the main body of infantry, whereupon the attack was broken off.[27] The wording of Herodotus's account strongly suggests that the Scythians were actually charging and chasing the Persian cavalry off rather than merely sniping at them from a distance.

The Scythians are credited with the invention of the 'wedge' formation, later adopted by the Persians and Thracians and also put to devastating effect by Alexander the Great's Macedonian cavalry. This formation was particularly suited to shock action because its narrow frontage made it easier to manoeuvre at speed in close formation and because, according to the Greek tactician Asclepiodotus, it 'made it easiest for them to break through'.[28]

The Scythians may well have led the way in the improvement of horse breeds. Stronger, and incidentally bigger, horses were a general, if very gradual, trend. Although size alone, it must be reiterated, is not the most important characteristic of a cavalry horse, greater bulk increases the intimidating effect upon an opponent, while height can confer an advantage in close combat with hand weapons such as the sword or *sagaris*. Buried in the frozen soil below the Ukrainian steppe, archaeologists have found Scythian tombs containing remarkably well-preserved horses, sacrificed that they might carry their noble masters across the hunting grounds of the afterlife. Typically red bay in colour and standing between 14.2 and 15.1 hands high, these were high-quality horses which have been likened to today's highly prized Akhal-Teke breed, noted for extraordinary feats of endurance. Not all Scythian horses would have been of this quality, but even the more common type were noted for their toughness and endurance.

The Scythians' most significant contribution to cavalry warfare was probably the beginning of the development of the saddle. All previous riders had, at most, sat upon a flexible blanket or animal skin that shielded the rider's legs from chafing and horse sweat but had no real structure. The earliest structured seats for riders found to date come from Scythian tombs and date probably from the early or mid fourth century BC. These consist essentially of two leather cushions attached front and back by a wooden arch, one cushion resting either side of the horse's spine when in use. These would have offered the rider improved comfort as well as distributing his weight either side of the horse's spine to prevent damage. Over the centuries that followed, the spread and improvement of saddles greatly increased the ancient horsemen's security of seat, enhancing their already-ample ability to give and receive blows, and reducing the damage to their horses' backs caused by increased weight of armour. While also adopted by skirmishing cavalry, the advantages of the saddle had particular relevance to shock cavalry. It must be emphasized, however, that development was gradual, not an overnight revolution, and we shall see that many of the finest glories of ancient cavalry were accomplished without saddles.

Unsurprisingly the Scythians and Massagetae were at the forefront of the return of effective horse armour, which had been common on chariot horses but was not much used on early ridden cavalry. When Herodotus was writing in the middle of the fifth century BC, the wealthiest Massagetae were already using bronze chest protection for their horses, probably in the form of a scale apron.[29] The Persians followed this trend through the fifth century BC and into the fourth, and they in turn influenced Greek ideas on the matter. In the fourth century BC, Massagetae and related Bactrian cavalry fighting as allies of the Persians provided the toughest challenge to Alexander the Great's Macedonian cavalry. Some, at least, of these were riding horses protected with trappers covered in iron scales.

Suitably impressed, Alexander's Successors continued the development of armoured heavy cavalry, producing shock troops heavier than anything the Assyrians had dreamt of. In the mid third century BC the cycle came full circle when the Parthians, a Scythian people who had infiltrated southwards over many generations, overthrew Macedonian rule and took most of the former empire of the Assyrians, Medes and Persians for themselves. Heavily armoured lancers formed the core of the Parthian armies that for three centuries thwarted the might of Rome.

From the first domestication of the horse onwards, the influence of steppe peoples upon the development of cavalry was enormous. With regard specifically to heavy cavalry we can see the influence of the steppe was greater than has often been appreciated, but it remains true that light cavalry remained more characteristic of those cultures, while heavy cavalry was more often associated with urbanized ones. This is partly a question of the resources required for large-scale production of metal armour and weapons. Perhaps more significant is the confrontational form of warfare forced upon settled communities tied to specific territories. Forced to protect cities and farms and without the space or means for prolonged evasion, civilized peoples settled their wars with pitched battles in which a quick and definite decision was at a premium. Finally, there is an artificial bias due to the nature of the surviving evidence which comes mainly from the more settled, 'civilized' cultures. In the following chapters we must concentrate on those cultures where surviving accounts allow us to follow the role of heavy cavalry in action.

2

Classical Greece

The generally accepted view of classical Greek warfare accords little significance to the role of cavalry. While numerous books discuss every possible aspect of the heavy infantryman, or hoplite, in the minutest detail, the horseman usually gets a couple of picture captions or a paragraph explaining why he was largely restricted to the secondary roles of scouting and raiding. The cavalry's role in battles is dismissed, at best, as a bit of skirmishing with javelins or maybe cutting down a few fugitives after the battle had been decided by the infantry. Almost invariably the following passage from Xenophon, recording events in 401 BC, is used to show that the hoplites had nothing to fear from cavalry whose seat was 'precarious' and who were too busy just staying on to do much harm to anyone but themselves:

> You must remember that ten thousand cavalry only amount to ten thousand men. No one has ever died in battle through being bitten or kicked by a horse; it is men who do whatever gets done in battle. And then we are on a much more solid foundation than cavalrymen, who are up in the air on horseback, and afraid not only of us but of falling off their horses: we, on the other hand, with our feet planted on the earth, can give much harder blows to those who attack us and are much more likely to hit what we aim at. There is only one way in which cavalry have an advantage over us, and that is that it is safer for them to run away than it is for us.[1]

This, however, overlooks the fact that Xenophon made his speech to the 'Ten Thousand', a group of tough, experienced mercenaries, precisely because they *were* afraid of the enemy's cavalry. And with good reason because, although faced with Persian cavalry in this instance, the Ten Thousand were mainly veterans of Greece's recently concluded Peloponnesian War and had seen there what Greek cavalry could do. For, although it cannot be disputed that the hoplites were still the dominant arm in Greek warfare, by the end of the fifth century BC cavalry were already playing a much more significant role on Greek battlefields than is often appreciated. They went on to assert themselves even more in the following decades. Moreover it can be shown that the increasing success of Greek cavalry was achieved by greater enthusiasm for closing with the enemy and settling the issue at close quarters.

Several things limited the role of cavalry and subordinated it to the hoplites. The first was the terrain. Much of mainland Greece consists of rugged, rocky mountains with little rainfall for much of the year. Those areas of good fertile ground that existed were needed for agriculture, so there was little good pastureland for the grazing of large numbers of horses. With agricultural land at a premium and the need to feed the human population, the necessary supplementing of grazing with grain feed was expensive. There were significant exceptions, including Thessaly and parts of Boeotia, where there are large open plains. Unsurprisingly, these were also the areas that produced the best cavalry. 'Classical Greece' included not only modern Greece, but also those areas colonized by Greeks. Many of these areas, in Southern Italy, Sicily, Asia Minor and Thrace, had good grazing land and produced good cavalry. Contact with neighbouring peoples who had strong equestrian traditions would also have reinforced this, not least because it allowed the introduction of 'new blood' to produce improved breeds of horses.

Apart from discouraging horse rearing, unsuitable terrain also provided a disincentive to cavalry's actual use in battle, depriving them of their greatest assets, their speed and mobility. To fight most effectively cavalry needs plenty of open space. On rough or obstructed ground horsemen are less able to manoeuvre into an advantageous position for an attack and make slower, more vulnerable targets. It is true that the hoplite phalanx was also best suited for combat in close order and was even more dependent on cohesion for its survival, and for this reason hoplites also preferred to fight on good level ground. But in mainland Greece, and many other areas, it was easy for them to form up in one of the many narrow valleys, their vulnerable flanks protected by steep slopes, rivers or some other obstacle, and advance straight ahead to attack the enemy head on. Cavalry's best chance against hoplites was an attack from the flank or rear, so the cavalry was far more disadvantaged if the nature of the ground did not allow room for manoeuvre.

The second limiting factor, partly deriving from the first, was the great expense of raising horses and developing suitable breeds for war. To give some idea of the financial constraints, the average price of a cavalry horse at Athens in the mid fourth century BC was around five hundred drachmas; the average price of a house was a little over four hundred.[2] Another good indicator of the relative expense of maintaining cavalry compared to other troops is the money required by the

Spartans from allies who did not provide the agreed number of troops, each cavalryman carrying the same tariff as eight light infantrymen or four hoplites.[3] As citizens had to provide their own equipment for most of the period, clearly only the wealthiest could afford to serve in the cavalry. This purely economic factor alone was enough to ensure that most Greek cities could only field a very small number of horsemen.

Finally we must consider how social and cultural factors led to an emphasis on hoplite warfare and placed constraints upon the employment of cavalry beyond those imposed by purely practical and economic concerns. In many Greek states a powerful belief seems to have existed that the tactics of the hoplite phalanx, the close-packed block of heavily armoured spearmen, was the only truly acceptable way to fight. Because economic factors meant that only the very richest had access to horses, there was an inevitable link between cavalry and aristocracy, while hoplites were drawn from a much broader base. As a result it has long been fashionable to describe the supremacy of the hoplite in class terms. The phalanx, the close-packed body of spearmen, each protecting the man to his left with his shield, can be seen as the embodiment and reflection of the relatively egalitarian and democratic values often associated with the Greek city state, or *polis*, which emerged from the Dark Age as the dominant form of society throughout most of the Greek world.

Mycenaean civilization had collapsed in the twelfth or eleventh century BC. The centralized monarchical authority which had provided the organization and resources for large-scale chariot production and horse breeding was destroyed and replaced by isolated, impoverished communities struggling for survival. The warfare of the early Dark Age, whilst endemic, was on a small scale and probably largely a matter of local raid, counter-raid and ambush between small war bands. Such fighting would be easily dominated by the local aristocracies who could afford bronze weapons and armour, and under whose protection and leadership such communities slowly began to recover. Archaeology suggests at least some of these chieftains fought as cavalry. Vase paintings portray horsemen with breastplates, helmets and spears; and there are grave finds such as one at Athens that contained a long sword, spears and horse bits. There is some evidence, such as a fresco from Mycenae itself, that the Mycenaeans had started to experiment with true cavalry before the collapse. Quite apart from any purely military considerations, the great financial benefit of replacing a chariot and two horses with a single horse would have hastened the transition, although chariots remained for sporting and ceremonial purposes.

Trade with the Near East resumed by the ninth century, allowing the importation of iron-working skills. Iron was cheaper than bronze because the ore was available locally, whereas bronze required tin imported over great distances, and meant cheaper and more efficient weapons and agricultural tools. Population growth, iron tools and a general recovery of stability boosted a return to agriculture. This allowed further population growth and, in the Peloponnese and Attica at least, created a growing class of independent farmers and artisans who could afford armour and iron arms for their own security. These came to expect a stake in society in keeping with their growing contribution in labour and defence. Village farming communities coalesced into groups around leading market centres, dictated by the pattern of increased local trading as surpluses grew. These developments set the stage for the reordering of society around the *polis* (plural *poleis*) or 'city state', recognizable from around 750 BC and exported through colonisation round the Aegean coast to the east, and to Sicily, Italy and Spain in the west.

These city states were relatively egalitarian societies, based upon the equality of all free citizens before the law. Although many might still be ruled by narrowly based oligarchies or even monarchies, most executive magistrates were elected and thus dependent upon the will of the hoplite class, whose interests could not be ignored.[4] In return for full citizenship, with voting rights and the possibility of office, men were obliged to equip themselves with the necessary armour and weapons to serve in the phalanx. At a minimum this would mean spear, helmet and the characteristic large, round shield that distinguished the hoplite, but preferably also body armour. While the poorest residents might be called upon to serve as lightly equipped skirmishers, and the wealthiest might choose to accept the extra expense of serving on horseback, the hoplites could expect to outfight the former and outvote the latter. It was the hoplites that formed the backbone of the army as they did of the economic and political life of the polis.

As citizens had to equip themselves, and only the wealthiest could afford to keep horses, there was an obvious link between cavalry and the aristocracy. As the egalitarian ethos of the hoplite class developed alongside the tactics of the phalanx, the horsemen were increasingly suspect. Generals were most often elected by the hoplite class from the hoplite class, and were expected to take their place in the front rank of the phalanx. The horse-riding aristocrats, or *hippeis*, literally setting themselves above the phalanx, were often suspected of putting their personal status before the interests of the polis. This mistrust can still be seen in literature from the late fifth century BC, even though cavalry was by then reaffirming its military worth. According to Thucydides, when the young aristocrat Alcibiades urged the Athenians to invade Sicily, Nicias warned them

[that Alcibiades] entirely for his own selfish reasons, will urge you to make the expedition ... He wants to be admired for the horses he keeps, and because these things are expensive, he hopes to make some profit out of his appointment. Beware of him, too, and do not give him the chance of endangering the state in order to have a brilliant life of his own. Remember that with such people maladministration of public affairs goes with personal extravagance.[5]

The hoplite class literally stood side by side in time of war, each sharing his shield with his neighbour. A single hoplite, or any number that did not work together, was clumsy and slow compared to a horseman and could be ridden down. But when they retained their cohesion, they were more or less impregnable to a frontal assault except by other hoplites. The aristocracy's increasing political marginalization, was therefore also translated into literal marginalization on the battlefield as the cavalry was forced to move out to the wings.

This political explanation for hoplite dominance, with the phalanx as the politically correct way to fight, is a very attractive perspective, not least because Aristotle adopted this approach when looking back on the Classical period from the fourth century BC. It is important, however, not to overemphasize notions of class identity to the exclusion of more basic and personal motives. Nor should we imagine the hoplite class as proto-communist idealists, most of them were slave owners after all. Far from believing all men should be equal, Greek men grew up in a culture of competition, each eager to outdo his peers in every field, particularly displays of manly virtue. Jealousy could be said to be the driving impulse. The same mentality that gave us the Olympic games drove citizens to seek to outdo each other in time of warfare also. But to be valid, such competition had to be seen as fair. With the majority of citizens fighting as hoplites, it is easy to see how those who turned up on horseback might be seen as somehow cheating. This is perhaps the more important reason why service in the phalanx, a particularly intensive and traumatic form of combat, came to be seen in many cities as the proper way for men to fight, the one true test of manhood.[6]

During much of the Archaic period most city states probably still fielded cavalry. There are plenty of vase paintings of mounted warriors, including several that are well armoured with breastplates, helmets and greaves, from Athens and Corinth. A magnificent late sixth century vase shows two such horsemen, each with helmet, breastplate, greaves and long thrusting spears, clashing over the body of a fallen hoplite.[7] Unfortunately, although the sources for this period are better than for the Dark Age, they still do not include the historical narratives that would allow us to recreate the cavalry warfare of this period with any real confidence.

By the late sixth century BC it seems that some *poleis* had decided they could do without cavalry altogether, placing their faith almost completely in the phalanx. This was particularly the case in the Peloponnese. The Spartans are known to have fielded cavalry in the seventh century, but by the late sixth they had none, although the king's bodyguard retained the honorific title of 'hippeis'. It seems the Spartan cavalry was disbanded during the egalitarian reforms undertaken during the Second Messenian War (c. 640–20 BC) by their great lawgiver, Lycurgus, because, as one scholar neatly put it, 'an elite, privileged, mounted force would have, in fact, shown that equality of hardship and service was a falsehood'.[8]

By the start of the Classical Period (c. 500–338 BC) the hoplite phalanx had become the chief characteristic of Greek warfare. This was partly due to the fact that wars between city states in the Archaic period had tended to become ritualized, limited disputes, usually over contested farming land. The hoplites marched out, decided the issue in a single 'fair' fight between phalanxes, hedged about with all sorts of conventions and rituals, and went home again. As the Classical Period went on, however, there was a tendency towards much less restrained warfare, either against foreigners such as the invading Persians, or between rival Greek states as these became more ambitious and aimed at dominating the others. Under these conditions, with longer campaigns and battles against enemies who were themselves less dependent on the phalanx, purely military considerations started to overcome political or cultural prejudices and the value of cavalry reasserted itself. By the winter of 425 BC, when the Peloponnesian War had been dragging on for half a decade, even the Spartans, acknowledged both then and now as the best hoplites, were forced to reconsider and 'raised a force of 400 cavalry ... something quite at variance with their normal way of doing things'.[9]

In most of Greece economic factors kept these forces small at first, and some minor states did not have a cavalry force worth mentioning until the mid fourth century, relying instead upon allies. But, despite all the constraints, cavalry played an increasingly influential part in Greek battles.

Of course, in those areas where the city state never fully developed and the aristocracy remained dominant, and where the geographic conditions were more favourable to horse rearing, large cavalry forces were fielded and arguably were even the main arm, but these areas are often omitted from historical discussions predominantly interested in the poleis. In 511 BC, the Thessalians sent one thousand cavalry to defend their Athenian allies from an all-infantry Spartan invasion force under Anchimolius. The Spartans were defeated with heavy losses, including Anchimolius himself, by a single cavalry attack.[10] In the early 480s the Thessalians were again 'expecting to sweep all before them' until the opposing Phocians stooped to the strategem of secretly burying large jars in the soil so that when 'the Thessalians galloped up ... their horses fell through into the jars and broke their legs'.[11] The Macedonians for their part, when facing an invasion by Thracians in 428 BC,

> never even thought of opposing them with infantry, but they sent for further reinforcements of cavalry from their allies of the interior, and though in greatly inferior numbers, they made cavalry attacks on the Thracian army when they saw their opportunity. Whenever they did so, being excellent horsemen and armed with breastplates, no one could stand up to them, but they found themselves running into danger by being surrounded by the enormously greater numbers of their enemies.[12]

After Thessaly and Macedonia, the most successful and largest cavalry arm in mainland Greece was provided by the Boeotian cities such as Thebes, which were city-states (much of the time linked in a loose confederation) but had plenty of good open grassland. The Theban cavalry fighting for the Persians at Plataea in 479 BC performed strongly and the threat this posed prompted neighbouring Athens to develop its own mounted arm. This took time and the Athenians continued to rely heavily upon their Thessalian allies to counter the Theban cavalry superiority, until their defection at Tanagra in 457 BC cost Athens the battle. By the Peloponnesian War, Athens could call on an impressive one thousand horsemen, usually fielding one cavalryman to ten hoplites, but this was only achieved through state intervention and the use of public funds to subsidize horse ownership. In the colonies, Syracuse in Sicily also produced a powerful cavalry arm, having the advantages of being a wealthy autocracy with some good grazing land and long contact with the cavalry traditions of the Carthaginian rulers of Western Sicily. These played a prominent part in the destruction of Athens's ill-fated Sicilian expedition in 415–13 BC.

Historians do not dispute the existence of classical Greek light cavalry, which performed the roles of messengers and scouts, and which could harass enemy foragers or have some minor nuisance value on the fringes of battle with their javelins. But many are reluctant to accept that there was any heavy cavalry worth speaking of, by which we mean cavalry equipped and prepared to close with enemy units and disperse or defeat them in close combat. Vase paintings of armoured horsemen are often dismissed as being of mounted hoplites who would ride to the battlefield before dismounting to join the phalanx. Some may have done in the Archaic period, but in most depictions from the fifth century onwards most of them lack the shields essential for this. Alternatively, if those depicted are carrying two spears, it is assumed that, as these are obviously javelins, they must be intending only to use them for fighting at a distance. Yet there are representations of armoured horsemen actually fighting on horseback, clearly using their spears to thrust at close quarters. Furthermore, there is plenty of literary evidence for the effective use of cavalry in a 'shock' role.

From vase paintings and funerary sculptures, supplemented to some extent by literature and actual archaeological finds, we can reconstruct the equipment such heavy cavalry used. Throughout the period the well-equipped *hippeus* had a bronze breastplate and helmet (Xenophon recommended the Boeotian style because it offered good protection without excessively impairing vision and hearing). Existing examples of cuirasses come in longer and shorter versions. The cavalry would have favoured the latter because it allowed the wearer to bend at the waist more easily, an obvious advantage when riding a horse. Some would have had leather strips or *pteruges* hanging from the lower edge as protection for the groin and upper thighs. Cuirasses have been found from the Greek colonies of southern Italy that were undoubtedly designed specifically for cavalry. These are fuller-length cuirasses that flare out a great deal at the bottom, so they protect the lower abdomen but still allow sufficient movement at the waist to ride a horse comfortably. Shins might be protected by bronze greaves, but long leather boots were commonly worn that would have been more comfortable for a horseman and allow him to feel the horse's flanks easily and apply leg aids more sensitively.

Through the fifth and fourth century hoplite equipment tended to become lighter, exchanging bronze cuirasses for lighter and cheaper body armour made of layers of thick, stiffened linen or leather. These corselets only weighed about 3.6 kilograms (some included metal plates and would weigh more) as opposed to 6 kilograms for a bronze cuirass.[13] Some horsemen adopted these in the fourth century, but the bronze cuirass stayed in use with the cavalry longer than with the infantry because the extra weight, while significant to a marching hoplite, had a much less dramatic effect on a rider's mobility and endurance.

In his *Peri Hippikes* (*On Horsemanship*), completed around 365 BC, Xenophon advises Greek riders to supplement their protection with a gorget to protect the throat, a jointed piece of armour for the whole of the bridle arm, and separate pieces for the right upper and fore arm. Xenophon was influenced by his experiences as a mercenary in Asia and his recommendations reflect contemporary Persian practice. Although there is no evidence of these last items actually being used in Greece in this period, it seems unlikely that Xenophon would have suggested anything that would not have served a useful function and they would have been a plausible option for the wealthiest *hippeis* at least.[14]

Xenophon also recommends the armouring of horses with

> a head-piece, a chest-piece and side-pieces (which will also act as thigh-pieces for the rider). But the most important part of the horse's body to protect is the flank, which is simultaneously the most vital part and the most vulnerable. The horse-cloth can be made to cover the flanks as well.[15]

Head-pieces were known in Greece in the form of a narrow metal plate running down the length of the horse's face, what medieval knights would call a chamfron, and are seen in some art. There is, however, little supporting evidence for the use of body armour on Greek horses in this period, although there is some evidence that the Ionian Greeks of Asia Minor may have used the combined side-piece and thigh protector Xenophon describes. An Ionian coin depicts a horse wearing a sort of mail apron, suspended from a strap around the base of its neck, with the lower corners of the apron apparently extending back over the rider's legs and attached to the back of his belt, or to the saddle cloth behind him. This would obviously be dangerous if the horse should fall.

As for weapons, the most commonly depicted armament is a pair of javelins, perhaps six feet long. This has often been taken as evidence of reluctance to close with the enemy (lack of stirrups is often slipped in here as an aside). However, this is not sound reasoning. Although javelins can be thrown and were used by skirmishing light cavalry and *psiloi*, this is not the only way they can be employed. The heavy infantry of the imperial Roman legions carried two javelins and no one tries to suggest that they were skirmishing troops incapable of shock action. They hurled their missiles at close range to disrupt an enemy immediately before charging them. These tactics would obviously be equally open to heavy cavalry armed with javelins.

Xenophon recommends that two javelins of strong cornel wood be carried, one to throw and one to use 'against adversaries in front or behind or to either side of you'. It is true he suggests throwing the javelin from as far away as possible (although this may not be very far), as this allows space to wheel away safely and ready the other javelin. Taken together we can perhaps imagine cavalry galloping up and loosing off a volley of javelins, each rider in turn wheeling away to prepare himself to approach again with his remaining spear. If the first volley has opened gaps in the enemy ranks, he could then charge in amongst them and use this as a thrusting weapon in close combat. Here the overarm grip, essentially the same as that used for throwing the javelin (and thus indistinguishable in sculptures and paintings) could have been used to thrust at a hoplite's face, or down over the top of the shield at his upper body. Significantly, Xenophon only expects cavalry commanders to train 'as many of your men as possible' to throw the javelin and gives the strong impression that this is a great bonus but not an essential skill. This is hardly what we would expect if their supposedly precarious seat restricted them to being skirmishing 'hurlers of javelins' rather than shock cavalry.

Some vase paintings show a single long spear being carried, of a type that is clearly meant as a thrusting spear rather than a javelin. These are more or less identical to hoplite spears, around eight or nine feet long, and sometimes wryly referred to as a *kamax* (literally 'pole' – also used for barge poles and vine props), but more often just as a *doru*, as are hoplite spears. It is clear that by the second quarter of the fourth century BC many horsemen were using thrusting spears, which Xenophon thought inferior to javelins because they are harder to handle, hence his call for a change to a pair of javelins as carried by the Persians. He refers to cane spears being prone to breaking, so some were clearly made of this, but his preference for cornel wood could presumably be applied to spears as well as javelins. The ash used for hoplite spears would also have been used.

Xenophon describes an incident in 396 BC when the Spartan king, Agesilaus, was campaigning near Dascylium in Asia Minor and the spears of his cavalry proved a liability against some Persians: 'Then the natives charged, and when they got to close quarters every Greek who hit his man broke his spear, but the natives with their javelins of cornel wood soon killed twelve men and two horses.'[16] But Xenophon's prescription of a training exercise in which a pair of horsemen each carried a spear *and* javelins suggests that he saw the weapon as having some value. The *doru* would often have a secondary spike on the butt end, which was one way of ameliorating the problem of broken shafts.[17] If the spear broke on impact then the rider could quickly turn the remaining portion round and use the spike as an emergency spearhead. The fact that cavalry were striking blows with sufficient strength for breakages to be a problem makes a mockery of the often repeated claim that solid blows could not be landed with a spear before the advent of stirrups and fully developed saddles with raised pommels and cantles.

With each cavalryman providing his own weapons, there was naturally some variety in armament, and various combinations of lance and javelin were probably found in the same unit. Still it is safe to say that the javelin that could also be used as a thrusting spear was the most popular weapon for most of the Classical period.

With all his spears thrown, broken or impaled in an enemy, the Greek horseman might have recourse to a sword. Again, Xenophon's *On Horsemanship* is particularly useful in giving a precise recommendation. In so doing he fired the first recorded shot in an often-passionate debate over the relative merits of cutting and thrusting that would rage as late as the First World War.

> I recommend a *kopis* rather than a *xiphos*, because from the height of a horse's back the cut of a *machaira* will serve you better than the thrust of a *xiphos*.[18]

The *xiphos* was a straight short sword designed primarily for thrusting. The *kopis* or *machaira*, literally a 'chopper', was similar in design to the famous kukri carried today by the Gurkhas, essentially differing only in its greater size and in having a 'knuckle-bow' to guard the wielder's hand. As in the kukri, the severely down-curved blade, widening towards its end, would have had the effect of concentrating the force of a blow in a small spot, combining the cutting action of a sword with the concentrated impact of a hammer. Xenophon's reference to a height advantage makes it clear that he envisaged its use against infantry, and, for sure, a heavy blow on the top of the head might well have concussed and stunned a hoplite even if it did not penetrate his helmet. The unprotected skull of a light infantryman could, of course, have been easily cleft or shattered.

The *machaira* was not the weapon to recommend if there is any truth in the claim that 'without stirrups your slashing horseman ... had only to miss to find himself on the ground' or that such a horseman could scarcely strike with any force.[19] Practical tests using a comparable sword from horseback have shown that it is possible, with or without stirrups, to land heavy blows and remain well seated.* Stirrups later offered very welcome additional security, especially with the sudden and unexpected changes of direction that must have occurred in any close combat, but the instability of riders who had never known them has been grossly exaggerated. Never having formed a dependence upon stirrups, the ancient rider's 'inner balance', to coin a favourite phrase of riding instructors, was probably developed to a very high degree.

The most essential part of the horseman's equipment was, of course, the horse itself. Artistic representations suggest that stallions were used for war. Although this could be the effect of heroic masculine ideals on artistic convention, it is reinforced by Xenophon's advice against purchasing a mount with overlarge testicles. Unfortunately there is very little direct archaeological evidence for the size of Greek horses. Only a small number of bone finds have been studied and these are all considerably earlier than this period.[20] What evidence there is, however, confirms the general picture given by artistic representations, that the horses used were not large, around the fourteen hands mark, although probably increasing slightly through the period, as the rise of cavalry prompted more selective breeding and the importation of blood stock from Scythia, Thrace and Persia.

In case a further reminder is required not to be too dismissive of the

---

* The author's own experiment involved cutting at cabbages on a fence post with an unwieldy and rather blunt sword. Even with this it was easy enough, with or without stirrups, to cut cleanly through the cabbage and into the fence post below. The only problem was that the horse on that occasion, Merlin, having no previous experience as a warhorse, took fright at the resulting loud 'thwack' and took off at high speed. Even without stirrups, the author was not unseated and was able eventually to regain control. The conclusions were reinforced by an impromptu demonstration provided during a visit to the Medieval Tournament School. Two concentric circles of riders cantered in opposite directions without their accustomed stirrups and landed decent blows on each other's shields with practice swords and maces. I remain indebted to Janet Rogers, Faris and, especially, to Brian James.

military potential of ancient horses on the grounds of height, we might consider the experience of the 21ˢᵗ Lancers who made their famous charge at Omdurman in 1899. They had exchanged their 'large troop horses … for Syrian and country-bred stallions'. These only averaged about fourteen hands in height and yet on the long approach march the 'smallest Syrian had to carry eighteen stone; with a heavy man the weight was well over twenty'.[21] If we then bear in mind that the average Greek man in this period was only about five foot six inches tall and weighed around ten stone, perhaps thirteen stone with his weapons and armour, there is no reason to assume the Greek horses were not up to the task.[22] It is undeniable, however, that a smaller mount imparts less of a height advantage in close combat and less of a psychological effect on the target of its charge.

Saddles as we know them did not exist in the Classical period and all the artistic evidence suggests that the rider sat on a simple blanket secured by a surcingle and breast strap. This being the case, it will be readily understood why Xenophon warns that a horse must be 'double spined': that the spine is naturally padded by well-developed ridges of muscle and flesh either side. Xenophon's recommendation that the horse cloth 'should be such that it affords the rider a safer seat and at the same time does not hurt the horse's back' strongly suggests, however, something with a little more structure was becoming available.[23] This may have been a simple padded construction fixed to the cloth. The Scythians are known to have had simple saddles with rigid arches at the front (pommel) and rear (cantle) by this time, so it is far from impossible that these were being adopted, although no trace of them yet shows in Greek art. Such a development towards 'a safer seat' would certainly tie in well with the increasing aggression of cavalry tactics.

The *hippeus* controlled his horse by means of a bridle much like a modern one, and of course with leg pressure, body posture and voice. Leg signals could be reinforced with spurs when necessary. A variety of bits were employed, some more severe than others. Most had crescent-shaped cheek pieces, some with plates studded or even spiked on the inside to act against the soft areas of the horse's muzzle when rein pressure was applied. These studded plates seem to have died out by the fourth century. Most surviving examples had jointed mouthpieces, like many modern bits, to prevent the horse getting proper hold of it with its jaws or teeth, a trick which would allow it to ignore the rider's signals (hence the phrase 'getting the bit between the teeth'). Similarly, the trick of adding rollers or short lengths of chain to the mouthpiece was well known, encouraging the horse to play with these with his tongue and to salivate, again making him less likely to 'set his mouth' against the bit. Some mouthpieces had quite severely spiked rollers, which Xenophon describes as 'hedgehogs', and others had oversized discs.

Of course a severe bit was not used gratuitously for cruelty's sake. It ensured that, even in the heat of battle, the horse 'heard' the rider's commands over the panic of the fray and the pain of wounds. The advantage, however, of training a horse to respond to a gentle bit is that it is more likely to trust you and want to obey your commands. Xeno-phon recommends the use of bits that hurt the horse's mouth if it tries to grip it between his jaws, but only for initial training so that it happily accepted the gentler bit that would be used henceforth.

Overall, Xenophon's comments on the training and riding of horses demonstrates a firm but humane approach, much of which is still prac-tised today. He seems to have understood that, to get the best from a horse, and to build that mutual trust that must have been vital in battle, that horse has to be treated with kindness and care, as the following passages illustrate:

> The single most important precept and lesson is never, in any of one's dealings with the horse, to get angry with it. The point is that anger and foresight do not go together, and so we often do something that we are bound to regret later. Suppose the horse is nervous of something and refuses to go near it; then you have to teach it not to be frightened of this thing. The best way to do so is to have a stout-hearted horse set an example, but failing that you should touch the supposedly frightening object yourself and gently lead the horse towards it. Compulsion and blows only make the horse more afraid, because any harsh measures that are inflicted on a horse in such a situation are thought by the horse to be caused by whatever it is that it is wary of.[24]

And to train it for the noise of the battlefield:

> You must also tell your groom to take the colt through crowds and to famil-iarise it with all kinds of sights and sounds; and if the colt finds any of this alarming, the groom must not lose his temper with it, but should calm it down and gently teach it that there is nothing to be afraid of.[25]

Also:

> By the same token, then, when surrounded by clamouring voices or the sound of the trumpet, it is important not to let the horse see you

discomposed and not to do anything to disturb it either. Instead, in a situation like this you should let the horse halt, if you can, and bring it its morning meal, if possible.[26]

Xenophon explains at some length that horse and rider must train together for all the contingencies that might be met on the field of battle, hunting being particularly useful for combining horsemanship with weapon handling. Such training will 'enable horse and rider to keep each other safe and, generally, because that seems to be the way for them to increase their usefulness to each other'.[27] The development of a good bond of mutual trust and confidence between horse and rider was vital to the survival of both in the tumult of battle. The poor performance of the Spartan cavalry in the prelude to the battle of Leuctra in 371 BC was attributed to lack of such familiarity between the horses and riders. This was a by-product of the persisting Spartan fixation with hoplite service; the wealthiest citizens provided horses for the good of the state, but they themselves fought in the phalanx. Others were appointed at the last minute to ride the horses, apparently those of lower status and worth; in short the men not wanted in the phalanx:

> the Spartan cavalry at the time was in very poor shape. This was because the horses were kept by the very rich, and it was only after mobilisation that the appointed cavalryman appeared to get his horse and whatever arms were given him; he then had to take to the field at once. Also the men who served in the cavalry were the ones who were in the worst physical condition and the least anxious to win distinction.[28]

Of course, individual equestrian expertise needed to be reinforced by group training. The Greek cavalrymen of the city states were not professional soldiers: there were no standing armies (with the exception of the Spartan hoplite force) and so no full-time units, although mercenaries became common in the fourth century. The almost constant and increasingly unrestrained warfare led, however, to an increasing appreciation of the need for collective peacetime training. Thus, when he raised a force of cavalry for his campaign in Asia Minor in 396–94 BC, Agesilaus went to great trouble to ensure that they were not only well equipped and mounted but also well trained as units. This was achieved by offering prizes to the cavalry unit rather than the individual horsemen that showed the best horsemanship, with the result that the 'hippodrome was full of riders'.[29] Xenophon's advice on being a *hipparchos*, or cavalry commander, emphasizes unit discipline: 'You must see that the men are capable of taking orders, because a good horse, a deep seat, and fine arms and armour are completely useless without obedience.'[30]

Xenophon also describes unit exercises ranging from long cross-country rides to 'friendly mock battles'. The latter largely concentrated on simulated engagements between two bodies of horsemen. One exercise consisted of two groups taking it in turns to chase each other back and forth across the hippodrome, simulating the retreat and pursuit. Some writers have seen this as further evidence that the cavalry's role was limited to evasive skirmishing tactics and the pursuit, but the repeated changes of direction would have been excellent for practising group cohesion and manoeuvre at speed, and for instilling timely obedience in the horses. Xenophon goes on to describe a further exercise where the two bodies lined up and charged through each other, excellent training for practising a shock charge, against cavalry at least. This helped accustom the horses to being driven forward directly towards and through an opposing unit. The fact that Xenophon does not describe any exercises for tackling hoplites need not mean that this was not foreseen, but simply reflects the difficulty of arranging a realistic exercise without undue risk to valuable horses or men. Furthermore, the hoplites were also part-time soldiers, mostly smallholding farmers, with little time to spare for training.

With regard to unit structure, it is again only the Athenian model of Xenophon's time that we can reconstruct in any detail. Two *hipparchoi* were elected each year and it was their duty to appoint junior officers and keep an eye on the equipment, training and condition of the horses. The nominal quota of one thousand was to be filled by recruiting equally from each *phyle* or tribe, of which there were ten, and this provided the basic tactical unit commanded by a *phylarchos*. Five such *phylai* were commanded by each *hipparchos*, thus forming a five hundred strong *hipparchia*. The *phyle* was subdivided into ten *dekades* of ten men, each of which would usually form a file when deployed in formation. One man was selected from each to be *dekadarchos* and he rode at the head of the file. These *dekadarchoi* formed the leading rank in battle and were selected as 'fit, ambitious men, who long for success and glory'. By contrast, the 'most level-headed veterans' were selected to ride at the rear of each file 'because it takes a brave man to stiffen the resolve of the men in front of him if ever they are called on to attack an enemy position'.[31] Between the youthful enthusiasm of the leaders and the solid experience of the veterans, the squadron was expected to find the best chance of success in a charge. 'To use an analogy,' explains

Xenophon, 'iron best cuts through iron when the blade's leading edge is strong and is backed up by sufficient impetus.'[32] (As any rider will appreciate, they may have also considered the character of the horses, as some horses are very 'forward going' when behind another horse, but unwilling to take the lead themselves.)

The basic formation of manoeuvre was a block ten files across and ten ranks deep, with each *dekas* forming a file headed by the *dekadarchos*. This was a very deep formation in which to attack and they could also form up in an extended line. For this reason leaders of five (*pempadarchoi*) were also appointed and these would lead the rear half of each *dekas* up alongside the front half to form a line twenty files wide and five ranks deep (diagram 1). As these were then in the front line, they were probably selected from promising young men on similar grounds as the *dekadarchoi*.

Phyle in Normal Order   ↑   *direction of movement*

D D D D D D D D D D

Δ Δ Δ Δ Δ Δ Δ Δ Δ Δ

Δ Δ Δ Δ Δ Δ Δ Δ Δ Δ

Δ Δ Δ Δ Δ Δ Δ Δ Δ Δ

P P P P P P P P P P

Δ Δ Δ Δ Δ Δ Δ Δ Δ Δ

Δ Δ Δ Δ Δ Δ Δ Δ Δ Δ

Δ Δ Δ Δ Δ Δ Δ Δ Δ Δ

O O O O O O O O O O

Phyle in Extended Order   ↑   *direction of movement*

P D P D P D P D P D P D P D P D P D P D

Δ Δ Δ Δ Δ Δ Δ Δ Δ Δ Δ Δ Δ Δ Δ Δ Δ Δ Δ Δ

Δ Δ Δ Δ Δ Δ Δ Δ Δ Δ Δ Δ Δ Δ Δ Δ Δ Δ Δ Δ

Δ Δ Δ Δ Δ Δ Δ Δ Δ Δ Δ Δ Δ Δ Δ Δ Δ Δ Δ Δ

O Δ O Δ O Δ O Δ O Δ O Δ O Δ O Δ O Δ O Δ

D = *Dekadarchos* (leader of *dekas*, or file of ten): 'fit ambitious men, who long for success and glory'.

P = *Pempadarchos* (leader of five).

O = *Ouragos* or File-closer: 'some of your most level-headed veterans'.

Xenophon also recommended that the *phyle* should often be divided in half so that half could act as a reserve. The *phylarchos* himself was to lead the first half while the *dekadarchos* most suited to the job would be nominated to bring up the reserve at the critical moment. Such practice would have been approved of by nineteenth century cavalry commanders, but we cannot be sure how often the part-time cavalry commanders of Xenophon's time adhered to such sound advice.

It is probably safe to assume that the cavalry of most other states was based upon a similar scheme. We know, for example, that the cavalry of the Boeotian confederacy was based upon units of a hundred cavalry from each of eleven districts. As far as formations are concerned, there were two very notable exceptions. The Thessalians apparently favoured a rhomboid or diamond formation while the Macedonians adopted the Scythian wedge, via the Thracians. By the end of the Classical period the Thebans too were experimenting with the wedge. The advantage of both was that the narrower frontage was thought to make it easier to change direction at speed and to break through an enemy formation, as was later the practice of the Macedonians, whose cavalry perfected use of the wedge.

Once trained and equipped, the role of the cavalry on the battlefield was largely dictated by the dominance of the hoplite phalanx, but it was still able to exert a powerful influence. Shock tactics had an important part to play in this. An appreciation of the relative strengths, weaknesses and vulnerabilities of horsemen to hoplites is crucial to understanding the use of cavalry in Greek battles. The power of cavalry lay in motion, that of the phalanx in solidity. Superior speed gave the horseman the initiative in as much as he could decline combat by riding away, and it is speed that multiplied the power of his attack. Stationary the horse was a large and vulnerable target, but motion transformed its bulk into a potentially devastating force. This was true in both a purely physical sense (power = mass x velocity) and a psychological one. But of course one cannot move through a solid object, which is what the hoplite phalanx tried its best to be. The cavalry therefore had to try to maintain their freedom of movement, committing themselves to the charge only when the situation offered the chance to do so decisively.

It was very difficult for cavalry to attack a hoplite phalanx frontally. On the purely physical level, because he had half of the length of the horse in front of him, the horseman, even if armed with the same length spear as the hoplite, effectively had a much shorter reach to his front than the hoplite, who would therefore be able to strike his horse first. To attack his opponent the horseman has to be able to ride past him, which he obviously could not easily do if the hoplites were in close order with their shields overlapping and spears levelled. He needed gaps in the enemy ranks, to be able to get in amongst them in order to strike back with spear thrust and sword stroke.

Psychologically, too, gaps were vital. This was obviously so for the rider, who had no desire to see himself or his valuable mount skewered on a bank of spears, but even more so for the horse. Because horses are prey animals that usually escape predators by running away, the horse needs to think it has somewhere to go. Its overriding urge in a situation of stress is to keep moving as fast as possible. It was, and is, difficult enough to make a horse charge straight at a dense mass of men. When these men were armed with spears it was even harder, for the leading horses, like their riders, would see the obvious threat of being impaled.

For the horse the crucial moment came about three strides out from the line of spears. It then had to decide whether to obey its rider's commands to go forward, transmitted by spur and bit and voice, or its instinct to run for safety. If there was a gap in the line of spears, or if the hoplite line was not deep, there was much more chance of a horse seeing a compromise solution to its dilemma and trusting that obedience was the shortest route to safety. At this point the psychological state of the rider again feeds back into the equation. It is a fact that horses are adept at sensing fear, tension and hesitation in their riders. This is no riders' folklore but has a sound scientific basis: horses are herd animals with strong social bonds that require them to pick up the subtlest nuances of mood or anxiety. If the cavalryman is not fully committed to the charge, if he is panicking and thinking of escape, the horse will sense this and will also hesitate. The domesticated horse looks to its rider for guidance and leadership, as in the wild it looks to the herd leader. If the rider can remain positive and focused on driving forward, the horse is more likely to take the plunge; and, if the leading horses decide they can see a way through, the herd instinct means the rest will probably follow.

The psychological aspect must also be considered from the other side. However hard it tried to be one, the phalanx was not in fact a solid object. It was made up of hundreds of individual men of all ages and varying degrees of experience and courage. As a group of horsemen bore down on them out of a cloud of dust, each man had to fight an individual inner battle. The hoplite might have been told by officers or veterans, as Xenophon told his men, that he was safe as long as he stood firm in his place; but what if they were wrong? It is hard to imagine what it must have been like standing there, hemmed in and weighed down, as the ground beneath started to throb with the thunder of hundreds of approaching hooves. The speed with which a cavalry charge happened made this threat a different one to deal with than the measured approach of another phalanx, although this too must have been daunting. If an infantry fight went wrong the hoplite might have the chance to withdraw, or, if it came to it, throw down his shield and outrun his encumbered enemies. Against cavalry, the temptation to turn and run must have been intense. What if others ran first? Of course a man would know that he could not outrun a horse, but if he outran most of his comrades he might get away while they perished, and the very difficulty of escape made a good head start all the more desirable.

A hoplite's spear, less than two inches thick and prone to breakage, must have seemed frail protection indeed against the approaching avalanche of horseflesh. The cavalry charge effectively became a game to see who flinched first, played for very high stakes. Armed only with his spear, the hoplite could do nothing to test the cavalry's resolve until they were a few strides away. Even two thousand years later, when infantry were armed with muskets that could start to kill the cavalry and test their resolve long before the latter reached them, the experience was traumatic, as this passage from a British officer of the Napoleonic period demonstrates:

> It is an awful thing for infantry to see a body of cavalry riding at them full gallop. The men in square frequently begin to shuffle, and so create some unsteadiness. This causes them to neglect their fire. The cavalry seeing this have an inducement for riding close up, and in all probability in getting into the square, when all is over. When once broken, the infantry, of course have no chance. If steady it is almost impossible to succeed against infantry, yet I should always be cautious, if in command of infantry attacked by cavalry, having seen the best of troops more afraid of cavalry than any other force.[33]

In this way there was the possibility that this psychological impact could cause enough panic in a phalanx for a determined frontal cavalry charge to succeed. This may indeed be what happened at Phalerum in 511 BC when one thousand Thessalian cavalry charged and sent the Spartans rushing back to their ships with heavy casualties. Herodotus makes no mention of any Thessalian losses, nor of a hard fight or any special manoeuvres. He simply tells us the Thessalians launched a cavalry attack and that 'the attack succeeded; many Lacedaemonians were killed, Anchimolius among them, and the survivors driven back to their ships'.[34] This would be consistent with the Spartans panicking and fleeing as the horsemen bore down on them, as a result being overhauled and cut down at will. We do not have enough details to be sure, however, and such instances were rare. This is chiefly because, whatever the possible benefits, the risks to the cavalry making a frontal attack on hoplites were always great, so they tended to adopt more sophisticated tactics.

It is generally true that cavalry could not, or would not, charge a well-ordered hoplite phalanx frontally. Fortunately they did not often have to. Greek cavalry is often said to have been incapable of effective shock action against hoplites except in certain 'special circumstances', that is in flank or rear attacks or if disorder or panic created gaps in the shield wall. What is not always mentioned is that their speed, mobility and versatile armament made them ideally suited to exploiting just these circumstances, which were not rare, or even creating them for themselves.

Cavalry exposed one of the phalanx's vulnerabilities early in the Classical period, at Plataea in 479 BC. The nature of the hoplite phalanx meant that it was prone to disruption when moving at anything faster than a deliberate march. The whole essence of the phalanx, and the source of both its offensive power and its security against attack, depended upon presenting that united front, the left half of each man's shield protecting the right of the man next to him, the levelled spears of the front two or three ranks forming a lethal bank of iron points. But in order to catch a fleeing opponent, who had jettisoned his shield and spear and whose legs had the adrenalin added by fear, the victorious hoplites had to run. This meant that some loss of cohesion was inevitable as younger, fitter or bolder men outstripped the older, less healthy or more cautious ones. As they tried to run forward over uneven ground, discarded equipment and the bodies of the dead and dying, the phalanx would start to fray at the edges and break up into smaller groups and individuals pushing forward to secure victory. With well-led cavalry around, this could be their downfall.

At Plataea the combined forces of southern Greece faced the much larger forces of the Persians and the Boeotians, including the Thebans, who had thrown in their lot with the invader. The Greek army, having refused the offer of two thousand heavy and two thousand light cavalry from Gelon of Syracuse, found themselves with no cavalry force to counter the huge numbers fielded by their opponents. For twelve days the Persian cavalry could make no real impression upon the Greek infantry, who simply stood in formation on high ground each day under repeated barrages of arrows and javelins. Eventually the Greeks were forced to shift position because the Persian cavalry had ridden round them and deliberately fouled the spring that had been their water supply, and had cut up a train of five hundred mules carrying food supplies. They attempted this tactical withdrawal under cover of darkness but it was mishandled, leaving the Spartans and Tegeans still withdrawing in full view of the Persians the next morning. Thinking the enemy beaten and withdrawing in disorder, Mardonius, the Persian commander, launched a badly coordinated attack that resulted in his own death and the collapse of his army. The Boeotian cavalry, however, were made of sterner stuff.

> the rest of Mardonius' force took to their heels simply because they saw the Persians in retreat, and before they had even come to grips with the enemy. The only section of Mardonius' army which was not hopelessly routed was the cavalry – especially the Boeotian cavalry: this force did good service to the fugitives, keeping all the time in close contact with the enemy and acting as a screen between their friends and the pursuing Greeks.[35]

Of these Boeotians, it was the Theban contingent in particular that made a name for itself. When the news of the Persian rout reached those Greek contingents that had got safely away in the previous night's withdrawal, they rushed to join in the pursuit and grab a share of the honours and, perhaps more importantly, the plunder. The contingent led by the Corinthians had the sense to keep to the high ground of the foothills as they approached, but the 'Megarians, Phliasians and others' took the direct route across the plain.

> These last had nearly got in touch with the enemy when they were seen by the Theban cavalry under Asopodorus son of Timander, who, taking advantage of their complete lack of order and discipline, promptly attacked, killing six hundred of them and driving the remainder in headlong flight into the hills – an inglorious end.[36]

No mention is made of any Theban losses in this action. Thanks to Asopodorus' quick decision to attack, his men, emerging from a cloud of dust, must have cantered in amongst these incautious footmen before the latter realized what was happening and before any sort of front could be formed. It was not surprisingly a one-sided affair.

Plataea demonstrated that hoplites had to move with caution when enemy cavalry were around. Even if the main battle was won, cavalry often played an important role in covering the retreat of a defeated army. At Mantinea in 418 BC the Athenian phalanx was in danger of being surrounded and destroyed after their allies broke and fled. According to Thucydides, they 'would have suffered more heavily than any other part of the army if they had not had their cavalry with them to help them'.[37] With this experience under their belts, the Athenians were suitably cautious when the boot was on the other foot. In the first battle of their ill-fated Sicilian expedition (415–13 BC) the Athenians, having brought no cavalry with them, defeated the Syracusan infantry but were unable to exploit their success fully:

> The Athenians did not pursue them far. They were prevented from doing so by the numbers of still undefeated Syracusan cavalry who charged and drove back any of the hoplites whom they saw pressing their pursuit in advance of the rest. Nevertheless they followed up the enemy as far as it was safe to in compact bodies.[38]

On a later occasion the Syracusan cavalry again prevented defeat turning into complete disaster, and managed to make some of the Athenians' best infantry pay dear for their lack of circumspection:

> The right wing of the Syracusans fled to the city and the left to the river. Wishing to cut them off from the crossing, the three hundred picked Athenian troops hurried toward the bridge at the double. The Syracusans, most of whose cavalry was also in this part of the field, rallied under the influence of fear and went against the three hundred Athenians, routed them and drove on into the Athenian right wing, the first detachment of which was also thrown into confusion by their attack. Lamachus, seeing this, came up in support from the Athenian left, bringing with him the Argives and a few archers. After crossing a ditch, he and a few others who had gone with him were left isolated there, and he and five or six of his men were killed. The Syracusans immediately and hurriedly snatched them up and took them to a place of safety beyond the river before they could be recovered; then, as the rest of the Athenian army was approaching, they fell back themselves.[39]

Important and impressive as these rearguard actions were, cavalry's effectiveness against hoplite armies was not restricted to reducing the damage suffered in defeat. We have examined the difficulty for cavalry of charging against an intact phalanx head on, due to the horses' sensible reluctance to impale themselves on the levelled spears of the hoplites. The wall of overlapping shields and bristling spear points presented no such obstacle to flank attacks. These had to be delivered at speed before the relatively cumbersome hoplites could turn and form a new front, or when they were already engaged in combat to their front. For this reason, cavalry were usually deployed on the flanks where they could manoeuvre around the ends of the opposing battle line or at least protect their own hoplites from being similarly outflanked. The battle of Solygia, early in the Peloponnesian war in 425 BC, offers a good illustration of the efficacy of a cavalry attack delayed until the attention of the enemy hoplites was fully fixed on their front.

An Athenian force of two thousand hoplites and two hundred cavalry, under Nicias, landed in Corinthian territory. They had sailed by night to achieve surprise, but the Corinthians had been forewarned and were alerted by beacons. As the Athenians were forming up on the beach overlooked by the hilltop village of Solygia, a strong force of Corinthian hoplites under Lycophron formed up and attacked down the slope against their newly landed right wing. The Athenians managed to hold the attack and the whole phalanx of both sides became engaged. The fighting was fierce, 'it was hard hand to hand fighting throughout'.[40] The advantage shifted back and forth several times. The Corinthian left wing at one point retreated back up the hill to regroup, hurled some rocks down, then raised the *paian* battle hymn and charged back down again. Again the Athenian line held, although the arrival of Corinthian reinforcements drove them right back to the ships for a time.

It was the Athenian cavalry that eventually broke the deadlock between the struggling and pushing phalanxes. It is not clear why they had waited so long; perhaps it was because they were the last ashore, as the horses had to be unloaded from their specially converted ships, or perhaps they had contented themselves with hurling their javelins until the Corinthian right had advanced off the rock-strewn slope. Although Thucydides seems reluctant to elaborate much on their actions, it is clear that their intervention was the decisive factor:

> So for a long time both sides stood firm and yielded no ground. The Athenians had the advantage of their cavalry in the battle (the Corinthians having no cavalry at all), and finally the Corinthians were routed, and retreated to

the hill, where they halted and stayed still without making any attempt to
come down again. Most of their fatal casualties, including Lycophron their
general, took place in this rout of their right wing.[41]

The following year at Delium, the Athenians found themselves on
the wrong end of a similar flank attack. The Athenian army and that of
the Boeotian confederacy approached from opposite sides of a large hill.
Warned of each other's presence by their cavalry scouts, they formed
up and prepared for battle. The Boeotians, commanded by a Theban,
Pagondas, had around seven thousand hoplites, over ten thousand light
troops and peltasts, and one thousand cavalry; an impressive force for
the time. Pagondas drew up the various contingents of hoplites side by
side, with the Thebans massed twenty-five deep on the right, Thespians
in the middle and the rest on the left. He then divided the light troops
and cavalry between the wings to protect the flanks of the phalanx and
began to advance.

The Athenians under Hippocrates had a similar number of hoplites,
which formed up eight men deep, but no proper light troops. Thucydides says they too divided their cavalry between the two flanks, but he
does not give their number. Given, however, that the Athenians often
dispatched expeditionary forces with a 10:1 ratio of hoplites and cavalry,
and given also that we know that three hundred were left at Delium,
four hundred might be an educated guess. While Hippocrates was still
addressing his troops, the Boeotians appeared over the crest of the hill.
Hippocrates ordered the Athenians forward and the two phalanxes met
at the run.

The hoplites crashed into each other and a fierce fight ensued on the
slopes of the hill, but the cavalry and light troops on the flanks found
that watercourses prevented them from closing. The deep mass of the
Thebans on the right began to push back the Athenian left by sheer
weight of numbers, despite stubborn resistance. But elsewhere the more
experienced Athenians were enjoying great success. The contingents
on the left of the Boeotian line were routed and the Athenian hoplites
began to turn in on the now-exposed flank of the Thespians, cutting
down many of them. But Pagondas was alert and saw an opportunity
to make good use of his superiority in cavalry: 'It also happened that
Pagondas, seeing that his left wing was in difficulties, had sent two
squadrons of cavalry round the hill out of sight of the Athenians.'[42]
Presumably Pagondas had drawn these from his right wing, while
those on the left kept the attention of the Athenian cavalry opposite,

perhaps exchanging javelins and taunts with them across the gullies and streams.

Imagine the horror of the Athenian hoplites on the right wing, cutting their way victoriously through the Thespians, when they suddenly heard the pounding of eight hundred hooves behind them and, glancing nervously over their shoulders, saw the Theban cavalry charging down on them. Unable to disengage and form a solid barrier of shields and spears before the cavalry were upon them, the hoplites must have known the havoc those horsemen would wreak among them. Before contact was even made, the Athenian phalanx disintegrated into a mass of frightened individuals thinking of their own safety. The psychological impact of the Thebans' flank charge was out of all proportion to their numbers, magnified by the element of surprise and the fact the attack was launched against the unshielded right-hand side of the hoplites.*

> When they suddenly came into view they caused a panic in the Athenian wing that had been victorious, since the soldiers imagined this was another army bearing down on them. And now, what with this panic on one wing and with the Thebans pushing on and breaking through on the other, the whole Athenian army took to flight.[43]

With all organization lost, the hoplites became easy prey to the faster horsemen and their heavy armour became a curse. Shields were cast aside in the desperate, often futile, race to get away. Many were felled by a downward slash of a *machaira* as a Theban horseman swept past, before the gathering dusk rendered fast riding too risky.† 'The Boeotians followed them up and cut them down – particularly the Boeotian cavalry and the Locrians … The pursuit, however, was cut short by the coming on of night.'[44]

The siege of Syracuse offers us an example of a commander learning the value of flank attacks by experience, and of the importance of giving cavalry room to manoeuvre into an advantageous position. The Spartans sent a general, Gylippus, to organize the Syracusan defence.

*Note that at Solygia, too, it was the Corinthians' unshielded flank that the Athenian cavalry helped to rout.

† The philosopher Socrates was among these fugitives, but Alcibiades, serving as a cavalryman, escorted him off the field, keeping the Theban horsemen at bay. By doing this, he repaid Socrates for defending him against all comers when he lay wounded at Potidea some years earlier.

In his first battle, aimed at preventing the Athenians from completing a surrounding wall to cut off supplies or reinforcement from the city, the Syracusans were defeated because 'the battle was fought at close quarters between the two lines of fortifications, where no use could be made of the Syracusan cavalry'.[45] Taking this lesson on board, Gylippus tried again:

> This time when Gylippus joined battle he had led his hoplites out rather farther from the fortifications than on the previous occasion. His cavalry and javelin-throwers were posted on the Athenian flank in the open ground beyond the ends of the two walls. In the battle the cavalry charged and routed the Athenian left wing, which was opposed to them, with the result that the rest of the army also was beaten by the Syracusans and driven back headlong behind its fortifications.[46]

So lethal was the impact of such flank or rear charges that the mere threat of such an attack became sufficient to halt an otherwise victorious phalanx. In 370 BC some Mantinean hoplites had just managed to come to grips with and defeat some lighter infantry and peltasts from Orchomenus, under Polytropus:

> There Polytropus fell fighting; the rest fled, and great numbers of them would have been killed if it had not been for the arrival of the Phliasian cavalry, who rode round to the rear of the Mantineans and made them give up the pursuit.[47]

Here we see the Phliasian cavalry commander sensibly making the most of the horseman's inherent advantage in mobility to get in the optimum position to threaten a charge. With their rear threatened, the Mantinean hoplites had no choice but to forego the chance to slaughter the fleeing Orchomenians and face about to meet the new threat, hastily reforming their line to present that forbidding wall of shields and spear points to deter the cavalry. Of course, the Phliasians might have stood a fair chance of defeating the Mantineans if they had caught them while they were trying to move forward quickly in pursuit, as we have already seen from the example of Plataea, but there was no need for them to risk valuable horses for a defeated ally.

If the enemy phalanx did not oblige by hurrying forward in disorder, or was not conveniently engaged in slugging it out with their opposite numbers, the cavalry had to work harder and make its own chances. This could be achieved by making repeated limited charges by small groups, those with javelins hurling them into the huddled ranks. As

demonstrated at Plataea, where hoplites stood for hours under fire
from Persian cavalry, missile fire alone could not be relied upon to do
much damage to the well-armoured phalanx. A volley of javelins might,
however, create momentary gaps as encumbered hoplites ducked the
missiles, stepped or tripped over comrades who were hit and had gone
down, or as they attempted to drag the wounded into the interior of
the formation. If insufficient gaps appeared, the horsemen could wheel
away and let another group try. While turning they were vulnerable, but
with other groups hovering menacingly nearby it was a brave hoplite
that risked breaking ranks to take his revenge. It was not so much the
casualties from javelins as the constant threat of shock action that could
prove decisive. The sustained mental stress of facing repeated charges
could lead to a panic. These were probably just the sort of tactics
adopted by the Chalcidian cavalry against Athenian invaders in 429 BC:
'The Chalcidian cavalry also kept riding up and charging whenever
they saw their chance. Indeed, they were largely responsible for causing
a panic among the Athenians, who were routed and then pursued for a
considerable distance.'[48]

If threatened by cavalry, an unsupported hoplite force might adopt
one or both of two defensive measures. They could form a square so
there was no vulnerable flank or rear. A force could march in a square
but had to halt when actually under attack to allow the men forming
the rear and sides to turn and face outwards. Squares were used by
the Athenians in Sicily in 415 and 413;[49] by Xenophon and the 'Ten
Thousand' during their epic retreat from Asia Minor in 401–399 BC;[50]
and by the Spartan king Agesilaus when crossing the territory of the
Thessalians, although the latter had the luxury of his own cavalry which
he posted in front of and behind the square for added protection.[51]

The other option was to make for high or broken ground where it
was more difficult for cavalry to charge effectively, as they would have
to move more slowly. On landing in Sicily, the Athenians, conscious
that the enemy's main advantage was his powerful cavalry arm, chose
'an excellent position ... where the Syracusan cavalry would have the
least chance of doing them damage either during a battle or before it,
since on the one side there were walls, houses, trees, and a marsh in
the way, and on the other side there were steep cliffs'.[52] In addition,
steep slopes also conferred an immense psychological advantage on the
infantry looking down on the horsemen, reversing the usual intimidating effect. After the Athenian cavalry had broken their right wing
at Solygia, the Corinthians 'retreated to the hill, where they halted

and stayed still without making any attempt to come down again'.[53] At Amphipolis in 422 BC, an Athenian army was overwhelmed by a force composed largely of cavalry and light infantry sallying from the city, with the cavalry playing a leading role. The Athenian general, Cleon, was killed while fleeing, probably ridden down by cavalry, 'but his hoplites formed up in close order on a hill, where they beat back two or three attacks'.[54] But, although forming square or taking refuge in difficult terrain could save hoplites from disaster, this was not the way to win battles and in either case their actions were seriously constrained.

A more satisfactory way to protect a phalanx against cavalry was to fight fire with fire and have some cavalry of one's own to protect the flanks. So as cavalry became more common, and as Greek armies ventured further afield against non-hoplite armies, it inevitably became more common for Greek cavalry to meet other cavalry in combat. In the winter of 415/14 BC the Athenian leaders in Sicily made a cavalry force of their own the top priority for the next season's campaign. Cavalrymen were shipped in with their equipment, but without horses, the idea being that the horses could be procured in Sicily. Similarly, when Agesilaus was campaigning in Asia Minor in 396 BC, the unsuccessful cavalry skirmish near Dascylium convinced him that there was only one satisfactory answer to the Persian superiority in this arm. Agesilaus

> realised that without an adequate force of cavalry he would be unable to campaign in the plains, and so he decided that he must acquire such a force rather than have to fight a campaign in which he must always be, as it were, on the run. He therefore had a list made of all the richest people in the area and told them to provide horses. It was proclaimed that whoever produced a horse, arms and a good man would be exempted from military service himself, and, as people were very willing indeed to find others to die instead of them, the result of the proclamation was that the plan was carried out with remarkable efficiency.[55]

This new cavalry force underwent intensive training and had its first major test when Agesilaus invaded Sardis the following year. It failed in the traditional role of light cavalry, to which it has often been thought that ancient cavalry was limited, allowing a large force of Persian cavalry to approach undetected and attack Agesilaus' foragers. But it soon redeemed itself by means of decisive shock action:

> When Agesilaus saw what was happening he ordered his own cavalry up

in support, and at the sight of the approaching reinforcements the Persians drew together and formed up against the Greeks in line of battle, with squadron after squadron of cavalry ... He also ordered his cavalrymen to attack with the knowledge that he was backing them up with all the rest of the army. It was the crack Persian troops who received the Greek cavalry attack, but they fell back in the face of the all-out shock of the assault. Some of them were cast down there and then in the river, while the rest fled. The Greeks set out in pursuit and captured the Persian camp as well.[56]

Mounted opponents presented cavalry commanders with a different tactical problem to tackling the phalanx. Against the infantry, as we have seen, their tactics were those of the opportunist. They took advantage of their superior mobility to choose the moment of decision, feinting and probing until they saw a weakness. Against other cavalry they could not so easily count on being able to keep their distance, and to try to do so meant exposing their backs to the enemy, so they had to change their tactics.

Faced with enemy cavalry there were two plausible options. The first was to keep a safe distance and avoid combat, although this meant they could not hold a position if attacked and was no good if they were supposed to be covering the flank of a phalanx. The other was to attack. Even if in a defensive role, it might well pay to attack first and hit the enemy before he was prepared, or before he could build up any momentum. Generally the side moving fastest, in the tightest formation and with the most resolution won. Most often the slower, less organized or less confident side gave way before the two sides met. If not, then the tighter, faster group of horses more easily barged past any horses that didn't move aside in time and their riders' blows had more impetus as they ploughed through the channels that had opened. Unlike for the phalanx, for cavalry to receive a cavalry attack at a standstill was no real option at all. The rules of this deadly game were simple and easy to learn. But in the heat of battle, when decisions had to be made quickly and under pressure, and no accurate assessment of the enemy's intentions and resolve could be made, even the best cavalry got it wrong on occasion.

Decisive leadership was often the determinant of success. In 394 BC Agesilaus was marching through Thessaly, returning from Asia Minor to rescue his native Sparta from Corinthian and Athenian attacks. His army soon found itself being harassed by Thessalian forces allied to Sparta's enemies.

For some time Agesilaus led the army forward in a hollow square, with half his cavalry in front and the other half at the rear. However, the Thessalians continued to slow up the march by making charges on the rear guard, so he sent back to the rear all the cavalry in the van except for his own personal guard. The two forces formed up against each other, but the Thessalians thought it would be unwise to engage in a cavalry battle in such close proximity to the hoplites [thus engaged they could not maintain their mobility and retreat if the hoplites attacked them]; so they turned round and retired slowly, with the Greeks following cautiously after them. Agesilaus saw that both sides were making a mistake. He therefore sent his own guard of picked cavalry and told them to pass on the word to the others, and then all together to go after the enemy as fast as they could and not give him a chance to face around.

As for the Thessalians, when they saw Agesilaus' men charging down on them so unexpectedly, some of them fled, some of them turned to face the charge, and some, while trying to do this, were caught with their horses only half turned. Polycharmus the Pharsalian, who was in command of their cavalry, turned round and fell fighting, as did the men who were with him. After this the Thessalians fled headlong, some being killed and others taken prisoner. Certainly they never stopped running until they got to Mount Narthacium ... [Agesilaus] was particularly pleased with this action, seeing that with a cavalry force chosen by himself he had defeated the people who, more than all others, pride themselves on their horsemanship.[57]

In some battle narratives from this period, the cavalry are listed among the forces present and their position in the battle line is recorded, almost always on the flanks of the infantry; then no more is heard of them until the battle is over. This has been used to strengthen the case for their ineffectiveness, reducing them to the role of mere spectators or even as evidence that the horsemen dismounted and fought with the phalanx. This is the case at two of the best-known battles, Nemea and Coronea, both in 394 BC. At Nemea the cavalry are not mentioned after the initial deployment, and at Coronea they seem to have played no part until some Spartan cavalry rode up to inform Agesilaus that a number of the defeated enemy had taken refuge in a nearby temple. If the closest contemporary account of these came from anyone other than Xenophon, we might suspect that this was due to social bias of the historian not wanting to pin credit anywhere than on the egalitarian phalanx. This cannot be the case with Xenophon, but it is easy to find other good reasons why the cavalry appear to have achieved little in these two major battles without returning to the idea that they were generally impotent.

In both cases it is probably significant that the two armies were more or less evenly matched in terms of cavalry. At Nemea, there were six hundred on the Spartan side (Spartans, Eleans and other allies) and six hundred Athenian horsemen on the Corinthian side, while at Coronea 'the horsemen of either side were about even in number'.[58] They probably acted to cancel each other out. Lacking the cavalry superiority enjoyed by the Athenians at Solygia, or by Pagondas' Boeotians at Delium, they may well have spent the whole day eyeing each other at a distance or engaging only in minor skirmishes. The size of the forces involved at Nemea would have allowed each cavalry commander to send some units forward while retaining others in reserve to exploit any opportunity. Because cavalry is at its most potent in the initial charge into contact, it is an axiom of cavalry fighting that the side with the last reserve usually wins. A fresh squadron charging in on a flank when all the enemy's units are already bogged down in a mêlée, their formation lost and their horses tiring, often settles the matter. With both sides playing the same game, neither could be sure of finishing the affair with a single decisive charge and, perhaps, exercised sensible restraint. In addition, at Nemea the ground may well have been unsuitable for cavalry action, as there was so much scrub and ground cover that the Spartan commander was unaware that the enemy was advancing until he heard them singing the paean.[59]

At Coronea, assuming the terrain was not similarly adverse, the traditionally superior Boeotian cavalry might have been expected to give a similar number of Spartans short shrift. But Agesilaus still had with him the well-trained cavalry that he had brought with him from Asia Minor and with which he had defeated the even more famous Thessalian cavalry the year before. At both Nemea and Coronea the cavalry forces played a crucial role simply by enforcing a stand-off. By so doing they prevented the phalanxes of their own side suffering the fate of the Corinthian hoplites at Solygia or the Athenians at Delium and in Chalcidice.

When the terrain and tactical situation allowed two cavalry forces to come to blows, this action tended to be fast and furious. Xenophon says of a fight between Athenian and Theban cavalry that 'none carried a weapon so short that it would not reach the enemy';[60] a euphemistic way of saying that the fighting was at very close quarters and that none hung back.* His own son, Gryllus, was killed in this combat. A good illustration of the fast, furious and fluid character that increased use of cavalry brought to Greek battles occurred in 382 BC. A Spartan army of around ten thousand men, commanded by Agesilaus' brother Teleutias, marched on Olynthus. In addition to Spartan cavalry, there were contingents of Theban and Macedonian horsemen. Teleutias

> halted the army about a mile and a half from the city and himself took command of the left wing. In this way he would advance in the direction of the gates from which the enemy came out; the rest of the line, made up of the forces of the allies, stretched away to the right. Also on the right he posted the cavalry from Laconia and Thebes and all the Macedonian cavalry who were there; he kept by him Derdas and his [Macedonian] cavalry, about four hundred in number; this was a force of which he thought highly ...
>
> After the enemy had come out and formed up in line in front of the city wall, their cavalry in massed formation charged on the Laconians and Boeotians. They struck Polycharmus, the Spartan cavalry commander, down from his horse and covered him with wounds as he lay on the ground; they killed others, and in the end forced the cavalry on the right wing to turn and run. As the cavalry fled, the infantry on their left began to give way [sensibly given that their unshielded right flank had been exposed]. Indeed, the whole army might well have been defeated if Derdas and his force had not charged directly at the gates of Olynthus. At the same time Teleutias advanced with his own troops in order of battle. Seeing this, the Olynthian cavalry feared that they might be cut off from the gates; they turned round and retreated as fast as they could, and many of them were killed by Derdas as they rode past him. The Olynthian infantry also retreated to the city.[61]

The Olynthians' opening gambit had been a massed cavalry charge to sweep away the opposing cavalry and thus threaten the whole enemy line with being outflanked on its vulnerable, unshielded side. It very nearly succeeded. The only thing that saved the Spartan army was the intervention of Derdas' cavalry, which in turn threatened the Olynthians with being outflanked and cut off from retreat.

It is highly significant that Teleutias deliberately kept his four hundred

---

* There was a well-known story used to illustrate the Spartans' courage in battle and appetite for close combat. When a young Spartan complained to his mother that his short sword, or *xiphos*, was too short to reach the enemy, she told him to add a good step forward to it.

best horsemen by him when he deployed. The retention of a reserve to exploit an opportunity or negate a setback is now considered one of the fundamental principles of warfare. The first identifiable, deliberate use of such a reserve is, however, often said to be the product of Alexander the Great's genius at Gaugamela, some half a century later.[62] It cannot be doubted that Teleutias beat him to it, and he in turn may have picked up the idea from his brother Agesilaus, who, as we have seen, only sent his picked mounted guard to help his rearguard against the Thessalians when he saw 'both sides were making mistakes'. The latter had, until then, been acting as a vanguard on the march, rather than acting as a true reserve kept back to meet a contingency.

Rather than attributing the use of reserves to one individual's flash of inspiration, it is sense to see it as an evolving response to the more fluid tactical situations created largely by the increased use of cavalry. Cavalry provided both the need and the means for effective reserves. By making outflanking of a single line more likely, they increased the need to have a force that was held back to deter or reverse this. Their greater mobility made it far more likely that they would reach the critical point in time. They could match other cavalry and had early on proved that they could deliver a quick and decisive blow against infantry who exposed a flank (as they had to if they turned in on the flank of the first line, attempting to roll it up); or against those already engaged or pursuing a beaten enemy in disorder – all of which meant they were ideal for use as a reserve as a battle reached its climax.

The earliest explicit example of a reserve being kept in Greek warfare is actually that of the Athenians' first battle against the Syracusans, where 'Half of the army was drawn up in advance, eight deep; the other half was in a hollow square, also eight deep, covering the tents, and had orders to be ready to move up to the support of any part of the front line which they saw to be in difficulties'.[63] It is true that this was an infantry reserve, the Athenians having no cavalry with them at this stage, but such care was taken because the Syracusan cavalry was 'at least 1200 strong' and the Athenians recognized that 'the greatest advantage they have over us is in the number of their horses'. As it turned out, the Athenian reserve was not put to the test; the important point is that the presence of cavalry was already encouraging more sophisticated tactics.

Cavalry were not the only force challenging the pre-eminence of the hoplites. Increasing use was also being made of lighter, more mobile types of infantry. Hoplite armies had always been accompanied by their personal servants and large numbers of men of lower status who could not afford the necessary equipment to fight in the phalanx. On campaign they carried out most of the foraging and the deliberate devastation of enemy property that was intended to provoke the enemy into coming out from behind their city walls and engaging in a decisive hoplite battle. They were, however, very vulnerable to cavalry if caught in the open, and this gave cavalry great strategic importance. When the Peloponnesian War broke out in 431 BC, the Spartans set out with the time-honoured strategy of devastating the farmland of the Athenians to goad them into a battle where they could be crushed by the superior Spartan phalanx. But the Athenian statesman, Pericles, sensibly decided against this and proposed an alternative strategy whereby the Athenians would sit behind their walls and rely on their seaborne supplies until the Spartans went home. Pericles was only able to maintain the support of those of the hoplite class whose farms were in danger of being stripped and burned by using Athens's carefully nurtured cavalry force, now numbering about one thousand, to limit the devastation: 'Pericles was convinced of the rightness of his views about not going out to battle ... He did, however, constantly send out cavalry in order to stop enemy patrols from breaking into country near the city and doing harm.'[64] The policy was successful for some years, Thucydides recording that in 427 BC: 'As on previous occasions, the Athenian cavalry went into action wherever possible and prevented the mass of enemy light troops from leaving the main body of the army and doing harm in the districts close to the city.'[65]

The Athenians were on the other end of a similar strategy in Sicily. The Syracusans withdrew their army within the walls but used cavalry to harass the besiegers. Although their main army made several major sorties resulting in pitched battles, the pressure was maintained in between with cavalry patrols interfering with the collection of supplies:

> the water they [the Athenians] used was in short supply and was not available near at hand, and when the sailors went out to collect fuel, casualties were always occurring because of the Syracusan cavalry which controlled the land.[66]

During the protracted and less restrained wars of the fifth and fourth centuries BC, light infantry were increasingly used in pitched battle too. For this purpose they were usually equipped with javelins, or occasionally slings or bows, and some would also carry a dagger or sword if they could afford it. A small shield might be carried, or a cloak or animal pelt draped over the left forearm, but no armour was worn. Their light armament suited them to hit and run skirmishing tactics in loose formation. Being unencumbered, they were particularly useful in rough terrain, but even on the plains they could eventually wear down and destroy a phalanx if there was sufficient room for them to keep falling back as the hoplites advanced. If caught in the open, however, they were very vulnerable to cavalry who could easily ride in amongst them and butcher them.

From the Peloponnesian War onwards, increasing reference is made to peltasts. These were versatile troops recruited from, or modelled on, Thracian tribesmen. In the fourth century BC they were often specialist mercenaries. Basically enhanced skirmishers, they were better armed than the ad hoc bands of skirmishers, with more effective shields, javelins, swords and, later, thrusting spears as well. They combined the mobility and skirmishing power of out-and-out light infantry with some close fighting value, making them excellent for chasing and catching skirmishers trying to harass the phalanx. They were very valuable as flank protection to the phalanx as they could quickly change face to meet an outflanking manoeuvre, and, if they could close up their formation in time, they stood more of a chance against cavalry attack than the lighter infantry. But as they were trained and accustomed to fight in looser order, their formations lacked the physical and psychological solidity of the hoplite phalanx and they remained vulnerable to a determined cavalry shock charge. Once the cavalry was in amongst them, their lack of armour meant they were relatively easily cut down.

Faced with skirmishing missile-armed infantry, cavalry had a simple choice. Even if carrying javelins, copying their skirmishing tactics was not a realistic option. The horsemen would come off worse for the simple reason that they presented a much larger target. The much greater space needed for horsemen to skirmish successfully also meant they could return a much smaller volume of fire for a given length of front. The effective range and accuracy of a javelin is also shorter when thrown from horseback. In addition, the horseman, needing to hold spare javelins and his reins in his left hand, could carry fewer projectiles, especially compared with an archer or slinger, and would run out of ammunition sooner. Therefore, unless they were prepared to keep well out of range and be effectively neutralized, the only option that made any real sense was a shock charge. As long as the light infantry were not too close to the protection of the enemy phalanx, or in unsuitable terrain, there was nothing to stop the cavalry riding them down. Closing in as rapidly as possible minimized the casualties from missiles by crossing the field of fire quickly. It also increased the sense of impending doom in the light troops and caused them to panic. Quickly reloading a bow or sling with a squadron of horses bearing down on them would suddenly have become very difficult.

As peltasts, a little better equipped to defend themselves, began to be regularly encountered by cavalry, they were accorded more respect than pure skirmishers. At Lechaeum in 390 BC, a group of mercenary peltasts under the Athenian Iphicrates humiliated a Spartan force by use of evasive skirmishing tactics. This is usually lauded as a triumph of the new peltasts over the traditional and much vaunted Spartan phalanx, which it was. But little attention is given to the fact that the Spartan hoplites were accompanied by cavalry, which made their defeat inexcusable.

> Now, when the best men had already been killed, the cavalry came up and they once again attempted a pursuit with the cavalry in support. However, when the peltasts turned to run, the cavalry charge was mismanaged. Instead of going after the enemy until they had killed some of them, they kept, both in their advance and their retreat, a continuous front with the hoplites. So it went on, the same actions with the same results, and, while the Spartans were continually losing in numbers and in resolution, their enemies became bolder and bolder.[67]

Clearly this Spartan commander did not grasp how cavalry fitted into the increasingly complex tactical puzzle presented by more varied troop types. Eventually his force was penned in on a hill and destroyed, although most of the cavalry escaped. But cavalry commanders soon learnt that the peltast was little more than a glorified skirmisher and deserved to be treated in the same way as skirmishers when caught in the open. In 381 BC a force of Olynthian cavalry rode out to challenge a Spartan army, under Teleutias, that was systematically destroying their farmland.

> When Teleutias saw them he was enraged at their audacity and at once ordered Tlemonidas, the commander of the peltasts, to charge them at the double. The Olynthians, when they saw the peltasts charging down on them, calmly retired and went back across the river. The peltasts, however, came after them in a mood of overconfidence, following them across the river as though they were pursuing troops in full flight. As for the

Olynthian cavalry, they turned about and made their charge at the exact moment when it seemed that the peltasts who had crossed the river would still be easy to deal with, and there they killed Tlemonidas himself and more than a hundred of his men.[68]

A few years later the Olynthian cavalry, now allied to the Spartans, again found themselves being shadowed by peltasts and gave them similar treatment:

But the Olynthian cavalry ... wheeled round and, bearing down on the peltasts, chased them up a slope and killed great numbers of them; for men on foot are easily overtaken by cavalry when going uphill where riding conditions are good.[69]

In 378 BC, the Theban cavalry learnt a similar lesson almost by accident. This incident not only demonstrated the peltast's vulnerability to cavalry, but also demonstrated the potentially crushing psychological impact of a determined cavalry charge, even on a fresh hoplite phalanx. A mounted Theban raiding party was withdrawing from Thespian territory, pursued by a combined Spartan and Thespian army with mercenary peltasts, under the Spartan Phoebidas.

Phoebidas pressed his attack boldly. He had the peltasts with him and had ordered the hoplites to follow in battle order. He now entertained the hope of routing the Thebans; he was leading on his own men with the greatest confidence, calling the rest of his army to join in the attack and ordering the Thespian hoplite force to come up in support. However, in their retreat the Theban cavalry had come to an impassable ravine. Here they first gathered into a compact body and then, not seeing how they were to get across, turned back to face the enemy. There were not many peltasts in front of them and the first of these fled in terror of the cavalry who, as soon as they saw this, took the lesson to heart and charged against the others. There, Phoebidas and two or three of his men fell fighting, and at this the whole mercenary force turned and ran. In their flight they came to the Thespian hoplites, men who had previously done a lot of boasting about how they would never give way to the Thebans. In spite of this, however, they too turned and ran, though there was not even a regular pursuit as it was now so late in the day. Not many were killed but the Thespians went on running until they were inside their city walls.[70]

The outstanding success of this charge was probably greatly helped by the fact that the intentions of the riders and their horses were perfectly matched. Having found themselves trapped by the impassable ravine, the horses' natural instinct would have been a desperate stampede back the other way.

The psychological factors at play upon the horses here, a kind of equine version of burning one's bridges, may have been recognised and utilized by Greek commanders as they gained experience in the use of cavalry. There were a number of instances where cavalry were ordered to attack, and then infantry ordered to follow close behind. Obviously this tactic could be justified straightforwardly in that it meant that, should the cavalry charge fail to rout the enemy straightaway, the infantry would arrive quickly to help them out or to exploit any confusion or disorder they had caused. Whether it was merely a fortunate side-effect or not, it would also have had a psychological effect on the horses that may have been a significant factor in the success of such tactics. Reluctant as the horses may have been to gallop into the enemy, the sight and sound of the infantry running up behind them would have herded them forward. In this situation the path of least resistance for the horse was to obey his rider's commands to go forward.

When they were available peltasts were ideal for this work, but on several occasions the Spartans used the youngest hoplites for this purpose, as when the Spartan Pausanius 'ordered the cavalry to charge at a gallop and the infantry in the age groups between twenty and thirty to follow the cavalry'.[71] As early as the Mantinea campaign in 418 BC the Thebans seem to have fielded troops specially trained in this role, 'five hundred cavalry and five hundred dismounted troops trained to operate with the cavalry'.[72] The idea that such troops held onto the horses' tails seems a dubious one, as this would have been likely only to result in many of them being debilitated by kicks from annoyed horses or dragged off their feet. More probably they ran behind as closely as they could manage.

This use of light infantry and cavalry in combination was part of a wider trend. More frequent and longer campaigns gave commanders greater scope for experimenting with the increasing variety of troops. The various states were mobilizing more of their resources; not only the small farm owners as hoplites, but the gentry as cavalry and the poor as light infantry. Specialized mercenaries flourished. In place of the old amateur levy of hoplites, followed by a smattering of armed servants and a few mistrusted cavalrymen, the wealthier states at least were fielding more sophisticated combined-arms forces. By the second quarter of the fourth century BC, the better Greek generals were learning to use all the elements together. As the mercenary commander Iphicrates is said to have remarked, an army was like a person: the general was the head, the phalanx the body and breastplate, the light infantry were the hands and the cavalry the feet.[73] The cavalry were the feet presumably because it was they that provided the ability to manoeuvre quickly. Although, as this makes clear, all the components were vital, it was the cavalry in particular, with their combination of speed and hitting power, that were largely responsible for injecting more variety and tactical sophistication into Greek battles.

To illustrate the importance that shock cavalry was attaining towards the end of the Classical period, it is only necessary to look at a remarkable string of victories won by the two Theban commanders, Pelopidas and Epaminondas. Theban and allied Thessalian cavalry played a key role in all of them, which is not surprising given their long-established tradition of mounted prowess, stretching back at least to Plataea and Phalerum. Ironically, both generals were killed in the moment of victory, but the legacy of their demonstration of the decisive potential of the cavalry charge lived on.

The first battle took place near Tegyra in 375 BC. Pelopidas was heading home to Thebes with 'a small force' of cavalry and the elite infantry of the Sacred Band, made up of 150 pairs of male lovers. They were travelling along a narrow strip between a mountain and the marshy flood plain of a river, making for a pass. The cavalry were riding at the rear, probably to prevent the slower hoplites from being left behind. According to Plutarch, one of the Thebans suddenly cried out in despair that they had fallen into their enemies' hands as two battalions of Spartan hoplites appeared from the pass, between seven hundred and a thousand in number and considered the best infantry in the known world at the time. Pelopidas supposedly replied, 'Why not they into our hands?'

With no room for manoeuvre, the only option was a head-on clash. As the Spartans bore down on them (Plutarch specifies that the Spartans advanced first), Pelopidas ordered his cavalry up from the rear of the column and told them to attack while he followed behind with the Sacred Band in close order. 'His hope', explains Plutarch, 'was that wherever the cavalry charged, this point would offer him the best chance to break through the enemy.' The Theban cavalry seem to have struck right at the centre of the line, for it was here that the two Spartan commanders were quickly cut down along with those around them. The Spartans, confused by this furious onslaught and the sudden loss of their leaders, opened a path for the Theban cavalry, assuming they were merely trying to break through to safety. But Pelopidas, not content with escape and spotting the chance for a clear victory, led the Sacred Band down this corridor before launching an attack into the soft belly of the Spartan phalanx. 'He cut his way through them with great slaughter, until finally the entire Spartan force turned and fled.'[74]

The Thebans won another victory over the Spartans at Leuctra in 371 BC. Expecting a Spartan invasion, the Thebans and their Boeotian allies hastily conscripted a force of 'not more than six thousand'.[75] Led by Epaminondas, this force seized the pass at Coronea, only to find that King Cleombrotus had taken the coastal route and reached Leuctra, outflanking them and threatening Thebes itself. Hurrying back, the Thebans took up high ground and, suddenly catching sight of the 'Lacedaemonians covering the entire plain of Leuctra, they were astounded at beholding the great size of the army'.[76] Undaunted by the odds and the protests of the other elected leaders, and supported by Pelopidas, who again commanded the Sacred Band, Epaminondas opted to give battle on the plain.

From this point there are many discrepancies between the accounts of Xenophon, Plutarch and Diodorus, particularly as regards the role of the cavalry, but certain basic facts are incontestable. The Spartans formed a line, with Cleombrotus commanding the right with his elite guard around him, while the left was commanded by Archidamus, son of Agesilaus. Epaminondas adopted what was, according to Diodorus, 'an unusual disposition of his own', massing his best infantry (the Thebans themselves) in an unusually deep column on his left, with the various allies stretching away to his right.[77] According to Xenophon, the Spartan phalanx 'was not more than twelve men deep' while the Thebans 'were drawn up in a massed formation of at least fifty shields in depth'.[78]

All the sources agree that Epaminondas' plan was to strike an overwhelming blow at the Spartan right where Cleombrotus and the best of the Spartans were. Battle was joined and all are agreed that there was a fierce fight in which Cleombrotus 'perished in an heroic resistance after sustaining many wounds'. The much-vaunted Spartan phalanx, still the best in Greece despite the debacle at Tegyra, collapsed into a rout with heavy casualties. The question is where the cavalry of both sides was while all this was going on.

Diodorus, writing centuries after the event, does not mention the cavalry at all and simply attributes the Theban success to 'their valour

and the denseness of their ranks'. But can this be the whole story? The
Spartan elite were schooled from boyhood to face death with equanim-
ity and no troops were more experienced and disciplined in keeping
their ranks welded in solid unity. True the Thebans had the weight
of numbers at the first point of collision on the right wing, but only
the front three ranks or so could actively participate at one time, the
remainder providing only psychological weight and replacements in a
prolonged fight. Diodorus himself noted that the Thebans were many
times outnumbered, and massed fifty deep their line was many times
shorter. If there was a long struggle on the right wing, and even if as he
asserts, the Theban right wing was ordered to retreat ahead of the Spartan left, avoiding battle, it should not have long prevented Archidamus
from outflanking the Theban attack column in flank. Epaminondas'
bold plan succeeded because he overwhelmed the Spartan right quickly,
before the rest of their line could be brought to bear. The mere sight
of the deep phalanx was unlikely instantly to overawe the descendants
of the three hundred who had fought to the death against the Persian hordes at Thermopylae. But both the other accounts suggest that
something beyond the ordinary clumsy clash of phalanxes happened
to disrupt the Spartan ranks, thus sowing the kind of disorder that no
phalanx could survive.

   Plutarch, having earlier mentioned that Cleombrotus had one thousand cavalry when he invaded, fails to mention the cavalry of either
side in his account of the battle. In his account, the main Theban column advanced obliquely to the left, hoping to entice Cleombrotus' elite
Spartans to follow and draw them away from the rest of their army,
while the rest of the Theban line hung back. The Spartans apparently
saw the danger and started 'to change their formation, extending their
right wing and starting an encircling movement so as to outflank and
envelop Epaminondas'. This was foiled by Pelopidas and the three hundred strong Sacred Band dashing forward, throwing themselves upon
the Spartans 'before Cleombrotus could either deploy his wing or bring
it back to its previous position and close up his ranks. His charge caught
the Spartans out of position: they had not yet formed their line and
were still moving about indecisively.' This appears to offer us an answer
as to why the Spartans were in disarray so that when 'Epaminondas'
main phalanx bore down on them … their spirit faltered, their courage deserted them'. Are we to believe that the Spartans were 'moving
about indecisively' close enough to be attacked by a force of hoplites
(for such were the Sacred Band)? Plutarch's account comes from his

life of Pelopidas and he naturally gives his hero the vital role; but, having done so, he seems to acknowledge that his own account stretches credibility:

> And yet the Spartans were the most skilled and experienced soldiers in the world, and in their training they paid special attention to the problem of changing formation without falling into disorder or confusion; each man was accustomed to take any one of his comrades as his right-hand or rear-rank man, and wherever danger might threaten, to concentrate on that point, knit their ranks, and fight as effectively as ever.[79]

Only the account of Xenophon, well placed to speak to survivors of the battle, both explains the whereabouts of the numerous Spartan and Theban cavalry and accounts for what rapidly became a 'rout and slaughter of the Spartans such as had never before been seen'. He clearly states that 'since between the two armies the ground was level, the Spartans stationed their cavalry in front of the phalanx and the Thebans stationed their cavalry opposite them'. Behind the cavalry Epaminondas formed his fifty-deep column opposite Cleombrotus' position, realizing that 'if they proved superior in that part of the field where the king was, all the rest would be easy'. Of the two phalanxes, it was the Spartans that advanced first, confident of their superiority in hoplite fighting, despite the Thebans' unusual formation. But then something happened that they could not have trained for: 'The cavalry had already engaged and the Spartan contingents had very quickly been worsted. Then in their flight they had fallen foul of their own hoplites.'[80]

The Spartan cavalry were chased back through the ranks of Cleombrotus' advancing hoplites, throwing them into confusion. This is why the Spartans were still moving about indecisively when the Theban infantry smashed into them. Possibly some of the Theban cavalry in hot pursuit even exploited the gaps thus opened and started to cut their way towards the king, but they may have veered off and ridden out to the flank as their infantry came up. Pelopidas and the Sacred Band may well have been the first Thebans to wade into Cleombrotus' floundering phalanx, having followed the cavalry as closely as they could. Cleombrotus stood his ground and was cut down as the Spartans desperately tried to recover from this unaccustomed confusion and reknit their ranks. They resisted long enough to carry their king's mortally wounded body clear, but soon Epaminondas' main force came up to finish the job. The Spartan elite broke and fled, followed by the rest of the army. No doubt the Theban cavalry took up the pursuit until the fugitives reached the relative security of their camp, which was on higher ground, contributing to the heavy one-sided casualties.

It was a crushing defeat. Diodorus says more than four thousand Spartans were killed and only approximately three hundred Thebans. Xenophon, more plausibly, puts Spartan deaths at nearly a thousand, but this included one king, one polemarch (a senior officer of the phalanx), two of the king's tent companions and four hundred of the seven hundred elite Spartans present. Such was the physical and psychological damage that when news of the defeat reached Sparta, where Xenophon may have been present, they reacted by urgently mobilizing men up to sixty years old for hoplite service. As a direct result Thebes replaced Sparta as the leading state in Greece.

In 364 BC some of the Thessalians asked the Thebans to send an army under Pelopidas to help rid them of the tyranny of Alexander of Pherae (the most powerful Thessalian city). The Thebans prepared an army, but an eclipse at the time of its departure was seen as a bad omen. Only Pelopidas, who had once been imprisoned by Alexander, and three hundred cavalry were prepared to go. The Thessalians joined him in large numbers but Alexander still had a much larger army when the two encountered each other at Cynoscephelae ('the dogs' heads'), where a range of steep hills rose from the plain. Both armies possessed strong forces of cavalry and peltasts in addition to their hoplite phalanxes.

Both generals sent their cavalry onto the plain, while sending peltasts to seize the heights, their phalanxes forming up in the plain. Pelopidas' cavalry quickly put Alexander's to flight but then got carried away and attempted to charge uphill at Alexander's peltasts, who had won the race to secure the high ground. This was asking too much even of Thessalian cavalry. The slopes were steep and the peltasts hurled javelins down upon them, driving them off with heavy casualties. Pelopidas then directed the cavalry to attack some of Alexander's infantry down on the level ground, which they did, while he personally led an infantry assault upon the slopes. It is unclear what kind of infantry the cavalry attacked at this point, or whether this action was in conjunction with Pelopidas' phalanx, but it seems they did so with some success. Some of the cavalry at least returned to support Pelopidas' peltasts, whose assaults had also been thrown back more than once. Finally, with cavalry and infantry acting in proper concert, Alexander's peltasts were finally driven back down the other side. As Alexander's troops were wavering and falling back, Pelopidas saw his arch-enemy trying to rally some of his mercenaries. Unable to control his personal feelings,

Pelopidas heroically, but unwisely, rushed down the slopes and hurled himself upon them, single-handedly cutting down several as he tried to get at Alexander. Unsurprisingly he was quickly riddled with javelins and killed. Seeing him fall, his troops were enraged and redoubled their efforts. The cavalry in particular took a terrible revenge:

> The cavalry launched another charge in which they routed the whole of the enemy's phalanx. They pursued the infantry to a great distance, cut down more than three thousand of them, and left the countryside strewn with corpses.[81]

The tyrant had been defeated and was soon to be murdered by his own wife, who had earlier become an admirer of Pelopidas while he was imprisoned in Pherae. But the battle was followed by mourning for Pelopidas rather than celebration on the part of the Thessalians, who begged the Thebans to be allowed the honour of burying him. Interestingly, their display of profound grief included shearing off their horses' manes and tails, perhaps indicating the extent to which Greece's most equestrian society identified themselves with their mounts.

Cynoscephelae demonstrated once again the potentially decisive power of determined heavy cavalry. Even though the climactic charge may have been launched against a phalanx that was already wavering, this itself was largely due to the softening up of the cavalry's earlier attacks, although Pelopidas' phalanx may now have been closing in on them too. Equally significant is the outcome of the assaults on the ridge. Both the cavalry and the infantry were repulsed when attacking separately but succeeded when finally combining their efforts.

The harnessing of the shock charge into a combined arms battle was taken to a new level by Epaminondas at Mantinea in 362 BC. Here the lessons of Tegyra and Leuctra were put into effect in unequivocal style. Tegyra might be dismissed as a small-scale, surprise encounter rather than a proper battle. At Leuctra, it might be argued that the Theban cavalry were only intended to chase off their opposite numbers, and that the subsequent disruption of the Spartan infantry was no more than an unlooked for bonus. But in the encounter at Mantinea, which has many similarities to the two previous battles, the decisive role was planned for them from the start.

Epaminondas had invaded Lacedaemonian territory and even made an attack on Sparta itself. Deterred by an aggressive defence under Agesilaus, he turned to attack Mantinea. He sent his cavalry ahead with the aim of catching the Mantineans and their livestock outside of the walls.

In this, too, he was thwarted as the Athenian cavalry happened to arrive on the scene and defeated the Theban horsemen in a ferocious clash that claimed the life of Xenophon's son, Gryllus. Mindful of the effect of repeated defeats on his personal prestige and the loyalty of the allied contingents, Epaminondas was determined to achieve something solid before returning to Thebes and so decided to risk a pitched battle.

Diodorus gives figures of thirty thousand infantry and not 'less than three thousand cavalry' for Epaminondas' army. Facing him was a combined force of Mantineans, Athenians, Spartans and various other allies, which Diodorus numbers at twenty thousand infantry and two thousand cavalry, all under the command of the ageing Agesilaus.[82] The two sides were perhaps more evenly matched than these numbers suggest. Much of Epaminondas' numerical advantage in infantry was due to large numbers of Thessalian light infantry armed with javelins and slings. The Spartan phalanx, though not of the uniformly high calibre it had been before the disaster at Leuctra, was still a potential battle-winner if allowed to fight on its own terms, and the Athenian hoplites were also experienced and likely to put up a good fight. Epaminondas' strongest suit was his cavalry, which was not only numerically superior but also of excellent quality, being comprised of Thebans and Thessalians. This said, the Athenians probably had five or six hundred cavalry with them whose confidence had been boosted by their recent victory. Finally, in Agesilaus the Thebans faced the most experienced commander in Greece, a wily and experienced general who knew how to use cavalry and infantry and had never suffered a major defeat.

Agesilaus' deployment gave priority to his flanks, a wise precaution against a more numerous enemy, especially one superior in cavalry. The honour of holding the extreme right of the line he gave to the Mantineans, who, fighting on their own doorstep, might be expected to fight bravely. This had the advantage that they protected the unshielded side of his own Spartan hoplites who made up the rest of the right wing. The left wing of the phalanx was entrusted to the Athenians, who comprised the biggest and most renowned of the allied contingents, with their cavalry guarding their flank. The hoplites of the various other allies filled up the centre. According to Diodorus, there was cavalry on both flanks, but there was also a body of Elian horsemen posted in reserve.[83]

Epaminondas formed his army up in line, Thebans on the left (opposite the Mantineans and Spartans) with Arcadians in support. The right wing he entrusted to the Argives and he filled the centre with 'the remaining multitude'. But, instead of advancing towards the enemy line, Epaminondas marched his men off towards some hills as if declining to give battle that day and had them ground arms as if in preparation for making camp. This had the desired effect of lulling Agesilaus into a false sense of security: he allowed his army to leave their positions, the infantry turning their minds to food and rest; the cavalry, as is the timeless lot of horsemen, first saw to the needs of their horses. Epaminondas then had his men retrieve their arms, formed them up in a new formation and advanced quickly on the enemy. The ruse had the desired result:

> when they saw him advancing there was a total lack of steadiness. Some were running to take up their positions, others forming into line, others bridling their horses, others putting on their breastplates. The general impression was one of people expecting to suffer rather than to cause damage.[84]

The formation Epaminondas had adopted for this advance was a refinement of the one he had used at Leuctra. The Theban hoplites were again massed on the left, but this time, according to Xenophon, it was in a wedge-shaped formation: 'His next move was to bring up company after company to the wing where he was himself and to wheel them into line, thus adding weight to the wedge like formation of this wing.'[85] This was unusual in the extreme, and has been the subject of controversy ever since as to exactly what Xenophon was describing. However this wedge was formed, the Theban infantry was clearly being massed for another decisive blow on a narrow front, aimed at the enemy right. This dense mass led the way forward while the rest of the army, in which Epaminondas had less faith, were allowed to trail behind so that the right wing of the phalanx was well behind the left.

> Epaminondas led his army forward prow on, as it were, like the ram of a trireme, believing that if he could strike and break through at any point, he would destroy the whole enemy army. His plan was to fight the battle with the strongest part of his army, and he left the weakest part far in the rear, since he knew that, if it were defeated, this would discourage the troops that were with him and give heart to the enemy.[86]

The plan was for the leading left wing to deliver a quick knockout blow and overwhelm the unprepared enemy, with the aim of making his whole army collapse before the weaker elements of his own army were put to the test.

Leading this assault was a large part of the Theban and Thessalian cavalry, providing the cutting edge that was to strike the first demoralizing blow and start the collapse of the enemy. These too were formed up in a wedge, probably at the suggestion of the Thessalians, to whom it was well known as a formation particularly appropriate for breaking through enemy units. Perhaps the novel infantry wedge was an experimental attempt to adapt the same formation to the phalanx. Cooperating with the cavalry were detachments of infantry, perhaps the Sacred Band or possibly peltasts who could more nearly keep up with them. Their role was to exploit any openings or disruption made by the cavalry, as Pelopidas had at Tegyra and Leuctra.

Agesilaus meanwhile had managed to deploy some of his cavalry in the path of the oncoming Thebans while his right wing got itself into order behind. These were the first to meet the onslaught as Xenophon explains:

> The enemy had drawn up their cavalry like a phalanx of hoplites in a line six deep and without infantry to act together with the cavalry. But Epaminondas had formed up his cavalry, too, in a strong wedge formation, and he had infantry with them in support, believing that when he had broken through the enemy cavalry he would have defeated the whole force opposed to him, since it was very difficult to find men who will stand their ground when they see any of their own side in flight.[87]

The biggest threat to the success of his bold plan was that the Athenians opposite his right wing, which he wanted to leave out of harm's way, might come to the assistance of the Spartans and assail the big wedge on its flank with their own cavalry and hoplites. To forestall this Epaminondas sent his remaining Theban cavalry with masses of javelinmen and slingers, as well as some peltasts, to keep the Athenians occupied, posting these on low hills opposite them. The Athenian commander, Hegesileos, sent forward his cavalry with a few supporting javelinmen to attack them, but they were driven off by heavy missile fire from the skirmishers and controlled counter-attacks by the Theban cavalry. Light infantry armed with missiles, particularly those armed with longer-range weapons like the sling, could do great damage to vulnerable horses when they were protected from being ridden down, as they were in this case by the presence of the Theban cavalry.

> Now as the Athenian horse attacked the Theban they suffered defeat not so much because of the quality of their mounts nor yet on the score of the riders' courage or experience in horsemanship, for in none of these

departments was the Athenian cavalry deficient; but it was in the numbers of light-armed troops and in their tactical skill that they were far inferior to their opponents ... Consequently the Athenians, who were continually being wounded by the light-armed and were harried to exhaustion by the opponents who confronted them, all turned and fled.[88]

Diodorus makes a point of praising the Athenian cavalry because they managed *not* to get in the way of their own hoplites as they galloped back past their flank to safety. The pursuing Theban cavalry let the routed horsemen go and charged into the now unguarded flank of the Athenian phalanx instead, plunging into their ranks and laying about them in a chaotic mêlée. They quickly gained the upper hand and the Athenian phalanx collapsed into a panicking mob, with the Thebans hot on their heels, each picking their victims and riding them down with a well-timed spear thrust or a slash of the sword to the back of the neck. But it was now that Agesilaus' foresight and experience paid dividends. 'The battle was a hot one; the Athenians were exhausted and had turned to flee, when the Elian cavalry commander, assigned to the rear, came to the aid of the fugitives and, by striking down many Boeotians, reversed the course of the battle.'[89] The Athenian horsemen meanwhile had rallied and returned to attack the light infantry and peltasts who were now without cavalry protection. Catching them as they made for some high ground on the Athenian flank, 'they gave battle and slew them all'. The Athenians were now victorious on this flank but both their phalanx and their cavalry had taken a mauling. More importantly they had been kept busy while the main Theban spearhead was thrust towards the Mantineans and Spartans on the right.

Xenophon, pro-Spartan as he was, quickly passes over the details of the ensuing clash on this flank: 'All his [Epaminondas'] anticipations were fulfilled. By overwhelming the force against which he struck he caused the whole enemy army to turn and fly.'[90] The Spartan cavalry gallantly bore the first impact of the cavalry wedge but did not manage to buy much time for the hoplites behind them, as Diodorus recounts:

Both cavalry forces lashed at one another and the battle hung for a short time in the balance, but then, because of the number and valour of the Boeotian and Thessalian horsemen, the contingents on the Mantinean side were forced back, and with considerable loss *took refuge with their own phalanx*.[91]

It was Leuctra all over again. The defeated cavalry was driven back upon their own phalanx. But this time the Thebans and Thessalians followed through, driving their wedge into the resulting gap, carving an ever widening breach in the Spartan ranks. Startled hoplites tried to fling themselves sideways out of the path of the pounding hooves, sending a convulsion of confusion and disorder along the phalanx to either side of the point of attack. Those that could not get out of arms' reach in time were felled by spear thrusts to the face and limbs, the slash of a machaira to the neck or a stunning blow to the top of the head. Others may well have been trampled as the horses were funnelled through the confined space, until they burst out of the other side of the phalanx, still in pursuit of the beaten Spartan and Mantinean cavalry.

As at Leuctra, the massed Theban infantry arrived to find the job half done and quickly routed the disrupted enemy phalanx. Diodorus describes a fierce and protracted fight, but his account of this stage of the fighting is discredited by his description of the hoplites of both sides fighting with javelins. Xenophon would surely have made more of it if the Spartans had put up a fight worthy of their reputation. Both historians, however, are agreed that Epaminondas was mortally wounded even as the enemy broke and took to their heels before him. According to Diodorus, he was carried from the field barely alive, impaled by a spear that had passed clean through his breastplate, clinging to life long enough to hear confirmation that the enemy were beaten before declaring 'it is time to die'.

When it was realized that their general was stricken, the demoralized and leaderless Thebans failed to pursue the beaten enemy, instead sounding the recall by trumpet. Having skated over the flight of Agesilaus (his hero and patron), Xenophon elaborates on this limitation of the Theban victory.

> Those who were left, even though they had won, failed to take full advantage of the victory. The enemy phalanx was on the run, but the hoplites did not kill a single man of them, nor did they advance beyond the point where they had made their first impact. The enemy cavalry had also fled, but again the Theban cavalry did not pursue them and kill either cavalrymen or hoplites. Instead they fell back timidly, like beaten men, *through the routed lines of their enemies.*[92]

This last line removes any doubt that they had earlier charged through the enemy phalanx, otherwise they could hardly have fallen back through it. Had the cavalry fight occurred out beyond the flank of the Mantinean phalanx, as might easily be deduced from Diodorus's assertion that 'both sides divided the cavalry and placed contingents on both wings', then the Theban cavalry could have much more safely retreated that way rather than picking their way through the routed hoplites and over ground now churned up by thousands of fleeing feet and strewn with bodies, weapons and discarded shields.

Although it was the attack of the Theban and Thessalian cavalry against the Spartan right wing that paved the way for victory, the performance of the opposing cavalry units on the other wing is equally instructive. The Thebans, having cooperated with their supporting light infantry to drive off the Athenian horse, then outflanked and routed the Athenian phalanx thus exposed. Given that the allied infantry on this flank had been left far in the rear, the Athenian phalanx must have been fresh and intact before this attack. The Athenian cavalry had then rallied, itself no mean feat, and destroyed the now unprotected Theban and Euboean light troops. Finally the Elian squadron again proved that Agesilaus at least had grasped the value of a cavalry reserve when they rescued the fugitive Athenian hoplites from the pursuing Theban horsemen.

After Mantinea neither the Spartans, having suffered their second heavy defeat in a decade, nor the Thebans, now bereft of the inspired leadership of Pelopidas and Epaminondas, proved capable of dominating Greece. But the tactical lessons were well heeded by those who would fill the power vacuum: the Macedonians.

During the course of the Classical period, an increasing number of Greek states made use of cavalry forces. From the first they did, as is widely acknowledged, fulfil roles peripheral to the traditional clash of the heavy infantry, who were still the arbiters of victory or defeat. Cavalry could act as scouts before the battle, they could pursue fugitives once it had been won, or cover a retreat if it had been lost. Increasingly, however, the potential offered by their combination of mobility and striking power began to be realized.

Greek commanders increasingly found that there were a number of situations in which the hoplite phalanx was vulnerable to attack by cavalry during the battle itself. Using their superior mobility, horsemen could exploit opportunities to charge the phalanx from flank and rear, preferably once it was already engaged frontally, throwing it into confusion and hastening its collapse into panic. Such attacks proved decisive more frequently than has often been recognized. Increasingly, Greek cavalry were fulfilling the role of heavy cavalry, equipped and prepared to engage in close combat. As the best way to protect the phalanx was to counter like with like, cavalry came to be almost essential offensively and defensively.

The increased danger of being outflanked encouraged a better use of terrain features that, by hindering the rapid orderly movement of horses, could protect a flank against envelopment. By providing Greek generals with a force that could manoeuvre rapidly and which, largely through its intimidating aspect, could be particularly devastating when attacking from an unexpected direction, cavalry also made battles less predictable and more fluid. They gave commanders more options. In so doing they stimulated the use of tactical reserves to guard against unexpected developments and to exploit opportunities. It is true that the concurrent increase in the use of light infantry also contributed to the greater tactical sophistication of Greek warfare, but the fact that these were even more vulnerable than the phalanx to a mounted charge only increased the usefulness of shock cavalry.

The full potential of shock action by cavalry was beginning to be realized by the Thebans in their victories over the Spartans. At Tegyra and Mantinea, possibly also at Leuctra, the Theban cavalry were not left to look for an opportunity for a charge to arise during the course of the infantry fighting. Instead they were given from the outset the task of disrupting the enemy line by means of a shock charge, supported by the infantry. Cavalry was now more than an auxiliary to the phalanx. They were now an equal partner, and even capable of playing the leading role in coordinated tactical plans.

3

The Macedonians

Amongst the generally poor picture painted of ancient horsemen, the cavalry of Alexander the Great have always been treated as a dazzling exception, galloping victoriously onto the pages of history fully formed from nowhere. While classical Greek cavalry is often dismissed as hard pressed even to stay on their horses due to their lack of stirrups and proper saddles, Alexander's horsemen, still without these aids, are described delivering decisive hammer blows that punched holes through the enemy lines.[1] The Macedonian heavy cavalry did indeed play the decisive role attributed to them but they were not invented overnight. As seen already, Greek cavalry had become a powerful force on the battlefield by the mid fourth century BC. The Macedonians merely continued and refined the developments already underway elsewhere in Greece, particularly in Thebes.

The cavalry force with which Alexander ran amok across half the then known world was, like the rest of his army, and indeed the Macedonian kingdom, largely created by his father, Philip II. When Philip first took up the reins of power in 359 BC, initially as regent for his young nephew, Macedon's prospects of survival, let alone major power status, were not good. Philip's brother, King Amyntas III, had just been defeated and killed by Bardylis and his invading Illyrian army, which now occupied much of the north-western marches of the kingdom. Inhabiting the mountains to the north were the equally hostile Paeonians, while the Thracian tribes of the forests and plains to the east were so numerous and ferocious that Herodotus thought they would conquer the world if they ever stopped fighting each other for long enough. No help was likely to come from the south either, for that way lay Thessally and other Greek states that, although they worshipped the same gods, considered the Macedonians to be uncouth foreigners. For decades the Thessalians, Thebans and Athenians had interfered in Macedonian affairs, and now Athens actively supported a pretender to the throne.

Fortunately, Philip proved equal to the task. With a mixture of bribery, diplomacy and decisive military action he managed to stabilize the situation and secure Macedon's remaining territory against further

invasion. He then set about reforming his army: re-equipping, reorgan-
izing and subjecting it to a thorough training regime of manoeuvres,
mock battles and route marches. Philip had inherited a small permanent cavalry bodyguard, the *hetairoi* (Companions), and an infantry
bodyguard, the *pezhetairoi* (Foot Companions). In time of war these
cavalry and infantry were supplemented by calling up the aristocracy
and the peasantry respectively. Because the Macedonian landowners
had a long tradition of producing efficient and well-equipped horsemen,[2] Philip made them his main strike force. By 358 BC, Philip was
ready to go on the offensive.

Having first invaded the territory of the Paeonians and forced their
new king to sign a treaty of alliance, Philip was ready to settle the score
with Bardylis, who had defeated his brother, and recover the lost territories of upper Macedonia. According to Diodorus, Macedonians and
Illyrians each fielded about ten thousand infantry, but Philip had six
hundred cavalry to Bardylis' five hundred and the latter were probably
less well equipped. His account of the battle is short of detail but the
contribution of the cavalry is at least clear.

> The valour of both armies was such that the issue of the battle was for a
> long time doubtful; many fell, but many more were wounded ... At length,
> when the horse charged both upon flank and rear [presumably having seen
> off the Illyrian cavalry], and Philip, with his stoutest soldiers, fought like a
> hero in the front, the whole body of the Illyrians was routed and forced to
> fly outright; whom the Macedonians pursued a long way ... There were slain
> of the Illyrians in this battle above seven thousand men.[3]

The close coordination of cavalry and heavy infantry here was a mark
of the influence upon Philip of three years spent as a hostage at Thebes,
where the methods of Epaminondas and Pelopidas would have become
well known to him. Their victories at Tegyra, Leuctra and Mantinea had
hinted at the potential of cavalry to rupture the enemy's line and pave
the way for the main infantry assault.

The keystone of the reformed army's success was the careful integration of various types of troops – each individually more specialized but
making up part of a versatile and balanced force. The native cavalry's
tactics and equipment were now thoroughly specialized for shock action,
while the levy infantry was turned into an ultra-specialized phalanx: at
once more lethal and impenetrable frontally and yet more vulnerable
than ever to flank and rear attacks unless protected by good cavalry.
Heavy cavalry and the phalanx formed the core of the army, but as

Macedonian power and wealth grew these were supplemented with specialist mercenaries such as Cretan archers, Rhodian slingers and siege engineers, while allied or vassal states such as Thracians and Paeonians provided most of the light cavalry and light infantry components.

Over the next twenty years Philip campaigned almost continuously, all the while honing his military machine and its tactics on the whetstone of experience, so that it effectively became a permanent professional army. In 356 BC Philip seized Crenides, where Greek settlers had started exploiting gold deposits, and renamed it Philippi. This massive boost to the royal coffers allowed for more troops to be equipped, fed and paid. By his death, the Macedonian heavy cavalry had grown to around 2800. This expansion was achieved largely by recruiting new squadrons from the liberated provinces of upper Macedonia and granting land in return for cavalry service in newly conquered territory. In 344 BC Philip intervened in the affairs of the Thessalian League, defeating the tyrant of the rogue city of Pherae, and was elected head of the league for life. This coup added the magnificent Thessalian cavalry to Philip's resources.

By 340 BC Macedonian power had been greatly extended over most of southern Thrace, the Paeonians and many of the Illyrian tribes had been reduced to tribute-paying satellites, and Philip's nephew had been placed on the throne of Epirus. The southern Greek city states, particularly Thebes (his nominal ally) and Athens, were now becoming nervous to say the least, with good cause as Philip was already planning to unite the Greeks under his influence, by whatever means, and then 'liberate' western Asia from Persian rule at the head of their combined forces. When Philip attacked Byzantium and Perinthus, which guarded both the shortest crossing to Asia and the main route for Athens's vital corn imports from the Black Sea region, an Athenian-led coalition of Greek states declared war. This move proved to have come too late: when a combined Athenian and Theban army finally stood up to the Macedonian host at Chaeronea in 338 BC, the Greeks were decisively crushed.

The surviving accounts of Chaeronea are frustratingly deficient, particularly as to the movements of the Athenian and Theban cavalry. These were probably at least equal in number, if not quality, to the two thousand Macedonian and Thessalian horsemen fielded by Philip. The Greeks, who probably had a few thousand more infantry than Philip's thirty thousand, seem to have formed their phalanx up across the whole plain, with their right flank resting on the River Cephisus and their left upon the hilly ground beneath Chaeronea itself. They preferred, quite reasonably, to entrust the protection of their flanks to these natural

obstacles rather than their own cavalry, presumably arraying their horsemen some way behind the phalanx to counter any breakthrough. As far as
we can tell, however, they did not intervene in any meaningful way when
the infantry was defeated, perhaps suggesting that the latter collapsed too
quickly or that the cavalry knew themselves to be outmatched.

We do know that Philip entrusted his left wing, facing the Thebans, to
the eighteen-year-old Alexander, while he himself faced the Athenians.
Ancient and modern writers alike are agreed that at the climax of the
battle Alexander led the Companion cavalry in a decisive attack upon
the elite hoplites of the Theban Sacred Band. According to Diodorus,
he did so 'with a more than ordinary heat and vigour ... was the first
that broke through the main body of the enemy next to him, with the
slaughter of many, and bore down all before him'.[4] It is most likely that
this charge was delivered on the Sacred Band's left flank after an over-
eager advance by the Athenians had opened a fatal gap in their line.
The Athenians' error was possibly prompted by a deliberate retreat by
Philip on the right wing, trying to lure them out of their sound defensive position. If Philip did indeed withdraw his right while his cavalry
paved the way for his left to launch a decisive assault on the enemy's
elite troops, it can be seen as an interesting variation on the theme of
Epaminondas' tactics.

The Sacred Band was utterly destroyed and the Greek army collapsed
into rout, leaving over a thousand Athenians and 'a great number
of the Boeotians' dead, and thousands more as prisoners. The anti-
Macedonian alliance was smashed and all the Greek states (except
Sparta, which stubbornly refused) now fell over themselves to ally
themselves with Philip, who forced them to form a federation now
usually referred to as the 'League of Corinth'. This was to be eternally
allied to Macedonia and recognise the Macedonian king as commander
of the league forces that the member states would provide for the
invasion of Persia. Philip of course, did not live to fulfil this role, but
by the time of his assassination in 336 BC he had set the stage for Alexander's dazzling career of conquest – not least by providing Alexander
with a thorough education in the art of war and the fine cavalry force
with which he would seal victory after victory.

The cavalry were recruited regionally, each area providing an *ila* or
squadron, a little over two hundred strong. Many volunteers were also
attracted from Greek cities by the prospect of regular pay. By Alexander's reign the title 'Companions' was applied to the whole of the
Macedonian heavy cavalry, of which the old bodyguard now formed the

Royal Squadron (*ile basilike*). This was larger than the others, probably numbering around three hundred. Although there is no direct evidence for it, practical considerations suggest that there must have also been subdivisions into much smaller groups, perhaps the ten-man *dekas* of Xenophon's proposed system, but it does seem there was no other subunit at the intermediate level. For most of Alexander's campaigns, the Companions were commanded by Philotas, although Alexander himself usually took over direct command of them in battle and placed himself at the head of the royal squadron.

Philip had developed a system to ensure a steady supply of suitable recruits for the Companions. The leading families of Macedon were to send their sons to him from the age of about fourteen to be educated as royal pages (*paides basilikoi*) at the king's expense, although non-Macedonians might also be accepted. The syllabus included writing and academic study but concentrated on horsemanship and weapon skills. They had special privileges and only the king himself was allowed to punish their misdemeanours. This helped foster personal loyalty to the king, even as they acted as hostages for the good behaviour of their noble fathers. Upon reaching maturity they were ready to serve in the cavalry, with suitable candidates joining the royal squadron. Alexander himself went through the same system, Philip having hired Aristotle as his tutor. Whenever he charged at the head of the Royal Squadron Alexander did so in the knowledge that he was followed by many of his childhood classmates, an important factor in the esprit de corps of this most elite of units.

To fulfil the decisive role that they were expected to play in battle, the Companions were thoroughly specialized for shock combat. Philip is usually credited with two significant innovations in this respect, although in both cases it may be more a case of regularising earlier trends rather than of true innovation. One was the adoption of the wedge formation and the other was the exclusive use of a long lance as the primary armament of every rider. Both these features deserve closer attention.

The wedge was devised by the Scythians and then taken up by the Thracians, with whom Philip had fought on numerous occasions. In reality it is likely that use of the wedge had spread south via Macedon as far as Thebes before Philip's reign. The Thessalian diamond or rhomboid was almost certainly a development of it and Epaminondas' Theban cavalry experimented with it at Mantinea. But Philip probably systematized and developed its regular use for the Macedonian cavalry through the rigorous training he was noted for.

As its name suggests, the wedge took the form of a triangle, with a single rider forming the leading point and each successive rank containing more men. If each full squadron formed a single wedge, this would mean something like sixteen ranks. The neat diagram given by Asclepiodotus suggests a geometrically precise placement of ranks and files that could never have been maintained in action at anything more than a trot. But both the academic Asclepiodotus and the experienced cavalry officer Arrian agree that the benefits of this formation were two-fold. First, the narrow frontage meant that wheeling to change direction could be done relatively quickly, as the formation just followed the leader 'as is the case in the flight of cranes'.[5] Secondly, the narrowness of the front made it 'easy to cut through any enemy formation', which is what fitted it particularly to shock action.[6] This is rarely explained any further, but one way to understand it is as follows. When a squadron in line charged an enemy unit, only some of the horsemen in the front rank were likely to find a convenient gap in the enemy's line through which they could ride. Men in the target unit moving aside in one part of the line would cause denser crowding in others, so, unless the enemy broke and scattered altogether straight away, many riders would not find a way through and would have to come to a halt. By contrast, when a wedge charged the lead rider needed only to find a gap for himself to ride at and the rest of the squadron would pile into it behind him. The passage of the lead horse, assisted by its rider's weapons, widened the breach for the two or three horses immediately behind and they for the next rank, and so on.

Although the wedge proved its effectiveness in Alexander's Persian battles, where it was well suited to his aggressive battle plans, it should not by itself be seen as a decisive factor, as the Persians were also using it. However, the Companions did derive a definite advantage from their main armament. In place of the mixed armament of Xenophon's time, they were uniformly armed with a single long thrusting spear or *xyston*. Quite apart from outreaching their opponents in close combat, this also affected the Companions' psychological approach as a cautious exchange of javelins was no longer an option. We know the *xyston* was made of tough cornel wood (a type of cherry) and had a spearhead at either end, the second acting as a counterbalance and as a reserve if the lance was broken. We also know that it was relatively long because Arrian, drawing on the eyewitness account of Ptolemy, cites its length as a decisive factor in the defeat of javelin-armed Persian cavalry at the Granicus.

The exact length has been the focus of a huge amount of debate, however, and although it may seem a small point it will be discussed a little more. The confusion of modern scholars arises from the fact that some sources seem to refer to a cavalry *sarissa*, leading many to believe the Companions' lance was identical to the *sarissa* carried by the Macedonian infantry. This is compounded by the scarcity of surviving examples. In the very few cases where sarissa heads and fittings have been found, the shafts have obviously perished and they were not found in such a manner that the weapon's length could be estimated from their position. Even if their length could be determined, there was nothing to say definitively whether they belonged to a cavalryman or a phalangite.

The infantry sarissa was at least fifteen feet long and very heavy, consisting essentially of two spear shafts joined by an iron coupling sleeve (of which one possible example has been found).* At one end it had a spearhead and at the other a heavy finial to act as a counter-balance and possibly as a butt spike to allow it to be planted in the ground. We know that the Macedonian phalangites (members of the phalanx) replaced the traditional hoplite shield with a much smaller and lighter one borne on a strap, both hands being required for the sarissa. The obvious awkwardness of such a long and clumsy weapon, especially for troops riding in the close wedge formation, is the main reason why many writers, including myself, believe the Companions carried something shorter and lighter.

Just to confuse the issue Alexander's army included a unit of cavalry sometimes specifically referred to as the *sarissophoroi*, that is sarissa-bearers. Their usual name of *prodromoi* (literally forerunners, or scouts) indicates that they were light cavalry, not part of the Companions, but their name clearly suggests that sarissae could be used by horsemen, although we cannot say whether these were identical to those used by the infantry. On the other hand, the fact that this unit could be distinguished by this name possibly suggests that the other cavalry units, including the Companions, were not so armed. It is possible that

---

* A replica made from the specifications of the few surviving pieces by Minor M. Markle III, was eighteen feet long and weighed 14.5 pounds. Even the lighter version which he conjectured for cavalry use weighed over twelve pounds and had to be held in the middle.[7] It is not surprising that Markle's practical testing of the weapon, it appears, extended only as far as getting an 'expert horseman' to sit on a stationary horse with it.

the *sarissophoroi* were distinguished with that name precisely because they were the only ones using a sarissa (possibly a short cavalry version but still longer than other cavalry spears) and that they were a specially selected, even experimental, light cavalry unit.

There is nothing inherently impossible about a fifteen-foot lance being carried by a horseman. The famous Polish 'winged hussars' of the late seventeenth century AD carried heavy lances over fifteen feet long, although it will immediately be countered that they had the advantage of high saddles and stirrups to keep them in place.[8] Perhaps more significantly, their lances were heavily tapered from butt to tip so that the point of balance was closer to the rider.*

*Peter Connolly recently made a lance based on the same artefacts as Markle, measuring over sixteen feet but with a tapered shaft that meant it was balanced if gripped just four feet from the butt end.[9] Apart from the relative ease of handling, this left more of the weapon in front of the hand at the business end, in this case giving the rider twelve feet of 'reach'. Connolly's lance was tested by an experienced re-enactor striking a dummy at the canter. He used both of the techniques of wielding the lance shown in ancient art with good results. The two techniques can be referred to as 'overarm', where the spear is held up above the shoulder with the thumb pointing back, as though it was going to be thrown; and 'underarm', where the lance is held at waist or thigh level, thumb forward. 'Couching', where the shaft is gripped between arm and body under the armpit, was not introduced until the middle ages. However, the rider in the experiment did find that the lance was very heavy when wielded overarm and that the shaking of the spearhead did impair his aim, although this was less pronounced in canter than in trot. The underarm technique was found to be easier to aim but its length made retention of the lance after a strike very difficult. Usually a lancer achieves this by rolling his wrist as he passes the target so that the head describes an arc downwards and back until it is clear of the now fallen target. In this case the rider, mounted on a horse of authentic size, maybe even a little large by Alexandrian standards, could only keep the lance clear of the ground by swinging it out horizontally, rather than vertically, so that the butt end passed behind him over the rump of the horse and the spearhead out to the side. This must have required a lot of space, something that would not have been available to heavy cavalry charging in a tight formation. While this was a very valuable and laudable piece of practical research, Peter Connolly's conclusion that this was the weapon of the Companions does not seem fully justified. The thought of them swinging a lance with a twelve-foot reach out to the side with riders alongside conjures up images of chaotic mayhem. It might of course have been less of a problem for the *prodromoi* operating in looser formation as light cavalry.

Fortunately there is some artistic evidence to shed some light on the question. The stone relief sculpture known as the Alexander Sarcophagus is nearly contemporary and shows Alexander and the Companions in action. Unfortunately all the weapons were made separately, probably of bronze, and have long since been pilfered. From the holes where these were attached, it seems that Alexander and another rider were depicted wielding lances of which the forward portion was about seven and a half feet or longer. They are wielding the weapons 'overarm' so the shafts would have passed level with their ears. Unfortunately, there are no fixing holes for the rear portion of the spears, which would have projected beyond the edge of the frieze. If these riders were holding their spears a third of the way along the shafts, this would indicate a lance between eleven and twelve feet long.

Another interesting depiction is a painting of a Macedonian cavalryman with a double-headed lance charging a Persian infantryman. The relative scale of horses and figures seem less good than the mosaic and sarcophagus, and the forward tip of the lance is obscured by his unfortunate target, but for once we can clearly see the butt end furnished with a second spearhead. It is hard to determine the total length, but it again appears to be around twelve feet long and is definitely gripped way behind the centre point, roughly one third of the way along.

Best of all is the famous 'Issus Mosaic', featured on the cover of almost every book about Alexander. It is believed to be a Roman copy of an original painting by Philoxenus produced during Alexander's life or shortly thereafter. It clearly shows Alexander in the act of skewering a Persian with a long lance that he is wielding with his right hand away from his side and roughly level with his horse's back. The mosaic is damaged where the rear portion of the lance shaft would be, but the tip of a secondary spearhead or butt spike is visible. Alexander is holding the spear about one quarter or a third of the way along the shaft.*

---

*The multi-talented Peter Connolly, a professional illustrator, has made a meticulous study of the mosaic and explains convincingly that it is accurately scaled and proportioned and can therefore be used to determine the length the artist intended to depict. Accurate in so many details of horse tack and other items that are checkable against actual finds, there is no reason to believe that the original artist was not equally careful about the lance. Connolly's careful measurements from the mosaic, when scaled up, show that the lance depicted was indeed tapered to bring the point of balance towards the butt, and would have measured 3.58 metres, very close to twelve feet. In view of this, it is hard to see why he opted to make his replica sixteen feet long.

A twelve-foot-long lance is still a formidably large weapon, requiring much skill and practice to use effectively. Tapered and balanced so it could be held one third of the way along, it would give the rider eight feet of 'reach', a significant advantage over an opponent with a general-purpose eight-foot spear, which gave only four or five feet of reach in front of the hand. It would, however, be much lighter and handier, altogether easier to imagine being of practical use to a formation of heavy cavalry than the considerably more massive sarissa. Whatever the Companions' weapons were actually called at the time, and this may have been inconsistent just as in English we switch between 'spear' and 'lance', the balance of probability and evidence seems to suggests a twelve-foot weapon, with a head at either end and a shaft tapered so it could be held about one third of the way along.

Apart from the lance, the rest of the Companions' equipment was little different from that of Greek cavalry. Cuirasses were most usually leather or stiffened linen with a varying complement of metal reinforcing plates, although some may have switched to lighter body armour as the campaign in Asia progressed.[10] Helmets were usually of the Boeotian type recommended earlier by Xenophon, or the so-called Thracian type. Both were open-faced and afforded the good vision and hearing vital equally for rapid cavalry manoeuvre in formation and in the confusion of a swirling cavalry mêlée. The swords carried as secondary weapons were probably a mix of the curved slashing *kopis* type and the straighter cut-and-thrust *xiphos*, with a blade that broadened slightly before tapering again to the point and usually described as 'leaf shaped'.

Horse tack had also probably developed little. Judging from actual examples and the Issus Mosaic, many of the bits used were of the familiar type with crescent-shaped cheek pieces, some also have even longer 's'-shaped cheek pieces. Longer cheek pieces help in turning the horse's head, being particularly helpful when trying to ride one-handed.* The lower half of the 's', curving under the horse's chin, may also have acted as an early type of curb bit, pressing on the lower jaw when the reins are pulled to reinforce the restraining action of the bit. This last point remains uncertain as it is not clear from depictions if the method of attachment to the cheek straps would allow this action.

---

* During the practical research for this book our trainee warhorse had his usual simple 'egg-butt snaffle' bit replaced with one having long sidebars (though straight ones) and this helped the author's ability to steer with one hand appreciably.

Those on the Issus Mosaic appear to have rollers on the mouth bit, and these may have been large and severe, judging from an actual example of a similar-looking bit excavated at Thebes.

Fabric saddlecloths and whole animal skins were used for the rider's comfort. It is tempting to speculate that the saddles being developed by the Scythians around this time were adopted, and that it was the additional security this afforded to the Companions that allowed them to charge confidently with their unwieldy lances. Artistic representations offer no evidence to support this development in Alexander's reign, however, although the Kazanlak tomb paintings show that a simple saddle was definitely known to the 'free' Thracians, those not directly under Macedonian rule, shortly after Alexander's death.

As for the horses themselves, Macedonia had always been better off than its Greek neighbours, with plenty of fertile grazing in the coastal plains. Thrace was also a region renowned since ancient times for its horse breeding and the conquered areas provided a ready source of breeding stock. Philip was well aware of the need to improve the native stock with new blood, as he demonstrated in 389 BC. Although he was then on his way south from the failed siege of Byzantium to deal with the Athenians and Thebans, Philip made a detour to chastise Atheas, a Scythian king who had seen Philip's troubles as an opportunity to renege on their alliance. After defeating Atheas, and despite his pressing engagement in the south, Philip took the time to organize the collection of twenty thousand selected Scythian mares, which were sent on to Macedonia. As the Macedonians themselves rode stallions, these were not to provide immediate remounts but were the basis of a major breeding programme. Whether they ever reached Macedonia is unclear, as Philip was ambushed by another tribe on the way home and lost much of his plunder. The well-preserved horses from frozen tombs further north are evidence that the Scythians had finely bred animals which could also be large by ancient standards: fourteen and a half hands and occasionally even over fifteen hands.

Alexander of course rode his stallion Bucephalus, which was apparently bred from a famous Thessalian strain and cost Philip a staggering thirteen talents (enough for a Greek labourer to live on for a hundred years).[11] The close bond between the two is famous. Bucephalus would let no other rider upon his back, and when he was stolen by some local tribesmen in Asia a distraught Alexander threatened to have the entire tribe slaughtered unless he was returned – which worked.[12]

Although Bucephalus carried Alexander all the way to India, the toll of his master's campaigns on cavalry horses was horrendous; one extended forced march after the battle of Gaugamela killed a thousand of them. Although batches of reinforcements from Macedonia were sent to Alexander at intervals, losses often had to be made good from local sources, which in many cases would have been of superior quality anyway. At Aspendus Alexander accepted the surrender of the town on the condition that they hand over horses that were being specially bred for Darius in lieu of taxes. Most of the cavalry would have started off with more than one horse of their own, and a groom to look after them. In battle, the grooms would sometimes be ready behind the fighting lines to bring up fresh horses if a lull in the fighting presented itself. Some of the wealthier officers would have had many horses.

If remounts were scarce these could be commandeered and given to those whose horses had become casualties. There was an administrative officer dedicated to the task of maintaining the supply of horses and of redistributing them where necessary. When an officer, Amyntas, was on trial for suspected treason, part of the evidence against him was brought by Antiphanes, 'the clerk to the cavalry', who accused him of refusing 'to follow the normal practice and give some of his horses to those who had lost theirs'. Amyntas 'explained that he had started with ten horses, of which Antiphanes had already requisitioned eight, and that he had no choice but to hold on to the last two unless he was prepared to fight on foot'.[13] The situation got better once Alexander had conquered the Persian empire. When he marched into India he was able to give a new ally 'thirty horses from his own stable'.[14]

The Persian, and later Macedonian, armies had access to two horse breeds of particular note. The most famous are the Nisaean horses (also Nesean or Nysaean). They are first mentioned in the fifth century when Herodotus described ten sacred Nisaean horses in procession behind Xerxes' bodyguard as his army set off to invade Greece. Herodotus explains, 'they were so called because they come from the great Nisaean plain in Media, where horses of unusual size are bred'.[15] This passage makes it unclear whether these ten 'sacred' horses were the only Nisaean horses with the Persian army. Later in his invasion Xerxes had some of his horses race against some Thessalian horses, apparently gaining an easy victory, but whether they were Nisaeans is unknown.[16] These horses were probably tall by ancient standards, possibly sixteen hands high, as well as very muscular and well able to bear the weight of heavier equipment.[17]

By the time Alexander was shown the Nisaean plain, five or six days'

march south of Ecbatana (Hamadan) in north-western Iran, the breeding herds had been reduced by one hundred thousand by theft and
the demands of war, still leaving an impressive fifty or sixty thousand
remaining.[18] The exact location of the 'Nisaean plain' is unknown, but
one plausible recent suggestion is the Vale of Borigerd. Here 'Median
grass' still grows, more commonly known as alfalfa. This is a fodder
highly valued for its exceptional protein content and a high level of cal-
cium which promotes the growth of big, strong bones. The geographer
Strabo stated that Nisaean horses, 'not inferior to those of Media' were
also bred in Armenia.[19] Strabo was writing much later, in the first century BC, but it is not unlikely that Persian kings would have attempted
to increase production of such a valuable military asset by establishing
other studs where possible.

Further north and east in Bactria and Sogdiana, which between
them encompassed modern Afghanistan and much of Turkmenistan
and Uzbekistan, the various tribesmen rode horses similar to the
modern Turcoman and Akhal-Teke. These would have been tall by
ancient standards, perhaps 15.2 hands high, but more finely built and
less bulky than the Nisaeans. Modern Akhal Teke horses are famous
for two characteristics. First, their prodigious stamina. Second, their
amazing coats. These can be chestnut, dun or bay but often have a
metallic sheen that makes them blaze like gold or copper in bright
sunlight.[20] The city of Balkh, the ancient capital of Bactria, was then
known as Bactra-Zariaspa, 'Bactra of the Golden Horses'.[21]

The very best area was the Ferghana Valley at the far eastern extrem-
ity of modern Uzbekistan. This was beyond the Tanais River (Syr Darya)
in Scythian territory, just beyond the limits of direct Persian control but
within its sphere of trade and influence. Alexander's conquests stopped
short of this valley, Alexandria Eschate (Alexandria the Furthest) being
established just a little to the west. The fame of the Ferghana horses
was so widespread that the Chinese Emperor Wu Ti set his heart on
securing a stock of them from which to breed mounts for his own army.
Between 138 and 126 BC he sent several trade missions to Ferghana for
this purpose but these were halted when his envoys were murdered.
But the horses, known to the Chinese as 'heavenly horses' or 'celestial
horses', were too highly prized to give up on and in 104 BC an armed
expedition was mounted which, at the cost of fifty thousand casualties, seized three thousand of them by force and took them back to
China, where they were used to establish imperial studs.[22] According
to a Chinese source of the first century AD, the Ferghana horses all

measured just over 15.3 hands high, although selective breeding may
have resulted in some size increase since Alexander's day.[23]

Although both the Nisaean and the Bactrian/Ferghana type horses
were highly prized and generally accepted as superior to their Macedonian counterparts, it must be noted that none of our sources directly
refer to them as giving a specific combat advantage to the Persians in
the way that the longer weapons of the Macedonians are. In the one
instance that Macedonian cavalry were explicitly unable to match the
'swifter horses' of their opponents, it is noted that their own horses were
already 'in poor condition from long forced marches and poor fodder'.[24]
Indeed, in one pursuit it was some of the Persians who found that
their horses could not maintain the pace set by the Macedonians and
were caught as a consequence.[25] On the other hand, heavier armour,
including horse armour, is mentioned as a Persian advantage at Gaugamela, and this was largely made possible by the greater capacity for
sustained weight-carrying of their horses. It is perhaps for this characteristic rather than speed or sheer size (although this was welcome)
that these breeds were most highly prized and they continued to play
an important part in the development of heavily armoured cavalry
under Alexander's successors.

The problems associated with feeding the horses must have been
immense, as local grazing was quickly exhausted in all but the most
fertile regions if the army did not keep moving, so hay had to be collected and transported on the march. In any case, horses in the wild
have to graze for about sixteen hours a day to remain fit. Each hour
spent working for their human masters is one less hour available for
eating, so working horses have to have their grass diet supplemented
with various grain feeds. Alexander had around five thousand cavalry
when he began his Persian expedition. In 1939 a typical German infantry division had 5375 horses to pull its guns and transport and required
over fifty tons of hay and oats a day.[26]

This then was the cavalry spearhead of Alexander's invasion of the
Persian Empire. He led them, and the rest of his army, to a string of
stunning victories with decisiveness, conspicuous gallantry and the
sort of supreme self-confidence that perhaps can only come from having gods, heroes and kings in one's family tree. Alexander crossed the
Hellespont into Asia in the spring of 334 BC with around thirty-five
thousand infantry (of whom only thirteen thousand were Macedonian
pikemen) and five thousand cavalry, including 1800 Companions in
eight squadrons, and a similar number of Thessalians.

What followed was an eight-year run of military victory and conquest. In three years the western half of the Persian empire had been conquered, three major Persian armies smashed and Darius' throne taken. The remaining years essentially consisted of a triumphant armed tour of the far-flung eastern provinces, asserting Macedonian authority and quelling all resistance. Accompanied as it was by official surveyors, botanists and geographers, the expedition was also a methodical scientific exploration. In early 326 BC Alexander crossed into India and fought the last of his great battles in June of that year, at the River Hydaspes. The Macedonians gained another victory, but it was not an easy one. Fuelled by an unquenchable thirst for further kudos and an insatiable curiosity, Alexander pressed onwards into India, thinking he was close to the ends of the earth and the surrounding ocean. At the River Beas, however, his men had finally had enough and refused to go any further eastwards. They had fought and marched almost twenty thousand miles and won for Alexander the largest empire the world had yet seen. Alexander grudgingly agreed to turn back, although the return began with a last campaign down the Indus to the Indian Ocean. The army finally came to rest back at the Persian city of Susa early in 324 BC. Alexander set about reforms of his army, using it as a model of integration between his Macedonians and his new Asian subjects. When he died in 323 BC, he was, according to some sources, already planning to lead this revamped army westwards to conquer the Carthaginian empire in North Africa.

No blow-by-blow account of Alexander's campaigns can be given here. For the present purpose it is enough to know that, besides innumerable sieges and skirmishes, he defeated the Persians in three major set-piece battles: at the Granicus River in 334 BC, Issus in 333 BC and Gaugamela (also known as Arbela) in 331 BC. He also fought two other major battles that were recorded in sufficient detail to repay study: against the Scythians at the River Tanais in 328 BC and against the Indian king, Porus, at the Hydaspes in 326 BC. To make a worthwhile assessment of Alexander's tactics and the performance of his cavalry, we must first assess the available literary sources.

Given that Alexander is among the most famous men in history, it is perhaps surprising that no contemporary, or even nearly contemporary, account of his life and deeds has survived intact, although references in later works confirm that there were many written.[27] The oldest surviving account is in the seventeenth book of the *Universal History* written by Diodorus Siculus in the mid first century BC. The other

surviving accounts are those of Quintus Curtius Rufus (first century
AD), Plutarch (early second century AD), Arrian (mid second century AD)
and Justin (third century AD). All of these authors, however, had earlier
accounts at their disposal and so indirectly preserve contemporary and
even eyewitness testimony.

Justin's work can quickly be set aside. It is an epitome of the *Histo-riae Philipiccae* of Pompeius Trogus (written in the late first century
BC, with only the prologue now surviving outside of Justin). It is very
poorly regarded by modern scholars and of little value for the current
purpose. Of the others, it is ironically the latest, Arrian, which is gen-erally considered the most reliable because he specifically named his
main sources. These were the accounts of Ptolemy and Aristobulus.
Ptolemy was one of Alexander's childhood friends and later an officer
in his army; he was therefore an eyewitness to many of the events he
described and would have been well informed even about those he did
not observe first-hand. Aristobulus accompanied the army as Alexan-der's chief engineer and would have picked up around the campfire
what he did not see with his own eyes. When Ptolemy and Aristobulus
wrote their accounts some years after the actual events, by which time
Ptolemy was king of Egypt, they could supplement their own memo-ries not only by conversation with other veterans but by reference to
official records and correspondence. The Macedonian invasion force
was accompanied by an official historian, Callisthenes of Olynthus,
the nephew of Alexander's famous tutor Aristotle. He kept a journal
of the expedition and was apparently also responsible for compiling
the official bulletins sent back to Macedon and the Greek cities for
public consumption. Callisthenes was executed on a charge of treason
in 327 BC but his work up to this point, including all the major battles
against the Persians, certainly formed an invaluable source, directly or
indirectly for later writers.

Plutarch wrote a short biography of Alexander as one of his series of
Lives, which were intended as moral lessons. He drew on and named
a wide variety of contemporary sources, including Aristobulus, Cal-listhenes, Ptolemy and Chares the royal usher, and seems to have
applied a critical eye when selecting from them, sometimes discussing
discrepancies. He quotes frequently from Alexander's correspond-ence, presumably kept as part of the official records with the journal.
According to one modern biographer, Plutarch must have been among
the best-read men in antiquity.[28] It must be remembered that he was,
by his own admission, writing 'biography, not history', and his *Lives*

accordingly 'dwell upon those actions that illuminate the workings of the soul'.[29] Even so, his brief account contains much that is reliable and useful.

Diodorus and Quintus Curtius are both thought to have relied chiefly on the work of Cleitarchus, which was probably written around 310 BC. It was certainly written before Ptolemy's account because Arrian passes on Ptolemy's reference to it where he differs on a minor point. Cleitarchus is among the most quoted writers by later historians and his work may have been the best known in antiquity, although he was not always well regarded. Although he was not an eyewitness, he seems, as far as we can tell, to have referred to a wide range of sources including Callisthenes' dispatches but also, interestingly, the testimony of Greeks in mercenary service with Darius. Through Diodorus and, especially, Quintus Curtius he passes on interesting information and perspectives not found elsewhere.

Because Diodorus was writing a 'universal history', his treatment of Alexander is thought to be merely a précis of Callisthenes. Quintus Curtius, on the other hand, gives a full and florid account which also drew on other sources, but perhaps not excluding his own imagination. The usefulness of both Diodorus and Quintus Curtius has often been questioned, but the value of the latter at least is now more highly regarded than previously. There are many details preserved only in Quintus Curtius that must have come from a well-informed contemporary source, such as the information regarding the clerk of cavalry and the systematic redistribution of cavalry horses already described.

There are sometimes major discrepancies between the accounts these various sources give of Alexander's battles. The number of troops present always varies while the sequence of events within a given battle sometimes appears in a different order, or what appears as a major event in one source is not mentioned at all in another. Some of this can be attributed to the different primary sources used. It is well to remember the Duke of Wellington's famous explanation that a battle was like a ball, with no two attendees later remembering every episode or the order they occurred in. Given the wide chronological spread of the surviving sources and the much vaster array of sources available to them, it is perhaps more remarkable that so much does tally and can be fitted into a coherent synthesis which should be reasonably close to the 'truth'. All in all, when trying to assess the Macedonian cavalry in action, we are not so badly served for reliable literary evidence as might first appear.

Alexander's set-piece battles suggest that he had a basic tactical plan, with variations to take into account the local situation. This, like all good tactical systems, was built upon sound appreciation of the characteristics and armament of the various units and followed from Philip's reforms. It is most likely that Philip's battles, if only we knew more about them, would reveal a similar system emerging as he worked out how best to use his new army.

Alexander's character and his tactical method ordained that he would always take the offensive, seeking to seize the initiative and overawe the enemy, even though he was usually outnumbered. To this end he usually launched a concentrated assault on one wing, usually his right, seeking like Epaminondas at Mantinea to strike an early morale-shattering blow with his best troops.* Spearheading the advance at the right of the main line were the Companions with Alexander at the head of the royal squadron, although they were often preceded and flanked by screening forces of light cavalry and light infantry until the moment to charge arrived.

At Gaugamela Alexander definitely employed an oblique approach with his right wing forward and the rest of the line staggered so that the left wing was deliberately held back or 'refused'. At Granicus and Issus he may have deployed in line parallel to the enemy, but the rapid advance of the right-wing cavalry had much the same effect, making sure this wing went into action first. The left flank of the phalanx was guarded by the Thessalian cavalry and light troops. The bulk of the main line was of course formed by the bristling pike phalanx with the elite foot guard, the Hypaspists, as its right-hand unit. These were therefore next to the Companion cavalry, so that Alexander had both his best cavalry and his best infantry concentrated around himself at the decisive point. This arrangement ensured that, when the Companions led the attack, the first infantry to arrive in support were the elite unit, just as the Sacred Band had followed up the Theban horse at Tegyra, Leuctra and Mantinea.

---

* Epaminondas had chosen to concentrate his force on his left because he wished to attack the Spartans' best troops, who held the position of honour on the right. Macedonian custom may have dictated that Alexander placed himself on the right wing and, as he intended to lead the decisive attack himself, this meant his oblique advance had to be with the right leading. Philip had been on the right at Chaeronea, even though he possibly refused this wing, but he had Alexander to lead the Companions for him on the left.

In most Classical Greek battles the cavalry's main role was to protect the phalanx's flanks until it could win the battle in the middle, with an increasing propensity as the fourth century wore on to intervene in the central struggle when the opportunity arose. For the Companions it was the other way around. Alexander's first objective was always to create an opportunity to lead the Companions in a charge on the enemy's left or left centre, disrupting their line and starting the disintegration before driving inwards towards the centre. The centre was the traditional post for Oriental commanders, and it seems that in his Persian battles Alexander was not only rolling up the rest of the enemy line but aiming specifically for Darius. The advance of the infantry meanwhile pinned the enemy line in place and then finished off the job once the cavalry had started the collapse.

If it is possible to criticize Alexander's battlefield performances for anything it is that he attempted to apply the same basic plan regardless of the situation. Thus at both the Granicus and Issus the Companions were committed to a charge across a river or stream with a numerically superior enemy holding the far bank. Alexander's courage and belief in heroic personal leadership sometimes also took on the appearance of foolhardiness. Had he been killed at Granicus, as he so nearly was, he would have gone down in history as one of the great military blunderers, deservedly cut down while dashing into the enemy ahead of his troops. There were numerous occasions when only the skill, training and morale of his men prevented the full price of his rashness being paid. On the other hand, he won consistently, so his faith in the power of the Macedonian army was well founded.

Soon after crossing to Asia Minor, Alexander found his way blocked by a Persian army at the River Granicus. The Persians opted to place their twenty thousand cavalry in front, parallel with the river, with their twenty thousand mercenary Greek hoplites kept in the rear on a low ridge, for which they have been condemned by most writers ever since. With hindsight, a more conventional strategy would have been to defend the actual riverbank with the solid defensive line of hoplites, with the cavalry held back to charge into any troops that managed to break through or outflank their phalanx. The Persian commanders may have been influenced by snobbery or mistrust of the Greek infantry, but it was also reasonable to expect that the disruption caused by the fast-flowing river, along with a preliminary barrage of javelins, would provide plenty of opportunity for them to get in amongst the Macedonians and cut them down as they struggled up out of the water.

Alexander faced this challenge with only a select part of his army. Those troops left near the coast included all of the League of Corinth forces (in which he had little faith) except perhaps six hundred cavalry. He may have had with him just thirteen thousand infantry (including seven and a half thousand pikemen, the rest being assorted light infantry) but all of his cavalry. The Companions and Thessalians, eighteen hundred of each, were of course excellent front-line cavalry; the six hundred Greeks were less uniformly equipped and trained (and less enthused by Macedonian leadership) but nevertheless not the impotent force often supposed. The balance was composed of various light cavalry units well versed in skirmishing and screening duties, including javelin-armed Paeonians and Thracians as well as four squadrons of the *prodromoi* or scouts.[30] These were the troops also known as *sarissophoroi*, and although used like light cavalry were apparently equipped with the unwieldy sarissa.

Alexander, faced with an enemy in a strong defensive position, was outnumbered by more than two to one overall and four to one in cavalry, the favoured arm of both himself and his opponent. Alexander ignored the warnings of Parmenio, his late father's most trusted officer, and decided on an immediate attack. The motives which Arrian, drawing on the eyewitness accounts of Aristobulus, Ptolemy and Callisthenes, attributes to Alexander at this point may well be accurate. Alexander was apparently concerned that any hesitation would 'give the Persians added confidence ... and they would begin to think they were as good soldiers as we are'.[31] Alexander wanted to establish psychological dominance early on in the campaign. In short he was going to teach the Persians to fear him.

He drew up the phalanx, posted the Thessalian and Greek cavalry on their left flank and posted himself at the head of the Companions on the right wing. In advance of the main body of Companions was a cavalry screen consisting of the *prodromoi*, the Paeonians and Socrates' squadron of Companions. These troops were ordered to cross first, supported on their left by the right-hand company of the Hypaspists. As they forged across against the swift current, Alexander 'leapt upon his horse and called upon his bodyguard [the Royal Squadron] to follow and to play the man'. Then, 'with trumpets blaring and the shout going up to the God of Battle', he led the rest of the right wing forward into the river.[32]

The Persian commanders, meanwhile, had spotted Alexander and had massed their best units opposite him. These showered the foremost men with javelins as they struggled against the swift water and then quickly started to get the better of them in close combat as they emerged. Meanwhile, it seems that the right wing crossed obliquely, edging upstream to the right and passing behind the advanced screen so as to emerge to their right, extending the line. They were supported by light infantry; archers and Agrianian javelinmen following behind as best they could. From this point Arrian's dramatic narrative must be allowed to unfold for a while uninterrupted so the reader can savour the atmosphere of Alexander's audacious attack and the ferocious cavalry mêlée that ensued. Arrian not only drew on contemporary accounts, he was also himself an experienced cavalry commander who knew what was credible.

The first to engage the Persians were cut down and died a soldier's death, though some of the leading troops fell back upon Alexander, who was now on his way across: indeed he was almost over, at the head of the army's right wing. A moment later he was in the thick of it, charging at the head of his men straight for the spot where the Persian commanders stood and the serried ranks of the enemy were thickest. Round him a violent struggle developed, while all the time, company by company, the Macedonians were making their way over the river, more easily now than before. It was a cavalry battle with, as it were, infantry tactics: horse against horse, man against man, locked together, the Macedonians did their utmost to thrust the enemy once and for all back from the river-bank and force him into the open ground, while the Persians fought to prevent the landings or hurl their opponents back into the water.

Things soon turned in favour of Alexander's men; their experience and the weight of their attack began to tell, added to the advantage of the long cornel-wood spear over the light spears of the Persians.

During the fight Alexander's spear was broken. He called on Aretis, one of his grooms, for another, but Aretis was himself in difficulties for the same reason, though still fighting gallantly enough with the remaining half of his weapon [thanks to the second spear head]. Showing it to Alexander, he called out to him to ask someone else, and Demaratus the Corinthian, one of Alexander's personal bodyguard, gave him his spear. The fresh weapon in his hand, he caught sight of Mithridates, Darius' son-in-law, riding with a squadron of horse in wedge formation far ahead of the main body; instantly he galloped out in front of his men, struck Mithridates in the face with his spear, and hurled him to the ground. Rhoesaces then rode at Alexander with his sword and, aiming a blow at his head, sliced off part of his helmet, which nevertheless dulled the force of the impact. A moment later Alexander was on him, and he fell with a spear-thrust through his cuirass into his breast. Now Spithridates had his sword raised, ready for a blow at Alexander from behind; but Cleitus, son of Dropides, was too quick for him, and severed his shoulder sword and all. Meanwhile Alexander's party was being steadily reinforced by the mounted troops as one after another they succeeded in getting up out of the river and joining him.

The Persian were now in a bad way: there was no escape for horse or rider from the thrust of the Macedonian spears; they were being forced back from their position and, in addition to the weight of the main attack, they were suffering considerable damage from the lightly armed troops who had forced their way in among the cavalry. They began to break just at the point where Alexander in person was bearing the brunt of things.[33]

Not much evidence here of precariously perched riders hesitating to engage, prodding ineffectually at each other lest they unseat themselves, or falling off when they tried taking a good swing with a sword.

As the Persian cavalry started to stream away, their mercenary hoplite infantry now found themselves isolated. Although in a strong defensive position, they were no doubt badly shaken by this unforeseen turn of events. It was towards them that Alexander now turned his attention:

Alexander soon checked the pursuit of them [the Persian cavalry] in order to turn his attention to the foreign mercenaries, who had remained in their original position, shoulder to shoulder – not, indeed, from any deliberate intention of proving their courage, but simply because the suddenness of the disaster had deprived them of their wits. Ordering a combined assault by infantry and cavalry, Alexander quickly had them surrounded and butchered to a man, though one or two may have escaped notice among the heaps of dead.[34]

This account of Arrian's sounds very calculated and efficient and there is no suggestion that the cavalry were ineffective against this phalanx. But because this looks like a force of cavalry successfully charging an unbroken body of heavy infantryman, and because this has so often been declared impossible, we need to consider exactly what happened here.

Historians have assumed that Alexander, having started to pursue the Persian cavalry, turned back and charged the hoplites in the rear while they were fighting the Macedonian phalanx, and indeed this fits with them being 'quickly surrounded' and with the course of Alexander's later battles.[35] If surprised from the rear then the destruction of the phalanx by cavalry is unremarkable. Arrian's account closely followed that of Ptolemy, who supplemented his own memory of these events by reference to the king's journal that recorded, amongst other things, Alexander's orders and actions in battle. Arrian was apparently very precise about what he reported as a specific order from Alexander. Where Arrian wrote that Alexander 'ordered' something then it is very likely that he did so.[36] So if Alexander *ordered* a combined assault by infantry and cavalry this does not fit with him already having ridden past the mercenaries' position and delivering an opportunistic attack on their exposed rear. It rather seems to suggest a more organized attempt to coordinate the two arms. If the Companions' pursuit had already carried Alexander beyond the flank of the Greek position, it would have taken time to get an order back to the other units to attack. If not, then it would have taken time for Alexander and the cavalry to ride beyond the Greeks and round to their rear. In either case the Greeks would have used the time to form into a square. Plutarch's account even suggests there was time for the Greeks to send an appeal for quarter to Alexander.

Can it be that the Companions took an equal part in the destruction of an unbroken body of spearmen, not by attacking their exposed backs while they faced the other way, but by actually breaking into a defensive square, albeit a hastily formed one? Alexander probably regrouped his forces and passed the word to the other units to attack the hoplites' position. It may have been at this point that he mounted a fresh horse to spare Bucephalus. The Macedonian phalanx and cavalry would have each attacked separate faces of the enemy square to avoid disrupting the other's formation, the faster cavalry presumably riding round to the far side if their abortive pursuit had not already brought them there.

When the signal was given to attack, the cavalry were still faced with the undesirable prospect of attempting to urge their mounts into a wall of hoplites. This was not achieved, as has been suggested, just because their longer lances allowed the lead rider to hit the hoplite in front of him a fraction of a second before the hoplite could hit him; it surely had more to do with the psychological state of the mercenaries and of the Companions than anything else. Having already witnessed from the higher ground the unlikely success of Alexander's headlong attack across the river, and the rapid defeat of their own more numerous Persian paymasters, the Greeks were half beaten already. By contrast the

Companions' blood was up, and having just routed the flower of the famous Persian cavalry, they were probably feeling almost invincible. It is a great tribute to their discipline and control of their horses, not to mention Alexander's presence of mind, that he had been able to halt their pursuit at all. There was probably plenty of shuffling and wavering of spear points in the Greek lines to encourage them as they spurred their horses forward into one last hell-for-leather effort. Then of course there was the inspiring example of their king in front. Even so, charging a line of hoplites was hazardous, as Plutarch's account makes clear. 'In this instance he allowed himself to be guided by passion rather than by reason, led a charge against them and lost his horse (not Bucephalus on this occasion), which was pierced through the ribs by a sword thrust.'[37]

Despite this mishap, the low casualties suffered by the Macedonians suggest that organized resistance soon collapsed and what followed was a one-sided slaughter. Contradicting his earlier statement that the Greeks were butchered to a man, Arrian says two thousand were captured and sold into slavery, but this still means up to eighteen thousand were cut down. The cavalry must of course share the credit for this with the infantry of the Macedonian phalanx, who drove irresistibly into the front of the hoplites with almost complete impunity, as their much longer weapons formed a deadly barrier now that they were clear of the river and formed up in good order. The Macedonians lost eighty-five cavalry, including twenty-five Companions killed in the opening assault across the river and only around thirty infantry.[38]

The imbalance of losses has been used to suggest that Arrian's figures are false, but it was a common feature of pre-gunpowder warfare that relatively few fatal casualties were sustained while both sides were still actively fighting in an organized manner. Individuals tended to play for safety first, looking to ward off the enemy's blows and passing up the opportunity to strike a big blow if this would expose them to counter attack. It is harder for a cavalryman to duel cautiously, especially if unshielded, as he can hardly sidestep or duck blows, although the length of their lances might have allowed Macedonian cavalry that failed to break into the enemy ranks in the initial rush to jab at them and hold them at bay while keeping their horses head-on to the enemy. Even so the opportunities to strike a clear killing blow were relatively rare while the enemy was still fighting back as a group. The vast majority of casualties were always suffered by troops whose will to continue this struggle had cracked under the massive strain of prolonged close proximity to danger and who, in seeking to flee, exposed their backs to an enemy who could then release their stress in unrestrained killing with little risk to themselves.

In fights between two heavy infantry units, comfortingly crowded behind their wall of shields and spears, it could take a long time for either side to reach this crisis point. It was always one of the great merits of cavalry that the unnerving, knee-weakening effect of their charge offered a short cut to the breaking point. In part it was the apparent irrational disregard for their own safety of men galloping headlong into danger on the back of a herd of animals that made it clear that the cavalry were not playing for safety first, and it is this as much as any logical calculation of their specific fighting ability that could cause panic. If their victims lost their nerve straight away the horsemen could literally cut to the chase and proceed straight to the phase of one-sided destruction, which their greater mobility allowed them to prolong by pursuing the enemy. Of course at the Granicus the Greeks were surrounded and very few escaped.

With the local Persian army eliminated, Alexander proceeded systematically to conquer Asia Minor, starting with the cities of the coast and then subduing the interior. Most towns were overawed without a serious fight, although there were exceptions, most notably the important port of Halicarnassus, which had to be besieged and stormed, which was not cavalry work. For his part, the Persian king was busy raising an army with which he intended to face Alexander himself.

Meanwhile there took place an incident which neatly epitomizes the character that made Alexander such a brilliant leader of shock cavalry. At the town of Gordium Alexander was taken to an ancient chariot, the yoke of which was fastened with a particularly thick and complex knot with the ends all hidden. Local legend had it that the man who could undo the knot would become king of all Asia. Where many an aspiring king before had doubtless tugged his beard, scratched his head or torn his nails on the thick ropes before walking away confounded, Alexander sized up the puzzle, drew his sword and sliced through the ropes. Whether or not this was a real incident, one could not invent a better metaphor for Alexander's generalship.[39] As at Granicus before, and at Issus shortly after this incident, he met a tricky tactical problem by simply cutting to the heart of the matter. This decisive, supremely self-confident, no-nonsense approach was guaranteed to make the most of the power of shock cavalry.

In the summer of 333 BC, Alexander was ready to leave Asia Minor and head south along the coast of Syria. Parmenio had been sent ahead

with a force to secure the Pillars of Jonah, a narrow pass leading from
Cilicia to Syria. He now reported that Darius was encamped only two
days' march inland from his position with a huge army, waiting on
a broad plain 'good for cavalry action and suitable for manoeuvring
the vast numbers under his command'.[40] Alexander, urged on by the
Companions, although he scarcely needed encouragement, immediately marched south, leaving the sick and wounded at Issus, and led his
army through the pass. Meanwhile Darius, eager to crush the invader
and believing that 'the Persian cavalry would ride over the Macedonian
army and trample it to pieces' began to worry that Alexander would not
come to join battle and so moved from his well-chosen position on the
plains.[41] Believing Alexander to be procrastinating in Cilicia, Darius
moved north and then west, coming down to the coast by an unguarded
pass near Issus and finding himself behind Alexander's army and sitting across his lines of supply. Now sure that Alexander would have to
fight him, he took up position on the narrow coastal plain behind the
River Pinarus.

   He did not have long to wait. As soon as Alexander had confirmed
the reports that Darius was behind him, he sent a force of cavalry
and archers to secure the Pillars of Jonah and turned his army round.
Although no doubt embarrassed at being outmanoeuvred, Alexander
instantly realized that Darius had miscalculated by opting to give battle
on a narrow coastal strip where his vastly superior numbers, particularly in cavalry, could not easily be brought to bear because they would
be crammed between the sea and the mountains.

   At dawn the next day the Macedonians marched back into Cilicia.
At first the narrowness of the pass forced the Macedonians to advance
in column but, as soon as sufficiently open ground was reached, Alexander then deployed his men so they could advance in line of battle.
Reinforcements had reached Alexander at Gordium, including three
hundred Macedonian cavalry (it is unclear whether these were Companions or *prodromoi* or a mixture of both), two hundred Thessalian
cavalry and one hundred and fifty Greek cavalry from Elis. The whole
army now numbered 5300 cavalry and 26000 infantry. The deployment
was basically the same as at the Granicus: the phalanx in the middle
with the Hypaspists at the right-hand end next to the Companion
cavalry, who were flanked and screened by the light cavalry of the Paeonians and *prodromoi*. Light infantry was divided between both flanks.
As usual, Parmenio commanded the left half of the line and Alexander
the right. The one major difference was that Alexander initially kept the

Thessalian cavalry with himself on the right wing, leaving Parmenio only the cavalry supplied by the other Greek states, and some light Thracian cavalry, to protect the left flank. This was perhaps because Alexander intended him to keep that end of the phalanx as close to the sea as possible.

When Darius learnt of the Macedonians' approach he sent a powerful force of cavalry and light infantry across the Pinarus to screen the deployment of his massive host. According to Arrian, this screening force alone outnumbered Alexander's total force. It is impossible to give remotely accurate figures for the total size of the Persian army, even the generally meticulous Arrian giving the fantastic figure of six hundred thousand, stating that this was 'on record'. Unusually the lowest figure comes from Diodorus and is still a massive four hundred thousand. All that is certain is that Darius' army was many times larger than Alexander's, although of greatly varying quality and containing large mobs of untrained levies from various parts of the empire.

Darius anchored the left of his line in the foothills with a mass of light infantry, some of which crossed the river and began working their way along the rugged slopes to threaten the right flank of the Macedonian army as it advanced past them. The main core of his first line was formed by his thirty thousand mercenary Greek hoplites, flanked on each side by thirty thousand Kardakes. Arrian says these were Persian heavy infantry but modern historians refute this largely because of the short shrift they were about to receive from the Macedonian cavalry and because of references to archers. The two are not mutually exclusive. Xenophon's *Cyropaedia* suggests the Persians had been experimenting with mixed units of spear- and bow-armed infantry, with armoured spearmen in the front ranks and several ranks of archers behind.[42] The Greeks and Kardakes lined the river bank which was steep in places and which in others had been made more formidable by hastily erected palisades. Some way in the rear of the heavy infantry was a second line consisting of 'a great mass of light and heavy infantry. These were organized according to the countries of their origin and drawn up in greater depth than was likely to prove of much service; mere numbers made this unavoidable'.[43]

Once he had his infantry in position, Darius had his screening cavalry recalled by trumpet call. The greater part of these, including many heavily armoured units, he sent straight to his seaward right flank where, according to Arrian, 'the ground was rather more suitable for cavalry manouevre'. Initially some were sent to the hilly left flank, but,

due to the ground and the lack of space next to the infantry, all but
a small number of these were redirected to the right. Darius himself
took up the traditional position behind the centre of these and presumably had his mounted guard around him. Darius was depending
on his heavy infantry, assisted by the riverbank, to meet Alexander's
main attack, while his cavalry was massed on the right to smash the
Macedonian left.

As the Persian dispositions became clear, Alexander saw that the
Persian cavalry was concentrated next to the sea and realized Parmenio
would need more cavalry to deal with them. Accordingly he sent the
Thessalians to him, ordering them to ride across behind the Macedonian army, rather than in front, to conceal the move. Yet despite this,
and the fact that the ground most suitable for cavalry was on the left,
Alexander did not alter his plan to launch his own best cavalry (and
himself) into the attack on the right flank where the best Persian infantry held a naturally strong position.

As his army advanced, Alexander spotted the threat of those Persians
in the foothills, some of whom were now behind his right flank. He
detached the Agrianian javelinmen, some archers and three hundred
light cavalry to contain the threat while the rest of the line continued
to advance cautiously, careful to maintain a good line. Two squadrons
of the Companions took up post among the remaining screening units
on the extreme right flank as a further precaution. The detached force
quickly chased these Persians further up the slopes of the mountain and
Alexander recalled all but the three hundred cavalry, these being left to
deter the Persians from coming down again. This flank was now secure
and the Macedonians were nearing the river. Alexander halted his army
and rode along the line to check their alignment and encourage them
by recounting past victories before returning to his place at the head
of the royal squadron. All was now ready for the battle proper and the
line rolled forward again.

The pace of the advance was again kept steady at first, while Alexander's
experienced eye no doubt scanned over the enemy ranks for any signs of
weakness or a promising gap between units. All the leading riders must
also have been scanning the ground ahead for the easier points to plunge
down into the river and scramble up the other side. But when the first
Persian arrows started to land close to the Royal Squadron the time for
caution was over and Alexander spurred Bucephalus forward.

But once within range of missiles, Alexander, at the head of his own troops on the right wing, rode at a gallop into the stream. Rapidity was now everything: a swift attack would shake the enemy, and the sooner they came to grips the less damage would be done by the Persian archers. Alexander's judgement was not at fault: the Persian left collapsed the very moment he was on them – a brilliant local success for the picked troops under his personal command.[44]

Darius, seeing his whole left wing heading the wrong way and Alexander's squadron now carving their way through the fugitives towards his own position behind the centre, turned his ceremonial chariot and fled, 'indeed he led the race for safety'.[45] Most of the second line now took this as their cue to excuse themselves too.

Meanwhile, on the seaward flank, the Persians had seized the initiative and launched a massive cavalry attack on Parmenio's wing. Leading these attacks were several Persian commanders who had been at the Granicus, keen to redeem their honour in the presence of the King of Kings and determined not to repeat their mistake of sitting waiting for the Macedonians. To use their cavalry offensively was undoubtedly correct, especially as this included some heavy shock units in which both horse and rider were armoured, possibly Armenians on Nisaean horses.[46] But the lack of room for an outflanking manoeuvre meant a frontal assault was the only option and did not allow their huge numerical advantage to come into play at once. According to the account of Quintus Curtius Rufus, one squadron of Thessalians was smashed by the initial Persian onslaught while the rest used the superior mobility of their less heavily burdened horses, aided by the rhomboid formation, to ride away and then quickly wheel round and fall upon the Persians once the momentum and cohesion of their leading units was lost.[47] Even so the Thessalians and the rest of Parmenio's cavalry were soon embroiled in a boiling mêlée that Arrian describes as 'desperate enough'.[48]

In the centre things also looked dangerous for the Macedonians. When Alexander galloped off on his glorious charge, the phalanx had inevitably been left lagging behind but started to attack as promptly as possible. The right-hand units were speeding up and drifting to the right to support their king, while the left-hand units were pinned down by the Persian cavalry attack and could not advance beyond their own cavalry without exposing their flank. The result was that a potentially fatal gap opened up in the centre of the line and worsened as it negotiated the river banks. Darius' Greek mercenaries saw the chance to get past the pikes and tear into the soft belly of the Macedonian phalanx and on their own initiative launched an attack 'precisely at that point where the gap was widest'.[49] This was a critical moment for the pike-men, who started taking heavy casualties as they fought to seal off the gap and re-establish a proper line. If the enemy hoplites got into the heart of the phalanx in force the whole thing could quickly collapse. During the ensuing struggle 'Ptolemy, son of Seleucus, and about one hundred and twenty Macedonians of distinction died a soldier's death' and many more were wounded.[50] Fortunately there was no panic. The discipline and morale of the infantry enabled them to hold together just long enough.

At this critical juncture Alexander, who was trying to pursue Darius, had the presence of mind to realize that the rest of his line was teeter-ing on the brink of disaster. As at the Granicus, he managed to bring the Companions back in hand and then led them in a charge on the flank of the opposing hoplites, throwing all into confusion and blow-ing their formation apart as the squadron wedges penetrated between the ranks of spearmen 'and were soon cutting them to pieces'.[51] Men who moments before had been sensing victory as they watched their comrades in the front ranks breaking into the vaunted Macedonian phalanx, now found themselves herded together by the mass of the horses that suddenly appeared amongst them and attacked with lance and sword by the riders. Seasoned professionals though they were, this sudden change of fortune was too much for the mercenaries, and those at the rear started jettisoning their heavy shields and making their escape. There was some resistance from those trapped by the press of their comrades, Alexander himself received a superficial wound in the thigh, but soon all had degenerated into a panic-ridden mob stampeding to the rear and making for the mountain passes.

The Persian cavalry, still battling to overcome the stubborn resist-ance of the Thessalians, now realized that their king and the rest of the army had left them in the lurch and in danger of being cut off. They too joined the rout, trying to force their way through the remnants of the infantry, but the heavy units in particular were unable to outrun the vengeful Thessalians.

> The horses with their heavily equipped riders suffered severely, and of the thousands of panic stricken men who struggled to escape along the narrow mountain tracks, almost as many were trampled to death by their friends as were cut down by the pursuing enemy. The Thessalians pressed the pursuit

without mercy, and the Persian losses in both arms, infantry and cavalry, were equally severe.[52]

The fleeing Darius kept to his chariot until forced to abandon it, along with his shield and bow, by the increasingly rough terrain and the press of the crowd. He then took to a horse and made good his escape. Alexander's men kept up the chase as long as it was safe to do so in the gathering gloom.

Alexander had gained another stunning victory that depended upon the shock of the Companions' charge to cripple the enemy line. The risks had been enormous, and not only because of the immediate physical danger that had earned Alexander another battle scar. Had the Kardakes resisted just a little longer the Greek mercenaries might have broken the Macedonian centre, but the Persians had been unable to bear the psychological trauma of a determined cavalry assault. Equally, if the Thessalians had been unable to contain the more numerous and heavily equipped Persian cavalry, the outflanked Macedonian phalanx would have suffered the same fate as Darius' Greek mercenaries. In the event the results justified every risk and the Companions fully repaid Alexander's faith in them. Their high morale allowed them to deliver the first charge with conviction, despite the factors seemingly stacked against success. Discipline, training and experience then allowed them to be rallied from the pursuit to deliver the battle-saving attack on the hoplites' flank. It must have been a mightily relieved Alexander who now limped from the battlefield to soak off the dust and blood in Darius' bath, captured along with his wife and mother in the Persian camp.

The third of Alexander's major battles with the Persians was fought near Gaugamela in 332 BC. In the interim, while Alexander had conquered Syria and Egypt, Darius had gathered near Babylon an even vaster army from every remaining corner of his still-vast empire. Notable among these was a large contingent of heavy cavalry under Bessus, satrap of Bactria (modern Uzbekistan), drawn from the semi-nomadic Bactrians themselves and the Massagetae, a Scythian tribe from the fringes of the empire. Not only were the riders well protected with armour of metal scales, so too were their excellent horses. Like the armoured cavalry at Issus, these represented the beginning of the cataphract, an ultra-specialized type of very heavy cavalry. Although some of Bessus' men, particularly the Scythians, probably carried shields for added defence, their usual offensive armament at this period may still have been less specialized for the shock charge than that of Alexander's Companions; a mix of javelins and lances was still employed, with some carrying bows too. It was probably around this time that the Scythians were making advances in saddle technology that would have given the rider extra security of seat to offset the top-heaviness of heavier body armour and shield.

Darius, determined to learn from his enemy, replaced some of the weapons that his various contingents came with, having 'ordered the swords and lances to be made much longer, thinking by that advantage Alexander gained the victory' at Issus.[53] This seems as likely to have applied to the cavalry as the infantry, especially as the Macedonian phalanx had not particularly distinguished itself at the last encounter. It may be that Bessus' men were among those re-equipped, or it may actually be that they were already equipped with lances and that it was actually their arrival that prompted Darius to re-equip others. Curtius claims that 'for the cavalry and their mounts there were protective coverings made of interconnected iron plates', presumably like those worn by the Bactrians and Massagetae.[54] It also seems likely that the Persian guard units would be given first priority for any new equipment. Whatever the case, we know that at Gaugamela the Macedonian cavalry was faced with at least some horsemen better protected than themselves and equipped with long lances similar to their own. Darius was going to fight fire with fire and was clearly banking on his superiority in cavalry to defeat Alexander. Despite the presence of the fine units mentioned, he even converted some of his abundant masses of infantry by ordering 'herds of horses to be broken in' and 'distributed among the infantry-men, so that his cavalry would be stronger than before'.[55]

Darius also learnt from his mistake at Issus and made sure there would be no sea, rivers or mountains to prevent the full might of the King of Kings swamping the impudent invader. Although Alexander, approaching by an unexpected direction, manoeuvred him off his chosen site just north of Babylon, Darius managed to find himself an open plain in Alexander's path:

> It was suitable for riding on, without even a ground covering of shrubs or low bushes, and one could get an unimpeded view even of things a long way off. So Darius gave orders for protrusions in the flat land to be levelled and any higher ground to be completely flattened.[56]

This was clearly cavalry country. This made things easier for Darius' secret weapon, scythed chariots. These odd weapons, which were revived intermittently in the Middle East, consisted of a chariot, pulled in this case by four horses, with long scythe blades and spearheads projecting from the axles and the yoke. The idea was that it was driven straight at an enemy unit to cause casualties if possible, but more importantly to sow disorder and panic in their ranks. Xenophon's account of Cunaxa, seventy years earlier, makes it clear they failed completely on that occasion, but he does describe a success against some of Agesilaus' Spartan infantry caught in the open.[57] On that occasion the scythed chariots were closely supported by Persian cavalry to exploit the disruption of the enemy formation, and just two of them were instrumental in the defeat of seven hundred veteran heavy infantry.[58] At Gaugamela Darius had two hundred. He is also said to have had around a dozen elephants, but these seem to have played no part in the battle and were probably left in the camp on the day, where they were later captured. The risk of them causing panic among the thousands of nervous, newly broken horses on their own side may have been deemed too great a liability.

Darius deployed his army in Alexander's path and waited. His dispositions are recorded in some detail because his orders for the deployment fell into Macedonian hands after the battle, although there are problems and discrepancies in the various ancient sources that pass these on to us. The biggest problem is that of numbers: totals range from wildly exaggerated to ridiculous, with Plutarch and Diodorus both giving Darius a million men. Modern scholars believe one hundred thousand may be nearer the limit of credibility, still a vast achievement. Fortunately we have a clearer idea of the numbers of the cavalry. The two sources that give detailed deployments, Arrian and Quintus Curtius, agree fairly closely on the total of cavalry, plausibly stating forty thousand and forty-five thousand respectively, even giving us a breakdown of many of the individual units.

Darius' front line consisted of all his cavalry, divided into two strong wings. Any cavalry would be wasted head-on against the Macedonian phalanx, however, so he selected some infantry units to fill the centre of the line. It would be their job to hold the centre as long as possible while the cavalry won the battle on the flanks, stripping the Macedonian phalanx of protection. This centre was built around the one thousand Persian infantry guard 'with the golden apples on their spear butts'. These were sandwiched between Darius' remaining mercenary hoplites, 'the only troops likely to be a match for the Macedonian infantry', one thousand on each side.[59] Alongside these were some of the more potentially useful tribal contingents: Mardian archers, Carians and Indians. The Indians may have been a mix of mounted and foot units as some Indian cavalry certainly appear to have been near the centre. The rest of the infantry were relegated to a second line some distance in the rear, where they were drawn up 'in depth' in their various national or tribal groups. Darius placed himself in the centre, presumably immediately behind the infantry guard, with his 'kinsfolk' and the rest of his thousand cavalry guard about his ceremonial chariot.[60] He also selected some of the best of the Bactrians and kept these 'posted by his side in the fight'.[61] In front of the centre were fifty scythed chariots.

The right wing held some superb units of cavalry: Parthians (another offshoot of the Scythians that had settled within the Persian Empire and would one day rule it); Medes, who centuries before had been the Persians' overlords and from whom the Persians had first acquired the secrets of horsemanship; and Sacae, yet another Scythian tribe, not under Persian rule but currently their allies. The majority of these were equipped as light cavalry. Placed in front of this line were the Cappadocian and Armenian contingents, which were probably more heavily equipped, and another fifty scythed chariots.

Darius placed most of his heavily equipped units in his left wing to meet the expected charge of the Companions on the assumption, correct as it turned out, that Alexander would use similar tactics to previous occasions. On the far left the pick of the heavy units, two thousand Massagetae and a thousand Bactrians, were placed out in front to meet the initial onslaught. To the right of these were one hundred scythed chariots, fully half those available, intended to break up Alexander's attack. Behind the chariots were the main body of Bactrians with Bessus, squadron after squadron amounting to eight thousand. These were supported by a thousand Dahae (another Scythian tribe who probably fought as mounted archers), and four thousand Arachotians from what is now Pakistan. Both of these were probably light cavalry and presumably covered the left flank of the main line. To the right of the Bactrians were contingents of Persian, Susian and Cadusian cavalry, each with an infantry unit of their countrymen interspersed to offer close support. Some of the newly converted cavalry may have been here, with the infantry intended to add extra stiffening and slow the Companions down if they attempted to break through at this point.[62] These mixed units linked Bessus' cavalry wing, in which Darius placed so much hope, with the infantry centre. This wing alone contained about twenty thousand cavalry.

Against this vast array, Alexander could only muster seven thousand cavalry, less than the Bactrian contingent, and forty thousand infantry including the light troops. When he first approached the Persian position and saw, from a range of low hills, what awaited him on the plain below, he behaved with commendable but uncharacteristic caution. The rest of that day was spent in careful reconnaissance of the Persian position as Alexander tried to work out how best to go about tackling the problem. The abundance of heavy cavalry massed on the enemy's left (the right as Alexander viewed it) probably gave the greatest concern. Even if he massed all his cavalry on that wing they would be outnumbered three to one, and of course his other flank would be left unprotected. In any case, the much longer Persian line and the open ground meant that encirclement from both flanks was almost a certainty. That night, we are told, the Macedonian army rested while the Persian stayed on alert in case of a night attack. Alexander meanwhile racked his brains before finally falling into a deep sleep.

The following morning, Alexander deployed his troops to attack the enemy position. Having been able to observe the enemy's dispositions closely the day before, and having pondered it half the night, Alexander adopted a familiar approach after all. The Companions, around two thousand of them in eight squadrons in wedge formation, formed the right of the main line where Alexander himself took his usual station with the Royal Squadron. To their left were the Hypaspist foot guards and beside them the rest of the Macedonian pike phalanx. Completing the main line on the left were around two thousand Thessalian cavalry, the squadron from Pharsalus acting as bodyguard to Parmenio in his usual position in charge of the left wing.

In view of the likelihood of having his flanks turned, Alexander took extra care to provide against attacks in the rear. Behind the pike phalanx he formed a second line of infantry from his Greek and Illyrian allies. These had orders to turn and face the rear in the event of encirclement. As usual the main line was screened and flanked by lighter troops. In front of the Companions were units of Agrianian javelinmen, Cretan archers and Thracian tribesmen. The right flank was screened by three successive rows of units, the better to guard against a flanking manoeuvre. In front was Menidas' mercenary cavalry, probably equipped in traditional 'multi-purpose' Greek style, and behind them the light cavalry of the Paeonians and *prodromoi* equipped with sarissas. The third line was light infantry consisting of the remaining Agrianians and Cretan archers and some veteran mercenary peltasts, ready to turn to meet an outflanking move or to intervene in a cavalry mêlée once the light cavalry had taken the initial momentum out of the enemy charge.

His dispositions made, Alexander addressed the troops and had Bucephalus brought to him, having ridden another horse to spare Bucephalus until the actual moment of battle because he 'was now past his prime'. Then together they took up their place at the head of the Royal Squadron and began the advance. As he advanced, right wing leading, Alexander was heading directly for Darius' infantry centre, with the much longer Persian line overlapping his massively on both sides. If he simply attacked straight ahead, not only would the Companions have to charge a solid line of good spearmen, but the Persian left wing would simply fold in on their flank as they did so. So Alexander changed the direction of the advance, marching diagonally towards the right. This meant each successive unit in the Macedonian line turning their left side slightly towards the Persian line so the whole army was virtually marching in column across the face of the enemy. This was a very risky manoeuvre, presumably intended to reduce the overlap on this side (although worsening it on his left), and to bring the Companions opposite a softer spot in the line, while his own phalanx would soon be aligned with Darius' infantry. Alexander may also have been deliberately trying to tempt Darius into readjusting his line or launching a premature attack that might open up an opportunity. Again we may be seeing the influence of Epaminondas, as some accounts of Leuctra suggest he deliberately edged across to one flank as he advanced in order to lure the enemy into a hasty redeployment that led to their defeat.

Darius responded to Alexander's manoeuvre by ordering Bessus to extend his line to the left, moving units across to maintain the threat to Alexander's right flank. When Alexander was almost off the specially prepared ground, Darius ordered Bessus to send the forward units of Massagetae and Bactrians around the end of Alexander's line to 'encircle the Macedonian right under Alexander and thus check any further extension in that direction'. Alexander ordered Menidas' squadron to prevent this by charging the Scythians, but in so doing they were themselves charged by the one thousand picked Bactrians and driven back by weight of numbers. The battle was now joined and things started to happen quickly, each side committing more units in rapid succession to try to seize the advantage. Alexander now ordered in the Paeonians against the Scythians, Menidas' men now also returning to the attack with them, catching them in the flank as they tried to continue their encircling manoeuvre and forcing them to withdraw momentarily. Bessus in turn committed more and more Bactrian squadrons, also rallying the Scythians and sending them back into the fray. 'A close cavalry action ensued, in which the Macedonians suffered the more severely, outnumbered as they were and less adequately provided with defensive armour than the Scythians were – both horses and men.'[63]

While the Macedonian light cavalry were fighting desperately against the odds, Darius now unleashed the scythed chariots against the main line, forcing it to abandon its oblique march and face the front again. Arrian describes this attack as a complete disaster thanks to Alexander's foresight:

> for the chariots were no sooner off the mark than they were met by the missile weapons of the Agrianes and Balacrus' javelin throwers, who were stationed in advance of the Companions; again, they seized the reins and dragged the drivers to the ground, then surrounded the horses and cut them down.[64]

A few broke through the loose formation of the light infantry but the Companions had been warned in advance to open their ranks, making paths that the terrified chariot horses happily galloped through, eventually being rounded up once blown by the royal grooms and reserve infantry in the rear.

The group of fifty chariots that attacked in the centre were similarly allowed to pass through gaps opened between the files of the phalanx, the horses being speared from either side as they passed through. Curtius describes the awful carnage:

> Horses and charioteers fell in huge numbers, covering the battlefield. The charioteers could not control the terrified animals which, frequently tossing their necks, had not only thrown off their yokes but also overturned the chariots. And wounded horses were trying to drag along dead ones, unable to stay in one place in their panic and yet too weak to go forward.[65]

Yet he records that a few careered onwards to the second line of infantry 'inflicting a pitiful death on those they encountered' so that 'the ground was littered with the severed limbs of soldiers'.

On the Macedonian left the remaining fifty chariots may have had more success, contributing to a desperate situation in which Parmenio now found himself. It is probably to this attack that Curtius refers in his often jumbled account when he describes some Macedonians 'killed by the spears that projected well beyond the chariot-poles and others dismembered by the scythes set on either side. It was no gradual withdrawal that the Macedonians made but a disordered flight, breaking their ranks'.[66] If such a rout occurred it was presumably only the screening light infantry units, for the Persian attacks on this flank were held, albeit with extreme difficulty. While the chariots attacked, the Persian cavalry was soon folding itself around the Macedonian line and encircling them, embroiling the Thessalians in a desperate fight for survival.

When the chaos of the chariot attack had passed Alexander could see that the fierce fight on the extreme right was still raging, sucking in more and more Persian units. It seems likely that Alexander fed in a few squadrons of the Companions to prop up this flank, for the light cavalry, even with their supporting light infantry, could hardly have contained such a superior force for long. Eventually the excellent discipline and determination of the Macedonians turned the tide, 'and by repeated counter-charges, squadron by squadron, succeeded in breaking the enemy formation'.[67] By then Alexander had already struck the decisive blow elsewhere. Observing that the Persian left was now overstretched, Alexander saw his chance to cut another Gordian knot. 'Presently, however, the movement of the Persian cavalry, sent to the support of their comrades who were attempting to encircle the Macedonian right, left a gap in the Persian front – and this was Alexander's opportunity.'[68]

Alexander led the remaining uncommitted squadrons of the Companions at the weak point in the enemy line, with the foot guard and the right-hand end of the phalanx taking up the charge in turn as best they could. Plutarch describes the launching of the attack as 'with shouts of encouragement to one another the cavalry charged the enemy at full speed and the phalanx rolled forward like a flood', while Arrian vividly describes its ferocity.[69]

> He promptly made for the gap ... drove in his wedge and raising the battle cry pressed forward at the double straight for the point where Darius stood. A close struggle ensued, but it was soon over; for when the Macedonian horse, with Alexander himself at the head of them, vigorously pressed the assault, fighting hand to hand and thrusting at the Persians' faces with their spears, the infantry phalanx in close order and bristling with pikes added its irresistible weight, Darius ... saw nothing but terrors all around him, [and] was the first to turn tail and ride for safety.[70]

Darius' mounted Persian Guard had been resisting fiercely until Darius himself abandoned them, Curtius explaining that 'they had neither the desire nor the opportunity to reach safety, and each man thought it a noble fate to meet his end before the eyes of his king'.[71] As Darius fled, leaping on a horse, and abandoning his chariot, bow and shield to be captured a second time, panic again set in. In the centre and on the right the Macedonians 'pressed the pursuit, cutting down the fugitives as they rode', while Darius escaped in the dust and confusion.[72] It was only now, with the Persian centre crumbling into flight once more, that the dangerous situation on the right was finally resolved. One last charge from the *prodromoi* under Aretes finally finished the Massagatae. Aretes himself put his sarissa to good effect by killing the Scythian leader.

With Darius' flight another decisive victory was within Alexander's grasp, but it could easily have been different. When Alexander attacked, the right-hand units of the pike phalanx followed as best they could, but this caused a gap to open up between two of the units in the centre, just as it had at Issus. Into this gap rode a body of Persian and Indian cavalry, basically doing to Alexander what he was doing to the Persian line. Lacking an Alexander to lead them, however, and perhaps less well practised in the shock role, they did not take full advantage of the situation. Instead of ploughing into the vulnerable interior of the phalanx from the sides and rear, they took the path of least resistance and rode on to attack the Macedonian baggage, which means that they must also have found a way through the second line of Macedonian infantry. Whether they were simply after plunder or were trying to free Darius' mother, a prisoner since Issus, is unclear. They killed many of those left to mind the baggage before the Macedonian second line turned about, attacked them from behind and scattered those they did not kill.

Alexander halted the Companions and turned to go to the aid of his hard-pressed left wing. He is thought to have received a request for help from Parmenio but it is unclear at what stage this reached him, as it is hard to see how a messenger could have found him once he had plunged into the Persian line. It may be a fabrication intended to besmirch Parmenio, who was later implicated in a treasonous plot and executed. According to Curtius, Alexander was brought a fresh horse at this stage, so there must have been a temporary lull; perhaps the messenger found him then. Alternatively, the message may have arrived before the decisive charge was ordered but it failed to deflect Alexander from his chosen course of action, a great credit to his judgement if that is what happened.

In any case, Alexander was riding across the field, behind the original position of the now dissolving Persian line, when the final crisis of the battle occurred. A column of enemy cavalry units crossed his path, probably Parthians, Medes and Indians. Noting the collapse of their centre, they had been attempting to withdraw in good order from the fight with Parmenio's wing but now turned to attack Alexander before he could take them in flank as Arrian describes:

> The ensuing struggle was the fiercest of the whole action; one after another the Persian squadrons wheeled in file to the charge; breast to breast they hurled themselves on the enemy. Conventional [for the Persians] cavalry tactics – manoeuvring, javelin-throwing – were forgotten; it was every man for himself, struggling to break through as if in that alone lay his hope of life.[73]

According to Curtius, Alexander, riding as always at the head of the Royal Squadron's wedge formation, met this attack as he had a similar one at the Granicus. Riding straight at the leader of the enemy squadron, 'he transfixed with his spear the Persian cavalry commander'.[74] In the situation, this was precisely the thing to do. Any hesitation could have been the end of him. As it was, the Companions followed his lead and pitched in enthusiastically. 'Desperately and without quarter, blows were given and received, each man fighting for mere survival rather than any further thought of victory or defeat. About sixty of Alexander's Companions were killed.'[75] The Royal Squadron emerged victorious, although some of the Persians broke through and escaped. Ascertaining that the rest of the Persian right wing had also given up the fight and were on the run with the Thessalians in hot pursuit, Alexander also took up the chase again until nightfall once more put an end to the slaughter.

Yet again Alexander had used the speed and striking power of the Companions to crack open the enemy line. Resisting the temptation to feed any more than necessary into confused fighting out on the far right, he had kept the bulk of them together until he saw the opportunity to strike a really telling blow. Timing was everything. Instantly seizing the opening, the Companions struck hard and penetrated deep into the main enemy position, knowing that, until their infantry lumbered up, their safety lay in maintaining the momentum. Like a well-aimed spear thrust, they drove straight for the vital nerve centre – Darius – paralysing the enemy body and thus ensuring its collapse. Some twenty-three centuries later the Germans used a similar approach with their tanks, in what became known as *Blitzkrieg*, or 'Lightning War'. How appropriate that name would have seemed to Alexander, the supposed son of Zeus the Thunderer.

The Persians had tried to find an answer to the Companions: they had tried cavalry defending a river bank at the Granicus and then infantry defending a river bank at Issus. Now they had tried cavalry mixed with infantry and a theoretically superior cavalry force that was both more numerous and more heavily armoured. At Issus and again at Gaugamela Darius' troops had broken into or through the awesome phalanx, yet somehow the Companions' onslaught had pulled Alexander's chestnuts out of the fire. So far, Alexander had not even really been forced to stretch his tactical plan.

It would fall to others to find out whether anything could force Alexander to forego his cavalry charge. Although Darius raised another army, it melted away at Alexander's approach and Darius was murdered by Bessus as they fled towards Bactria. Bessus proclaimed himself king and conducted an effective resistance for a while with the assistance of some Scythian allies, until he in turn was betrayed by Spitamenes. It was a band of six hundred lightly armed Scythian cavalry, temporarily throwing in their lot with Spitamenes, that delivered the most severe blow to the invading Macedonians so far, mainly because Alexander wasn't there. A force of fifteen hundred infantry, eight hundred mercenary cavalry and sixty Companions were virtually wiped out because those in command of this detachment could find no answer to the age-old Scythian tactics of keeping their distance and pouring in volleys of arrows. Sporadic attempts by the cavalry to charge them failed because the Scythians simply scattered on their swift steppe horses, firing as they went, and then returned to pepper their pursuers again when the Macedonians' horses, which were in poor condition on this occasion, had run out of steam. Only three hundred infantry and forty cavalry escaped.

Alexander heard the news of this reverse when he was preparing to carry the war into the Scythian homelands across the River Tanais. A covering barrage from bolt-shooting catapults drove the Scythians back far enough from the far bank for the crossing to be made, but once across Alexander soon had to tackle a similar force of horse archers to that used by Spitamenes. Most of these were mounted on their small but fast and tough steppe ponies, but they were probably backed up by heavier, armoured cavalry on Ferghana horses, drawn from the nobility. Arrian says a catapult bolt pierced a Scythian through his shield and breastplate, suggesting that at least some of the Scythians were well armoured.[76] Alexander quickly showed how they could be dealt with by clear thinking and decisive action. He used the *prodromoi* as bait, sending them well ahead to be surrounded, while the rest hung back, presumably out of sight. Once the Scythians were fully occupied with attacking the *prodromoi*, Alexander ordered three of his four units of Companions to charge, supported by light infantry. Unusually, Alexander did not lead the charge himself, but brought up the rear with the fourth unit of Companions. This gave him control over a fresh mobile reserve to influence what promised to be a highly fluid cavalry battle. In the event the surprised Scythians were completely caught out by this unexpected development and fled in terror, with the Macedonian cavalry in hot pursuit. Many were too slow to escape and both Arrian and Quintus Curtius say they left one thousand dead. Quintus Curtius adds that eighteen hundred horses were captured while Alexander had only sixty cavalry and one hundred infantry killed and a further thousand men wounded.[77]

This victory cowed the Scythians and put an end to most of the unrest within the former Persian provinces, as Quintus Curtius Rufus explained:

> It was this expedition, with news of the timely victory, that brought Asia [that is the Persian Empire] into subjection, though most of it had been in revolt. People had believed the Scythians invincible, but after this crushing defeat they had to admit that no race was a match for Macedonian arms.[78]

The defeat of the Scythians demonstrated great tactical flexibility, but it was more of an ambush than a true pitched battle. A far sterner test was to be met when Alexander pressed on beyond the borders of Darius' old domain to conquer India, which then consisted of numerous independent kingdoms. Having received the allegiance of one king, Taxiles, he undertook to attack his rival, Porus, whose kingdom lay across the River Hydaspes (the Jhelum in Pakistan).

When he arrived on the banks of the Hydaspes in the early summer of 326 BC, he found Porus waiting for him on the other side of a broad river in full flood. What he saw gave him pause for thought. Although the Macedonians were alarmed by the size of the river, this was the least of their worries, as Quintus Curtius explained:

> the bank opposite provided an even more terrifying scene, covered as it

was with horses and men and, standing among them, those immense bodies with their huge bulk; deliberately goaded, these deafened the ears with their horrendous trumpeting. The combination of the river and the enemy suddenly struck terror into hearts which were generally given to confidence and had often proved themselves in battle.[79]

Those 'immense bodies' were of course elephants. Although the Macedonians had captured a dozen or so in Darius' camp after Gaugamela, and had seen those of their new ally, Taxiles, this was the first time they faced the prospect of fighting them. Porus may have had as many as two hundred. Of all Porus' large army, which probably included around fifty thousand infantry, four hundred chariots and four thousand cavalry, it was the elephants that most concerned Alexander, as they were likely to neutralize his main striking force if he tried to cross. 'He thought it likely', explains Arrian, 'that his horses ... would be too much scared by the appearance of these beasts and their unfamiliar trumpetings to be induced to land.'[80]

The two armies faced each other across the river for days while Alexander had boats brought up from the River Indus and flotation devices made of hay-filled hides prepared. Each night large bodies of Macedonian cavalry rode up and down the river bank noisily as though looking for a place to cross. Porus responded by sending out his men and elephants to shadow them along the opposite bank. After days of this the Indians, as Alexander had hoped, started to relax their guard and took less care over tracking the Macedonians. Alexander still could not risk a crossing immediately opposite Porus' army but his patrols could now move at will at night without giving anything away. Some miles from the camp a possible crossing point was found that was shielded from the view of the opposite bank by a wooded islet. Alexander had the boats and floats stashed there and then marched there by an inland route one night with a picked force. Craterus was left in command at the camp with the main force and strict instructions to attempt a crossing only if Porus moved all of his elephants away to meet Alexander. Alexander's force crossed early the next morning and was not spotted by enemy scouts until it was nearly across. The scouts promptly rode off to inform Porus while Alexander got his troops ashore.

Alexander had five thousand cavalry with him and six thousand infantry. He had selected the Royal Squadron, now referred to as the *Agema*, and the units of Companions commanded by Hephaestion, Perdiccas and Demetrius. The cavalry had been reorganized since

Gaugamela. Each *ila* (squadron) was for the first time subdivided into two *lochoi* of roughly 125 men, each commanded by a *lochagos*, giving greater tactical flexibility. Then the squadrons were paired up into larger units called hipparchies and commanded by a hipparch, which may have been largely for administrative purposes. The units were no longer divided along tribal lines and commanders were now appointed to them purely on merit regardless of ethnicity. The Companions now also contained many Persians, Bactrians and others, even in the *Agema*, as part of Alexander's policy of integrating and assimilating his new subjects. In addition to these three hipparchies of Companions he had brought along Bactrian and Sogdian units, some Scythian cavalry and some Dahae mounted archers. Apart from the Dahae, it is not specifically stated how these tribal contingents were equipped but we know there were only one thousand mounted archers in total, so at least two thousand of them were not archers. Bactrians and Scythians may well have been heavy cavalry of the type seen at Gaugamela and they were all to perform well in close combat against the Indian mounted troops. The infantry contingent consisted of the Cretan archers, and the Agrianian and Thracian light infantry, backed up by the pikemen of the *hypaspist* foot guards.

As they reached the far bank of the Hydaspes, Alexander led the cavalry off ahead, ordering the Cretan archers to follow as soon as they could, while the other infantry got itself into good order. Alexander was intending to strike fast and hard while he still had the element of surprise, not giving Porus time to react to the news his scouts would soon bring him. As always he had the psychological effect of decisive action in mind.

> The idea that was in Alexander's mind was that if Porus' army should attack in force he would either settle them straight away with a cavalry charge or, failing that, fight a delaying action until his infantry could come to his support; if, on the other hand, the Indians proved to be so badly shaken by the bold and unexpected crossing of the river that they took to their heels, he would be able to press hard on the retreating enemy.[81]

This is what heavy cavalry is for. They use their speed of manoeuvre to be upon the enemy quickly, throwing them off balance mentally and giving them no time to prepare, then striking hard to finish the job.

When news reached Porus that a force had crossed the river and threatened to outflank him, he dispatched his son (his brother, Spitaces, in one account – perhaps both were there) with two thousand cavalry and one hundred and twenty chariots to delay Alexander while he got the rest of his army in order. These chariots were not the scythed version encountered at Gaugamela. They were fighting chariots such as the Assyrians would have appreciated three centuries earlier. They were big and heavy and each carried six men: two archers, two shield bearers and two to share the driving and the throwing of javelins.[82]

As this force approached the Macedonian cavalry, Alexander first sent in the Dahae mounted archers to harass them while pressing on with the rest to go straight for the Indian main body, which he assumed to be following close behind. But, having ascertained that this force was unsupported, he decided to defeat it in detail, rather than leaving it threatening his rear as he advanced. It had to be eliminated quickly so that he could strike at Porus while the iron was still hot. The Macedonian cavalry set about it in characteristic fashion.

> He attacked at once, and the Indians, seeing Alexander there in person and his massed cavalry coming at them in successive charges, squadron by squadron, broke and fled. The Indians' losses in the action were some four hundred mounted men, Porus' son being himself among the killed; their chariots and horses were captured as they attempted to get away – speed was impossible, and the muddy ground had rendered them useless even during the fight.[83]

Porus' advance force was thus easily defeated, but it had achieved part of its aim, for even the brief resistance it had offered (perhaps not so brief as a first reading suggests, given that 'successive charges' were required) had cost Alexander vital time. Porus left part of his force with some elephants to keep an eye on Craterus' force, which was now making visible preparations to cross, then marched out of his camp to meet Alexander's force 'with the flower of his army'. He moved a little inland, away from the treacherous mud of the river bank, and deployed.

As usual the ancient sources differ in the figures they give for Porus' forces, but not as much as usual, the discrepancies no doubt stemming largely from the splitting of his force. It is safe to give him approximate figures of thirty thousand infantry and four thousand cavalry, including many of those that had just fled from Alexander, and around three hundred chariots.[84] The most important differences concern the elephants: the usually well-informed Arrian gives Porus two hundred; Diodorus one hundred and thirty (an encouragingly strange number to make up) and Quintus Curtius Rufus only eighty-five.

Porus deployed his troops to take full advantage of the immense power of the elephants and particularly the deterrent effect they would have on the enemy cavalry, whose horses, unlike his own, were not accustomed to them. He spread his elephants out in front of his infantry, at intervals of one hundred feet according to Arrian,

> to form a screen for the whole body of infantry and to spread terror among the cavalry of Alexander. He did not expect that any enemy would venture to force a way through the gaps in the line of elephants … terror would make the horses uncontrollable.[85]

Behind the elephants he placed his heavy infantry, with the units covering the gaps in the line of elephants, 'though on a front of lesser extent'. More infantry were placed on either wing, flanking the elephants, probably including archers with powerful longbows of bamboo that fired very long and heavy arrows, but were clumsy and slow to use.[86] Outside of these on either flank were the cavalry with a screen of chariots in front.

When Alexander arrived on the scene with his cavalry he was impressed by the sight of the Indian army, which apparently looked like a fortress; the infantry forming the walls and the elephants standing at intervals like great towers.[87] Porus himself made a magnificent spectacle, by all accounts a huge man, splendidly armoured and seated upon the biggest of the elephants. Diodorus and Arrian agree that he was five cubits tall and Plutarch claims 'his size and huge physique made him appear as suitably mounted on an elephant as an ordinary man looks on a horse'.[88] Alexander was probably as much impressed by the skill and generalship he had shown and realized that his chance of a swift victory was gone. He halted and let his cavalry rest their horses while the infantry caught up, then had the cavalry screen the infantry while they in turn rested, for he 'had no intention of making the fresh enemy troops a present of his own breathless and exhausted men'.[89] Surveying the opposition, Alexander is said to have remarked, 'At last, I see a danger that is a match for my courage – I must take on beasts and fine warriors together.'[90]

Alexander was outnumbered by approximately five to one in infantry, and was relying on a relatively slight numerical superiority in cavalry that might well be nullified by the enemy's elephants. In order to make sure of being able to strike an effective blow somewhere, Alexander massed four thousand of his five thousand cavalry on the right wing, where he characteristically intended to lead the first assault. Here he faced around two thousand Indian cavalry and one hundred and fifty chariots, assuming that Porus, deploying first, had divided his cavalry into two equal wings. Alexander could not put all his cavalry into this blow, however, as he needed some cavalry to protect the left flank of his infantry from cavalry attack. As the Thessalians, who usually performed this task, had long since returned to Greece, he took the unprecedented step of splitting the Companions up and sending two hipparchies to the left wing under the command of Coenus. Coenus was instructed, however, that if Porus moved all his cavalry across to meet Alexander's attack he was to leave his post on the left flank and follow them, ensuring that the Macedonians would have cavalry superiority on the right wing. The infantry were formed with the pikemen in the middle and the light infantry providing some protection on either side and also probably forming a skirmishing screen in front. They were given strict orders 'not to engage until it was evident that the Indians, both horse and foot, had been thrown into confusion by the Macedonian cavalry'.[91]

Alexander opened the battle by sending ahead his thousand mounted archers against the Indian left flank to start softening up the enemy chariots, hoping to cause confusion and 'shake the enemy by the hail of their arrows'. Behind them he began advancing with the rest of his right-wing cavalry, 'intent upon making his assault while they were still reeling under the attack of the mounted archers'. Meanwhile Porus, realizing that this was where the main threat lay, reacted as Alexander had hoped, by bringing all of his cavalry from his right wing across to the left in column behind his infantry line. As they arrived at the left wing, however, they found that Coenus and one thousand Companions had ridden round the end of the elephant and infantry lines and were following hard on their heels, presumably having driven off the chariot screen left opposite them unless these too had moved across with the cavalry. The Indian cavalry now tried to redeploy to face both threats but was still in some confusion when the converging Macedonian attacks hit home.[92]

Alexander's experienced eye saw the confusion among the Indian squadrons and 'saw his chance; precisely at the moment when the enemy cavalry were changing direction, he attacked'. The royal squadron and the rest of the cavalry ploughed into and through the chariot screen on Porus' left so that 'almost all the Indian chariots were presently broken in pieces' as stricken horses and drivers panicked and overturned the clumsy vehicles.[93] Porus ordered some elephants over to break up this charge but, although elephants can put on a good sprint in a straight line, were too ponderous to intercept 'the swift Macedonian horses'. So rapid was the charge that the archers on this flank could not fire their big bows quickly enough and were ridden down 'so that as they struggled to make a shot they were overtaken by their swift-moving enemy'.[94] The Indian cavalry was quickly thrown into chaos by the speed and ferocity of the combined attacks but, rather than fleeing the field, 'fled back in confusion upon the elephants, their impregnable fortress – or so they hoped'.[95]

So far all had gone much to plan for the Macedonians, the Companions as always throwing their opponents into chaos by a well-timed and ferocious attack. With the enemy's units now jumbled altogether and hemmed in, Alexander ordered his own infantry up. But now the nearest elephants counter-attacked the Macedonian cavalry, whose terrified horses could not be induced to approach them, and forced them to keep their distance. When the infantry came up a desperate slugging match ensued in which the Macedonian cavalry could do little to intervene:

> The elephants being made use of (by the mighty bulk of their bodies and their great strength), bore down and trod under foot many of the Macedonians; others were caught up with their trunks, and tossed into the air, and then fell down again with great violence upon the earth, and so miserably perished; many likewise were so rent and torn with their teeth, that they died forthwith.[96]

With the exception of the mounted archers, Alexander's cavalry could not intervene anywhere where there were elephants still active. They could charge any troops that were temporarily without such protection, as when the Indian cavalry made a foray. Then the strength and experience of Alexander's mounted troops were too much for them and they were driven back among the elephants again. Such was the general confusion that all the Macedonian cavalry units had become intermingled. They continued to launch controlled attacks where possible, encircling the Indians and making sure that they were all hemmed in one confused mass where complete chaos reigned, but it was left to the infantry to tackle the elephants. The Macedonian light infantry showered the elephants with javelins and arrows, wounding many and killing the mahouts of others, while the phalanx tried to use their long pikes to herd them back onto the huddled ranks of the cavalry and infantry they protected.

Many of the elephants went berserk and 'ceased altogether to play their expected part, and, maddened by pain and fear, set indiscriminately upon friend and foe, thrusting, trampling and spreading death before them'. The Indians 'jammed up close among them ... found them a more dangerous enemy even than the Macedonians'.[97] Arrian explains that the Macedonians were spared worse harm because, having room for manoeuvre, they 'were able to use their judgement, giving ground when they charged'. Even so the Macedonians suffered too as Quintus Curtius Rufus describes:

> Some however pursued the elephants too energetically, provoking them to turn on them by the wounds they inflicted. Trampled underfoot, they served as a warning to the others to be more cautious ... So the fortunes of the battle kept shifting, with the Macedonians alternately chasing and fleeing from the elephants.[98]

Porus at some point gathered other elephants together around his own. With infantry driving them on from behind, he made a concerted counter-attack which Diodorus says 'caused great slaughter among the Macedonians' and which Quintus Curtius Rufus states had the Macedonians on the verge of a rout and 'casting around for a place to flee'.[99] Some desperate moments followed, the Thracian infantry resorting to hacking at the elephants' feet and trunks with axes and *kopis* swords, before the Macedonians gained the upper hand and had them all boxed in again. This carnage went on for hours until eventually the surviving elephants had had enough and Alexander ordered the final attack.[100] Even then the Macedonian cavalry, which usually was so devastating in pursuit, played only a secondary role. Their horses by now must have been exhausted from the day's exertions and the strain of constant fear.

> In time the elephants tired and their charges grew feebler; they began to back away, slowly, like ships going astern, and with nothing worse than trumpetings. Taking his chance, Alexander surrounded the lot of them – elephants, horsemen, and all – and then signalled his infantry to lock shields and move up in a solid mass. Most of the Indian cavalry was cut down in the ensuing action; their infantry, too, hard pressed by the Macedonians, suffered terrible losses. The survivors, finding a gap in Alexander's ring of cavalry, all turned and fled.[101]

Porus, 'so long as a single unit of his men held together, fought bravely on', Arrian emphasizing that in this he was very different from Darius. Only when severely wounded did he attempt to leave the battlefield, and even then he attacked the first messenger sent by an admiring

Alexander to ask for his surrender. When he eventually was induced to surrender, Alexander was so impressed by his dignified bearing that he promptly confirmed his sovereignty over his subjects, gave him some additional territory, and 'from that time forward found him in every way a loyal friend'.

Allegedly, around twenty thousand Indians had been killed or captured in this battle. Only Arrian and Diodorus give casualties for the Macedonians, and although they vary enormously on the infantry losses, their figures for the cavalry killed are not too far apart at 230 and 285 respectively. Perhaps the most grievous loss to Alexander was that of Bucephalus, his comrade in arms and companion since boyhood, who died a few days after the battle. He was possibly approaching thirty years old, certainly well over twenty, and had played his part in most of Alexander's great victories. Alexander founded a city where he was buried and named it Bucephalia in his honour. The River Hydaspes was also to be the last of Alexander's great battles. His army mutinied and refused to go further into India, prompted partly by rumours of armies of even bigger elephants in the lands to come. The army soon headed for home, although not without adventures on the way. Alexander fell ill and died on the return journey in 323 BC, at the age of thirty-three.

The battle of the River Hydaspes had been the sternest test yet for the Macedonian heavy cavalry. They had proved themselves far superior to the Indian cavalry and chariots, but Porus' elephants had prevented them from turning this into a quick victory. The Companions had finally come up against something that could not be thrown into confusion and swept away by a bold charge, quite the reverse as it was they who were thrown into disarray. Although the Macedonians eventually won a crushing victory, the cavalry contributed little after the initial defeat of the Indian cavalry. Ironically it was the first major battle in which Alexander had enjoyed a numerical superiority in cavalry.

This points up an important limitation of heavy cavalry. At Granicus and Gaugamela, they had triumphed first over other cavalry and this had precipitated the collapse in morale of the rest of the opposing army. At Issus they had defeated infantry through sheer audacity and psychological shock. The Kardakes had 'collapsed the very moment [Alexander] was on them'. At all three battles the enemy collapse was also hastened by the neutralizing of the enemy command. The Persian officers at Granicus narrowly failed to kill Alexander before they were cut down, while Darius was targeted and chased off the field at Issus and Gaugamela. But when faced with troops that could hold their ground against the initial onslaught, preferably aided by determined leadership, the effectiveness of heavy cavalry was greatly reduced. At the Hydaspes it was their misfortune to come up against an animal that usually responded to the dilemma of 'fight or flight' by trying the options in that order and was not easily overawed, whereas the Companions' horses were terrified even when their riders were willing. The physical fighting power of heavy cavalry was considerable but it was nothing compared to the massive psychological impact that they derived from speed and sheer bulk. This remained true throughout the history of heavy cavalry and cannot seriously detract from the Companions' fine record of achievement.

Perhaps the most impressive attribute of the Macedonian cavalry was the degree of discipline and training shown in the way Alexander was able to keep them in control after the first charge. Even in the professional armies of the nineteenth century such control was still considered a vital but difficult goal for cavalry to attain. The Duke of Wellington's exasperation with the habit his British cavalry had of 'galloping at everything' and expending their usefulness in a single charge is well known. The importance of rectifying this was repeatedly emphasized in later training manuals as the cavalry, it was recognized, was 'of all branches the most liable to be thrown into confusion and the most difficult to rally'.[102] Certainly few instances of such control and flexibility were displayed by medieval cavalry. This control combined with their sheer élan and high morale surely marks Alexander's Companions as one of the finest cavalry forces in history.

The refinement of shock tactics by the Macedonian heavy cavalry provided Alexander with his main means of attacking an enemy force and projecting his will over them. He fully realized the psychological aspect in their employment, offering as they did the ability to shake an enemy's resolve at the onset by falling upon them in an early charge. The sheer audacity of the cavalry attacks at Granicus and particularly at Issus played a large part in initiating the collapse of a numerically superior enemy before the full weight of their numbers could come into play. The infantry, who at Granicus and Issus were in some difficulty, and whose line was penetrated at Gaugamela, were enabled to move up and help finish the job. It is important to remember that Alexander's cavalry were used as part of a balanced and coordinated combined arms force, but they certainly played the lead role.

Leading them personally, Alexander was able to take advantage of the mobility and discipline of the Companions to react quickly to changing circumstances and to grasp immediately any opportunity for victory in the midst of battle. At Gaugamela this allowed him to exact the full price for the overextension of the Persian line, thereby winning a battle that was still very much undecided. Like a well-balanced sword in the hand of a skilled fencer, the Companions allowed Alexander to fix his eye upon his target and launch a precise and lethally penetrating thrust at the heart of the opposing army.

4

The Successors

After Alexander's death his empire was soon broken up in a series of wars between his former governors and generals, usually referred to as the *Diadochoi* or 'Successors'. These wars were fought by armies largely modelled on Alexander's, although with an increasing admixture of eastern elements, such as elephants and scythed chariots. The Diadochoi generally continued to place their faith in the shock power of cavalry as Alexander had done. Although the cavalry arm of Macedon itself declined, Macedonian-style cavalry thrived in the eastern provinces and was to be joined by even more specialized shock varieties.

It may seem surprising that Macedonia, the birthplace of Alexander's all-conquering Companions, should have allowed its heavy cavalry forces to decline, but in fact the reasons are quite straightforward. Alexander invaded Asia with around five thousand cavalry and thirty-five thousand infantry, the cavalry thus contributing about 12.5 per cent of the total force. Of these, around four thousand were Thessalians and Companions fully capable of taking their place in the main battle line. This force had been deliberately built up throughout his father's reign to tackle the Persian cavalry on the broad plains of Asia. Antipater was left behind to guard the homeland and keep an eye on the Greek cities with only about one and a half thousand cavalry and ten thousand infantry. Further reinforcements of cavalry were periodically sent to Alexander, along with at least some of the *paides*, the officer cadets being groomed as the next generation of Companions. If Alexander had survived and established a stable regime, no doubt many horsemen would have come home, perhaps bringing Persian horses to replenish and improve the Macedonian and Thessalian bloodstock. But it was not to be. Instead his untimely death was followed by a period of endemic warfare and then the secession of the eastern provinces, ensuring that many of the horse-rearing and riding nobility who had joined Alexander's great adventure never returned – either through death or because they sought their fortune in Asia or Egypt. This one-way flow of men and horses was the main factor in a decline from which Macedon's cavalry would never really recover.

The weakness of Macedon's cavalry arm was soon exposed and further weakened when the Greek cities took the opportunity presented by Alexander's death to rebel against Macedonian domination. When he marched to quell this rising, Antipater could field only six hundred Macedonian cavalry. Worse still, the Thessalians, who had 'previously sent him many fine horses', had joined the rebels; in one stroke depriving Macedon of half their cavalry strength and an important supply of horses. Antipater was defeated at Thermopylae in the autumn and besieged in Lamia.

At this stage Alexander's generals were still cooperating. In the spring of 322 BC, Perdiccas, who had been appointed regent, sent an officer named Leonnatus back to Macedonia with a small force to assist Antipater. By urgent recruiting Leonnatus managed to raise a relief force of two and a half thousand cavalry and twenty thousand infantry. The new recruits, for the cavalry at least, may have consisted in large part of inexperienced youths and reactivated veterans; given the desperate situation and the enemy's known superiority of cavalry, this probably represents the utmost cavalry effort Macedonia was capable of at this point. But they were still outnumbered by the Greeks, who abandoned the siege of Lamia and came to face Leonnatus with twenty-two thousand foot and three and a half thousand cavalry 'amongst whom were two thousand Thessalians, brave and valiant men, on whose exertions they mostly relied for obtaining the victory'. The Greek and Thessalian cavalry was used en masse and managed, after a stiff fight, to drive off their Macedonian counterparts. Leonnatus himself was driven into a marsh 'and oppressed by his arms, after he had received many wounds, was there slain'. Stripped of their protective cavalry, the Macedonian phalanx 'in order to avoid the horse, withdrew from the plain and open field and betook themselves to the steep and rocky hills'. Here they successfully repelled further attacks from the Thessalians, but when Antipater's force joined up with them the next day, seeing 'that the Thessalians were too strong for him in horse', he had to beat an inglorious, careful retreat to Macedonia 'over hills and other craggy places'.[1]

The Greeks were defeated later that year, but only with the help of reinforcements, including fifteen hundred cavalry, returning from Asia with Craterus, who had been one of Alexander's most trusted generals. At Crannon in September 322 BC Antipater and Craterus fielded five thousand cavalry. The Greeks, now depleted by complacency and desertions, were heavily outnumbered but could still muster three thousand five hundred horsemen 'in whom they placed great confidence of victory' and these opened the battle. Although outnumbered, they were apparently getting the better of the Macedonian cavalry, most of whom must have been the demoralized survivors of the previous battle, but the issue was decided by the successful attack of the Macedonian phalanx, which included six thousand veterans of Alexander's campaigns. The Greek coalition fell apart soon after as the various participants each made a separate peace with Antipater, although the Thessalians were now obviously suspect as allies.

Had a sustained period of peace ensued, the cavalry might have started to recover in numbers – although of course not in experience. But the wars of the Diadochoi continued, and, on top of all this, in 280 BC Macedonia was among those areas swamped by an invasion of Celtic tribes. Quite apart from the actual losses in fighting and raiding, there was massive social and economic disruption and depopulation of the rural economy. Such conditions would have affected the numbers of available cavalry much more severely than of infantry. Any bunch of peasants could be given a pike and shield and drilled into a moderately effective phalanx much more quickly, and cheaply, than horses could be bred or riders brought up to reasonable competence as horsemen. As seen already, the cavalry was provided by the nobility because it was they who had the resources to breed horses, and the leisure time, while their slaves or tenants worked the fields, to get the daily riding practice required to make an expert horseman.

Up to 301 BC, it looked as if there was some chance that Macedonia and the newly conquered territories might be reunited under the hand of Antigonus Monopthalmus (the One-Eyed), Alexander's former governor of Phrygia.[2] But his death at the battle of Ipsus in that year confirmed the division of the empire into separate kingdoms: the two most important being the kingdom ruled by Seleucus and his descendants, centred on Persia and dominating most of western Asia; and Egypt, where Ptolemy and his descendants ruled. Although Antigonus' son, Demetrius Poliorcetes (the Besieger), later gained the Macedonian throne, he and his descendants, who retained it until the final defeat by the Romans, were limited to Macedonia proper and intermittent control of parts of Thrace.[3] Too many of the equestrian nobility and their horses had gone to seek their fortunes abroad and now these resources were permanently lost to Macedon.

By the time Philip V of Macedon faced the invading Romans at Cynoscephelae in 197 BC, he could raise only two thousand cavalry, less than nine per cent of his force, including Thessalians, light cavalry units and mercenaries. Only in the generation of relative peace that followed Philip's defeat at Cynoscephelae did the Macedonian cavalry start to recover. When his son Perseus made his stand against the Romans at Pydna he was able to raise three thousand Macedonian and one thousand allied Thracian cavalry. The Thessalians could not be induced to defy Rome. Perseus also tried to hire a further ten thousand horsemen from the Celtic Bastarnae but found he could not afford them; a sure indicator that Macedonian generals still appreciated the potential of cavalry and would take all they could get their hands on with the resources available. At Pydna the Macedonian phalanx was destroyed by the Roman legionary infantry before the cavalry had played any real part. These then followed their king's example and abandoned the footmen to their fate: an ignominious end to a fine tradition of mounted valour and to Macedonian independence. Thereafter Macedonian riders and horses served under the Roman eagle.

The legacy of Alexander's bold use of cavalry was best displayed in the eastern provinces where generals could draw on the vast equestrian resources of the former Persian empire. Here the veteran Macedonian cavalry and, increasingly, locally raised units fashioned in their image, played a decisive role in most of the battles, particularly while the first generation of Successors, those that had actually served under Alexander, still lived. The proportion of cavalry to infantry in eastern-based armies was therefore much higher than in Macedon itself. At Gabiene in 317 BC, Antigonus Monopthalmus had nine thousand cavalry, almost 30 per cent of his force; his opponent Eumenes of Cardia had a little over six thousand, comprising 14.5 per cent. Demetrius Poliorcetes, having commanded some of his father's cavalry creditably at Paraitakene and Gabiene, fought his first battle in overall command at Gaza in 312 BC with only eleven thousand infantry and between seven and eight thousand horsemen; the cavalry thus contributing around 40 per cent of the total. He was beaten by Ptolemy I of Egypt with four thousand cavalry and eighteen thousand infantry. This was a more balanced force but the cavalry content was still over 18 per cent, and it was largely these that won the battle for him.

It is generally considered that, after the first-generation Successors had passed away, the cavalry declined even in the east. It is true that the proportions of cavalry in some of the later battles were markedly lower, but this merely flags up one of the dangers of using this measure without careful scrutiny. At Raphia in 217 BC, the Ptolemaic army was back to less than 7 per cent cavalry and the Seleucids to a little over 10 per cent. Yet Ptolemy IV was still fielding five thousand cavalry, much the same as Alexander had taken to Asia, and Antiochus III could manage six thousand. It was just that the number of infantry in both armies had been inflated by desperate recruiting for this crucial showdown. The fact that effective cavalry requires well-trained horses and experienced riders placed a cap on the number of cavalry that could be raised at short notice. This limitation didn't apply to the infantry. Ptolemy IV, for example, fielded seventy thousand foot soldiers by arming the Egyptian peasantry: a measure that would not have produced horsemen worth having, given their lack of equestrian experience, even if adequate horses could have been found, which they could not.

Naturally the Macedonian rulers of Egypt and western Asia preferred to trust Macedonian or Greek troops rather than the conquered 'barbarians'. Alexander's conquests had left many small garrisons in captured cities, and many new towns had been founded and colonized by his veterans, and these provided an important core to early successor armies. Their descendants continued to be called upon but their limited numbers had increasingly to be supplemented with native subjects and new colonists. At all times mercenaries were also used.

Both the Seleucids and Ptolemies developed a system for securing the services and loyalty of sufficient recruits by granting land in return for military service. Surviving administrative papyri have ensured that more detail is known about the system as applied in Egypt. Basically the estate, or *kleros*, was awarded to an individual to derive a living from as he saw fit. In return he would be called up when the king required his services. The troops raised in this way were known as *klerouchoi* (the Seleucid equivalent were *katoikoi*). The system was used to raise both infantry and cavalry, but the size of the plots varied according to the service required, with those earmarked for the cavalry receiving more land. Cavalry *kleroi* in the third century BC were usually either one hundred acres or seventy acres, the latter being increased to eighty acres in the second century BC. This not only allowed plenty of space for raising horses, but provided the income required to produce good horsemen. The level of slave or indentured labour that the owner of such an estate could afford was evidently expected to allow him enough leisure time to train his horses, hunt and practise his weapon skills.

When called up, the *klerouchoi* were mustered into units. Those in receipt of one hundred acres were formed into hipparchies numbered from one to five. Those in receipt of seventy acres went into one of four hipparchies with ethnic names: Thessalians, Thracians, Mysians and Persians. These regimental names may have originally indicated the actual ethnic background of the recruits; but if so this soon ceased to be true. Another possibility is that the names reflected a style of equipment. The same reform that increased their *kleros* to eighty acres also replaced the ethnic names with numbers, perhaps indicating a standardization of their equipment. It has been suggested that the five hipparchies of one-hundred-acre men were heavy cavalry, with the lower status forming the light cavalry. This would make sense, especially if the riders provided their own arms and equipment, as the more expensive armour required by heavy cavalry would have been paid for by the higher revenues from their larger estates. Although state arsenals definitely existed, the *klerouchoi* cavalry may have supplied much of their own equipment. The horses at least were their own, as they are bequeathed in surviving wills, which they would not have been if they had been government property. This would make sense not only from the economic point of view but also in terms of fighting efficiency, as it ensured the riders were already familiar with the mounts that would carry them in battle. Horse tack and horse armour, as well as personal armour, would all be more efficient if made to measure, although perhaps the state arsenals provided standard patterns for purchase.

The hipparchies were divided into *ilai*, the *ilai* into *lochoi*, and these into *dekades*. Unfortunately we do not know even the nominal strength of any of these units apart from the *dekades* (singular *dekas*, from *deka* meaning 'ten'), but the division down as far as tens is interesting. The hipparchies probably still contained between four and five hundred men in two *ilai*. Each *ila* may, however, have been divided into more *lochoi*, perhaps four of them with around fifty or sixty men each. More subdivisions would have eased manoeuvring and deployment, giving commanders more tactical flexibility and encouraging the use of local reserves. At Paraitakene, for example, Eumenes' attacking wing was formed from a main line with four small units of fifty deployed as a flank guard. Were these an *ile* divided into four *lochoi*? It may be that Alexander's squadrons had actually been further subdivided than our sources reveal. Certainly it seems very likely on practical grounds that something akin to the *dekas* had always existed; but the evidence as it stands points to greater articulation of the levels in between being a further refinement of cavalry tactics under the Successors. Of course, Xenophon had long before recommended cavalry formations with subdivisions down as far as *dekades* and even half *dekades*.

Unsurprisingly the battles of the period were fought according to what were seen as Alexander's methods, although with varying degrees of modification and success. Thus the opening gambit of most generals was to concentrate the greater part of their heavy cavalry on one wing to launch a decisive charge, guarding the other flank with fewer or lighter cavalry with orders to delay the enemy. Sometimes the oblique order was used in an attempt to ensure that the weaker, defensive wing was last to be engaged. Thus, at Gaza, Demetrius Poliorcetes opted to place all but one and a half thousand of his eight thousand cavalry on one wing to 'make the onset'. The remainder were on the other wing with orders 'to keep an oblique line and make a running fight of it'.[4]

Whereas Alexander had always concentrated his main striking force on the right wing, the Diadochoi might favour either. This was largely because they were fighting with similar armies against generals with a similar system and so were always second-guessing each other. Which of his opponent's wings was going to be most heavily loaded with cavalry became perhaps the most important variable a commander had to consider when deploying. Once one side had committed to a deployment, the other general had to decide quickly how to counter this threat. One option was to oppose it with his own main attacking force, as happened at Gaza where Demetrius was opposed by Seleucus I and Ptolemy I. These two experienced generals had originally planned to weight their left, but when they saw Demetrius' massive concentration was on his left, they decided to mass three thousand of their four thousand cavalry on their right to meet it. This ensured that the battle opened with a fierce clash of heavy cavalry similarly armed with xyston and sword. 'Upon the first onset they fought with their lances, when many were killed, and as many wounded on both sides. Then they fell to it with their swords, and there, thronging together, thrust one another through, and fell in heaps together.'[5] Despite their superior numbers, Demetrius' cavalry were routed when the elephants he launched in support of them were made to panic by pre-prepared anti-elephant obstacles and stampeded back through the horses. Having committed himself heavily to this attack, Demetrius was now unable to prevent the rest of his army melting away.

The other option to counter a concentration of heavy cavalry was to oppose it with a defensive cavalry wing, hoping to delay it while one's own offensive wing tried to defeat the wing the enemy had left weakened. We have already noted the orders given to Demetrius' right wing at Gaza. At Paraitakene in 317 BC, Eumenes, Alexander's former chief secretary, intended to attack with a strong right wing containing most of his best cavalry, including 'nine hundred that are called Companions' and three hundred of his bodyguard regiment. Antigonus chose to counter this threat by guarding his left wing with javelin- and bow-armed light cavalry used to evasive skirmishing tactics, intending that 'by this means the strength of that part of the enemy's army, wherein they placed their greatest confidence, was wholly eluded'. These tactics initially worked very well and the attack of Eumenes' heavy cavalry stalled as they were unable either to catch their opponents or evade their missiles 'due to the weight of their arms'. Eumenes eventually restored the situation by sending for 'some of the swiftest horse from the left wing'. These managed to outflank the troublesome enemy and, with a supporting attack from some elephants, drove them all off. Antigonus meanwhile was making good use of his heavy cavalry on the other flank that Eumenes had just weakened further.[6]

A commander could of course choose to split his cavalry equally between the two wings to be prepared for all contingencies, but this might mean he didn't have a superiority, or even parity, on either. The aggressive legacy of Alexander meant most of his successors preferred to seek the opportunity for a decisive cavalry attack on one wing, even if it meant taking risks elsewhere.

Alexander's influence also led to an emulation of his heroic leadership style with the generals most often to be found exercising personal command of the heavy cavalry on the loaded wing. This had sound practical reasons. It put the general in question at the only point where he could really hope to exercise any sort of control over what was meant to be the decisive attack once it had been launched. If the main blow was going to be delivered by the heavy cavalry, it made sense for the general to do whatever he could to ensure its success. He could see what was happening and was on the spot to seize an opportunity or rectify a mistake.

We have seen how, at Paraitakene, Eumenes was able to take the decision to send for light cavalry from the other wing to rescue his stalled cavalry attack. Meanwhile his infantry phalanx, containing three thousand of Alexander's veterans, was driving Antigonus' infantry centre from the field. Most of Antigonus' heavy cavalry was under the command of his son Demetrius and was being delayed by Eumenes' light cavalry, but Antigonus was himself present on this wing with his three hundred most reliable heavy cavalry. Just as it looked like the battle was lost, he saw a gap open up in the enemy's line between his victoriously advancing phalanx and the cavalry. Seizing the opportunity, Antigonus charged into this gap, much as Alexander had done in a similar situation at Gaugamela. But whereas Alexander would now have turned towards the centre, charged the enemy's infantry in the flank and rolled up his phalanx, Antigonus turned outwards to aid his son by outflanking and scattering Eumenes' left-wing cavalry. Even so, the veteran pikemen could see the threat to their flank and rear and were forced to break off their pursuit and withdraw, probably forming a square or squares. Antigonus rallied some of his main body and remained in possession of the battlefield, allowing him to claim a victory despite having sustained more casualties, but only his timely cavalry charge had avoided a crushing defeat.[7]

One of the most important ways this personal command could be exercised was after an attack had succeeded. One of the things that marked Alexander as an outstanding leader of cavalry was that he always managed to keep his cavalry under control after a successful breakthrough, rallying at least some of them to exploit their success by turning to attack another target in the flank and rear. In 317 BC Antigonus and Eumenes faced each other for the second time that year at Gabiene. Antigonus had a sizeable cavalry advantage, nine thousand compared to six thousand, while Eumenes again placed his faith in his superior infantry phalanx. Antigonus again entrusted his right-wing cavalry to his son Demetrius, but once more he also took his own place there at the head of his bodyguard, 'where he himself intended to charge'. Eumenes also put himself on this flank with the best of his cavalry, including the bodyguards of various provincial rulers, but had this wing held further back, or 'refused', to delay the decision here, while his centre ran obliquely with the elite Argyraspidai (Silver Shields) on the right furthest forward to open the infantry fighting. In a confused fight amongst clouds of dust, Antigonus' own unit charged that of one of Eumenes' governors, who promptly fled with fifteen hundred troops. This started the collapse of Eumenes' left, despite his own efforts. Eumenes escaped to join the other flank where he could be more use, his remaining hopes now lying squarely with the phalanx, which was again quickly breaking its enemy counterpart. Antigonus now managed to regroup his cavalry, sending part under Python to take the Silver Shields in flank while he and Demetrius attempted to block off any escape by Eumenes. Again Eumenes' veteran infantry were quick to see the danger and formed a defensive square, thwarting Python's attempted flank attack and withdrawing safely to a river. For the second time Eumenes' troops had easily won the clash of pike phalanxes in the centre, only to have their efforts rendered irrelevant by Antigonus' bold, but controlled, use of heavy cavalry.[8]

The problem of keeping or re-establishing control after a successful charge was a perennial one throughout the history of cavalry warfare. It called for great discipline and presence of mind from all the riders, but particularly from the commander, who had to remain aware of the overall situation. You only have to picture yourself in this situation for a moment to appreciate this. Imagine that you have just managed to steel yourself and your horse sufficiently to dash upon a group of armed men who are going to try to kill you; with other frightened horses on either side and behind, your mount is probably merely following the herding instinct: the herd is in danger and on the move, so it is best just to keep on running. Perhaps the enemy wavers and flees before your approach, or perhaps there is a brief clash; spear thrusts and sword strokes are exchanged, men and horses start to go down. Then suddenly the enemy unit is fleeing and those men who were trying to kill you are now scattering before you, exposing their backs, trying to escape into the swirling dust kicked up by the thousands of hooves whose drumming reverberates in your ears. It is very easy then to forget the rest of the battle and just take up the chase of these fugitives. Even if an officer calls, or has a signaller sound a horn, the troopers may not be able to see or hear him in the dust and din.

It is therefore no surprise that few Hellenistic generals had as good a record in this matter as Alexander or Antigonus. In one of history's great moments of tragic irony, Antigonus met his death at Ipsus from this very cause. Instead of leading his mounted bodyguard on the wing, he opted to take his stand on foot with the phalanx, leaving his son Demetrius to command the cavalry alone. This should not be interpreted as any waning of faith or interest in the cavalry on Antigonus' part as he was now in his early eighties; hard riding is not kind to old bones. Antigonus' ten thousand cavalry were slightly outnumbered by those of his opponents, Seleucus I and Lysimachus (the former governor, and now ruler, of Thrace), but he did have about ten thousand more infantry than them. Seleucus' real advantage lay in his four hundred elephants, which could be a very effective deterrent to cavalry, Antigonus having only seventy-five. Despite this, Demetrius opened the battle when he led 'the strongest and best squadrons of cavalry in a charge against Antiochus, Seleucus' son'. According to Plutarch, 'He fought brilliantly and put the enemy to flight', but, instead of rallying his troops to take the Seleucid infantry in the flank or rear, 'by pressing the pursuit too far and too impulsively he threw away the victory'.[9] Seleucus, turning the situation to his advantage, now redeployed his elephants across the rear of his army as a screen, preventing Demetrius returning when he eventually tired of the pursuit. Meanwhile on the other flank the cavalry clash had presumably gone the other way, as Antigonus' infantry was apparently now left completely at the mercy of the remaining Seleucid cavalry.

The Seleucid cavalry did not in fact charge Antigonus' phalanx, perhaps in part because the infantry may have had time to form a square while Seleucus was rearranging his elephants, but the mere threat of this was eventually sufficient to bring about its collapse. Hoping to bring Antigonus' veteran troops over to his side intact, Seleucus had his cavalry repeatedly threaten to charge while intermittently calling upon the enemy to surrender. Demetrius meanwhile, finally returning with his riders on blown horses, could do nothing but skulk beyond the screen of elephants he found blocking his path. Eventually a large portion of Antigonus' phalanx, despairing of salvation, surrendered, triggering the rest to flee. Antigonus was ridden down by cavalry and died still wondering where his son was.

At Raphia, Antiochus III made the same mistake as Demetrius. Enjoying a considerable advantage in cavalry, having six thousand to Ptolemy IV's five thousand, but with fewer infantry, he led his right-wing cavalry in the opening charge. This was successful in that it drove Ptolemy's left-wing cavalry from the field. But Ptolemy, who had also been on this flank, extracted himself from the confusion to take command of his phalanx in the centre, while the Seleucid king got carried away with the thrill of the chase and disappeared off into the distance with his best horsemen. On the other flank the Ptolemaic cavalry had the better of it. Although it was the Egyptian infantry which then defeated the Seleucid phalanx, these horsemen were on hand to join in the slaughter. Antiochus eventually returned to find his phalanx scattered with ten thousand left dead on the field.

Apart from the question of control, the general's mere presence provided an important morale boost to the troops. This should never be underestimated. Napoleon's maxim that the moral factors are three times as important as physical ones in warfare was at least equally true in ancient warfare. The presence of a king or commander, with ultimate power to punish or reward, was a powerful incentive. There was probably also a large element of deliberate emulation of Alexander, especially among the first generation of Successors, and a general belief in the heroic ideal that a king or leader's place in battle was to set an example in the front rank. At Gaza, where Ptolemy I and Seleucus I were allies, they might logically have been expected to divide the command so that each commanded half the line. Instead, both kings positioned themselves with the heavy cavalry massed on the left wing 'amongst whom they themselves intended to charge', leaving the whole of the rest of the line in the care of subordinates.[10]

Pyrrhus of Epirus, who was a distant relative of Alexander, also commanded his cavalry very much in the heroic style. He displayed the same instinct for decisive action and the apparently reckless disregard for personal danger that had driven, or rather led, Alexander's Companions to perform such prodigies. During his retreat from a failed attempt to take Sparta in 272 BC, his personal example resulted in his bodyguard cavalry achieving the notable feat of charging and destroying an elite band of Spartan infantry.

> Pyrrhus himself had just learned of his son's death, and in an agony of grief ordered his Molossian cavalry to charge the Spartans. He himself rode at their head and strove to drown his sorrow in Spartan blood. He had always shown himself to be an irresistible and terrifying fighter, but this time his daring had surpassed anything that had been seen before. When he rode at Evalcus, the Spartan side-stepped his charge and aimed a blow with his sword that just missed Pyrrhus' bridle hand and sheared through the reins. Pyrrhus ran him through with his lance, but in the same moment fell from his horse: he went on fighting on foot, and cut to pieces the picked company of Spartans who were fighting round the body of Evalcus.[11]

The disadvantage of course was the risk of the general himself being killed. At the Hellespont in 321 BC, Craterus charged at the head of his Agema only to be killed in the early stages of the action when he was thrown from his horse and trampled by those following. This prompted the rest of the attacking cavalry to flee. Meanwhile, his opponent Eumenes was on the other flank, where he hoped to get revenge on Neoptolemus, his own former cavalry commander who had recently switched sides. When the opposing squadrons of cavalry charged and a fierce combat ensued, these two sought each other out and settled the matter one on one. According to Diodorus' highly detailed account, which has the ring of a true incident preserved, in the press of the mêlée neither could get in a good sword blow and they ended up grappling and pulling each other to the ground. Then they laid about each other with swords again. Eumenes quickly hamstrung Neoptolemus who, unable to stand, fought on his knees and inflicted three painful but superficial wounds on his former commander's arm and thigh. Eumenes then got in with a killing blow to the neck.[12]

Most heavy cavalrymen in Successor states continued to wear arms and armour similar to, or perhaps deliberately emulating, Alexander's Companions for a hundred and fifty years after his death. There were, however, two important developments in the rider's equipment: first, the introduction of shields; and, secondly, the development of the heavily armoured cataphract by the Seleucids.

Cavalry with shields first appeared in mainland Greece and Macedonia in the second quarter of the third century. It is unclear what influences were at work but two theories are commonly put forward. From 280 BC to 275 BC Pyrrhus of Epirus campaigned against the Romans in southern Italy on behalf of Taras, originally a Spartan colony, whose horsemen appear to have been using shields from the late fourth century, as evidenced by coin images. Perhaps Pyrrhus adopted shields for his cavalry and so imported the trend upon his return to Greece. Alternatively, shields may have been adopted from the Celtic invaders who overran Macedonia and northern Greece in 280 and 279 BC. The shields shown in use by Macedonian cavalry on the Aemilius Paulus monument appear to be of Celtic type, being circular with a raised central rib.

Shields are such obviously beneficial things to a soldier that we are immediately prompted to ask why Greek and Macedonian cavalry did not carry them earlier. Amongst foot soldiers other than archers, for obvious reasons, the shield was always the first bit of defensive equipment chosen. If he could afford nothing else, an infantryman would have a shield, as his primary concern was to be able to ward off the enemy's missiles or blows, the most likely source of injury. For a rider it was different because he had to control his horse or be completely useless. Handling a shield and the reins in one hand is awkward. To maintain good control of a horse, especially with a severe bit, only a very small movement of the hand is necessary. If a rider is carrying a small shield in his bridle hand he would have to move his arm around a lot to parry incoming blows and would jerk the horse's mouth all over the place giving all manner of confusing signals. To be really useful to a horseman who needed to keep his left hand still a shield needed to be large, so that it covered much of the body without needing to be moved. But of course big shields are heavy and make the rider more top heavy. Thus it is easy to see why a horseman, for whom staying on his horse was the prime factor in avoiding injury, would much more readily forego the protection of a shield. The sheer awkwardness of handling a decent-sized shield also explains why those Hellenistic cavalry armed with lances are never portrayed with shields, the combination of these two weighty and awkward items being excessively difficult to manage on horseback.

What was it that changed to make the extra encumbrance worthwhile? One possibility is that the trade-off between greater protection and the demands of riding was always a fine one and that therefore cultural influences alone were enough. That is to say both options, shielded or unshielded cavalry, were more or less equally rational choices and would thus be adopted in some cultures and not others, only to be transmitted later, along with other fashions, after contact with other cultures; in this case perhaps the Celts or southern Italians.

Alternatively, the spread of cavalry shields may have been linked to the development of the saddle by the Scythians. Xenophon seemed to be aware in the middle of the fourth century BC that something more than a simple blanket was available, or at least possible.[13] The spread of Scythian saddles, however, probably came after the conquest of the Persian empire. It is most likely that knowledge of it passed from tribes such as the Massagetae to the Seleucids and thence to the other Successor states. Or it may have been transmitted via the Thracians: the Kazanlak tomb paintings, dated to the late fourth or early third century BC, show that a simple saddle with slightly raised pommel and cantle was in use by the Thracians. It is perfectly possible that both routes of influence operated simultaneously.

The Celts later played an important part in the development of the structured saddle, but there is no evidence for the now-famous Celtic 'horned' saddles being earlier than the Scythian types. The Celts may, however, have already adopted these Scythian saddles (the 'horned' saddle later developing from it) and then helped to transmit to the Hellenistic world both the saddle and the cavalry shield during the Celtic invasions of northern Greece and Asia Minor. These early saddles may have offered riders enough extra security to tip the cost/benefit analysis in favour of carrying a shield, although this was not the only reason for using saddles. Extra comfort alone would be enough, not to mention the reduction of sores and damage to the horse's back.

Those cavalry units that adopted shields also seem to have reverted to carrying multiple javelins as their main armament. This is no surprise considering that riding with the weight and unhandiness of the twelve feet long xyston by itself was no mean feat, even with a primitive saddle.[14] This return to the pair of javelins has led some, including Ian Heath, to argue that Macedon's cavalry was reverting to a skirmishing and harassing light cavalry role. Certainly there were units of so-called 'Tarantine' cavalry equipped in this manner and employed as light cavalry in many successor armies.[15] Livy's description of an encounter between Macedonian and Roman cavalry at Athacus in 200 BC, in what the Romans called the Second Macedonian War, is often used to support the view that the Macedonians had abandoned shock cavalry altogether. Livy states that the Macedonian cavalry were expecting to skirmish from a distance and were seriously surprised when the Roman squadron charged in to close quarters. Philip V of Macedon's

> forces took it for granted that the type of fighting would be what they were used to, that is, that the cavalry would advance and retreat alternately, discharging their weapons and then retiring ... but the Roman attack was as stubborn as it was spirited, and this threw the enemy's tactics out of gear. The Romans behaved as if it were a general engagement in line ... and the cavalry, as soon as they had reached their enemy, reined in their horses and either fought from horseback or jumped down and mingled with the foot soldiers [the Macedonian cavalry were supported by light infantry] in the fight. Thus the king's cavalry, unaccustomed to a stationary fight, were no match for the Roman horse.[16]

Compelling as this evidence may initially seem, it probably tells us only about Macedonian light cavalry, which had always existed alongside the shock cavalry. The forces engaged at Athacus were actually only light screening forces. Besides, even clashes between shock cavalry units can often involve advances and retreats as squadrons disengage, reform and wheel to charge in again with renewed impetus, sometimes by tacit mutual consent. The unusual Roman tactic of reining in their horses completely, and even dismounting to fight on foot, would have produced 'a stationary fight' by comparison with the tactics of Companion-style heavy cavalry, or most other cavalry over the following two thousand years. It is not surprising if it wrong-footed their opponents. Furthermore, the passage in question comes just a few paragraphs after Livy's description of another cavalry clash that took place when the invading Romans first ran into Macedonian cavalry:

> These two squadrons, coming from different directions ... finally encoun-

tered one another on the same road. Each body had heard the noise of the mounted men from some distance, and they were well aware of the enemy's approach. And so, before they came into sight of one another they had made ready their horses and arms for combat, and there was no delay in charging as soon as the enemy came into sight. As it happened the two forces were well matched in numbers and in spirit, both being made up of picked men, and the fight went on for some hours on equal terms. Finally the exhaustion of men and their mounts put an end to the battle without a clear victory for either side. The Macedonians lost forty horsemen, the Romans thirty-five.[17]

Clearly the Macedonian cavalry on this occasion were perfectly willing and able to engage in shock action. The whole evidence adds up to the Macedonians having several specialized types of cavalry. Some undoubtedly were 'Tarantine' light cavalry armed with javelins and shields, wearing little armour and trained to skirmish at a distance. It was probably a unit of this type that was overwhelmed at Athacus. Others were heavy cavalry, some wearing body armour as well as shields, and although similarly armed with javelins perfectly capable of shock action. As has been seen from Xenophon's writing, the use of javelins did not preclude shock action, although it did give the option of engaging an enemy from some distance, at least while the limited supply of javelins held out. Finally, Macedon probably still retained some units armoured and armed with the xyston, but without shields, specializing purely in the shock role, into the second century BC alongside the other types.

The Macedonians were not defeated at Cynoscephelae and Pydna because their cavalry had forgotten or abandoned the techniques of shock combat, nor were they outclassed by Roman cavalry. Cynoscephelae took place in heavy mist, across a ridge line, hardly ideal conditions for decisive cavalry action; yet the cavalry gave a good enough account of itself in the early stages, only joining the rout when the phalanx was broken up. At Pydna, most, if not all, of the Macedonian cavalry were held back in reserve behind the infantry, which was sent to attack the Roman position across a stream and into rough ground. The Macedonian left wing, which may have contained some cavalry, collapsed in the face of an attack by elephants supported by the Roman allied cavalry, which included Pergamene heavy cavalry armed in Hellenistic style. Perseus then quit the field and most of the cavalry then followed suit without having been tested.

To return to the second development in equipment, the emergence of the cataphract must be examined. This term is now generally used for cavalry where both the riders and the horses are heavily armoured. The term is first used in reference to some of the Seleucid cavalry at the battle of Magnesia, where Antiochus III fielded six thousand *cataphracti*. The reliefs on the temple of Athena at Pergamum depict arms and armour believed to be the spoils taken from the defeated Seleucids.[18] These show a metal horse's facemask (the medieval term is *chamfron*), probably in bronze, with a transverse feather crest, and a panel of lamellar armour (rows of metal rectangles laced together, usually with a fabric or leather backing) that is almost certainly chest protection for a horse (in the middle ages rigid chest armour for a horse would be called a *peytral*).[19] For the rider there was a metal helmet with a full face mask, complete with sculpted beard, the usual style of cuirass with *pinions* and *pteruges*, and articulated full-arm defences which appear to have been made up of overlapping horizontal hoops which may be metal or rawhide.

The cataphracts may indeed have been provided with even more armour than this. We have already seen how the wealthiest Scythian and Massagetae nobility had probably been armouring their horses since the fifth century BC. Some Persian cavalry had adopted this practice by the fourth century BC with chamfrons and aprons of scales that protected the horse's chest. Xenophon advocated the adoption of Persian-style cavalry armour for the Athenians and a few decades later, as we have seen, it was those units in the Persian army whose mounts had 'protective coverings made of interconnected iron plates' that proved the most dangerous components of the Persian armies defeated by Alexander.[20] It is therefore likely that Seleucid armies, drawing on Persian and Bactrian manpower, included some cavalry on horses armoured in this way from quite early on, alongside the traditional Macedonian-style cavalry raised from the settlers (called *katoikoi* in the Seleucid kingdom). Indeed, where Livy introduces the *cataphracts* at Magnesia, he implies that the royal squadron used some horse armour, but that the cataphract horses wore even more.

> On the right ... three thousand cavalry in breastplates – cataphracti is the name for them ... On the left ... three thousand cataphracti and a thousand other cavalry, the royal squadron, with lighter protection for riders and their mounts but in their other equipment not unlike the cataphracti.[21]

Livy, following a contemporary source, is clearly introducing the cataphracts as something new in the extent of the armour for riders and horses, which the horse armour on the Pergamum relief does not really warrant. Perhaps the head and breast armour shown is all that would have been worn by the mounts of the royal squadron. If this inference is correct, the most likely candidate for the additional horse armour worn by Antiochus' cataphracts is something akin to the examples found at Dura Europos. Consisting of overlapping metal scales fixed to a fabric backing, these were trappers shaped like those modern horse rugs that cover the whole body and fasten at the chest.

Although the Dura Europos finds were much later Roman pieces, their style was adopted from the Parthians, many representations being found in Parthian art. By the time the Romans adopted cataphract equipment the Parthians were rulers of the core of the old Persian Empire, having overthrown the Seleucids. The Parthians were a Scythian people who had settled within the Persian Empire and had thus become subjects first of Alexander and then of his Seleucid Successors. In the mid third century BC they, along with the Bactrians, rebelled and then went on to seize control of much of the eastern part of the Seleucid empire (incidentally cutting off important horse-breeding regions). Interestingly, Antiochus III waged a successful campaign against them in 209 BC, which may well have provided the inspiration for the introduction of cataphract units in the years before Magnesia.

Heavily armoured and equipped with lances (the xyston, or later the *kontos* which may have been heavier), the cataphracti took specialization for shock combat to the extreme. Their additional protection made both horse and rider less vulnerable to enemy weapons. This carried with it an important psychological advantage as it allowed them to plunge into close combat more confidently, the rider's confidence and added sense of invulnerability being transmitted to the horse through the subtle unspoken clues that horses are so good at reading.

But this came at a price. The weight of the armour was a significant encumbrance for man and beast and put great demands on both. Even more so than the use of shields by cavalry, the development of fuller armour was certainly linked to the development of the saddle, which helped negate some of the associated top-heaviness. Nor is it a coincidence that this development took place first amongst Scythian peoples with their tradition of equestrian skill and in those areas where the horses of greatest strength and stamina were bred. The Seleucids no doubt used the sturdy Nesean breed for their home-grown cataphracts. Even so the clumsiness of the equipment probably reduced their manoeuvrability and endurance compared to conventional cavalry.

Tactically this restricted them to an all out charge in close order. Although well protected from most weapons, the cataphract might be unable to keep off more mobile opponents for long if he found himself isolated amid the cut and thrust of a fluid, fast-wheeling cavalry fight. It was therefore even more important for these troops than for other cavalry to maintain good order and discipline in the attack. At Magnesia they neatly demonstrated both the potential power and the weaknesses of their type.

Antiochus III had sixty thousand infantry and twelve thousand cavalry. Of these six thousand were cataphracts, showing the extent to which Antiochus placed his faith in them. He must have been truly impressed to convert half his cavalry, especially given the expense of the equipment. Another two thousand were more conventional heavy cavalry divided equally between two elite units, the Agema and the royal guard, on partially armoured horses. Another two and a half thousand were Galatians (the Greek name for the Celts who had settled in Asia Minor after being expelled from Greece in the third century BC). Some Galatian noblemen would have worn chainmail or other body armour but mostly they acted as multipurpose cavalry on unarmoured horses and equipped with shields and an assortment of thrusting spears, javelins and swords. The balance of the Seleucid cavalry were unarmoured mounted archers of the Dahae and other tribes.

The Romans were in position first, resting their left flank on the river. They were heavily outnumbered with only around three thousand cavalry, of which eight hundred, commanded by their ally King Eumenes of Pergamon, were heavy cavalry of Hellenistic type. Nearly all of these were massed on the open right wing with only about one hundred and twenty cavalry between the infantry and the river. Antiochus divided his cataphracts equally, placing three thousand on each side of the main line of heavy infantry interspersed with elephants. He took station on the right with the *agema* with the infantry guard, horse archers and light infantry filling the rest of the gap between his flank and the river. The other cataphracts had the royal squadron on their immediate left, then the Galatian cavalry, some 'Tarantine' light cavalry and masses of light infantry making the line much longer than that of the Romans. In front of this wing was a screen of scythed chariots and Arab archers mounted on camels intended to disrupt the opposing cavalry.

Eumenes opened the battle on his own initiative, sending forward light infantry supported by small units of his Pergamene cavalry to attack the scythed chariots before they could get under way. These were soon thrown into confusion and driven back towards their own troops, where they 'turned their terror on their own men'.[22]

> The storm as it were that broke upon them so terrified the horses – partly because of the wounds inflicted by missiles aimed at them from all sides, partly because of the discordant shouts – that they suddenly rushed off blindly in all directions at once ... and the cavalry in pursuit increased the confusion and panic of the horses, and of the camels, since these were likewise terrified ... the auxiliaries in support who were stationed nearest to the chariots, were terrified by their panic and confusion, and they also turned and fled, exposing the whole formation as far as the cataphracti.[23]

The left flank of the cataphracts was suddenly wide open and unexpectedly exposed to the threat of a flank attack. Some tried to escape, throwing the close-packed ranks into such disorder that they were quickly swept away by the enemy cavalry. In the ensuing confusion they paid the full price of sacrificing mobility for armour.

> And the cataphracti, now that their supports were scattered, did not withstand even the first onset. Some of them rushed away in flight; others were overwhelmed, burdened as they were by their armour and weapons.[24]

The panic of the left wing exposed the heavy infantry in the centre and the Roman infantry advanced to exploit this. On the other wing, however, the cataphracts made a much more impressive contribution, at least to begin with. With the king there in person and their flanks both secure, at least for the present, they were able to deliver a straightforward charge which soon had the Roman left fleeing back towards the safety of their camp. Livy says it was the Roman cavalry which Antiochus first attacked with his cataphracts and light armed troops, but this seems hard to reconcile with the initial deployments he described:

> What had happened was that Antiochus, on the right flank, had observed that the Romans, because of their reliance on the river, had no auxiliaries there except four troops of cavalry; and these, in keeping contact with their comrades, were leaving the river bank unsecured. He had therefore attacked the Roman cavalry with his auxiliaries and *cataphracti*, and he did not attack them in front only; he outflanked them by the river and kept pressing them hard on that side, until first the cavalry and then the infantry next to them were driven headlong towards the camp.[25]

As the Romans had only a small number of cavalry between the river and the flank of their legionary heavy infantry, while the cataphracts were flanked by thousands of infantry, the cataphracts must have been opposite part of the Roman infantry line. Even though the Roman line was evidently drifting across to the right as it advanced, enough to allow some Seleucid troops to work round the flank of the cavalry, it is hard to see how three thousand horsemen and thousands of archers, slingers and javelinmen could all have attacked effectively on the short frontage occupied by the Roman cavalry detachment. It seems more likely that the Seleucid light infantry on the right flank were sent in first, harassing the Roman cavalry with sling stones and arrows while others worked their way round the right flank of the Roman cavalry along the river bank. When the Roman cavalry broke, the cataphracts, probably supported by the Agema since the king appears to have joined the advance, charged the legion opposite them. These broke and ran for the camp.

As the Romans claimed only to have lost twenty-four cavalry and three hundred infantry killed in the whole battle (although there were 'many wounded'), it seems that the cataphracts did not inflict that many casualties on the fleeing infantry. This is probably due again to the weight of their armour. Horses under heavy armour, particularly the kind that covered the whole body, would not have been able to sustain much more than a steady trot for long. One of the flaws of horse anatomy is that they have great trouble losing excess body heat. Overheating causes rapid tiring and, in extreme cases, complete seizure of the muscles. The temperature under an armoured trapper in the Middle Eastern climate would soon have soared. With this in mind, the cataphracts probably kept to a walk as they began to advance, moving up to a steady trot at maybe a hundred yards out and only breaking into a canter to gather momentum (psychological as much as physical) for the final few dozen yards if at all. For the same reason, once they had an enemy on the run they probably could not sustain the pursuit at speed for more than a short distance without the risk of rendering the horses completely blown.

Having succeeded in making a breakthrough, the *cataphracti* had shot their bolt. Although the fleeing Romans were chased almost to their camp, the Seleucid cavalry were not so hard on their heels as to prevent them being rallied by an officer and making a stand. Nor did the *cataphracti* wheel inwards and roll up the enemy line. The arrival of just two hundred enemy cavalry from the other flank was enough to convince Antiochus that he could ask little more from his men and horses. He turned his own mount and fled the field. The Roman and

Pergamene cavalry 'pursued the enemy all over the plain ... and they cut down the hindmost as they came upon them'. Three thousand of the Seleucid cavalry were killed.

Cataphracts have come in for particular criticism from those modern historians who believe mounted shock combat was not viable before the invention of the stirrup.[26] It is curious then that they should have gone on to enjoy an operational history of over a thousand years, longer than the plate-mail-clad knight of western Europe so beloved of Hollywood and popular imagination. True, Magnesia was a less than impressive historical debut, the Seleucids being forced to cede all of Asia Minor west of the Taurus to buy peace from the Romans and their allies. Within fifty years they had been overthrown and replaced by the Parthians. Cataphracts were a vital element in Parthian armies for the next three and a half centuries and then in those of the native Persian dynasty, the Sassanids, who ousted them in turn and ruled the region until engulfed by the Arab conquests in the mid seventh century AD. The Romans also adopted the cataphract, although not until much later when the similar cavalry of the steppe-dwelling Sarmatians threatened their borders.

It is inconceivable that cataphracts would have enjoyed such longevity and wide emulation if they had not performed successfully. They must have fulfilled their shock role more than adequately to make the huge expense of such troops acceptable. Horses are expensive, and selective breeding for greater weight carrying would only have made them even more so. Who would put their best, most valuable, horses in heavy armour under a hot Middle Eastern sun, with all the attendant risks of heat stroke, dehydration and debilitation, unless it was going to produce results? And this is besides the actual business of fighting. Who would so compromise that mobility which had always been cavalry's greatest asset unless it was to operate in situations where full armour would confer a significant advantage, that is in the thick of close combat? The notion that they were some kind of impotent rich man's folly does not stand up to the tests of historical evidence and common sense.

Assyrian lancers: The first regular heavy cavalry. Armoured Assyrian lancers ride down an unarmoured enemy horseman.

Bronze Statuette: Bronze statuette of a Greek horseman wearing a Corinthian helmet. Sixth century BC. © Copyright the Trustees of The British Museum.

Pelike vase: A Greek heavy cavalryman of the mid fifth century BC. He is armed with two spears and protected by a helmet and a cuirass with shoulder flaps that fasten down on the chest. Courtesy of The University of Arkansas Museum.

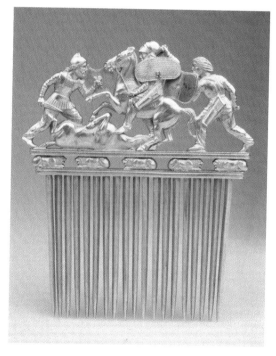

Comb with Scythians in Battle: A heavily armoured Scythian warrior seeks to finish off his opponent, having already maimed his horse with a spear thrust. Late fifth or early fourth century BC gold comb from the Solokha burial. © Copyright the State Hermitage Museum, St Petersburg.

Grave of Dexileos: Grave stele from Athens, depicting the deceased riding down a hoplite heavy infantryman, *c.* 390 BC. The Art Archive / Kerameikos Museum, Athens / Dagli Orti.

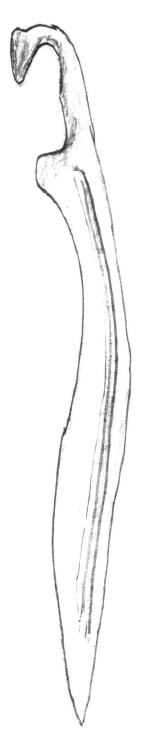

Iron sabre: A *kopis* or *machaira* of the sort recommended by Xenophon for use on horseback. It is an unwieldy weapon, useful only for vigorous hacking.

Pelinna: Armoured Macedonian horseman, with Phrygian-style helmet and cuirass with pteruges.

Alexander Sarcophagus: Alexander the Great defeating the Persians on the so-called Alexander Sarcophagus. The weapons were originally added separately in bronze, but have long since disappeared. The Art Archive / Archaeological Museum Istanbul / Dagli Orti.

Alexander at Issus: The most famous image of ancient cavalry in action. Alexander the Great skewers a Persian at the battle of Issus as Darius prepares to flee. Note the composite cuirass and the length of his lance. The tip of the secondary spearhead on the butt end is just visible to the left of the damaged portion. The Art Archive / Archaeological Museum Naples / Dagli Orti.

Tombstone of Titus Flavius Bassus: Tombstone of Titus Flavius Bassus, a Roman auxiliary cavalryman. He is armed with a spear and a long *spatha* sword and protected by a mail shirt, oval shield and helmet. His horse's face is protected by a chamfron and the horns of the saddle are just visible. The Art Archive / Museo della Civilta Romana Rome / Dagli Orti.

Relief from stoa of Athena: Captured arms and armour on a relief from Pergamum celebrating the defeat of the Seleucids at Magensia (190 BC) by the Romans and their Pergamene allies.

Parade Helmet: A masked helmet of the first century AD. Such early examples are usually dismissed as parade helmets but they later became standard combat equipment for the cataphract units that Ammianus Marcellinus described as looking like polished statues.

Trajan's Column: A scene on Trajan's column shows Roman cavalry pursuing Sarmatian horsmen during the conquest of Dacia, early second century AD. The Sarmatians are armed in cataphract style, with both riders and horses covered in scale armour, although the sculptor has surely misinterpreted the design of this.

Arch of Constantine: Roman heavy cavalry in action, riding down barbarians, in a scene from the Arch of Constantine, Rome. Fourth century AD.

5

Early Rome

No ancient army is more often studied or more highly vaunted than that of Rome, but it is their foot soldiers that usually take all the glory. Cavalry, by contrast, is an arm in which they are considered 'notoriously weak', at least throughout the Republican period.[1] The common view has it that the Romans were simply no good at cavalry warfare but more than compensated for this by the excellence of their infantry. This view is largely based on the apparent failings of the Roman cavalry in the wars against Carthage in the third century BC. There is a persistent belief that they had little equestrian tradition and consequently lacked an adequate supply both of skilled riders and of generals with a proper understanding of cavalry warfare. Yet there are grounds for believing that the citizen cavalry was initially the republic's most valuable asset and that cavalry warfare, and shock tactics in particular, were no mystery to Roman generals.

Romans dated the foundation of their city to what we would now call 753 BC.[2] It evolved into a small kingdom on the northern edge of Latium, home to numerous Latin-speaking cities with whom Rome had strong cultural and ethnic ties. It was bounded on the north by Etruscan cities that also had a strong influence upon it, its last three kings being of Etruscan origin. The republican period began when the last king, Tarquinius Superbus (the Proud), was expelled; an event traditionally dated to 510 BC.

Unfortunately, the first two centuries or so of the republic's history are not recorded in any contemporary account of the sort that Herodotus, Thucydides and Xenophon provide for Greece in the fifth and fourth centuries BC. It seems that nobody at Rome was moved to write narrative history until increased contact with Greek culture and the momentous events of the wars with Carthage prompted some to do so in the third century BC. When writing about previous centuries this first generation of writers had to depend heavily upon the administrative records kept by the *pontifex maximus* (chief priest) since at least the beginning of the republic. As well as recording those elected to the various magistracies and military commands, these recorded declarations of war, the enrolment of forces, the distribution of captured spoils and the awards or punishments due to returning generals. Quite possibly they included brief summaries of the course of major battles, if only for the purposes of apportioning blame or praise. The historians would have fleshed out such data with oral tradition and information preserved by the leading families in the form of funerary orations and tomb inscriptions. Although none of the work of the first generation of writers has survived to the present day, they provided source material for those later writers whose work has. Most of our information for the early republic therefore comes from writers of the first century BC, most notably Titus Livius (better known as Livy).

In general outline, warfare under the kings is thought to have been similar to that in Greece, consisting basically of a citizen levy divided into cavalry, a phalanx of heavy infantry and more lightly equipped supporting infantry, according to what equipment the citizens could afford. Archaeology has revealed strong Greek influences in arms and armour throughout most of Italy, emanating from the Greek colonies in the south of the peninsula and on Sicily, although these were blended with native features. The first clear description of military organization comes from Livy's description of reforms instituted by the penultimate king, Servius Tullius, and it is likely that this system was adopted with few modifications when the republic was founded.

Under this system, the population was divided into seven classes according to a property qualification and this determined both their voting rights and their role in time of war (which was virtually an annual occurrence). As those selected for service each year were expected to provide their own equipment, the cavalry were, in Livy's words, 'drawn from the most wealthy and prominent citizens'; these were the equestrian class, their social identity defined by the fact they served as horsemen (*equites*) rather than foot soldiers (*pedites*). The purchase of warhorses was subsidized by a tax levied on rich widows, but wealth was still necessary. Only men of the richest class, chiefly landowning families who lived off their estates outside Rome itself, were likely to be accustomed to horsemanship and be able to afford the horse's tack and a groom in addition to their own personal weapons and equipment.

Of the remaining six classes, which were numbered, the next five provided the infantry. The first class had to provide themselves with the full hoplite panoply of body armour, helmet, greaves, shield and spear and are believed to have fought as a phalanx. The subsequent classes had progressively lighter equipment, the fifth class being unarmoured and armed only with slings. The sixth class (actually the seventh when including the *equites*) were not only too poor to arm themselves effectively but were also considered to have too little stake in society to be motivated to defend it reliably in any case. They neither voted nor fought.

In return for bearing the greatest expense in time of war, the equestrians were rewarded not only with the honour and status that accrued from cavalry service, but also with political power. A man of the equestrian class was liable for a maximum of ten years' cavalry service between the ages of seventeen and forty-six, compared to sixteen years' infantry service for the lower classes, and when these were completed he was eligible to stand for the first rung of magistracies. When it came to voting, the equestrian class voted first and the voting system was so heavily weighted in their favour that, unless the equestrian vote was evenly split, it was often unnecessary to call upon the remaining classes to vote. Over the centuries the lower classes were progressively enfranchised and even given access to high office, but the *equites* continued to dominate the political life to the end of the republic, continuing to fill most of the magistracies and the benches of the senate.[3]

The main change to the Servian system upon the expulsion of the last king was that henceforth the army was commanded not by a single king but by two annually elected magistrates or consuls. In times of extreme danger a dictator would be appointed over the consuls, usually for a six-month period. He would then appoint his own deputy, or master of horse (*magister equitum*). The latter obviously had a special responsibility for the cavalry at some point, but this may have been largely administrative. In battle, where some of the cavalry would often be deployed on each wing, it is likely that common practice was for the dictator and master of horse each to command both horse and foot, each taking half of the battle line.

The troops mustered were organized into legions consisting of several thousand infantry, each with a contingent of cavalry. Usually four legions were raised, each consul commanding two as independent armies. The strength of a legion in the earliest period cannot be known with any real certainty. Livy, describing events in 340 BC, says the strength of a legion was then fixed at three hundred cavalry and five thousand infantry. Although it has to be suspected that he is taking his understanding of Polybius' description of a later period and projecting it back in time, he may not be far off the mark and usual practice may have been much the same long before it was regularized. More securely, from various references in Polybius, it seems that by the mid third century BC the norm was for each legion to consist of three hundred cavalry and 4200 infantry, although the infantry could be expanded in times of dire need to five thousand per legion, as it was in the Second Punic War.[4] The cavalry could not be so easily expanded due to the more limited pool of eligibly wealthy and suitably skilled manpower.

The cavalry of each legion was divided into ten squadrons, or *turmae*, each consisting of three *decuriae* (literally 'tens' - although these may not have actually contained the ten men their name suggests). Each *decuria* was commanded by a *decurio*, the most senior of whom also commanded the whole *turma*. Each *decurio* nominated another man as his *optio*.

The proportion of cavalry may seem small, a normal consular army of two legions having only six hundred cavalry to 8400 infantry, giving a mere 6.6 percent of the total, or only 5.6 per cent when necessity called for the infantry to be increased. But as Rome dominated or defeated successive neighbours, starting with the loose confederation of Latin cities, followed by various Etruscan cities and tribal peoples such as the Samnites and Umbrians, they were granted the status of *socii* or allies. In return for autonomy over their internal affairs, they surrendered control over their foreign policy and had to contribute troops to fight alongside Roman forces and under Roman command. The usual arrangement was for the allies to match each Roman legion with an equal number of infantry but three times as many cavalry. With these allied troops included, a standard consular army actually consisted of 2400 cavalry (600 Roman and 1800 Latin) and 16,800 infantry, bringing the cavalry content up to a much more impressive 12.5 per cent, comparable to most late Hellenistic armies. Of course it is actual numbers rather than proportions that matter on the battlefield. The cavalry of one consular army was more than virtually any classical Greek city-state had managed, and the two consular armies fielded each year were not far off the five thousand cavalry Alexander took to Persia. It is far from negligible and certainly far too large to be explained away as scouts and messengers.

The fact that the Romans depended upon their allies for three quarters of the legion's cavalry need not be taken as an acknowledgement of their superior expertise in this field, although the Campanians did enjoy a particular reputation as horsemen. The link between wealth and equestrian service limited the number of *equites* available in Rome, and the link with social prestige and political opportunity meant that the ruling elite must have been reluctant to widen this exclusive circle significantly in any case. Furthermore, because cavalry was the most expensive arm to field, what with the subsidizing of suitable horses and the limited supply of these, it made sense for the Romans to shift this burden onto the allies as far as was possible, without denying their own leading citizens the opportunity to serve in a manner fitting their station. The more cynical might even suggest that a useful function was served in maximizing the number of young nobles from the allies who were kept where the consuls could keep an eye on them in time of war, although to use the word 'hostage' might be putting too fine a point on it.

Once the allied troops were mustered with the consular army, one third of the cavalry and one fifth of the infantry, apparently the best of them, were separated out to form the *extraordinarii*, or picked men. These formed the vanguard and rearguard on the march, and in battle they may have formed a reserve under the consul's direct control. It is not clear, but likely, that the allied cavalry were also organized into *turmae*.

On the march, it is likely that a *turma* rode with the *decuriae* side by side, each in a single file led by the *decurio* and closed by the *optio*, the whole forming a column three wide by ten deep. When deploying into line of battle, the column could wheel to one flank, preferably the right so that the shielded side was presented as the column marched across the face of the enemy force. Each trooper then had only to perform a 'quarter turn on the forehand' to the left, so the formation was now ten files across and three deep, each *decuria* forming a rank with the *decurio* on the right and the *optio* on the left.

Because wealth, political power and social status were linked particularly to cavalry service, the *equites* developed an ethos of conspicuous and competitive striving to distinguish themselves on the field of battle. A reputation for courage and virtue on the battlefield was a great, almost essential, asset for those with political aspirations. Plutarch relates how the candidates for office would walk in the forum wearing togas but no tunics beneath, in order to show their battle scars.[5] Great importance was attached to single combat. The ultimate honour was to gain the *spolia opima*, that is to kill an enemy leader in single combat, strip him of his armour and be granted the right to dedicate these in the temple of Jupiter. Rome's legendary founder, Romulus, was supposedly

the first to do this, and many men died trying to emulate him, only two
succeeding. Livy describes how, in a battle outside Fidenae in 437 BC, a
cavalry officer spotted the Etruscan king, Tolumnius, valiantly attacking Roman horsemen even as they chased the rest of his broken army
from the field. The Roman cavalry officer, Aulus Cornelius Cossus,
seized his chance for glory and confronted him.

> Putting spurs to his horse he rode at his enemy with levelled spear. The
> blow struck home and Tolumnius fell; instantly, Cossus dismounted and,
> as Tolumnius struggled to rise, struck him down again with the boss of
> his shield and with repeated thrusts of his spear finally pinned him to
> the ground. Then he stripped the lifeless body of its armour, cut off its
> head and, sticking it on the point of a lance, returned to the fight with his
> spoils.[6]

Although Livy may have embellished this incident a little, he claims
that the Emperor Augustus himself, in whose reign he wrote, examined
the captured armour then still hanging, suitably inscribed, in the shrine
of Jupiter Freterius.

The eagerness of young *equites* for such enduring fame is illustrated
by the example of Titus Manlius. In 340 BC when a Roman cavalry
patrol came across an enemy Latin squadron, the leader of the Latins
issued a challenge to single combat 'to show how much better a Latin
cavalryman is than a Roman'. Titus Manlius readily accepted, motivated
'by shame at the thought of refusing the challenge', despite the fact that
the consul, who also happened to be his father, had issued strict instructions against acting without orders. He was victorious but did not long
enjoy his victory. His father had him executed for disobeying orders,
making a fearsome example of him.[7]

The influence of Homer's *Iliad* may have coloured the telling of
such individual combats, but there is no reason to doubt that such a
practice existed or that it formed an important part of the equestrian
ideal. There are obvious parallels with the 'chivalrous' ethos of medieval knights, stemming largely from the same need to legitimize social
privilege and to enhance personal prestige. But for the equestrian class
the hunger for personal distinction existed in tension with the need
to be seen to be serving the common good and it was through their
group actions in battle rather than showing off in single combat that
the *equites* really paid their dues.

Our most detailed descriptions of the struggles of the early Republic
come from Livy. He gives the *equites* a glorious role in many of these

battles, although he does also record failures. There are many examples
of them attacking the enemy line in the flank when they were already
engaged frontally, as against the Volscians in 385 BC when 'the cavalry
added their own terror', just as the contemporary *hippeis* of Greece
were doing. He also describes instances where the cavalry's ability to
cover ground quickly was used to seize the initiative by opening the
battle with a shock charge to disrupt the enemy line, supported by the
infantry. Enticingly these are attributed to dates much earlier than the
Theban victories at Tegyra, Leuctra and Mantinea that pointed the way
for cavalry-led combined-arms assaults of Philip and Alexander. For
example, a swift victory was apparently won in 490 BC when the Roman
consul Valerius noted that the Sabine enemy 'by extending their flanks
too widely, had weakened their centre, and Valerius, after a devastating
cavalry charge, sent in his infantry to finish the work'.

The cavalry certainly appear as a more reliable element than the
infantry. Outside Veii in 483 BC it was just as well that 'one unsupported
cavalry charge broke the enemy resistance', because the Roman infantry
walked off the battlefield in an early example of industrial action linked
to political unrest over land tenure. On another occasion the cavalry
charged but the infantry only followed up in support once a standard
bearer had been summarily decapitated for hesitating to advance. In
two instances the cavalry were ordered to cut down some of the fleeing
Roman footmen to force the rest to return to the fight.

In a number of these early battles, the Roman cavalry apparently
dismounted. This has fed the belief that they lacked confidence in their
own ability as horsemen, expressed by one author as follows: 'neither
were they known as great horsemen, preferring to fight on foot whenever they could, thus Roman cavalry had a decided tendency to devolve
into infantry as riders dismounted, like Homeric warriors, to join the
mêlée'.[8] In the first 250 years of the Republic as described by Livy, this
'decided tendency' consists of just six instances set against dozens of
examples of mounted action. Indeed, a quick survey of even those six
occasions reveals that far from being a preference, dismounted action
was a last resort for the *equites*.

In 496 BC the forces of the young Republic faced a combination of
Latins and supporters of the exiled last king of Rome, Tarquinius Superbus. As the battle reached its climax, the dictator's mounted bodyguard
were ordered to cut down those soldiers starting to slip away from the
rear ranks of the infantry as the Roman centre began to give ground to
the enemy. This desperate measure forced the infantry to return to their

task for the moment, but things still looked shaky. The horsemen then launched a counter-attack against some of the exiles and began to 'cut them to pieces'. When the Latin commander, already wounded in an earlier duel with a Roman cavalryman, approached with enemy infantry reinforcements, he was recognized by a mounted Roman tribune, who instantly challenged him to single combat and quickly killed him, only to be killed himself as he dismounted to strip his armour with a view to claiming the *spolia opima*. Meanwhile the dictator had ridden off to fetch more cavalry from the wings to prop up the infantry who were now on the point of complete collapse.

> Postumius now galloped off to make a final appeal to his mounted troops; and urged them to abandon their horses and fight shoulder to shoulder with the infantry. The appeal was answered; every man leapt from his horse and moved up at the double to the front line, which they covered with their shields. The effect was instantaneous, the infantry fighting with fresh determination once they saw the young nobles ready to share their dangers on equal terms. From that moment the issue was no longer in doubt; the Latins wavered, and then broke; the Roman cavalry remounted and began the pursuit, followed by the infantry.[9]

The victory at Lake Regillus held an important place in the Roman collective memory of the Republic's founding and struggle for survival. The central role of the cavalry in this achievement formed a central pillar of equestrian class identity and pride. Later legend had it that the Dioscurii, the mythical twin riders Castor and Pollux, had aided the Romans at the battle before almost simultaneously appearing on sweating horses in the forum at Rome to announce the victory. The anniversary of the battle was marked by an annual parade of the cavalry through the streets of Rome to the temple of Castor and Pollux.

At Satricum in 381 BC and Lake Vadimonis in 310 BC the cavalry were ordered to dismount to stiffen the resolve of the wavering infantry by setting an example of steadfastness, just as they had at Lake Regillus. At Signia in 362 BC the cavalry were ordered to dismount only after repeated frontal mounted charges had been made on the main enemy battle line but had failed to disrupt it sufficiently for the infantry assault to be assured of success. The dismounted cavalry then led the attack on foot, in what Livy called 'a novel way', defeating the elite infantry of the enemy in a signal example of their indomitable esprit and refusal to accept defeat.[10] At Satricum in 315 BC the cavalry of both sides, Roman and Samnite, dismounted; but only because they were trying to carry off the bodies of the Roman master of horse and the Samnite general who both lay wounded from the preceding mounted clash.

None of these instances really supports the idea that the Roman cavalry or their generals lacked confidence in their own ability to fight on horseback. Medieval knights, even once all the technical aids of stirrups, saddles and lance rests were fully developed, also often dismounted to fight among the infantry in situations where holding a line or specific position was a tactical priority. For them, too, a sense of class identity and the link between martial prowess and prestige drove the dismounted horsemen to set an example of steadfastness for their social inferiors. Were they also inadequate horsemen?

Given the nature of Livy's sources for the fifth and fourth centuries BC and particularly the lack of clarity over the nature of the enemy forces, due to his habit of presenting the enemy as an undifferentiated mass, any attempt to reconstruct precise tactics of the Roman cavalry in this earliest period remains speculative. We can certainly say, however, that what came down to Livy was a tradition that they had been effective and largely successful against both enemy cavalry and infantry. Such evidence as there is certainly cannot support the conclusion that the Romans of the later republic 'had no local tradition of horsemanship' to draw on, as has been claimed by some.[11]

As we move into the third century BC, the surviving sources are on a better footing as they had contemporary or near-contemporary narratives to draw on. Interestingly, in this century Rome faced three enemies to whom most historians have happily attributed far stronger cavalry traditions and generally superior aptitude for cavalry warfare; the Celts, Pyrrhus of Epirus with his Macedonian-style army, and the Carthaginians. The more detailed accounts of battles include cavalry versus cavalry clashes, which allow us to directly compare the Roman cavalry's performance with that of their opposite numbers and assess their relative effectiveness.

Before surveying their combat performance it would be useful to consider how the Roman cavalry were equipped. Unfortunately, it is surprisingly difficult to say how Roman cavalry were equipped before the second century, for it is only then that they can be surely identified in the surviving artistic representations. There are archaeological finds of weapons from Italy, but few that can be identified certainly as those of Romans, let alone Roman cavalry. The earliest textual evidence is irritatingly ambiguous and rests almost entirely on a single passage in Polybius, written around 160 BC, which is worth quoting in full:

The armour worn by the cavalry is now very similar to that which is used in Greece. In earlier times they had no breast-plates, and fought in tunics which allowed great ease and agility in mounting and dismounting, but exposed them to great danger in hand to hand fighting, as their bodies were almost completely unprotected. Besides these disadvantages their lances were also unserviceable in two ways. In the first place they made them so slender and pliant that it was impossible to take a steady aim, and the shaking of the weapon from the motion of the horse caused many of them to break before the iron tip became fixed in anything. Secondly, the butt end was not fitted with a spike, so that they could only deliver the first thrust with the point, and if the weapon then broke it became quite useless. The cavalry shield was made of oxhide and was somewhat similar in shape to those round cakes with a boss in the middle which are used at sacrifices. These shields were of little value in attack as they were not hard enough, and when the leather cover peeled off and rotted after exposure to rain they became not merely awkward, as they had been before, but quite useless. Since this equipment proved so unsatisfactory in use, the Romans lost no time in changing over to the Greek type. The advantage of this was that in the case of the lance the horseman could deliver the first thrust with a sure and accurate aim, since the weapon was designed to remain steady and not quiver in the hand, and also that it could be used to deliver a hard blow by reversing it and striking with the spike at the butt end. The same may be said of the Greek shields, which, since they were firmly and solidly made, render good service against both attack and assault [probably meaning both missile attack and blows landed in close combat]. As soon as they made these discoveries the Romans began to copy Greek arms, for this is one of their strong points: no people are more willing to adopt new customs and to emulate what they see is better done by others.[12]

The first of several problems this passage presents is that we cannot say when Polybius, who was writing in the mid second century BC, thought this switch to a heavier armament took place. The passage is a digression upon the Roman military system in the middle of his narrative of the Second Punic War (218–202 BC) and some scholars have suggested that it was in that war that the earlier armament was found wanting and replaced.

Others have thought it necessary to pinpoint the change to a time when conflict with Greek arms proved their superiority by direct comparison in action, raising the possibility that the invasion of Pyrrhus of Epirus was the catalyst, although Polybius did not say the weapons were found wanting against the Greeks, only that it was to Greek arms that they looked for replacements, and that the Greek colonies in Italy had long provided a ready source of inspiration and supply for Italian weapons and armour.

Whenever Polybius, who is our earliest surviving source and usually the most reliable, thought the adoption of heavier equipment took place, there are other problems with taking it too literally. Artistic evidence from around the period in which he wrote, such as the Aemilius Paullus monument, shows Roman cavalry wearing Celtic-style chain-mail armour, not Greek breastplates, so he may simply have meant that the Romans adopted comparably heavy armour to that of Greek cavalry, but not necessarily the type. But the biggest question it raises is whether earlier Roman cavalry ever really went into battle with no body armour. These were the wealthiest citizens and well capable of affording the best equipment around.

The *equites* could have chosen from Greek-style 'bell' or 'muscled' bronze cuirasses available to them from the earliest days of the Republic, and presumably hardened linen, leather or composite versions too. Variants of Greek helmets are known to have been used through much of Italy, although horsemen may well have preferred the better vision afforded by the simpler open-faced type with attached cheek-pieces and a rounded knob on the crown. A small terracotta figurine of a horseman dated to the late fourth or early third century BC wears a muscled cuirass and open-faced helmet. Found at Canosa in Apulia, around two hundred miles from Rome as the crow flies, it presumably depicts one of the nobility of an as-yet-unconquered Apulia, but he may not have differed at all from his Roman contemporaries.

Fourth century BC murals depicting Rome's Samnite neighbours show horsemen wearing a strapped-on bronze plate covering only the chest, rather than the whole torso, but still showing Greek influence in the replicated musculature. Archaeological evidence also attests the use of even simpler chest protection in the form of a simple disc or plate around 20–25 cm across used through much of Italy from an early date. This is the *cardiophylax*, or heart protector, which Polybius tells us was worn in his own time by the poorer infantry, those who could not afford chain mail. Chain mail is believed to be a Celtic invention, the earliest archaeological fragments, from Romania, dating from the third century BC, but conceivably existing earlier. When Roman cavalry first appear for sure in artistic evidence they are wearing chain mail.

Regardless of theoretical availability, it remains possible that the heaviest armour was eschewed deliberately for the sake of balance and ease of movement, although they might at least have worn the small *cardiophylax* without much encumbrance. Or did they eschew armour out of bravado, as did that minority of Gallic warriors who fought completely naked? The *equites* shared the Gallic warriors' thirst for individual glory and single combat, and proudly exposed the battle-scars on their bodies, so why not share this disdain for armour?

We must remember that there was probably a lot of variation both within a given levy and across the huge period encapsulated by Polybius' phrase 'in earlier times'. With each horseman providing his own armour, the exact extent of an individual's wealth, personal attitude towards physical risk and the trade-off between protection and encumbrance would all have played their part alongside questions of taste and fashion. Polybius was probably grossly oversimplifying a general trend toward a more universal adoption of body armour, which was intensified by the major military challenges faced in the third century BC. Even by Polybius' own day there would have been variations in style. A coin commemorating the Roman victory at Cynoscephelae in 197 BC appears to depict a victorious Roman cavalryman in Hellenistic helmet and composite cuirass, complete with *pteruges*, supporting Polybius' description. Yet, nearer his own time, the Aemilius Paullus monument, depicting the battle of Pydna in 169 BC, shows two Roman horsemen in chainmail, although Hellenistic influence can be seen in the shape of the pinions protecting the shoulders which mimic those of the Greek cuirass.

If early Roman cavalry, or some of them, were happy to wear less armour than their Greek contemporaries, it may have something to do with the fact that they appear to have carried shields from an earlier date, even if these weren't of the best design. Certainly they would have needed shields on those occasions when they appear to have dismounted to bolster the infantry lines. Greek cavalry, it may be recalled, appear not to have started carrying shields until some way into the third century BC, prompted by either the Galatian invasions or Pyrrhus' contact with shielded Italian cavalry. A cavalryman's equipment has always been dictated by the trade-off between protection and balance and ease of movement. Classical Greek cavalry generally opted for armour but no shield, while some early Roman cavalry opted for a shield (*parma equestris*) but relatively light or no armour.

It is also interesting to note that the Romans had the same trouble with excessively flexible long spears that Xenophon warned Greek horsemen against in the fourth century BC. The Greek type Polybius describes being adopted by the Roman cavalry was most probably like the traditional hoplite spear, about eight feet long with a butt spike, rather than the twelve-foot Macedonian lance. The passage quoted above seems to suggest that the Greek spears (Polybius uses the generic word *doru*) were used in conjunction with the Greek shield, and we have noted that in Hellenistic art there is no example of the longer lance and the shield being used together. There is plenty of room for uncertainty over even this though, as the chainmailed Roman cavalry on the Aemilius Paullus monument, whose weapons no longer remain, do not appear to be carrying shields. What appears to be one of the opposing Greek cavalry carries a large round shield with a pronounced reinforced spine. A Roman coin minted in 210 BC depicts two horsemen, probably representing the Dioscurii and thought to commemorate victory over the Capuans. They appear to be charging with lowered lances, wear Hellenistic-style armour and helmets (although with the characteristically Italian side feather crests), but no shields. Again it is likely that Polybius oversimplifies things and that the *equites* carried various combinations of armament. Some may have carried lances but no shields, others shorter spears and a shield; the larger Greek shield probably replacing the older Roman type gradually. Finally, although Polybius makes no mention of the type of swords carried, either in 'earlier times' or his own, we can be confident they were always carried as a back-up to the easily broken spear.

Their equipment has some bearing on whether the Roman cavalry were used as light or as heavy cavalry (or perhaps both). In asking this question we must remember that although form usually follows function, especially in military affairs, the term 'heavy cavalry' doesn't necessarily directly relate to heavy armour, although in practice there was a strong correlation in the ancient world. It is the psychological weight of their charge that mattered – so 'shock cavalry' is perhaps a better term to use. In the Napoleonic period, when firearms had generally rendered armour obsolete, the distinction between light and heavy cavalry regiments was maintained. It was not merely a matter of regimental tradition but of the roles they were intended to specialize in, even if circumstances often forced each type to turn their hand to the other's tasks. What is clear from all the literary evidence is that, however they were equipped, the Roman cavalry appears to have specialized in shock tactics from early on. We should bear the muddled question of their armour and armament in mind as we survey their actual performance and role in battle.

Celtic tribes, or Gauls as the Romans knew them, had first troubled the Romans in the early fourth century BC, when a massive invasion from northern Italy crushed a Roman army and went on to sack Rome. Livy, however, gives no details of their forces beyond describing 'an immense host, covering miles of ground with its straggling masses of horse and foot'.[13] They were bought off with gold after the sack of Rome. Another invasion was defeated in 358 BC, the Roman cavalry completing their destruction with a flank charge once they were already half-beaten – but again Livy does not give enough detail about the Gallic army for us even to know if they had any cavalry. But in 295 BC the Gallic threat returned, various tribes having now overrun most of northern Italy, irreparably weakening Etruscan power.

'The Gauls', wrote Plutarch, 'are particularly formidable at fighting on horseback, and in fact they have the reputation of excelling in this arm above any other.'[14] Gallic horsemen carried shields, usually circular or oval, and fought with a variety of spears and also with long swords that were generally of good quality, although some Roman writers denigrated them (as they denigrated most things Celtic). Surviving examples vary greatly in length but the general trend across the period was for this to increase, some examples having a blade three feet in length. The design of these swords meant they were of little use for thrusting or delicate fencing, being more suited to powerful, sweeping blows, putting the Celtic horsemen firmly on the side of the cut in the cut-versus-thrust debate that has continued throughout the history of cavalry.

The same mastery of metalworking that allowed them to make such long and often beautiful swords also allowed the Celts to invent chainmail by around 300 BC. Heavy but flexible and offering excellent protection against blows (although less so against thrusts or arrows), such armour was laborious to make and very expensive, so only the wealthiest warriors would wear it. Celtic chain mail was made into long shirts, the 'hem' usually split at the side for horsemen, with a double thickness on the shoulders in a cape-like arrangement, invaluable against other swordsmen employing the same hefty sword strokes. Many more could afford iron helmets, the type now known as the Montefortino being among several adopted and adapted by the Romans.

A word must be said here about Celtic saddles. In recent years some historians have latched on to the discovery of the Celtic horned saddle as the solution to the problem of how ancient cavalry managed to be so widespread and so successful without the supposedly indispensable stirrup. Some see the use by Gallic horsemen of long, heavy swords, body armour and sizeable shields as direct evidence that they were already using this advanced type of saddle from an early date. There is, however, no direct evidence for the use of such saddles before the later second century BC at the earliest. Their use in the wars of the third century BC is entirely possible but remains speculative.

Be that as it may, the Celts enjoyed a fine reputation for equestrian expertise in the ancient world that is happily accepted by modern historians. Romans would later adopt from them the 'horned' saddle and their patterns of cavalry armour and swords. Once conquered, Celts provided a large number of cavalry troopers to the Roman army. It might be expected then that the invading Gallic armies of the third century BC should have had little trouble from the supposedly negligible cavalry force of Rome.

In 295 BC the Gallic Senones intervened in Rome's latest war with their Samnite neighbours. They quickly besieged a Roman camp near Camerinum and destroyed the garrison by surrounding them as they tried to break out. The consuls in the field with the main Roman forces only learnt of this setback when 'some Gallic horsemen came in sight, carrying heads hanging from their horses' breasts and fixed on their spears, singing their customary song of triumph', perhaps directed to Epona, the Celtic goddess of horses.[15] According to Polybius, the earliest and most respected surviving Roman source for this period, it was only 'a few days' later that the Romans faced a combined army of Samnites and Senonian Gauls in battle near Sentinum. The two consuls had combined their forces and fielded 'four legions and a strong contingent of Roman cavalry [presumably stronger than the twelve hundred that would have been their standard allotment] plus a thousand picked horsemen from Campania, dispatched for this campaign, and an army of allies and Latins who outnumbered the Romans.'[16] Neither Livy nor Polybius gives meaningful figures for the Gallic/Samnite army, although the Senones had allegedly 'gushed with great hordes' at Camerinum.

The younger of the two consuls, Publius Decius, took the left wing, facing the Gauls. The fighting was opened with the infantry in the centre, but Decius quickly became impatient:

> And since the infantry battle seemed to be going rather slowly, he called

on the cavalry to attack, and, riding himself amongst the bravest of his youthful squadrons, summoned the young nobles to join him in a charge: they would win double glory, he said, if victory came first to the left wing and the cavalry [the right being the traditional post of honour, here appropriately taken by his senior colleague]. Twice they forced back the Gallic cavalry.[17]

Up to this point then the Roman cavalry seems to have acquitted itself well, twice driving back the Gauls in spirited charges. A perennial problem now arose, however, in that they followed up their success too far and soon got themselves entangled amongst enemy infantry units and thrown into some disarray. Then, probably as they sought to disengage from the enemy infantry and regain some semblance of good order for a third charge, they were counter-attacked by a fresh force of Gallic chariots. Even if they had featured in earlier Celtic invasions, which is likely but uncertain, they were a new experience to these particular Romans and, perhaps more importantly, to their mounts.

> They were alarmed by a new style of fighting; for the enemy, standing up and holding their weapons in chariots and wagons, bore down on them with a fearful noise of horses' hooves and wheels, and terrified the Romans' horses with the unusual din. Thus the victorious cavalry were scattered by a sort of panic frenzy, their blind flight overthrowing them, both the horses and riders. Their confusion spread to the standards of the legions, and many of the first line were trampled underfoot by the horses and vehicles sweeping through the army.[18]

This is a very rare instance of chariots scoring a success against cavalry and was due partly to them catching their opponents in disarray after a pursuit, but it also owed much to the fact that the Roman horses were not accustomed to this specific spectacle and noise. Despite the collapse of their left wing, the Romans went on to win the battle. The Gallic cavalry and chariots appear to have played no further part, presumably lacking the discipline to rally from the pursuit and send part of their force into the flank of the Roman centre and right as Alexander would have done. Instead the Romans, supposedly inspired by a deliberate act of self-sacrifice by Decius, were able to bring up infantry reserves from the third line in time to meet a renewed assault by the Gallic infantry.

The affair was finally settled late in the day when the other consul managed to manoeuvre the bulk of his cavalry onto the flank of the Samnites and deliver a devastating charge that sent them fleeing from the field. Again we are forced to wonder where the Samnite cavalry were to allow this. Had they already been defeated? Whatever the answer, it left the Gallic infantry isolated and quickly surrounded, although they tried to withdraw in close order with locked shields. Five hundred of the picked Campanian horsemen charged them from the rear and threw them into confusion. The Roman infantry were then ordered to 'press in to the kill while panic reigned'. Allegedly, twenty-five thousand Gauls and Samnites were killed, another eight thousand captured. Eight thousand seven hundred Romans had been killed, of whom seven thousand were on the left flank, most cut down by the cavalry and chariots. The Roman and allied cavalry had at least matched the Gallic opposite numbers, if not the chariots whose unusual success was largely due to their novelty.

More new challenges faced the Roman cavalry when Pyrrhus, king of Epirus, landed in Italy at the request of Tarentum, one of the Greek colonies in the south that was resisting the accelerating Roman expansion. His was a Hellenistic-style army, that is to say it was basically modelled on the Macedonian army of Alexander, with some developments. The sarissae, or pikes, of Hellenistic phalanxes were now even longer than in Alexander's day, sometimes over twenty feet, rendering them more impervious than ever to a cavalry frontal assault as long as they maintained good order, although they were also more vulnerable to a flank charge. On the flanks, however, the Roman cavalry would face the famous Thessalian heavy cavalry and others modelled on Alexander's Companions, commanded by the king himself. Pyrrhus was distantly related to the great Macedonian and successfully emulated his heroic leadership style and personal prowess in cavalry charges, if not always the finesse of his timing. Also, the Roman cavalry were about to meet war elephants for the first time in battle.

The armies first met near Heraclea in 280 BC, when Pyrrhus' advance guard reached the River Siris to find a Roman army fully deployed and waiting for him. The Roman cavalry started crossing at several points, forcing the advance guard to retreat. Pyrrhus led forward three thousand cavalry, hoping to fall upon the Romans as they emerged from the river in disarray. He soon saw, however, that the Romans were crossing with a discipline that he found surprising in 'barbarians', according to Plutarch. He needed to buy time for his infantry phalanx to deploy, so 'while their [the Roman] cavalry advanced against him in good order, he closed up his own ranks and led them in a charge'.[19]

Far from being overwhelmed by Pyrrhus' Epirot companions and

Thessalians, the Roman horsemen actually held their own in a hard-fought mêlée and eventually started to gain the upper hand. Pyrrhus' personal efforts were Alexandrian in character and, according to Plutarch, 'he stood out at once amongst his men for the beauty and brilliance of his elaborately ornamented armour, and he proved by his exploits that his reputation for valour was well deserved'.[20] His armour, however, almost ended up in the temple of Jupiter in Rome, as another example of the *spolia opima*, when one of the Romans' allied cavalry singled him out:

> The Italian wheeled his horse, levelled his lance and charged at Pyrrhus. Then in the same instant that the Italian's lance struck the king's horse, his own was transfixed by Leonnatus [one of Pyrrhus' companions]. Both horses fell, but Pyrrhus was snatched up and saved by his friends, while the Italian, fighting desperately, was killed.[21]

The Epirot cavalry was already falling back when the Roman infantry emerged from the river and Pyrrhus ordered the phalanx up to engage them. The cavalry fight on the flanks remained stiffly contested for a long time, as the advantage in the infantry fighting apparently shifted back and forth seven times, which would not have happened if either side had been able quickly to drive off the opposing cavalry sufficiently to expose the infantry to a flank attack. Before returning to the fray on a new horse, Pyrrhus exchanged his conspicuous armour and cloak with one of his friends, who was in turn attacked and killed by the Roman cavalry, forcing Pyrrhus to ride along the lines to show his disheartened men that he was alive, just as William the Conqueror much later did at Hastings.

The Roman cavalry were only beaten when Pyrrhus was finally able to bring his elephants into play. They may have been deliberately kept back as a reserve, but the lateness of their intervention suggests they may have been lagging some way to the rear of the army on the approach march. The elephants were sent in against the Roman cavalry on the flanks and their unaccustomed horses 'started to panic and bolt'. The Roman infantry still battled valiantly to make headway against the hedge of pikes, but their flank was now stripped of its protection. Pyrrhus seized the opportunity, 'launched a charge with his Thessalian cavalry and routed the enemy with great slaughter'.[22]

The following year, at Asculum, the Romans again faced Pyrrhus. According to Plutarch the battle was a two-day affair, although he does acknowledge the varying account of Dionysius of Halicarnassus, which does not mention the second day and gives few coherent details in any case. On the first day it seems Pyrrhus was forced to fight 'on rough ground where his cavalry could not operate, and along the wooded banks of a swiftly flowing river where his elephants could not charge the enemy's infantry'. Clearly the Roman cavalry could not operate here either. Plutarch seems to imply that the Romans deliberately chose this ground, but there is no reason, in the light of their performance the previous year, to think that they did so because they did not trust their own cavalry against Pyrrhus' horsemen. If the choice of ground was deliberate, it was no doubt the elephants that they were keen to neutralize and the broken ground would also favour the more flexible legionary infantry over the unwieldy phalanx. In any case Plutarch gives few details of this first day's action except that there was fierce fighting with heavy losses to both armies before they retired to their camps.

On the following day, Pyrrhus managed to seize and occupy the broken ground with part of his force and deployed the rest in such a way as to ensure that the main fighting would take place on level ground. Plutarch is frustratingly vague about the course of events that led to another costly victory for Pyrrhus, especially as regards the cavalry, which are not specifically mentioned. His statement that the Romans gave way 'where Pyrrhus himself was pressing his opponents hardest' does not make it clear whether he thought Pyrrhus was fighting on horseback, as we would expect him to have been. In any case, Plutarch is clear what the main agent of Roman defeat was.

> The factor which did most to enable the Greeks to prevail was the weight and fury of the elephants' charge. Against this even the Romans' courage was of little avail: they felt as they might have done before the onrush of a tidal wave or the shock of an earthquake, that it was better to give way than to stand their ground for no purpose, and suffer a terrible fate without gaining the least advantage.[23]

The likeliest explanation is that the Roman cavalry was again unable to resist the elephants and were driven away off the wings, leaving the Roman infantry to be easily broken by flank attacks by elephants and cavalry.

Pyrrhus finally suffered a definite defeat in his third major clash with the Romans in 275 BC near Maleventum (subsequently renamed Beneventum). Cavalry played no part in the fighting which followed a bungled attempt at a surprise nocturnal attack on a Roman camp.

Pyrrhus' cavalry were probably not even present and the Roman cavalry receive no mention; either because it took time for them to ready their horses or because they were again neutralized by Pyrrhus' elephants, which achieved some initial success before the Romans managed to stampede them back through their own lines, leading to a general collapse. Pyrrhus' Italian adventure was over. In the one battle where the contribution of the Roman horsemen is clear, they were beating the professional Epirot and Thessalian cavalry until the intervention of the elephants, just as they had been getting the better of the Celtic cavalry at Sentinum until the chariots had panicked them.

With Pyrrhus sent packing, the Romans went on to establish control of the whole of Italy south of the River Po. But north of the Po, the Gauls still resisted Roman encroachment. The next clash with the Gauls of which we have sufficient information is the major incursion mounted by the Insubres and Boii in 225 BC. Polybius explains that this was 'the largest which the region had ever sent out, and contained more leaders and celebrated warriors than ever before', and gives figures of fifty thousand infantry and twenty thousand cavalry and chariots.[24] Polybius carefully details the military resources available to Rome in this crisis. Each of the two consuls was given two citizen legions, each of which consisted of 5200 Roman infantry and three hundred Roman cavalry. They were supported by a total of thirty thousand infantry and two thousand Latin allied cavalry, giving each consular army six hundred Roman and one thousand Latin cavalry. In addition to the field armies, another twenty thousand infantry and fifteen hundred cavalry were recruited from the Roman citizens and kept in the capital as a strategic reserve along with allies amounting to a further thirty thousand infantry and two thousand cavalry. When news came of the Gallic invasion, the Etruscans and Sabines, making common cause with their ancient enemy against the Gallic threat, supplied fifty thousand infantry and four thousand cavalry, which were put under the command of a Roman praetor and posted on the Etrurian frontier. One of the consular armies was sent north to block the Gauls' expected route down the Adriatic coast near Ariminum, but the other had already been shipped to garrison Sardinia and had to be hastily recalled.

The Gauls quickly overran Etruria, sidestepping the frontier forces and reached Clusium, just three days' march from Rome. When they learned that the Etruscan and Sabine force was following them, they turned back and used their cavalry to lure them into a massive ambush near Faesulae (modern Fiesole), destroying six thousand of them and besieging a large body of the survivors on a steep hill. Lucius Aemilius Paullus now arrived posthaste from Ariminum and encamped nearby. The Celts, heavily laden with plunder, decided not to risk it all on an open battle and withdrew north, allowing Paullus to link up with the besieged force before dogging their trail. By chance, the other consular army, under Gaius Atilius, returning from Sardinia, blundered into their path from the north, near Telamon, capturing the Celts' advanced scouts. Alerted, Atilius personally led his cavalry ahead to seize a hill dominating the route the Celts had to take, ordering his tribunes to deploy the infantry for battle and then advance. The Celts sent some of their own cavalry to contest the hill with light infantry support, only belatedly realizing that the Roman cavalry were not Paullus' and that they were now trapped between the two consular armies. They then formed their infantry line facing both ways.

As he approached from the south, Paullus sent his cavalry off to the flank to assist in the fight for the hill while his infantry deployed for battle. Thousands of cavalry now swarmed over the slopes, drumming up swirls of dust. Squadrons wheeled and manoeuvred for advantage, charged and clashed, their formations mingling and dissolving into small clusters of horsemen desperately thrusting and cutting, then riding clear to regroup, turn about and re-enter the fray. The two Roman armies had 3200 Roman and Latin cavalry between them, plus whatever remnant of the 4000 Etruscan and Sabine cavalry Paullus had brought along, but even if all of these were committed to the fight for the hill, they were greatly outnumbered by the Gallic cavalry. According to Polybius' account, the drama of this spectacular clash was not lost on the other combatants.

> At first the conflict was confined to the fighting round the hill, and because of the great numbers of cavalry which were locked in battle the rest of the three armies stood by and watched the contest. In this encounter the consul Gaius Atilius lost his life, fighting with desperate courage in the thick of the action and his head was brought to the Celtic king. But the Roman cavalry fought on stubbornly, and at length overcame their opponents and took possession of the heights.[25]

Having got the Celtic horsemen on the run, some of the Roman or allied cavalry may have pursued them to stop them returning, but the rest reformed their squadrons and gave their horses a breather. While they did so, the Roman infantry below had begun to advance on the Celtic lines from either side. Although Polybius describes the advantage the Roman legionaries enjoyed in close fighting due to superior shields and swords, the trapped Gauls resisted fiercely and the contest was more or less evenly matched. But whatever portion of the Celtic cavalry remained on the field to protect their army's flanks, either because they had not been committed to the hill or had withdrawn from it, proved too demoralized to fulfil that role when the Roman cavalry entered the battle once more, streaming down the hillside. 'The end came when the Celts were attacked by the Roman cavalry, who delivered a furious charge from the high ground on the flank; the Celtic cavalry turned and fled, and their infantry were cut down where they stood.'[26]

The Celts are alleged to have lost forty thousand killed, including one of their kings, Aenorestes, who committed suicide, while the ten thousand captured included King Concolitanus. The Roman cavalry had defeated a superior number of enemy horsemen in a prolonged fight and, despite the loss of their commander, retained sufficient discipline and cohesion to re-form and launch the decisive attack on the enemy's infantry. What commander of any age could have asked more?

Such a crushing victory can only have strengthened the *esprit* of the Roman cavalry, not to mention their reputation in the eyes of their enemies. The psychological edge possessed by a force that had achieved such things may have played a large part in what may be regarded as the finest hour of the republican cavalry, which occurred a few years later.

Two consular armies invaded the territory of the Insubres in northern Italy, between the River Po and the Alps, and besieged Accerae. The Insubrians responded by sending part of their army across the Po to besiege Clastidium. One of the Roman consuls, Marcus Claudius Marcellus, set off with a relief force consisting only of six hundred light infantry and two thirds of the cavalry, theoretically 3200 horsemen, leaving his colleague to continue the siege of Accerae with the rest of their combined consular armies. As this flying column approached Clastidium, the Insubres and Gaesatae raised their siege and formed up in battle order to block their approach, with one flank resting on the river. When the Gauls saw Marcellus' force, according to Plutarch,

> they felt nothing but contempt for his tiny force of infantry, and, since they were Gauls, had no great opinion of the Roman cavalry. The Gauls are particularly formidable at fighting on horseback, and in fact have the reputation of excelling in this arm above any other, while on this occasion they also greatly outnumbered Marcellus.[27]

According to Plutarch's account, as the opposing armies closed, Marcellus ordered his force into an extended line to prevent the much larger Celtic force enveloping his flanks too easily, although this must have made his deployment shallower and more easily punctured along its length. Ahead of the advancing Gauls came their king, a huge man resplendent in burnished armour and shouting a challenge. With an oath to Jupiter, Marcellus accepted the challenge and spurred his horse. 'So he charged the Gaul and pierced his breast-plate with his lance: the impetus of his horse hurled his opponent to the ground still living, and a second and a third blow immediately dispatched him.' [28] Marcellus leapt off his horse and started to strip the king's armour, dedicating it to Jupiter as *spolia opima*. Meanwhile, his troopers, inspired by his example, tore into the now leaderless Gauls, 'not only the Gallic horsemen but also their supporting infantry'. [29] Polybius does not mention Marcellus' single combat but is specific that, despite their initially holding their ground, the Roman cavalry routed the Celts 'without the [Roman] infantry having been engaged at all. Many of them plunged into the river and were swept away by the current, but the greater number were cut down where they stood.' [30] 'Never before nor since', declares Plutarch, 'had so few mounted troops overcome such a large combined force of cavalry and infantry.' [31]

Just a few years later the Roman Republic would face its sternest military test since the first Gallic invasion. The poor reputation that the citizen cavalry have been saddled with in modern histories is based above all upon their performance in the Second Punic War of 218 to 202 BC, fought against the Carthaginians. The disasters of the early part of that war, and particularly the spectacular defeat at Cannae in 216 BC, are blamed to a large degree on the failings of Rome's horsemen and are usually used as the only case study by which a supposed lack of a Roman cavalry tradition is illustrated. Yet Rome entered that war with a cavalry force that must still have been riding high on the successes of Telamon and Clastidium. Veterans of these victories must have still been serving in the early battles against the Carthaginians – the riders certainly and perhaps even some of the horses. The trophies and spoils from them must have still been among the newest hanging in the temples and the retelling of them would have been among the freshest of that institutional lore and legend by which elite military units sustain their élan.

Against this, it is true that the previous war with the Carthaginians offered no illusions as to the challenge faced by the Roman cavalry.

The First Punic War of 264–241 BC had been fought largely at sea, but the one pitched battle of note occurred in 255 BC when a Roman army crossed to North Africa in an attempt to threaten Carthage itself. After initial successes this army was roundly defeated when a Spartan mercenary commander pointed out to the Carthaginians that, instead of lurking defensively on the high ground, they should make use of their advantage in cavalry and elephants by giving battle on the plains. Polybius states that the Roman cavalry were 'quickly routed' by the Carthaginian cavalry, who were then able to surround the Roman infantry already in the process of being demolished by the devastating assault of the elephants. In mitigation, Polybius makes it clear that the Roman and Latin cavalry, probably totalling around two thousand, were 'far outnumbered' by the 'overwhelming numbers of the Carthaginian cavalry', who were thus easily able to outflank them and charge them from front and sides simultaneously.[32]

The Second Punic War opened in 218 BC with the famous march of the Carthaginian army under Hannibal Barca from Carthaginian-controlled Spain to Italy via the Alps, designed to carry the war into Rome's backyard. He left Spain with fifty thousand infantry and nine thousand cavalry, a far higher proportion of horsemen than any Roman army.

The bulk of Hannibal's cavalry were Numidians, semi-nomadic tribesmen from what is now Algeria, supplied by tribes allied to Carthage. These were possibly the most accomplished riders in the ancient world, riding bareback and without even a bridle. Their only tack being a loose braided strap around the horse's neck, they controlled their horses almost entirely by leg and voice aids. Numidian horses were considered small but agile and shared with their riders a reputation for exceptional hardiness and stamina, the Roman historian Appian noting that they 'never even taste grain; they feed on grass alone and drink but rarely'.[33] The riders wore no armour, but each carried a light leather shield and several javelins. These were light cavalry, adept at all the scouting and screening work required on campaign, but in battle largely restricted to harassing tactics in loose formation.

Most of the remainder of Hannibal's cavalry, perhaps one third, were made up of troops enlisted in the Iberian peninsula, large parts of which had come under varying degrees of Carthaginian control since the First Punic War. These were from many tribes, some of indigenous

Iberian stock and others described as Celtiberian, that is a mixture of Celtic and Iberian blood and culture.*

To anyone familiar with modern breeds it will come as no surprise that Spanish horses were of high quality, fast, agile and intelligent. They were ridden with a bridle and bit and some may have had the basic saddles becoming common in the Hellenistic world by this time, although representations suggest a simple blanket or fur secured by a girth strap was most common. Some bridles included a plate to protect the horse's forehead and nose (*chamfron* is the medieval term).

Most Spanish horsemen probably wore little armour at this date, although some would have worn metal helmets and simple circular breastplates and the wealthiest could choose from Greek-style plate or linen cuirasses or corselets of scale or even, particularly for the Celtiberian nobility, Celtic chain mail. A small round shield, or *caetra*, was used for defence. Although it had a central handgrip, this could be strapped to the left forearm so the fingers of the left hand could be freed for handling the reins if desired. Most horsemen would have carried thrusting spears with the secondary spike on the butt, others perhaps preferring shorter ones that could double as javelins, but all would have carried a sword, with which weapon they were held to be particularly skilled.

Spanish swords were of two types. The *falcata* was virtually identical to the Greek *machaira* or *kopis* that Xenophon had recommended to Greek horsemen, except the downward curve may have been slightly less exaggerated and the point so shaped to permit a useful thrust as well as a powerful slash. The other type was a short, straight, two-edged sword, more handily balanced and equally useful for cut or thrust. The falcata seems likely to have been more popular with horsemen. Regardless of the design, the quality of their manufacture exceeded that of Roman weapons and they so impressed the Romans that captured Spanish smiths were sent to Rome to pass on the secrets of their manufacture. The *gladius Hispaniensis* was subsequently adopted as the standard Roman issue.

The first clash with the Romans came even before Hannibal made his famous crossing of the Alps. One of the consuls for that year, Publius Scipio, was en route to Spain by sea and had put in at Massilia (Marseille), a Greek-speaking colony allied to Rome, when rumour reached

*In the following descriptions of battles I have referred to these simply as 'Spanish'.

him that Hannibal had reached the Rhône and crossed it despite the resistance of the local Celtic tribe.* Scipio sent 'three hundred of his bravest' Roman cavalry and some mercenary Celtic horsemen working for Massilia to confirm this shocking news. As Polybius says they were to act as supporting troops, the Celts were probably fewer in number than the Romans. Hannibal, meanwhile, had learnt of the Roman fleet's arrival and sent five hundred of his Numidian cavalry on a similar reconnaissance mission. When these two scouting forces, roughly equal numerically, clashed, the Numidians may have been surprised, as they allowed their enemies to come to close quarters:

> the engagement was fought with such courage and fury that the Romans and Celts lost some 140 men, and the Numidians more than two hundred. After the action the Romans rode in pursuit right up to the Carthaginian camp, surveyed it, and then galloped back to warn their general that the enemy had arrived.[34]

First blood to the Roman cavalry.

When the next encounter occurred later that same year, however, the odds were stacked in Hannibal's favour. Having eventually negotiated the Alps and descended into northern Italy, he had only twenty thousand infantry and 'not more than six thousand cavalry in all', but he soon started recruiting among the Celtic tribes there, adding numbers of highly rated Gallic horsemen to his seasoned Spanish and Numidians. He was opposed again by Scipio who, after the clash on the Rhône, had sent most of his army on to Spain under the command of his brother Gnaeus, while he himself hurried back to Italy and took over the forces operating against the rebellious Celts in the Po valley.[35] Alerted by foragers that their two armies were drawing close to each other, both camped. The next day both generals led out 'all their cavalry, while Scipio took his javelin throwers (*velites*) in addition'; each was attempting a reconnaissance in force of their opponent's strength and position. The force Scipio had taken command of consisted of two

---

* Polybius' account of the innovative measures Hannibal employed to get his elephants across the river has been almost universally accepted ever since, despite an obvious flaw. Far from being terrified of water, as Polybius assumes, elephants love it and are strong swimmers. Their handlers are more likely to have had trouble coaxing them out of it again. If Hannibal built pontoons it was probably for his infantry and baggage animals. His cavalry crossed by swimming alongside their horses.

full legions and an under strength one that had already suffered heavily
in a Celtic ambush, so Scipio probably had a little more than three thousand Roman and allied cavalry, including some Celts from pro-Roman
tribes. Outnumbered at least two to one in cavalry, the *velites* available
to three legions would have made the total numbers roughly even.

In the vicinity of the River Ticinus, tell-tale clouds of dust thrown up
by thousands of horses warned each army that the other was approaching and they deployed their forces to engage. Scipio placed his light
infantry and Gallic cavalry in front and formed the rest of his cavalry in
line behind and advanced cautiously. Hannibal put his 'bridled cavalry',
including all the heavy cavalry units, in the centre of his line, with the
unbridled Numidians massed out on either flank, 'ready to make an
outflanking movement'. He attacked straightaway.

The approaching mass of horses was too much for the Roman *velites*
and they promptly fled back through their own cavalry without throwing a single javelin. Polybius' statement that they 'retired through the
gaps to a position behind their cavalry' sounds like an orderly manoeuvre utilizing the gaps left between the *turmae*. But, as he goes on to
say that they did so 'in terror of the approaching charge and of being
trampled underfoot by the horsemen who were bearing down upon
them', it almost certainly involved disruptive jostling and scrambling
through the Roman cavalry lines. Once the Carthaginian centre had
been engaged with the Romans for some time, the Numidians swept
around both flanks and attacked from the rear. The hapless light infantry sheltering there 'were now ridden down by the weight of numbers
and the furious onslaught of the Numidians'. Light cavalry they may
have been, but the Numidians knew when the situation favoured shock
action and happily closed with the virtually defenceless skirmishers.
With the *velites* cut down, scattered or driven back in amongst their
own cavalry again, the Numidians pressed their attack against the rear
of the Roman cavalry, who broke and fled.

Livy's prognosis on the outcome was that 'it showed clearly that in
cavalry the Carthaginians had the advantage'. Undoubtedly true, but
it was an advantage in numbers, not necessarily in quality. Until the
attack in their rear, which would have defeated any cavalry force in history, the Roman horsemen had actually been giving at least as good as
they got against Hannibal's assorted heavy cavalry. According to Polybius, 'they had lost many men, but had inflicted even heavier losses on
the enemy'. Even once broken by the attack in the rear, a group of them
rallied and managed to escort the seriously wounded Scipio to safety.[36]

True, Scipio might have handled them better by keeping a reserve to counter the encirclement but the horsemen themselves fought well.

Polybius states that it 'became a mixed action of cavalry and infantry because of the large number of men who dismounted in the course of the fighting'. Like the earlier examples of Roman cavalry dismounting in battle, this forms part of the 'evidence' supporting the belief that Roman horsemen lacked confidence in their mounted combat skills. It may be, however, that, because neither side gave way at the first onslaught, as often happened in cavalry combats, the fight had degenerated into a closely packed brawl. With any hope of forward manoeuvre lost and the flanks and rear penned in by encircling Numidians and the panicking masses of *velites*, individual *equites* might well have started to dismount to squeeze their way through to the front lines. Livy says that many 'dismounted to bring aid to hard-pressed comrades'. True, he also says that many 'fell from their horses', but this might be expected if the two dense masses of horsemen met in an unusually solid collision and would also have accounted for many on the Carthaginian side, whose testimony and viewpoint would not have reached Roman historians. When Livy says 'things were assuming the aspect of an infantry battle', what he is most trying to convey is that the two lines were locked in a stationary struggle, neither prepared to give ground. If the *equites* displayed a greater readiness to dismount than many cavaliers, it had less to do with a lack of riding ability than with their ingrained fear of failure under the gaze of their fellow citizens. As in the earlier occasions when they dismounted, the *equites* were merely demonstrating that determination to excel and win the respect of their colleagues that seems to have bred a peculiar strain of stubbornness amongst Romans.

Scipio, keen to avoid a pitched battle in the face of the Carthaginian advantage in cavalry, hurriedly withdrew across the Po and fortified a camp near the Trebbia river, where he was reinforced by the other consular army under Titus Sempronius Longus. Longus took over command from his wounded colleague and scored an early minor success when his cavalry and *velites* successfully drove off a force of Hannibal's Celts and Numidians who were raiding the surrounding farmland. Longus was now eager for a decisive battle and Hannibal, camped across the river, was happy to oblige, but only on his terms.

Hannibal hid a thousand picked Numidians and an equal number of light infantry in some overgrown watercourses on his side of the river. Early the following morning, Hannibal sent out his Numidians to cross

the river and attack the Roman camp, while the rest of his force ate
their breakfast – the cavalry first feeding, watering and grooming their
horses – and warmed themselves by their fires. When the Numidians
started lobbing javelins over the palisade, Longus took the bait and
immediately sent his cavalry out on hungry horses to tackle them, while
he mustered the legionary infantry. When he led out the main force
behind a screen of six thousand skirmishers, none of them had eaten
either. It was December and squalls of chilling rain would continue
throughout the morning.

The Roman cavalry were unable to get to grips with their opponents
'for the Numidians easily evaded their attacks by dispersing and withdrawing, after which they would wheel round and charge with great
dash, these being the peculiar tactics in which they excelled'.[37] This
comment from Polybius strongly suggests that he believed the Romans
were already operating as heavy cavalry. It is not only that they were
not as good as the Numidians at the hit and run tactics of light cavalry
skirmishers – he specifically says these tactics were 'peculiar' to the
Numidians. If the Romans were already so specialized in the close-
order heavy cavalry role, then they had probably already adopted the
heavier equipment and Greek-style lances described by Polybius. The
Numidians led them a dance and lured them across the flood-swollen
river, followed by the Roman infantry, who waded through icy water
up to their chests.

As the Romans drew near, Hannibal led out his army and formed
them up with his Celtic, Spanish and African infantry in the centre.
His cavalry, swollen by Celtic allies to 'over ten thousand', was divided
between the two wings. His elephants he also divided into two parts,
placing them in front of each end of the infantry phalanx. Scipio
recalled his four thousand horsemen, who were achieving little beyond
the exhaustion of their own horses against the screening Numidians,
and posted half on either side of his infantry as they deployed in the
traditional Roman triple line (*triplex acies*) behind the screen of skirmishers. When all was ready, the skirmishers withdrew through the
gaps left for this purpose in the Roman formation, and the heavy infantry moved forward to engage.

As soon as this happened the Carthaginian heavy cavalry, mainly
Spanish and Celtic, charged the Roman horsemen. The Roman cavalry
were not only outnumbered but already wet, hungry and tiring and
'fell back for the Carthaginian charge' which may well mean they fled
instantly. According to Livy, the elephants played a large part in the

rout of the Roman cavalry, 'as the horses were terrified by the sight and smell of these strange beasts they had never seen before'. As the heavy cavalry galloped off into the distance, the Carthaginian skirmishers and the 'main body of the Numidians' swarmed in to attack the exposed flanks of the Roman heavy infantry, who were already 'hard pressed from the front by the elephants'. To complete the Romans' destruction, the two thousand troops hidden in the watercourse rose up and attacked the legions from the rear. Ten thousand Romans and Italians managed to cut their way through the Carthaginian line and escape in good order, while 'the greater part were killed by the elephants and cavalry'. Taking refuge in Placentia, they were soon joined by 'most of the cavalry', suggesting that these had made a getaway without hanging around to resist. For the Romans, the only positive thing was that many of the Carthaginian horses and all but one of the elephants died shortly after the battle due to exhaustion combined with the intense cold and snow.[38]

In June of the following year, a further disaster was suffered at Hannibal's hands, at Lake Trasimene. It tells us little about the cavalry on either side, however, beyond the fact that the 2400 cavalry available to a Roman consular army were not there as a reconnaissance force, or at least were not consistently used in this role. The whole army blundered blindly into a massive ambush and was attacked from three sides as it marched in column along the mist-shrouded shore of the lake. According to Livy's version, some legionaries made a stand around the consul Flaminius for three hours, until he was cut down by a Celtic horseman. The final act of the tragedy was of Roman legionaries standing up to their necks in the water, having waded out as far as their armour would allow, waiting for death as the Carthaginian cavalry rode through the waters to finish them off.[39]

The other consul, hoping to join forces with Flaminius, had already dispatched his whole cavalry force ahead, evidently reinforced with more than the usual quota of allies, as they numbered four thousand. On hearing of their approach, probably from patrolling Numidian light cavalry, Hannibal sent a mixed force of spearmen and cavalry under Maharbal to intercept them. Maharbal killed half of these 'in his first attack', trapped the remainder on a hill and forced their surrender the next day. Our sources give few details but it seems likely that this was another ambush that gave little chance for response.

Hannibal, however, was not in a position to follow up his victory with an advance on Rome. Prior to Trasimene his army had undertaken a long forced march through marshy country and the cavalry horses were suffering from malnutrition and the men from scurvy. Accordingly he moved into an area near the Adriatic, 'which was extraordinarily rich in all kinds of produce', until the better grazing and, apparently, repeated bathing with old wine restored the coats of the horses to good condition. At the same time he re-equipped his African troops with captured Roman arms. Polybius is almost certainly referring to the Libyan heavy infantry rather than the Numidian cavalry. The latter continued to operate as unarmoured light cavalry, although they may conceivably have been given Roman swords and the javelins of Roman *velites*.[40] Hannibal had released all the non-Roman prisoners he had taken, sending them home with the message that his war was with Rome alone. Yet none of the Latin cities wavered from their alliance with Rome. As soon as his army was sufficiently recovered, Hannibal led them on a long trail of devastation and looting to demonstrate Rome's inability to protect these cities, and to tempt the Romans into another pitched battle.

In this phase of the war the movements of both sides were to a great extent dictated by the Carthaginians' cavalry dominance. The direction of Hannibal's rampage across Italy was determined in part by the need for good pasturage for the horses. For example, as winter drew near he seized Gerunium to serve as his winter quarters. There he could store the large amounts of corn he had gathered which, Polybius explains, 'was to feed not only his men but also his horses and pack animals, for the cavalry was the arm he relied on the most'.[41]

For their part, the Romans took the emergency measure of appointing a dictator, Fabius Maximus, to exercise sole command over their forces. For the next few months Fabius followed a strategy of shadowing the Carthaginians but refusing to be drawn into a pitched battle. By keeping his army on high and rough terrain and utilizing the defensive qualities of the Romans' trademark fortified camps, he made sure Hannibal could not attack him without throwing away the advantage of his cavalry. In addition to the numerical disparity of their mounted troops, Fabius was aware that the Carthaginian army was full of experienced, battle-seasoned troops, whereas his own newly raised legions were not. His strategy was very unpopular in Rome, and particularly with those allies whose land was devastated, but just by keeping his force in proximity of the enemy and attacking isolated parties of foragers where opportunity presented itself Fabius interrupted the enemy's supplies, gradually increased the morale and effectiveness of his own troops, and bought time for the raising of more forces in Rome and the allied cities. It was the abandonment of this strategy the following year, 216 BC, that led to the greatest defeat ever suffered by a Roman army.

The battle of Cannae has gone down in history as one of the most decisive, at a tactical level, of all time, and has been studied ever since by generals seeking the secret of victory. The German Schlieffen plan of 1914 and Operation Desert Storm in 1991 are but two strategic plans consciously influenced by it. It is this battle above all that has earned the Roman cavalry their reputation for impotence. In what was becoming a familiar pattern, the Romans, although they outnumbered the Carthaginians roughly two to one, were surrounded and massacred. Because the Roman cavalry clearly failed to protect the flanks of the legions from the Carthaginian cavalry, it has been concluded they must have been inferior.

The Romans had used the time won by Fabius' delaying tactics to bring together an unprecedented force of eight legions, which were matched as usual by the same number of allied infantry, giving them around eighty thousand infantry. The more limited recruiting pool for the cavalry may, however, already have been reaching its limits as the legions were accompanied by only six thousand cavalry, a lower proportion than usual but still a greater number than they had ever concentrated in one place before. We cannot say whether each legion had its full three hundred citizen cavalry, a total of 2400, with the allies failing to provide the standard three times as many, or whether the shortfall started with the Romans and the allies stuck to the formula. In the latter case, the citizen cavalry would have been only 1500 strong.

As this army marched to confront Hannibal, who had recently seized the important grain store at Cannae, he attempted a surprise attack on them with only his cavalry and light troops. Although the vanguard of the Roman column was thrown into confusion, the attack was first contained by some legionary infantry brought up from the rear and then repulsed by Roman cavalry and light infantry. The Romans proceeded on their way and the two armies encamped on opposite sides of the Aufidus river.

Hannibal was as keen as ever to offer a set-piece battle, despite having only half as many infantry as the Romans, a sure sign of the confidence he drew from having about ten thousand cavalry to their six thousand. Two days after their arrival, he formed his army on the plain between the river and the foothills of the Apennines, challenging the Romans to fight. But the Roman army stayed resolutely in camp even when their water-carrying parties down by the river were attacked by Numidian horsemen. Paullus, the consul for that day (when both consular armies were combined the consuls commanded on alternate days), wanted to wait until lack of fodder forced the Carthaginians to move their camp and then try to force them to fight on less open ground. His colleague Varro, however, is characterized in the ancient sources as an inexperienced hothead. As soon as the next dawn heralded his day of command, he led the army out to offer battle. As the Romans deployed, a process that would have taken several hours, Hannibal responded in kind.

Both armies had their infantry in the centre with the cavalry on either wing. Varro placed the Roman citizen cavalry on the right wing next to the river, and the Latin allies on the open left flank. With the allies being the larger contingent, it must have seemed to make sense for the cavalry to have been divided in this manner, but another option would have been to concentrate all the cavalry on the left flank. This would have allowed the infantry line to extend right up to the river, which would have protected that flank, assuming it provided a sufficient obstacle to hamper a cavalry attack. Hannibal placed his Numidians out on the open flank where they had plenty of room for their usual fluid tactics, and his heavy cavalry between his infantry and the river, opposite the Roman citizen cavalry. We do not know exactly how Hannibal's ten thousand cavalry was constituted, but it seems likely that the assorted heavy cavalry were at least half of that total, so between 1500 and 2400 Roman *equites* were faced by two to three times their number.

The battle opened, as most ancient battles did, with exchanges of missiles between the lines of skirmishers strung in front of the centre, but the two Carthaginian cavalry wings soon attacked. On the more open flank, up to five thousand Numidians swarmed forward in loose groups to harass the Italian allied horsemen. It is possible that a third of the Italians had been separated off as *extraordinarii* – possibly forming the consul's bodyguards and reserve. In this case the Italians numbered at most three thousand.

> The Numidians on the Carthaginian right were attacking the cavalry opposite them on the Roman left; they did not inflict many casualties, however, nor did they suffer any serious losses themselves because of their peculiar methods of fighting.[42]

As we would expect from heavy cavalry, the allies had difficulty coming to grips with the amorphous flock of Numidians. But they did keep them sufficiently at bay to prevent themselves being outflanked in any great numbers and, by keeping the Numidians on the move, minimized their own casualties, being aided in this by their body armour. True, they may have allowed themselves to be lured away from their station on the flank of their infantry a little, but all in all they were not doing badly at this stage.

On the other flank, things went less well for the citizen cavalry and it is their performance here that really constitutes the main plank of the case against them. The number of horses packed into the relatively narrow space, with the river restricting any manoeuvre, forced the opposing forces to charge head on in close order, 'leaving them no option', says Livy, 'but to go straight ahead'.[43]

The surviving sources are in agreement that there followed a desperate struggle in which the Romans were overwhelmed and broken. Hasdrubal, commanding the Spanish and Celtic cavalry, made sure the Roman horsemen were completely out of the battle before leading his force across the field, behind the Roman infantry which had scored early success in the centre, and quickly scattered the Italian cavalry in turn by attacking them from behind while they were still busy with the Numidians. Leaving the Numidians to chase the fleeing Italians, Hasdrubal then launched the Spanish and Celtic horse in a third attack on the rear of the Roman infantry, completing their encirclement. Although their now-unprotected flanks had already begun to be outflanked by some Carthaginian infantry positioned specially for this purpose, the cavalry assault on their rear was the final nail in their coffin and slaughter ensued.

It should be no surprise that a force of cavalry was quickly defeated by another that was three times its size, but the *equites* do seem to have been overwhelmed rapidly given that they managed to cancel their enemies' initial impetus. Livy says 'it was fierce while it lasted but that was not for long'; and even Polybius, who makes their resistance sound more prolonged, says it was over by the time the Roman infantry had come into contact with the Carthaginian centre, which must have been early on given the apparent Roman tactical plan.[44]

It seems that a number of the *equites* dismounted to fight and this is the most often-cited evidence that they were uncomfortable fighting as cavalry, despite the fact that many of the Celtic and Spanish horsemen also ended up on foot. Worse still, where this fact has been noted it has sometimes been used in support of the notion that ancient horsemen in general were forced to dismount because of their lack of stirrups.* So what exactly happened on the banks of the Aufidus?

Polybius covers this crucial fight in four sentences.

> But as soon as the Spanish and Celtic horse on the left wing came into contact with the Roman cavalry, the action began in earnest and the fighting which developed was truly barbaric. There was none of the usual formal advance and withdrawal about this encounter: once the two forces had met they dismounted and fought on foot, man to man. Here the Carthaginians finally prevailed, and although the Romans resisted with desperate courage, most of them were killed in the hand to hand fighting. Their opponents drove the rest remorselessly along the river bank, cutting them down as they retreated ... [45]

Clearly this was no premeditated decision to fight dismounted as infantry, for they only dismounted after contact was made. Had such been their intention they would, like the dragoons of a later period, have deployed on foot with their horses held a safe distance to the rear but close enough to be brought up if success meant they were needed for the pursuit. Advancing into contact and then trying to dismount and form a fighting line was obviously inviting confusion and disorder; one cannot fight effectively and hold a horse, nor would you want to risk the scared horses of the front rank running to the rear through the supporting ranks still moving up and then galloping off.

It may actually have made more sense for the Romans to have fought a purely defensive dismounted action. With their flank protected by the river, the Carthaginians would have been forced to attempt to charge a line of spearmen. But this would have been a waste of the cavalry, as there was plenty of true infantry available for this job. Most Roman infantry, it is true, were no longer armed with the long thrusting spears that could form such a deterrent to cavalry, but the *triarii* who usually formed the third line were and there were six hundred of these to each legion. All the Roman heavy infantry carried the long shield, the *scutum*, that gave much better protection than the cavalry shield and could form a more imposing shield wall. The deployment of the Roman cavalry on this flank only makes sense if they were intended to fight mounted.

---

* One otherwise-fine recent study of Cannae showed that this old view still persists: 'It is difficult to estimate how effective such cavalry would actually have been ... Cavalry without stirrups could hardly have made good shock troops'.[46]

Although heavily outnumbered the Roman cavalry may well have fancied their chances in a straight fight against the Spanish and Celts; they had, after all, beaten one numerically superior force of Celtic horsemen in a prolonged mounted fight at Telamon and blown away another with its infantry supports at Clastidium. True, we cannot know how many veterans of these earlier battles had survived the multiple calamities suffered already in the current war, nor how much damage these had done to morale. But the casualties at the Ticinus, Trebbia and Trasimene could be put down to outflankings and ambushes by the Numidians which would not be possible here. The plan of the Roman cavalry was to meet the enemy charge with their own and rely on superior resolve to drive them off, it always being the Roman belief that barbarians, and the Celts in particular, had no stomach or stamina for a prolonged fight.

The Romans did not give way at the first onrush of the bigger mass, as the Spaniards and Celts would have been hoping they would, but managed by their own resolve to hold their horses' obedience and urged them forward in a countercharge. At the last moment many of the horses on either side may well have tried to 'nap' or shy away from the apparent oncoming collision, but with rank upon rank bunching up from behind, some at least may well have tried to barge their way between those of the opposing front rank. With seven or eight thousand cavalry now trying to get at each other on a short front the leading ranks on either side soon became entangled.

'The horses', explains Livy, 'soon found themselves brought to a halt, jammed close together in the inadequate space.' With the initial impetus of the charge lost, he describes riders starting to pull one another from their horses, 'turning the contest more or less into an infantry battle'.[47] While some of the front ranks actually grappled with each other like this, some perhaps having irretrievably impaled or broken their lances upon an opponent in the initial attack, many must have retained their weapons or resorted to swords. In a tight press the Spanish, who were particularly famed for their individual swordsmanship, may indeed have been at an advantage. Those not in the front rank would have had little chance of getting their horses forward, especially as the ground became littered with dead and wounded men and mounts. Eager to assist their compatriots, many may have decided to slip from their horse and pick their way into the front line on foot just as had happened at the Ticinus where many 'dismounted to bring aid to hard-pressed comrades'.

In such a fight we would expect the deeper formation to have an advantage. In large measure this was because the sheer physical obstacle presented by the rear ranks, and the fact that they were watching, made it harder for those closer to the immediate danger to slip away and save themselves. The much deeper formation of the enemy (many times more numerous on the same frontage, they must have been in many more ranks) made it unlikely that the Romans could cut their way through. If the odd individual horseman carved and barged his way through a few ranks, he and his horse would soon find themselves swallowed up in the enemy mass and open to simultaneous attack from several directions, those from the left rear being most difficult to ward off.

Once the fight had become static, it must have been clear to the Romans that they were not going to sweep the opposition away as they had at Clastidium. With forward mounted movement impossible and no room to skirt round the flanks, the options were to fight it out on the spot or try to run. Unlike at the Ticinus, the Romans were not obstructed to their rear, so turning and riding away was an option for those at the back, at least in a practical sense. But even if an orderly withdrawal from the confused situation had been possible, which is unlikely with five thousand enemy cavalry at their heels, it would have exposed the flank of the Roman infantry to instant attack. Besides, honour demanded that they give no ground. As we have seen, scattered throughout their histories there were those occasions when the Roman cavalry had dismounted to show solidarity with their fellow citizens. What is more, Livy records that when the army was mustered every man had taken a formal oath 'never to leave the field in order to save their own skins, nor to abandon their place in the line for any purpose other than to recover or fetch a weapon, to strike an enemy or to save a friend'.[48] As the Celtic and Spanish numbers quickly began to tell, threatening to breach the shallower Roman line and break them into isolated pockets, many of those who dismounted may have done so the better to make a last stand.

Livy records such a last stand made by the consul Paullus with a 'guard of cavalry', which may indicate that he brought up the *extraordinarii* to attempt to retrieve the situation. Livy says these, still mounted and 'in close order', made several attempts to cut their way through to Hannibal and that Paullus, fighting at their head despite being wounded, managed to keep the resistance alive for a while. Only when he became too weak from his wounds to ride is he supposed to have dismounted, his guard then following suit to stand with him. Indeed this is the only point at which Livy suggests a sizeable body of cavalry deliberately dismounted to fight as a unit, adding that they did so 'in the full knowledge of defeat; they made no attempt to escape, preferring to die where they stood'. Hannibal supposedly exclaimed upon hearing that Paullus had made his men dismount, that 'he might as well have delivered them up in chains'. In Plutarch, the entire question of the Roman cavalry dismounting is implausibly portrayed as a mistake; Paullus was thrown from his wounded horse, upon which one after another of his staff dismounted to assist him, the rest of the cavalry assuming the order had been given for them to dismount also. Polybius, it must be noted, specifically says that Paullus emerged from the defeat of the cavalry on the right wing 'safe and unwounded' and rode off to join the fight in the centre, where he was eventually slain.

The exact details of what happened on the Roman right wing at Cannae will never be known, and were probably not clear to the participants, but the conclusions Polybius drew from it are telling.

> As in previous encounters it was the *superior numbers* of the Carthaginian cavalry which contributed most to the victory, and the battle demonstrated to posterity that it is more effective to have half as many infantry as the enemy and an overwhelming superiority in cavalry than to engage him with absolutely equal numbers.[49]

The Carthaginian cavalry was better handled than the Romans at Cannae, but were the cavalry themselves better? Perhaps. Leaving aside the Numidians, who were clearly superb in their light cavalry role, both the Spanish and particularly the Celts enjoyed a reputation as horsemen in the ancient sources that it is not for us to gainsay. But this should not be exaggerated. Stalin once answered concerns about the relative quality of Soviet and German forces by saying that quantity had a quality all of its own – and it seems to be this quality above all others that Hannibal's undoubted genius took advantage of in his early victories.

The battle of Cannae should have been a crippling blow for Rome, but this did not prove to be the case. News of the defeat was at first met with horror, but not despair. The Romans even refused to ransom back their prisoners; and those who had escaped the defeat, about ten thousand men including some cavalry, were later posted in disgrace to Sicily, not to be allowed to return while the enemy remained in Italy. Hannibal did not march immediately on Rome and the senate set about raising new armies, including two legions of freed slaves. It was the

vast reserves of manpower that Rome was able to mobilize, and the
political will to do so, that was the main factor in their eventual victory.
Legion after legion was raised, twenty-five eventually being in the field
at once. The drain on the limited pool of available *equites* and allied
horsemen must, however, have been very serious, 2700 having been
killed according to Livy. In Carthage, the news of the victory at Cannae
was announced with a dramatic flourish when sacks of the gold rings
worn by *equites* as a mark of status were emptied out on the floor of
the assembly. A few days later Rome's misery was further compounded
when another army, while passing through a forest, was ambushed by
the Gauls. Its utter destruction included all of its cavalry. The Romans
did manage to scrape together more cavalry, including some 'not yet
out of their boys togas', and these continued to give valuable service for
the rest of the war, but the heavy losses suffered between 218 and 216 BC
must have been more keenly felt in the cavalry arm than in the infantry
– and this before even considering the immeasurable damage done to
the pool of equine bloodstock.

After Cannae the Romans fell back on Fabian strategy again –
shadowing Hannibal, harassing him as safe opportunities arose, and
constraining his movements but avoiding pitched battle whenever
possible. Although the Latin allies and colonies held firm, most of the
cities of southern Italy went over to the Carthaginians, but the Romans
gradually retook these again, mopping up the small Carthaginian garrisons and nibbling away at Hannibal's irreplaceable veterans while
gradually gaining vital experience and confidence themselves. Polybius
maintained that Hannibal remained undefeated in a proper battle until
he left Italy in 203 BC. His ability to maraud in Italy for fifteen years
against huge numerical odds demonstrated his immense skill, yet at
the same time he failed after Cannae to force decisive battles on the
Romans – allowing them to turn the war in Italy into a war of attrition and of sieges, in short a war of manpower. In this kind of warfare,
cavalry still had an important role to play, protecting foragers, scouting, raiding and protecting armies while on the march, essentially light
cavalry functions, but there were relatively few opportunities for them
to score a decisive success through shock action.

Marcellus, the hero of Clastidium, seems to have been happier than
most Roman generals to operate close to Hannibal. As our sources
claim he generally had the better of the frequent skirmishes that
occurred between the armies' outposts patrols and foragers, this suggests that his cavalry was at least able to counter the Carthaginian

cavalry; for an army with a decisive cavalry superiority would have been expected to dominate such operations. Marcellus' cavalry also played an important role when he beat Hannibal outside Canusium in 209 BC, although we must suspect Livy and Plutarch have exaggerated the scale of the action, thereby contradicting Polybius' statement about Hannibal being unbeaten in Italy. Marcellus was ambushed and killed a short time later by Numidian cavalry while leading a small group of horsemen on a reconnaissance.

There was much fighting around Capua, the chief city of Campania and renowned in Italy for its horses and horsemen, which defected to the Carthaginian cause after Cannae. In 212 BC the besieging Roman infantry were in severe trouble against a foray by the Capuan horsemen until the Roman cavalry counter-attacked and checked them. Although Livy says the *equites* suffered the heavier casualties in their first charge, he adds that the action was broken off mutually 'with the honours more or less equal' when an unidentified body of troops appeared on a nearby hill.[50] Describing events of the following year, Livy says 'there were a number of engagements in which the Campanians usually proved their superiority in cavalry, though their infantry were regularly worsted'. He goes on to describe how the Roman cavalry found a way 'to make up by ingenuity what they lacked in strength'. Each horseman was to carry a light infantryman behind him into battle, 'all vigorous fellows, lightly built and quick on their feet', equipped with small shields and a bundle of seven short javelins. After several days of training these men to stay on the horse and then dismount on command, the new tactics were put to the test. The new formation rode out to confront the Campanian cavalry operating in the level ground between the Roman camp and the city walls. As the opposing forces closed, the signal was given and the infantry dismounted:

> The line of cavalry was transformed into a line of infantry, which immedi-
> ately charged, hurling its javelins in rapid succession and with great force.
> A great number were flung all along the line against both horses and men,
> inflicting many casualties; but an even greater shock was caused by the
> strange and unexpected mode of attack. The enemy were badly shaken and
> the Roman cavalry at once followed up the first assault, pursuing them to
> the city gates with great slaughter. From that moment on the Romans had
> the upper hand in both arms.[51]

We do not know how far this incident, with its 'great slaughter' of riders and mounts, helped to redress a numerical inequality, but it was very

probably the jolt to the Capuan horsemen's confidence that accounted
for the Roman cavalry's subsequent local advantage.

Hannibal attempted to raise the siege of Capua by a direct attack but
was unable to make much use of his cavalry in a battle that took place
across the trench lines and siegeworks, while a simultaneous sally from
the city was also repulsed. In a desperate last bid to save the city, he
made a rapid march on Rome itself, hoping to force the Romans to raise
the siege and race back to defend their capital. The dogged Romans
were not drawn, continuing to prosecute the siege more determinedly
than ever, but Fulvius Flaccus did hasten to Rome with one thousand
cavalry. Hannibal led two thousand of his cavalry right up to the out-
skirts of Rome, approaching the Porta Collina. Fulvius Flaccus, having
reached the city ahead of him, was unable to leave this insult unchal-
lenged and ordered the Roman cavalry to sally forth. It seems they
successfully drove off the Carthaginians without help, despite being
outnumbered two to one. Whether this should be attributed to Hannibal having only light cavalry with him, the Carthaginian horses being
more weary, or the sheer rapidity and ferocity of the Roman response
in defence of their city, it is impossible to say. Becoming aware that his
plan had failed, Hannibal withdrew; Rome was saved and Capua soon
surrendered.

Rome's superior ability to mobilize its manpower enabled it, even
while attempting to wear down Hannibal at home, to maintain armies
in Spain throughout the war, undermining the Carthaginian power
base there and ensuring that instead of sending reinforcements to
Hannibal in Italy, this theatre sucked in reinforcements from the home
government in North Africa instead. The cavalry of the various Iberian
and Celtiberian tribes were to be found fighting here on both sides as
fortunes swung back and forth and alliances were made and broken.

We have seen that Spanish cavalry were used to great effect in the
shock role by Hannibal in Italy, and Appian tells us that the Romans saw
these as 'such splendid fighters' that the Romans raised some in Spain
and sent them to Italy 'to contend against the others'.[52] But in the fighting in Spain, ironically, they do not stand out as having performed well,
although in some cavalry skirmishes with the Tartessi tribe, Hasdrubal
Barca, Hannibal's brother, did find 'the Numidan horsemen were not
a match for the Spanish'.[53] While individually skilled, courageous and
possessed of fine weapons and mounts, the Spanish troops were often
poorly motivated and proved unreliable, unsurprisingly given the situation with these two foreign powers fighting out their wars over their

homeland. At Ibera in 215 BC Hasdrubal's Spanish cavalry fled without a fight, thwarting Hasdrubal's first attempt to follow in Hannibal's footsteps to Italy.[54] Most of northern Spain then went over to the Romans under Gnaeus and Publius Scipio.[55] These in turn were deserted by their Spanish auxiliaries in 211 BC, contributing greatly to their deaths.

As in Italy, the African cavalry on the Carthaginian side caused the Romans particular problems. In 211 BC, Publius Scipio divided the Roman force with his brother and marched to intercept a force of Suessetani Spanish before they could join up with the Carthaginian armies converging on him. His force was located, however, and harassed on the march 'day and night' by a contingent of Numidian cavalry under their young prince, Masinissa. Not content with picking off stragglers and cutting up errant foraging parties, Livy says, 'often he would ride right up to the camp itself [the Romans fortified a camp every night] and charge at the gallop through the outposts guarding it, causing the greatest confusion'. Deserted by his own Spanish allies, Publius slipped away by means of a night march and engaged the Suessetani with some success until the Numidians appeared on both flanks and attacked. When Publius was run through the side with a lance and fell mortally wounded from his horse, the Romans broke in panic and were easily ridden down.

Gnaeus Scipio died twenty-nine days later in similar circumstances. His Spanish allies deserted the Roman camp at the first sight of the enemy and Gnaeus tried to slip away by night. Masinissa overhauled him the next day and, although his light cavalry alone could not decisively defeat them, they subjected him to such an intense harassment that he was forced to halt to fend them off, giving time for the Carthaginian main forces to arrive. Gnaeus spent the next night trying to make a makeshift fortification of pack saddles on a low hill, but this was stormed in short order the next morning.[56]

The command in Spain was awarded to the younger Publius Scipio, then only in his mid-twenties, when no other candidates stood for the post. Unsurprisingly he made it his policy to rely on Spanish allies as little as possible, although he was careful to cultivate their goodwill, and most of the cavalry he used in his brilliant rapid conquest of the peninsula was Roman and Latin. When he defeated Hasdrubal at Baecula in 208 BC, Scipio chose to send the Spanish prisoners back to their homes, replacing any horses they had lost with captured ones.[57] In a cavalry fight near Carmone the following year, Scipio personally led some of his squadrons against the Numidians whose usual hit and run tactics initially caused problems. But when Scipio ordered his men to 'pursue them without intermission, the Numidians having no chance to turn around, retreated to their camp'. Resuming the contest at the next encounter, Appian tells us 'the Roman horse prevailed over the enemy by the same tactics as before, by giving no respite to the Numidians, who were accustomed to retreat and advance by turns'.

At Ilipa in 206 BC, where Carthaginian power in Spain was effectively exterminated, only five hundred of Scipio's three thousand cavalry were Spanish, the rest Romans and Italian allies. Against these the Carthaginians had 4500 cavalry, including Masinissa's Numidians, and thirty-two elephants, as well as a greatly superior number of infantry. When the Roman army moved into the vicinity and began fortifying the camp, the Carthaginian cavalry, commanded by Mago Barca, another of Hannibal's brothers, attacked en masse:

> And the Roman working parties might have been roughly handled but for a timely and unexpected charge by a squadron of horse which Scipio had posted in concealment behind a convenient hill. Mago's leading cavalrymen were in loose order, and those of them who were quick enough to get close up to the rampart or actually amongst the working parties were soon scattered by the Roman squadron.[58]

Mago sensibly had the bulk of his cavalry following in close order and these continued the attack, but the Roman squadron resisted fiercely until their infantry began to arrive on the scene and drove the Carthaginians off.

This spoiling attack having failed, there followed a period of cautious posturing as both armies spent hours deploying for battle each morning and stood waiting for the other to make the first move, before retiring to their respective camps at dusk. Each day the armies adopted the same formation with their most reliable and heaviest infantry in the centre, flanked by the lighter Spanish infantry, and then cavalry on the extreme flanks. After several days of this Scipio sent his cavalry, who had been warned to have their horses groomed and fed before dawn, with light infantry in support, to attack the Carthaginian outposts at first light, while he deployed the infantry with their usual formation reversed. Surprised, Hasdrubal quickly roused his troops and ordered all his cavalry out to meet this attack while he hurriedly deployed in his usual formation.

Despite the Carthaginians' numerical advantage, this opening cavalry fight was indecisive. The restricted space between the infantry lines forced caution on the horsemen who could not pursue a beaten opponent effectively, nor charge through their line, without risk of running into the infantry behind so that, as Livy explains, 'the opposing squadrons, when overpowered, as happened more or less by turns, could safely withdraw to the protection of the infantry line'.[59] This continued until around midday, at which point Scipio ordered the cavalry and skirmishers to be recalled, which would have been done by trumpet signal, and they fell back through gaps opened in the ranks of the infantry.

Screened by his cavalry, Scipio had deployed with his legionary heavy infantry on the flanks instead of the centre and it is this surprise move that is generally credited with winning the victory that followed. In a plan that has strong similarities to Hannibal's at Cannae, both wings advanced rapidly, while the weaker Spanish auxiliaries in the centre advanced very slowly. The best Roman infantry were thereby brought against the weaker wings of the Carthaginian line and had them half beaten before the centre, where the Carthaginians had the better troops, was even engaged. What is not always mentioned in summaries of the battle is that it was the Roman cavalry, rapidly redeployed to either flank after their withdrawal through the lines, that led the attacks on either wing, still supported by the light infantry. With the enemy cavalry presumably still regrouping behind the centre, or perhaps belatedly feeding and watering their horses (they receive no further mention), the Roman cavalry easily outflanked the enemy line so that 'both wings were hard pressed and subjected to a double attack – on their flanks by the Roman cavalry, light troops and skirmishers, and simultaneously on the front by the Roman infantry'.[60]

As if this wasn't enough, Livy says it was the rapid movements of the cavalry and light infantry that startled the elephants, which had been posted ahead of the Carthaginian wings, so that they were herded towards the centre and became an equal nuisance to both sides. For a while the Carthaginians tried to make an orderly withdrawal but this soon ended in panic and unrestrained flight back to their camp.

Livy's version of the postscript to the battle may be distorted by literary device. The Carthaginians tried to withdraw during the night but were first abandoned by their Spanish allies and then caught on the march by the Roman cavalry the next day and subjected to persistent attacks on their flanks and rear which even Masinissa's Numidians could not adequately fend off. Forced to halt, they were caught up by the Roman infantry and 'what had been a field of battle was turned into a slaughterhouse'. The similarities with the deaths of Scipio's father and uncle may owe as much to Livy's poetic licence as to poetic justice, but we have no reason to doubt their general outline or the outcome. The rest of Spain soon came over to the Roman cause, apart from two towns that were quickly stormed and completely eradicated. Significantly, Masinissa and his Numidians changed sides too.

After his defeat at Baecula, Hasdrubal Barca had marched his remaining forces to Italy in an attempt to join up with his brother. Hannibal's march north to meet him was checked at Grumentum where the Roman cavalry launched a pre-emptive charge on his army as it emerged from the city in uncharacteristic disorder, forcing him to withdraw back within the walls. Meanwhile other Roman forces converged on Hasdrubal and forced his army to fight with their backs to the Metaurus river. Although there is no mention of the cavalry forces of either side in the battle, we know that whatever cavalry Hasdrubal possessed was unable to prevent his right flank being turned and his line rolled up, suggesting that they were successfully countered by the Roman cavalry. With defeat imminent, Hasdrubal rode into the densest part of the enemy line to seek death and was not disappointed, his severed head later being delivered by the Roman victors to Hannibal.

The Roman cavalry played a more definitely vital role in the final battles of the war when Scipio invaded North Africa in 204 BC from Sicily, with 1600 cavalry and sixteen thousand infantry, many of them the survivors of Cannae who had been sent to garrison Sicily. He was soon joined by Masinissa's Numidian forces and, when a large pro-Carthaginian force of Numidians was destroyed by a nocturnal attack that set their camps ablaze, the balance of cavalry forces was further tipped in Scipio's favour. Continued successes gave his forces an important psychological edge too: at the Battle of the Great Plains in 203 BC, the Italian horse drove back the opposing Numidian cavalry, while the Carthaginian citizen cavalry, despite being of heavier type, were driven back by Masinissa's light Numidians, 'for their spirit had been broken by their earlier defeats'. The Celtiberian mercenary infantry forming the Carthaginian centre refused to surrender but were surrounded and died to the man. The Carthaginian government was finally forced to recall Hannibal from Italy, as Scipio had intended. Lacking sufficient shipping to carry all his troops, he had to leave most of his cavalry behind and allegedly had four thousand horses slain rather than let them fall into Roman hands; another blow to Italy's equestrian gene pool.

In 202 BC Hannibal and Scipio met for the final showdown at Zama. For once Hannibal had a larger number of infantry, while the Romans had the advantage in cavalry. Each deployed their infantry in three lines and divided their cavalry between the wings, Hannibal adding a screen of eighty elephants that stretched across most of his front. Scipio put his 1500 remaining Roman and Italian horse on his left flank under the command of Laelius, and entrusted the other flank to Masinissa's four thousand Numidian cavalry. Opposite Masinissa, Hannibal put his own Numidians, but few if any of these were veterans of his Italian campaigns and they were in any case outnumbered roughly two to one. On the other flank, he opposed the Italian cavalry with native Carthaginian cavalry, again with little experience and again possibly outnumbered, although their number is uncertain.

The battle opened with some indecisive skirmishing between the two Numidian contingents, but the real fighting began when Hannibal ordered all his elephants to charge. The result was a disaster for Hannibal. The elephants on his left flank panicked straightaway and fled, apparently frightened by the sudden din of the charge being sounded, colliding with the Numidian cavalry en route and throwing them into confusion. Before they could rally, Masinissa attacked and drove them off. Elsewhere some of the elephants caused casualties among Scipio's light infantry, but these too were eventually killed, although some stampeded back through their own lines, now disrupting the Carthaginian cavalry on the other flank.

> It was at this moment that Laelius, taking advantage of the confusion caused by the elephants, launched a charge against the Carthaginian cavalry, drove them back in headlong flight and pressed the pursuit, as also did Masinissa on the right wing.[61]

For a long while the infantry were left to battle it out alone, the cavalry of both sides having disappeared into the dust. The Romans cut their way through Hannibal's first two lines, but when they came up against the fresh troops of the third, which consisted of his finest veteran troops, 'the issue hung for a long while in the balance':

> Many men fell on both sides, fighting with fierce determination where they stood, but at length the squadrons of Masinissa and of Laelius returned from the pursuit of the Carthaginian cavalry and arrived by a stroke of fortune at the crucial moment. When they charged Hannibal's troops in the rear, the greater number of his men were cut down in their ranks, while

of those who took to flight only a few escaped, since the cavalry were close upon their heels and the ground was level.[62]

Zama effectively ended the war, completing Rome's fight back from the brink of destruction. It had been won by Roman cavalry superiority and the ability of Masinissa and Laelius first to seize the fleeting opportunity presented by the flight of the elephants, and then to rally their victorious horsemen from the chase and lead them back to the danger of the battlefield to make the decisive intervention.

6

Later Republican Rome

Victory in the Second Punic War catapulted Rome into a prolonged period of rapid expansion and conquest. The citizen cavalry played an indispensable part in the numerous campaigns, but the ever-increasing demands of territorial acquisition wrought great changes on the army and its relationship with wider society. By the end of the second century BC, virtually the whole of the Mediterranean basin was under Roman domination, either as directly ruled provinces, through puppet rulers as 'client kingdoms', or as decidedly unequal allies; but the traditional citizen cavalry seems to have disappeared not long after. With the exception of possible brief revivals during civil war, their place in the final wars of the Republic was entirely taken by an increasing range of foreign auxiliaries and local allies.

The most spectacular achievements of the second century BC were the decisive battles that humbled the professional armies of those Hellenistic states founded by Alexander's successors, forcing them grudgingly to accept Roman domination. As we have seen already, when the Roman cavalry first clashed with Philip V's Macedonian cavalry in 200 BC, 'there was no delay in charging as soon as the enemy came in sight', and the two forces 'were well matched in numbers and spirit' so that the 'fight went on for some hours on equal terms ... without a clear victory on either side'.[1] Although on a small scale, the Romans losing only thirty-five men and the Macedonians forty, this action is interesting not only for establishing that there was no huge disparity in the quality of the opposing horsemen, but also for Livy's description of the aftermath, wherein the Romans may have inadvertently established something of a moral advantage. When Philip V had the bodies of his horsemen collected for proper burial, the Macedonian troops were apparently appalled by the degree of mutilation wrought upon them by the Spanish swords used by the Roman troopers.

> Now they saw bodies dismembered with the 'Spanish' sword, arms cut off with the shoulder attached, or heads severed from bodies, with the necks completely cut through, internal organs exposed, and a general feeling of

panic ensued when they discovered the kind of weapons and the kind of men they had to contend with.[2]

It is interesting that this passage has often been used to illustrate the power of this weapon in the hands of the Roman legionary infantry, despite the fact that, in this particular instance, the damage was definitely done by horsemen.

This was followed by another minor engagement, previously described, in which the Roman cavalry fell in with what seem to have been Macedonian light cavalry, supported by light infantry. The Macedonian cavalry were apparently expecting the Romans to skirmish cautiously, presumably due to the presence of the infantry, but the Romans 'acted as if this was a general engagement in line' and immediately closed with them. The initial charge seems to have failed to rout the enemy and their supporting infantry may have got in among the Roman horsemen and caused them some difficulty as it elicited the stubborn response we have seen earlier. Instead of withdrawing to regroup, they refused to retreat and stubbornly fought it out on the spot, some of them dismounting to fight among the footmen. Faced with this unexpectedly resolute response 'the king's cavalry were no match for the Roman horsemen'.[3]

The Roman cavalry were not much called upon at the battle of Cynoscephelae, in 197 BC, where Philip V of Macedon was decisively defeated. The initial cavalry skirmishes that did take place swung first one way and then the other, the Romans at one point having to be rescued by their Aetolian allies, but the terrain ensured that both armies were forced to rely chiefly on their infantry in any case.

The cavalry took a greater share of the laurels at Magnesia in 190 BC where the Seleucid army, the foremost proponent of shock cavalry at that time, was trounced. Magnesia, it may be recalled from the earlier discussion, was the first Roman encounter with cataphracts: mail-clad lancers on big, mail-clad horses. The Seleucid left wing, including three thousand cataphracts and 3500 other cavalry with infantry, camels and elephants in support, was routed by the charge of two thousand Roman and Italian cavalry and eight hundred Hellenistic cavalry supplied and led by King Eumenes II of Pergamum.

It was the Pergamene cavalry, supported by their contingent of light infantry, that had first stampeded the opening charge of Seleucid scythed chariots back through their own ranks, but the Roman cavalry played their full part in the timely exploitation of the ensuing chaos and clinched a decisive victory with very little loss to themselves.[4]

At Pydna, in 168 BC, the Roman cavalry were still giving good service. They took part in the successful attack that began the collapse of Perseus' army and effectively ended Macedon's last chance for independence from Rome, although it was the elephants supplied by Rome's Numidian allies that initially broke the enemy line.

The Roman cavalry had a solid if not spectacular record against the professional armies of the Successor states. These were wars decided by set-piece battles where heavy cavalry was in its element and where the penchant of the *equites* for aggressive, glory-seeking charges followed by stubborn refusal to give ground had a suitable stage. They had a patchier record in the long campaigns against various tribal peoples, which were actually much more typical of the second and first centuries BC as Rome secured its grip on the Mediterranean hinterland. These were wars mainly of raids and punitive devastation, of ambushes, skirmishes and the capture of tribal strongholds, often in almost inaccessible mountainous terrain.

The Roman cavalry probably performed their functions of patrolling, foraging and escorting columns adequately, but there were fewer chances for spectacular combat successes against elusive enemies using their familiarity with the local terrain to catch the Romans at a disadvantage before melting back into the landscape. The Roman and Italian heavy cavalry squadrons struggled against the Iberian cavalry in Spain, and particularly those of the Lusitani when pressing into what is now Portugal from 151 BC. The Lusitanian cavalry were well mounted even by Spanish standards and formed the mainstay of their long resistance under Viriathus, which destroyed several Roman armies and only ended when the Romans resorted to treachery in 140 BC.

The Lusitanian horses repeatedly demonstrated their stamina, agility and sure-footedness. Early in his career, Viriathus' army escaped entrapment in a valley when he remained behind with a thousand horsemen and held off the entire Roman army for a whole day by repeated attacks and withdrawals and clever manoeuvring before escaping at speed into the surrounding mountains. The Roman cavalry, Appian explains, were unable to catch him 'by reason of the weight of their armour, their ignorance of the roads, and the inferiority of their horses'.[5]

Although they generally fought in scattered groups and employed the hit and run tactics of light cavalry, some Lusitani cavalry may have been well armoured. Appian tells us that the traitors who agreed to kill Viriathus for Roman gold had to cut his throat because he had taken to sleeping in his armour and this was the only part of his body not protected. He also relates that, at his funeral, Lusitanian horsemen rode around his pyre wearing their armour.[6] Judging by Spanish vase paintings of the period, this armour was probably of chain mail or scale, or perhaps a combination of both, with scale for the upper body and chain mail for the abdomen, where its greater flexibility would have eased movement. Figurines represent horses with faces protected by chamfrons, and there is even some pictorial evidence for mail body armour for horses, although this was probably very rare.

The Roman cavalry was also severely tested in North Africa against the Numidian king, Jugurtha, between 112 and 105 BC. The Numidians had been allied to Rome since Masinissa's defection from Carthage in the Second Punic War. His successor, Mcipsa, supplied grain, elephants and light cavalry for the Third Punic War and the campaigns in Spain where his nephew Jugurtha, later adopted as a son, had personally led the cavalry with notable success. But after Mcipsa's death, Jugurtha refused to accept the division of the kingdom with Mcipsa's natural son, Adherbal.[7] When Jugurtha captured the port of Cirta and allowed his victorious troops to massacre resident Roman citizens there (many of them businessmen of equestrian status), war with Rome was inevitable.

The war initially went well for Jugurtha, who swiftly overran most of Numidia in the face of a half-hearted and poorly led Roman response. In 109 BC the intervening Roman army, under the consul Aulus Postumius Albinus, was surrounded, forced to surrender and made to endure the humiliation of passing under the yoke. The senate refused to accept the peace terms agreed to by Albinus and sent a new consul, Quintus Caecilius Metellus, to take command and exact revenge.

Jugurtha initially played for time by means of diplomacy and subterfuge but refused battle while he gathered his forces and looked for an opportunity to catch his new opponent at a disadvantage. Metellus responded with a policy of systematic conquest. Hoping to provoke Jugurtha into making a stand in open battle, he marched his force across Numidia, taking the surrender of numerous towns and storming or besieging those that resisted. Wary of the Numidians' favoured tactics, he took great care to guard against ambush or sudden cavalry raids. A screen of light infantry slingers and archers marched at the head of the column, while the auxiliary cavalry, which included locally raised Numidians as well as Thracian units, formed a protective screen to either side, with more light infantry units in support. The rear, always vulnerable against an elusive enemy in hostile territory, was entrusted to his talented subordinate, Marius, with the citizen cavalry.[8] That these were definitely Roman citizens of some status seems confirmed by the fact that an allied prince who asked for some of these cavalry as an escort was told it would be beneath the dignity of Roman horsemen to play bodyguard to a mere Numidian. The cavalry screen evidently did its job adequately as the Numidians, while a severe nuisance, were unable to prevent the inexorable Roman advance. Seeing that 'his country was explored by the enemy, and the affections of his subjects alienated', Jugurtha 'resolved to try the fortune of a battle'.

Advancing rapidly with a large force of infantry, vast numbers of cavalry and at least forty-four elephants, he fell upon the Roman column not long after it had crossed the River Muthul. Metellus was badly wrong-footed while manoeuvring to prevent the column from being cut off from fresh water and presented a flank to the Numidians. The sudden onslaught threw the column into complete disorder. Metellus struggled to coordinate a response as the Numidians dashed in amongst the Romans so that, in Sallust's words, 'horses and men, enemies and fellow countrymen were all mingled in confusion'. Surrounded groups had to rely on their own initiative so that 'nothing was done by direction or command'; but most stood their ground and fought back with fierce desperation.

Roman cavalry squadrons did their best to drive off the enemy horsemen, but it was like swatting at clouds of flies that would disperse momentarily only to swarm back in with their biting volleys of javelins as soon as the Romans halted or retired to regroup:

> Whenever a squadron of the Roman cavalry began a charge, instead of retiring in one direction, they [the Numidians] retreated independently, scattering as widely as possible. In this way they could take advantage of their numerical superiority. If they failed to check their enemy's charge, they would wait until the Romans lost their formation and then cut them off by attacks in their rear or on the flanks.[9]

Ultimately, however, the Numidians proved incapable of doing sufficient damage to cause the complete collapse of the Roman army, although they maintained their attacks throughout the whole of a hot African afternoon. Fortunately for Metellus, Jugurtha had not committed his elephants, which might have provided a sufficiently heavy shock force, against the main column. Instead he had despatched them to head off a Roman detachment sent ahead to secure a suitable campsite. Roman skirmishers counter-attacked the elephants as they tried to pick their way through an area of dense scrub, killing forty of the beasts and capturing four.

As the day wore on Metellus gradually reasserted some control, gathering scattered groups together and directing their resistance. As afternoon turned to evening both sides were growing weary and thirsty. Noting that the enemy attacks were finally slackening off, Metellus formed the nearest cohorts into good order and roused them to make a concerted counter-attack against a large body of the enemy infantry which had drawn off to rest on some higher ground. It was too much for the exhausted Numidians and the whole force melted away in panic-stricken flight. Jugurtha rode off into the wilds with only the horsemen of his royal bodyguard.

Jugurtha began gathering another army, but when Metellus resumed his methodical capturing and garrisoning of towns, the Numidian left the main body behind and conducted a cautious strategy of harassment and evasion with only a select body of cavalry. In addition to mounting lightning raids on the rearguard or any stragglers, they 'destroyed the forage and spoiled the water, which was scarce' in the path of the Roman advance.

Metellus besieged the important town of Zama; but, while most of the Roman forces were busy attempting a direct assault on the town Jugurtha led his horsemen in a daring attack on the Roman camp which seems to have been slackly guarded, and was only driven out with great loss. Metellus resumed his attack on the town the following day, but took the precaution of drawing his cavalry up in the open ground to guard the camp and the rear of the assault force.

Even so, when Jugurtha returned, he managed to surprise those cavalry outposts (or 'vedettes' to borrow a later term) furthest from the camp. This surprise was probably achieved by clever use of folds in the ground, wadis or areas of scrub to approach unseen before breaking cover for the final dash. When the rest of the Roman cavalry duly rode up in support, they were further surprised to find that the Numidians did not apply their normal tactics. Instead they pressed their charges home, managing to disrupt the Roman formations and engaging in a standing fight, despite their lighter armament. Furthermore, they were closely followed by detachments of light infantry who followed them into the fray and 'did great execution' among the Roman horsemen, who were vulnerable while they tried to duel with the skilled Numidian horsemen. Despite all this, Metellus' cavalry, of which the actual Roman contingent at least was better trained and equipped for close combat, eventually drove the Numidians off with heavy losses.

The following year Metellus managed to get a battle on his terms when he surprised Jugurtha's latest army and routed it, but without causing many casualties as most of them fled without a fight; 'for in almost every battle,' says Sallust scathingly, 'their feet afforded more security to the Numidians than their swords'. Jugurtha now fled with his few loyal troops: some cavalry and a number of deserters from the Roman army who could expect a horrible death if caught (possibly including the remnants of two whole *turmae* of Thracian auxiliary cavalry who are known to have deserted). He fled to Mauretania, where his father-in-law, Bocchus, was king. Presumably with Bocchus' blessing, he began to recruit from the Gaetulians, 'a people savage and uncivilized and, at this period unacquainted with even the name of Rome'. Drawing on his own experience and perhaps with the help of the deserters, he started to try to train them into a regular army along Roman lines and prepared to continue the war.

In 107 BC Metellus was replaced by Marius, his former cavalry commander, who had returned from leave in Rome as a newly elected consul and with newly raised reinforcements to pad out the ranks of what must by now have been well-seasoned veterans. He was later joined by his quaestor, Lucius Sulla and 'a numerous body of horse recruited from the Latins and Allies'. He continued Metellus' strategy and attacked one of Jugurtha's most important remaining strongholds at Capsa, despite the route lying across a broad desert supposedly filled with venomous snakes. The town was taken when a flying column of cavalry, with supporting light infantry following at their best speed, made a dash for the gates at dawn as the townsfolk emerged to work their fields. Capsa was sacked and razed to the ground. As clearly nowhere was safe, Jugurtha promised Bocchus one third of Numidia to secure his loyalty and determined on one last throw of the dice.

Jugurtha attacked late in the afternoon as the Romans rested towards the end of a hard day's march. Again he achieved complete tactical surprise, his cavalry descending upon them 'before the army could be formed up in battle order or its baggage piled – in fact before any signal or command could be given'. The Moorish and Gaetulian way of warfare was the same as that of the Numidians, relying primarily on masses of mobile but unarmoured light cavalry armed with javelins and leather shields. Despite Jugurtha's apparent attempts to instil some regular military discipline into them, they attacked 'not in line, or any regular array of battle, but in separate bodies', a rabble of infantry following to exploit the confusion sown by the charging horses. They succeeded in sweeping into the Roman column and surrounding groups of men as they ran to grab stacked weapons and as cavalrymen 'springing onto their horses, advanced against the enemy'. A good number were cut down in the initial onslaught, many more wounded and all thrown into confusion; only gradually did the veteran legionaries, a number of whom had been in a similar position with Metellus at the Muthul river, eventually organize themselves into circles 'and thus secured on every side ... withstood the attacks of the enemy'.

This situation, with the scattered and outnumbered clusters of Roman footsoldiers standing back to back like rocks amid the flood of enemy cavalry surging between 'and covering the field on all sides', calls to mind the afternoon of the battle of Waterloo in 1815. There, Napoleon's French cavalry were unable to break into the resolute British squares as long as they stayed put and their nerve held, and so it proved on this occasion also. The Romans of course did not have volleys of musketry to keep the enemy squadrons at bay, but when formed into a tight defensive wall, their armour and long shields would have given good protection against the enemy's javelins. Even so, it was a trying ordeal and some of the Romans would have given way to despair if it hadn't been for the intervention of Marius.

When the wave broke over his army, Marius did not panic. Realizing the impossibility of exercising proper command over any troops but those next to him, he took direct action. Leading his cavalry bodyguard, 'which he had formed of his bravest soldiers', he rode about the field, intervening wherever the need was greatest: 'sometimes supporting his own men when giving way, sometimes charging the enemy where they were thickest, and doing service to his troops with his sword, since in the general confusion, he was unable to command with his voice'.[10]

Marius and his horsemen did enough to keep the fight going until darkness fell, under cover of which Marius managed gradually to reunite his surviving troops, although enemy attacks continued. The Romans were now able to fight their way through to a more defensible position on a pair of rugged hills. Sulla and his Italian cavalry had evidently come through the long mêlée in reasonably good shape as they were entrusted with the vital task of seizing and guarding the lower of the two hills, with its vital spring of fresh water. The Numidians didn't risk a nocturnal assault up the rocky slopes. Thinking they had their enemy trapped and at their mercy, they surrounded the two hills and settled down for a night of celebratory drinking and feasting. Shortly before dawn, Marius had his army ready itself in silence and swept down on the slumbering enemy. The resultant slaughter was predictably one-sided and destroyed Jugurtha's last hope. Jugurtha himself escaped yet again, but was eventually betrayed to the Romans in 105 BC by Bocchus, his own father-in-law. He was paraded in Marius' triumphal return to Rome then starved to death in captivity.

The Jugurthine War is the last in which we can definitely say the Roman citizen cavalry took part. Henceforth Roman armies appear to have utilized only non-citizen cavalry recruited from the conquered provinces or loaned by allied states. The traditional explanation is that the Roman cavalry was so useless that, as soon as a new source of cavalry became available, they were replaced wholesale. As we have seen, the Roman citizen cavalry, although often in short supply, was far from being the token force that it has often been portrayed as, so we must look for other explanations.

By the end of the second century BC, the relationship between citizens and military service had changed. In the early centuries of the Republic, a number of citizens were enrolled each year to form the required number of legions, each providing their weapons and armour. The legions were then led out to fight a campaign of a few months against one of the neighbouring tribes before returning to Rome to be disbanded, the citizens then returning to their normal occupations, mostly to small farms. But by the second century BC the acquisition of overseas provinces was stretching this militia system to the limit as more legions were being called up and kept in the field for years on protracted campaigns of conquest and subjugation and providing an ever-increasing number of garrisons. When new consuls (and increasingly legates with pro-consular power) were elected each year, they were sent out to their assigned provinces with new drafts of replacements for the armies already operating there, but the bulk of those armies were left in place.

Military service became so unpopular in the mid second century BC, when Roman forces were suffering numerous casualties and embarrassing reverses in Spain, that the traditional method of enrolment had to be altered. Where the censors had previously selected individuals from those eligible citizens who presented themselves at the Campus Martius, they found such a poor turnout that the required number of troops for that year had to be conscripted purely by lottery. Apparently there were also insufficient candidates to fill the posts of military tribunes and legates, posts that had previously been hotly contested, with some eligible aristocrats feigning illness.

Changes in the Roman economy and agriculture also contributed to a shortage of suitable manpower to fill even the ranks of the legionary infantry by normal means. The richest sections of the nobility used the massive wealth derived from exploiting the new provinces to buy up huge tracts of land that were turned into industrial-scale farms, or *latifundia*, run almost entirely by slaves. The small-scale farmers who provided the bulk of those with the property qualification for legionary service were a vanishing breed, not least because farms were ruined by the prolonged absence of their owners on military service, who were then forced to sell their land to the *latifundia* in order to clear their debts.

When Marius was assigned to finish the Jugurthine War in 107 BC he was afraid that conscription by the usual means would not only be insufficiently fruitful, but would also lose him the popularity of the voters. He therefore took the deceptively simple step of recruiting from those below the usual property qualification, who therefore had to be equipped by the state with the arms and armour they could not afford for themselves. This used to be seen as the radical break that marked the birth of the professional Roman army. Henceforth military service was no longer linked to property qualification and was not a condition of citizenship. Although only full citizens could serve in the legions (others serving in auxiliary units of lower prestige), a Roman could enjoy all the social and legal benefits of citizenship without ever doing military service. Roman armies were now made up of volunteers who signed up as full-time long-service soldiers receiving regular army pay, and a share of any plunder, as their only income. In reality the process was probably a gradual one, although no less significant for that, with the incremental lowering of property qualifications and an increasing tendency towards state intervention in equipping those called up.

The so-called Marian reforms ended the distinctions between differ- ent classes of infantry in the legion – all now being uniformly equipped as heavy infantry by the state. The legion's integral light infantry com- ponent therefore vanished and it is conventionally assumed that the three hundred strong cavalry component was similarly abolished at the same time. Given that the Roman cavalry were evidently more efficient than often given credit for, this would seem an extremely foolish move just for the sake of the cost savings of regularization and uniformity. Given how central to their class ethos and prestige cavalry service had historically been, we must ask how the influential equestrian class could have allowed this to happen.

Rather than being abolished because of incompetence by a single reform, it is probably better to think of the equestrian class gradually *allowing* more of the burden to be taken by foreign auxiliaries, until eventually the citizen cavalry withered of its own accord. In the early centuries the ambitious equestrian welcomed his stints of cavalry service as a chance to win renown, which equalled social prestige and influence, to prove himself at least equal in virtue and courage to his ancestors. He also wanted to put in the required ten years that would qualify him to begin the career path of alternating civil and military magistracies, the *cursus honorum*, which could bring great influence and wealth. But the wars of the second century BC and the policing of the newly acquired provinces could require the serving cavalryman to be away from his estates and other business interests, not to mention the cockpit of political intrigue at Rome, for a long time. Obviously, regular army food and pay was a less alluring prospect for the wealthier citizen. Moreover the nature of the duties offered fewer chances of glorious deeds in relation to the dangers involved on long arduous campaigns against implacable barbarians in some unheard-of, disease-ridden backwater.

If military service was rapidly becoming a less attractive option for the *equites*, new alternative routes to wealth and influence were appearing to replace it. Indeed, wealth and influence became increasingly synonymous (regardless of birth or a reputation for civic virtue) as the new provinces opened up vast markets for commercial enterprise, cheap land and slaves for the establishment of *latifundia* – and opportunities for exploitative maladministration. 'Tax farming', whereby the tax collecting in a province was subcontracted out by the senate in return for a cash sum from the highest bidder, was only the most lucrative of many scams as Rome was flooded with exotic goods and dirty cash. The powerful senatorial elite, that tiny clique drawn from the equestrian class that was never more than a few hundred strong, had the best means to exploit such opportunities but still found it necessary to pay lip-service to the rule debarring them from commercial activity. There were no such limitations on ordinary equestrians who could happily turn their hands to making a quick profit on their own account or as the front men for senatorial patrons. The citizen cavalry was gradually replaced by foreign auxiliaries because the changing nature of Rome's military commitments and the exploitation of the new territories allowed cavalry service to be overtaken as the quickest route to wealth, and therefore influence, for the equestrian class. Some equestrians did still pursue military careers, but these were accommodated as officers in the legions or at the head of auxiliary troops.

This does not mean that the change to recruiting their cavalry solely from the conquered provinces (or the increasing number of enforced allies or client states) had no practical benefits for the efficiency of the Roman military system. Troops recruited from overseas, particularly from tribal warrior cultures, might be expected to be better suited to the nature of the warfare most commonly encountered, such as the use of Numidian light cavalry to counter those of their compatriots loyal to Jugurtha, and they could also be paid less. We cannot be sure of the extent of the damage inflicted on Italy's horse breeding stocks caused by the Second Punic War, alongside the replacement of traditional Italian farms by slave-run *latifundia* growing cheap grain for the swelling urban masses. But even if sufficient Italian horses had been available, the superb horse breeds available in Spain, Gaul, Syria and North Africa were too good a resource not to be used, and if you were going to recruit horses in the provinces, it made sense to employ them complete with their riders.

Although definite references to the citizen cavalry seem to peter out around the same time as Marius' campaigns, it is impossible to pinpoint when they last appeared. At Vercellae in 101 BC, when Marius halted the attempted invasion of Italy by the Cimbri, he is said by Plutarch to have chosen 'suitable ground for the Roman cavalry', despite the fact that the enemy allegedly had fifteen thousand heavily equipped horsemen with iron body armour (probably chain mail), shields and 'helmets like the heads and gaping jaws of terrible wild beasts'. Unfortunately Plutarch gives no details of Marius' own cavalry and few tactical details of the ensuing battle.[11]

The unpopularity and inconvenience of long foreign wars may have been largely responsible for the decline of the traditional citizen cavalry, but their waning may also have been hastened by events closer to home. In 91 BC, the discontent of Rome's forced Italian allies, the *socii*, erupted into open war. They were fighting not to regain their long-lost independence from Rome, but for a greater stake in the success of the state with the granting of full citizenship, which had previously belonged only to citizens of Rome or those cities actually established as Roman colonies. The Romans won the so-called Social War militarily but the senate was forced to concede full citizenship, first to all of Italy south of the Po but later extended to include Cisalpine Gaul. All free Italian men, from even the least distinguished backwater of the peninsula, now theoretically enjoyed the same political rights as someone of the oldest Roman family. If the old citizen cavalry had continued to be raised, it would have become a much less exclusive group, as any Bruttian, Lucanian or even – may the gods forbid it – an Italian Celt could be enrolled if they had the necessary wealth. It might have been preferable to the equestrian class, and the senate, to let the old cavalry tradition die rather than see it taken over by bumpkin upstarts.

By 88 BC, with Italy firmly back under control, Rome was able to turn her attention to a threat that had started much further afield, but now loomed ever closer. By then the forces of Mithridates VI of Pontus had overrun Asia Minor, occupied much of Greece and raised it in rebellion. They now threatened the Roman province of Macedonia. The severity of the threat was sufficiently obvious for the consul Sulla to take five of his six legions to Greece with him, even though Rome was teetering on the brink of civil war. Sulla had just seized power by a coup rather than hand over command of the legions to his rival Marius. Yet, despite the Mithridatic threat warranting his absence from Rome at such a critical time, Sulla landed in Greece with just 'a few troops of horse', and we cannot even be sure whether these were citizens or auxiliaries.

Sulla's first act upon landing in Greece was to send for reinforcements from Thessaly and Aetolia, the two areas of Greece then most famed for their cavalry. Mithridates was a formidable opponent and Sulla had every reason to be wary, particularly of his vast superiority in cavalry. The previous year the governor of the Roman province of Asia (western Asia Minor) had colluded with Nicomedes, the puppet king of Bithynia, to attack Pontus. Mithridates' total forces were then supposed to have included a quarter of a million foot soldiers, some of whom were Hellenistic-style pike phalanxes, but the cutting edge of the army was comprised of forty thousand cavalry and 130 scythed chariots. Mithridates' forces included allied troops from such equestrian cultures as the Scythians, Thracians, Armenians and the Sarmatians, the latter being a group of steppe tribes who were gradually displacing the Scythians (of whom they may actually have been an emerging subgroup) on the Eurasian steppes. All these peoples produced light cavalry as well as heavier armoured types drawn from the wealthiest sections of their societies.

At the Amnias river, the Pontic general Archelaus destroyed a Bithynian army of fifty thousand infantry and six thousand cavalry, using just his light infantry, ten thousand Armenian cavalry and a few chariots. For once scythed chariots scored a major success, causing panic in the enemy ranks. At Mount Scoroba, one hundred Sarmatian cavalry routed eight hundred of Nicomedes' remaining cavalry and took some of them prisoner. This incident reflects the high quality of Sarmatian cavalry (here making their historical debut but later to be a major power in their own right) and probably also the extreme demoralization of the Bithynian cavalry. Mithridates' forces had gone on to inflict a major defeat and ten thousand fatalities upon a Roman force of forty thousand infantry and four thousand cavalry. From then on the rest of Asia Minor was overrun with little resistance from Roman forces or their allies and Pontic armies had been sent to seize Greece and Macedonia.

Sulla managed to counter the enemy advantage in cavalry by marching rapidly through Boeotia and Attica (most of which came back over to the Roman cause) to attack Athens. Because Archelaus felt he could not abandon Athens, where a pro-Pontic regime had just been installed, he allowed himself to be tied to prolonged defensive counter-siege operations, in which cavalry were of limited use. Sulla kept doggedly at Athens until it was eventually captured and partially sacked in 86 BC. Archelaus, who Appian says was dumbfounded by the 'senseless and mad persistence' of the Romans, evacuated the remnants of his army by sea and united them with another Pontic force which had meanwhile invaded Macedonia and defeated the Roman garrison there.[12] When Sulla marched north in pursuit, he refused to join in open battle until he had manoeuvred Archelaus into favourable terrain, near Chaeronea.

From the histories of Plutarch and Appian, the former specifically referring to Sulla's own memoirs, it seems the combined Pontic force now comprised some 120,000 troops, including ten thousand cavalry and ninety-four scythed chariots. Plutarch gives Sulla a mere fifteen hundred cavalry and less than fifteen thousand infantry, while Appian suggests he may have had closer to forty thousand troops in total, the discrepancy probably lying in the uncertain number of Greek and Macedonian troops who now sided with the resurgent Roman cause. In either case, Sulla was clearly vastly outnumbered.

The two armies pitched camp at opposite ends of a narrow and rock-strewn plain bounded by rugged higher ground. Sulla seized the initiative by advancing rapidly towards the enemy forces, hoping to fight them on the broken terrain in which they had encamped. Archelaus only belatedly realized the weakness of his position, where his greater numbers and particularly his cavalry superiority could not be fully brought to bear. According to Appian, he first sent forward a detachment of cavalry to delay the oncoming legions while he deployed the rest of his army, but this force 'was put to flight and shattered amongst the rocks'. A force of sixty scythed chariots was then ordered to charge to disrupt the advancing legions and buy more time, but these were unable to build up enough impetus before the Romans were upon them and were routed. Appian describes some being funnelled along channels deliberately opened in the leading formations of the experienced and disciplined Roman formations, then encircled by those bringing up the rear and destroyed by volleys of javelins. Plutarch says the confident Romans acted as if they were at the circus, clapping and calling 'bring on more!'

Appian's account of the main event differs markedly from that of Plutarch, usually a well-informed source and himself a native of Chaeronea, but it does make more sense of the final outcome. In Appian's version Archelaus now attempted to regain the initiative by leading a massed cavalry charge. This succeeded in opening or exploiting a gap in the Roman line and cutting it in two, the Pontic horse then dividing to surround both portions. This would have been a potentially calamitous situation if Sulla had not kept most of his cavalry together in reserve. Seeing the approach of this fresh force threatening to take his own cavalry in flank and rear, Archelaus attempted to break off the attack and re-form further back, presumably alongside his infantry. Sulla however led 'the best part of his horse' and two infantry cohorts into an immediate counterattack that caught one wing of the Pontic army before it could redeploy, throwing it into a state of confusion that rapidly became a general flight. A counter-attack on the other wing soon produced a similar effect, the Romans pursuing ruthlessly all along the line. With the broken ground behind their original position hindering their escape, the enemy were slaughtered in great quantity, only ten thousand later rejoining Archelaus at Chalcis. Sulla claimed to have lost only thirteen dead. Plutarch accepts the Roman casualty figures even though he describes a much more formal battle with both lines fully arrayed and a long struggle between the Roman legions and Mithridates' elite pike phalanx, the 'Bronze Shields'.

Mithridates proved persistent and sent Archelaus reinforcements by sea that brought his total forces back up to ninety thousand men. Moving south again, Archelaus approached Sulla's force when it was near Orchomenus. Despite the outcome of the previous battle, Plutarch explains that Archelaus quite reasonably derived the confidence to give battle from the nature of the ground, 'unbroken and treeless' and 'an ideal battle ground for a side that was superior in cavalry'. Archelaus failed to attack immediately and Sulla set his men to digging a number of ditches, each ten feet wide, across the plain as anti-horse obstacles. Even so, when Archelaus finally attacked this position, the Romans 'fought badly because they were in terror of the enemy's cavalry'. At the crisis of the battle Sulla had to resort to running towards the enemy with only his shield-bearers to shame his terrified men into rallying. The counter-attack that followed eventually drove off the enemy and left ten thousand of their cavalry dead among the trenches that had hindered their retreat, Archelaus' son amongst them. After further entrenchments had penned the enemy in still further, the Romans stormed the Pontic camp with great slaughter.

Mithridates had been driven out of Greece and Macedonia but the war was not yet over. In Sulla's absence, Marius' faction had regained control of the senate, conducting a purge of Sulla's supporters and declaring him an outlaw. Another commander was appointed to conclude the war but was murdered en route to the east by his subordinate, Fimbria, who then assumed command of the army. Finally, Sulla invaded Asia Minor via Thrace, negotiated a treaty with Mithridates and then besieged Fimbria's army until he committed suicide and his troops surrendered. After attending to the security of the eastern provinces, Sulla and his veteran army set sail for Italy in 82 BC and the political crisis that had been simmering since his earlier coup was finally ignited into open civil war.

When Sulla landed in Italy his opponents were waiting to meet force with force, now led by the younger Marius, son of Sulla's now-deceased arch-enemy. Sulla had to fight his way towards Rome against similarly equipped and organized forces that were more numerous, but for the most part far less experienced, than his own. Among those who sided with Sulla was a twenty-three-year-old aristocrat, Gnaeus Pompeius, better known as Pompey. Pompey had inherited enormous wealth from his father, Gnaeus Pompeius 'Strabo' (the squint-eyed), a particularly unpopular general, described by Cicero as 'deeply hated by the gods and the nobility', who had captured Asculum during the Social War only to be struck by lightning as he lay sick in his tent and whose corpse was then mutilated by his own troops. Young Pompey was much more popular and used his inheritance to recruit and organize an army of three legions in the region of Picenum from his own funds, 'and provided them with food, transport animals, wagons, and all other necessary equipment'.[13] The force included a cavalry contingent of unknown strength, presumably from the other local landowning families. With this private army he set off to join up with Sulla's army.

Three Marian armies tried to converge on Pompey, but he seized the initiative and concentrated all his forces against one of them, which included a force of auxiliary Celtic cavalry.

> He stationed his cavalry, in which he was himself, at the front and when from the enemy's army also the Celtic cavalry rode out to engage him, he at once closed with the foremost and the strongest one of them and with a blow of his spear struck him down from his horse. The rest turned and fled, throwing the infantry also into confusion so that there was a general rout.[14]

The other two armies beat a hasty retreat, allowing Pompey to bring his force to the support of Sulla, whose forces were sweeping all before them en route to the capital.

Sulla's victorious progress almost fell at the last fence. At Signia he shattered the forces directly commanded by the younger Marius, who fled to Praeneste. Although the road to Rome now lay open, Sulla moved north to besiege Praeneste. Some Samnite troops allied to Marius started to move directly to the latter's relief, but with Pompey's force also converging on them, instead made a bold dash for Rome.

The Samnites had been citizens since the Social War, but they had once been the most implacable foe amongst Rome's neighbours. When the Samnite general camped just a mile from the Colline Gate, the prospect of the old enemy entering Rome under arms caused a panic in Rome. But 'at dawn the next day', Plutarch writes, 'the most distinguished young men in Rome rode out against him', the *equites* stirred out of their cautious neutrality by the threat to the city.[15] Many of them were killed but they bought enough time for Sulla, belatedly alerted to the danger, to hurry back.

First upon the scene were seven hundred of his cavalry, hard-riding veteran auxiliaries from his eastern campaigns, who 'came riding up at full speed'. Their officer, Balbus, here confronted an age-old dilemma of the cavalry commander: the need to make the most of speed and surprise had to be weighed against the inadvisability of going into action on blown horses, jaded from a long gallop. He ordered his men to dismount to rest the horses. According to Plutarch, he 'halted just long enough to let the sweat dry off the horses'; but as it is evident that they were unbridled, it was perhaps also long enough for them to have been brought water and corn, or at least to get their heads down for a little grass. With the savage, high-ported bits used by the Romans, they could not easily eat while bridled. Balbus 'then bridled them again as quickly as possible and engaged the enemy'.[16] Sulla's main forces pitched in as they came up and the battle of the Colline Gate, as it has become known, was the most desperately contested of the war. Indeed, the left wing under Sulla's direct command was routed and he thought the battle lost, only learning later that his subordinate, Crassus, had been victorious on the other wing and had saved Rome.

It is fitting that one of the last rides of the old Roman aristocratic cavalry was right outside the gates of the city itself and saved it from the Samnites. That they saved the city for Sulla is ironic as his two *coups d'état* prefigured the death of the republican ideal in civil war. More immediately, the direct aftermath of his return to Rome may well have put the last nail in the coffin of the traditional citizen cavalry. Having secured his grip on Italy, Sulla ordered a savage programme of purges. Those suspected of supporting the Marian faction were proscribed, that is to say their names were added to lists posted up in the forum announcing that there was a reward of two talents for their deaths. In this bloodletting it was the wealthy equestrian classes that suffered most, because the property of the proscribed was confiscated and resold. Plutarch relates the anecdote of one Quintus Aurelius who quipped, 'things are bad for me, I am being hunted down by my Alban estate', shortly before he was killed. Inevitably many informed on others innocent of any complicity with Marius, to wipe out debts or personal grudges. Untold damage was done to the old equestrian families, not only in terms of actual numbers but in depoliticizing and dampening down the ethos of civic duty in those that survived (or took their place through ill-gotten wealth).

The first civil war did not end with Sulla's return to Rome, as Marian forces remained at large in some of the provinces. Most were mopped up quickly enough but those in Spain under Sertorius held out against the central government armies until 73 BC, long after Sulla's death. Initially Sertorius had around eight thousand men, including seven hundred cavalry, against total government forces of 120,000 infantry and six thousand cavalry. He was, however, careful to cultivate the loyalty of the natives and later was often able to achieve local numerical superiority, himself possibly fielding up to six thousand cavalry.[17]

Although both sides made use of fine Iberian and Celtiberian horsemen, it was Sertorius who embraced the traditional Spanish way of

warfare, waging a guerrilla campaign characterized by 'his uncon-
ventional attacks, his ambushes, and his flanking movements', which
Plutarch says bewildered his first opponent, Metellus Pius, 'a man
whose whole training was in regular pitched battles and who commanded troops which were heavily armed and lacking in mobility'.[18]
Even Pompey, whose early career had shown a talent for improvisa-
tion and vigorous command, learnt some harsh lessons at the hands
of Sertorius, who allegedly dismissed him as a mere boy he would take
a stick to. Although mounted troops still played a useful role in raiding, patrolling and protecting marching columns and foragers, there
were relatively few opportunities for heavy cavalry to indulge in shock
action.

Eventually the rebels' power base was greatly eroded by a strategy
that centred on the systematic capturing of strongholds, similar to that
employed against the slippery Jugurtha. Sertorius responded with a
campaign of wide-ranging attacks on Roman supply lines. It was probably in this phase that his cavalry were most prominent. By the winter
of 75/74 BC Pompey was warning the senate that his troops were unpaid
and on the verge of starvation. Ultimately, Sertorius' failure to inflict
major defeats in battle allowed his war effort to be gradually strangled
by Rome's superior resources. His followers started to desert and in 73
BC he was assassinated and supplanted by one of his own commanders,
who proved far less skilful and was swiftly defeated.

Rome's military resources, meanwhile, were further stretched by the
resurgent threat at the other extreme of the Mediterranean. A second
Mithridatic war had been deliberately provoked in 83 BC by Murena, the
man left by Sulla to govern Asia. This resulted in a humiliating defeat
for Murena's forces and the loss, once more, of the client kingdom of
Cappadocia, which was only partly restored by a negotiated settlement
brokered by Sulla. In 78 BC King Tigranes of Armenia, the son-in-law
of Mithridates, invaded Cappadocia and reputedly sent three hundred
thousand of the inhabitants in chains to his capital, Tigranocerta. By
75 BC Mithridates had allied himself with Sertorius, who sent him some
Roman advisers, and prepared for war with Rome. When, in 74 BC, the
childless king of Bithynia died and bequeathed his kingdom to Rome,
Mithridates invaded. Pontic forces quickly swept through Paphlagonia
and Bithynia and on into the Roman province of Asia, besieging the
Roman governor in Chalcedon.

For this Third Mithridatic War, the Pontic king is alleged to have
gathered 140,000 infantry and sixteen thousand cavalry. The latter

included Armenians, Scythians, Bastarnae (called 'the bravest nation of all' by Appian) and Sarmatians of the Iazyge and Basilidae tribes. It was a markedly smaller mounted force than Mithridates had fielded in the first war, undoubtedly due in part to the depletion of horse stocks in the war-ravaged region, but it was still sufficient to give him a massive superiority over the Romans in this arm. This advantage was, however, frittered away by misuse and strategic ineptitude, skilfully exploited by the Roman commanders.

Even after urgent local recruiting, Lucius Licinius Lucullus, the consul sent out from Rome to restore the situation, was only able to field 1600 cavalry and thirty thousand infantry. He moved these forces up close to where Mithridates was now besieging Cyzicus. With a tenfold advantage in cavalry, Mithridates might have been expected to attempt a war of manoeuvre to force the Romans into a pitched battle on unfavourable terms. Instead he repeated the mistake his general Archelaus had made against Sulla in the first war, persisting with the siege and allowing himself to be tied to the positional warfare that best suited the Romans. Even if unwilling to abandon the siege, his horsemen should have been able to dominate the surrounding area to prevent the Romans foraging. In the event, the collusion of one of Mithridates' Roman advisers (one of those sent by Sertorius, who was by this time dead) allowed Lucullus to occupy a strategically located mountain, thereby cutting off Mithridates' supply lines and penning him in against the city.

As the siege progressed, Mithridates' cavalry horses rapidly lost condition from lack of fodder and suffered from 'sore hooves', probably from malnourishment causing the keratin of the hoof wall to become brittle. He therefore took the decision to send them back to Bithynia to preserve them for future operations. Lucullus got wind of this and ambushed them as they crossed a river. Some were killed but fifteen thousand men and six thousand horses were captured. With his cavalry effectively destroyed at a single stroke, Mithridates abandoned the siege and withdrew to Bithynia, suffering heavy losses en route due to the lack of cavalry protection.

By 72 BC Lucullus felt ready to carry the war into Pontic territory. His initial advance, however, was halted by defeat in a cavalry engagement in which his cavalry commander was captured. Although Mithridates had been able to muster only four thousand cavalry, they still heavily outnumbered those with the Roman forces. Lucullus took up a strong mountainside position and refused battle out of respect for the enemy's continued cavalry superiority. Fortune and his opponents' blundering, however, again came to Lucullus' aid. Mithridates sent a picked force of cavalry to ambush a vital Roman supply column. The attackers were beaten off with heavy casualties as they ineptly attempted to launch a mounted attack in a narrow defile. This need not have been more than a frustrating setback if the shaken survivors had not galloped back into the Pontic camp by night, causing widespread alarm that quickly escalated into panic and the flight of the whole army. The next morning Lucullus unleashed his remaining cavalry in pursuit and Mithridates was lucky to escape to Tigranes in Armenia with just two thousand cavalry.

In 69 BC Lucullus, having effectively secured and garrisoned Pontus, invaded Armenia with two legions and five hundred cavalry. Tigranes sent two thousand cavalry to slow the Roman advance, but these were routed in the first encounter and part of the Roman force laid siege to the capital. Tigranes had raised a vast army, said by Appian to include a barely possible fifty thousand cavalry. He sent six thousand of these to the capital, where they succeeded in breaking through the Roman lines and rescuing the royal concubines. Mithridates warned him against meeting the Romans in open battle, advising him instead to harass them with cavalry and devastate the country in their path to deny them supplies. Tigranes, however, was determined to fight and brought his army close to the Romans.

In the battle that followed it was Lucullus' tactical skill and clever use of the terrain that negated the enemy superiority in numbers. His tiny cavalry force was used to draw off a large portion of the enemy cavalry by means of a feigned retreat, a typically eastern ploy that may demonstrate that Lucullus had learnt a lot while in the east. Meanwhile, the legions marched under cover of dead ground to seize a hill in the rear of the enemy and then their camp. The sudden danger behind them, and the threat to their possessions, threw the whole Armenian army into chaos. When Tigranes' cavalry abandoned their chase to hurry back to assist, the Roman cavalry turned on their erstwhile pursuers and routed them, leading to the complete collapse of any remaining organized resistance. Tigranes escaped but his capital fell shortly after.

The following year Tigranes and Mithridates, having scoured the countryside to raise another army of 70,000 infantry and 35,000 (mostly Armenian) cavalry, tried again. This time Tigranes attempted to follow his father-in-law's advice, sending a large force of horsemen to attack a detachment of Roman troops out foraging. The legionaries, warned of the attack by the inevitable dust cloud, managed to take up arms and get into close formation in time to repulse the attack. Mithridates and Tigranes then decided to surround the whole of Lucullus' army by dividing their forces and marching around him on both sides. Lucullus, again warned by the dust cloud, sent out 'the best of his cavalry' to oppose them and delay their deployment while he led out the legions, which seems to have succeeded despite the odds. Although we lack any detail of exactly how this was achieved, it may well be symptomatic of Lucullus' cavalry having achieved a significant psychological advantage over their Pontic and Armenian counterparts, whose morale must by now have been at rock bottom.

While Tigranes withdrew to the depths of central Armenia, a dispirited but determined Mithridates marched towards Pontus with just eight thousand troops, half of them Armenian. Here he defeated the legate in command of the Roman garrison, who was then forced to arm freed slaves for a second battle. In this Mithridates was again carrying the day until he was severely wounded in the knee and face and forced to retire. Another legate, Triarius, assumed command of the local Roman forces and was able to hold off Mithridates in an inconclusive battle before both sides retired to winter quarters. In 67 BC, Mithridates again faced Triarius and scattered his army by means of a powerful cavalry charge. As he led the pursuit, a suicidally courageous Roman officer managed in the confusion to ride unnoticed for some time among his entourage until the opportunity presented itself to strike. Seeing that the king's body was too well armoured to wound him there, the Roman ran his sword into Mithridates' thigh, only to be cut to pieces by his bodyguard. Although his officers halted the pursuit, again preventing Mithridates from fully exploiting his advantage, the Roman casualties were already heavy and included twenty-four tribunes and one hundred and fifty centurions.

Lucullus, accused of deliberately prolonging the war, was replaced in 66 BC by Pompey, who had followed victory in Spain by mopping up the remnants of Spartacus' rebellious slaves in Italy and a dazzlingly successful campaign against piracy throughout the Mediterranean. Both Pompey and Mithridates, who must by now have been scraping the bottom of the recruiting barrel, fielded around thirty thousand infantry, although the Romans enjoyed a qualitative superiority. Mithridates' main hope still lay with his cavalry, of which he had three thousand compared to Pompey's two thousand. This was a much more slender margin of superiority than he was used to, but still significant, and Pompey initially showed the respect it deserved by encamping on wooded slopes.

As the two armies squared off near the Pontic border, Pompey showed that he had learnt more about cavalry warfare than the older Mithridates. When Pompey sent most of his cavalry towards the enemy camp, Mithridates obligingly sent his own cavalry out to meet the challenge. The Roman cavalry then feigned flight and led their pursuers away before turning on them just as the rest of the Roman cavalry, who had been waiting in concealment, attacked them in the rear. The Pontic cavalry could have guarded against such an eventuality by having part of their force follow at a safe distance to meet such a development, but instead they were easily surrounded. If Mithridates himself had not quickly come to their support with a large body of infantry, even fewer would have escaped than was actually the case.

With his one advantage severely diminished, and unable to draw sufficient supplies from countryside denuded by years of warfare, Mithridates retreated into the interior of Pontus, hoping that similar supply problems would halt Pompey. Pompey, however, had organized his supply lines carefully and again came up with Mithridates and started to encircle his army with fortifications. Mithridates stubbornly held his position until his men were starving and all the pack animals had been slaughtered before attempting to break out towards Armenia by night. The cavalry horses had not been slaughtered and had somehow been kept in sufficiently good condition to beat off Pompey's cavalry when they attacked the rearguard of the escaping army the following day.

Now it was Mithridates' turn to take to hiding in woodland and rocky slopes, marching only by night for fear of the enemy horsemen. He never reached Armenia, as he suffered a final defeat shortly after, although our main sources, Appian and Plutarch, are in disagreement as to how this came about. Plutarch describes Pompey ambushing the Pontic column by moonlight as it straggled through a narrow defile. Appian also places the action in a defile, but in broad daylight. The two armies were camped close together and the outposts had been skirmishing for some time. Due to the nature of the ground, some Pontic cavalrymen had left their horses in camp when going to the support of their outposts, only to be attacked by Roman horsemen. Perhaps these auxiliaries more readily accepted the risk of injury to their mounts on the broken ground because they knew that Rome would compensate them for any horses lost in action, whereas Mithridates' men probably provided their own and in any case knew that remounts were not going to be found easily. The Pontic horsemen rushed back to fetch their horses, but by suddenly bursting into the camp in disarray and mounting up they triggered a panic among the unprepared troops there. Pompey took full advantage and stormed the camp with great slaughter. In both versions about ten thousand Pontic troops were killed and many more captured. Mithridates managed to flee with a small number of cavalry, eventually reaching lands ruled by his son, who had failed to help him, north of the Black Sea. Here he continued to plot Rome's downfall until the rebellion of his son finally drove him to suicide.[19]

It is highly unlikely that any of the cavalry units used against Mithridates were composed of *equites* serving in the traditional manner, but it is not impossible. We can be certain, however, that they had vanished altogether by the time Julius Caesar began his campaigns of conquest in Gaul in 58 BC. That Caesar relied entirely on allied tribal cavalry is easily illustrated by an incident in that year. He was invited to parley with an enemy general, with instructions to attend accompanied only by a cavalry bodyguard. Because he had with him only Gallic cavalry, whom he didn't entirely trust, Caesar made them lend their horses to infantrymen from his favourite legion, the Tenth. Caesar himself records that one wag from the Tenth declared his pleasure at being elevated to equestrian status.[20]

Given the Celtic reputation as mounted warriors and of Gaul as a source of horses, it was inevitable that cavalry should play a major role in Caesar's campaigns there. His Gallic auxiliary cavalry fought in their native equipment in units led by their own chieftains, although large groupings of units would be put under a Roman officer. Most would have helmets of various designs, the best of which formed the basis of Roman legionary helmets, having cheek-pieces and good protection for the back of the neck. Those that could afford them would have chain mail shirts, and this would apply to an increasing number of warriors as the rewards of Roman service were accrued. All would have carried shields and various styles of spear, many of them suitable for both throwing and thrusting, in addition to long-bladed swords. With both sides fielding essentially identical troops, numbers should often have been the decisive factor, although in practice the smaller force often emerged victorious, demonstrating the supreme importance of leadership, morale and tactical handling.

Caesar's first campaign in Gaul was to repel an invasion by the Helvetii, an as yet unconquered Celtic tribe, attempting to migrate into the Roman province of Transalpine Gaul. Having apparently turned the enemy host back by ambushing part of their force as they crossed the Rhone, Caesar unleashed his four thousand cavalry in pursuit. Living up to the stereotype of brave but undisciplined Celts, they got carried away with the chase and slaughter and were in complete disarray when counter-attacked by a mere five hundred Helvetic horsemen. Panicking, they fled back to the protection of the legions. Perhaps Caesar had underestimated the fight left in the enemy and maybe he should have insisted on part of the force being held back in reserve, but in his account, which we are forced to rely upon as our main source, he prefers to blame the treachery of the leader of the tribal unit that fled first.

As a direct result of this débâcle, the Helvetic cavalry became bolder over the next few days, even attempting to provoke Caesar's cavalry into another massed attack, and their leaders were soon encouraged to turn on their pursuers with their whole massive force. The Roman legions were just encamping for the night, near a place called Bibracte, when a wave of Celtic warriors rushed upon them from a nearby wood. Caesar sent his cavalry to delay them but they could achieve little against the dense onrushing masses and were easily driven off, barely buying enough time for the legions to form a viable line of battle. The legions were eventually victorious and the Helvetii driven back to the Alps with massive losses, but it was this uninspiring start by the cavalry, which hinted strongly of indiscipline and fragile morale, which led Caesar to rely on his improvised cavalry as his bodyguard on the occasion referred to above.

Despite this and later setbacks, Caesar went on to make extensive use of his Gallic cavalry when, having secured his province, he proceeded to conquer the rest of Gaul. He completed the initial conquest by the end of the following year, 57 BC, by defeating a confederation of the Belgic tribes of the north east. Learning that the combined Belgic army was approaching the River Sambre, he crossed and fortified a strong position on the far bank to await their attack. Greatly outnumbered by enemies with a 'great reputation for bravery', Caesar began tentatively by sending out the cavalry to test them and 'soon found that his troops were as good as theirs'. When the Belgae detached a large part of their force to outflank Caesar's position and cut his supply routes by fording the river further along, they were intercepted and defeated by his cavalry and some slingers and archers. Many Belgic warriors were killed in the water by showers of arrows and slingshot, but those who had already crossed were surrounded and cut down by the cavalry.

The Belgic army fell apart soon after as each contingent fell back upon its own fortified towns. When Caesar learnt of this, he first sent out patrols to assess the situation and only then ordered the rest of his cavalry to harass the rear of the straggling columns. He had clearly learnt from the incident with the Helvetii. His cavalry overwhelmed a rearguard that 'put up a gallant resistance' and then pursued the rest, who were now in full flight 'for many miles'. 'Thus our troops were able, without any risk, to kill as many of them as there was time to kill', before nightfall caused them to halt.[21]

The fragmentation of the enemy effort allowed Caesar to defeat them one tribe at a time. The last major test of this phase came when the Nervii, who lived in particularly densely wooded country and so made less use of cavalry than most Gauls, ambushed the Romans as they were about to encamp on a hill overlooking a stream in a narrow valley. The Roman cavalry had been sent to the far bank, to provide a forward screen while the camp was built, and were keeping an eye on a few scattered enemy horsemen who would retreat into the dense woods behind them whenever threatened. Suddenly, the main infantry force of the enemy erupted from the tree line in a wild charge. Surprised and with little room for manoeuvre, Caesar's cavalry were quickly routed, just as they had been in similar circumstances against the Helvetii at Bibracte. The Roman infantry were even harder pressed this time, the camp was overrun and Caesar himself had to take up a shield and risk his life in the thick of the fighting to sustain the men's morale. This time, however, the cavalry did eventually manage to rally, albeit after the Tenth Legion had already defeated their immediate opponents and stabilized the situation by marching to the rescue of the camp. There was still a lot of hard fighting to be done: 'the horsemen,' explains Caesar, 'that they might by their valour blot out the disgrace of their flight, thrust themselves before the legionary soldiers in all parts of the battle.'[22] The Nervii were almost annihilated and their remaining allies forced to surrender soon after.

Although the whole of Gaul had now been made to bend its knee to Roman might, it was by no means fully pacified. Caesar's auxiliary cavalry, deliberately drawn from across most of the province, played a vital role in suppressing the annual rebellions of various combinations of tribes which broke out over the next few years. In addition to protecting the legions on the march, they often ranged ahead of them to devastate the rebel territory. Sometimes Caesar used his cavalry as an independent flying column to strike the enemy at the first hint of insurrection, before they could even properly gather their forces. In early 53 BC, for example, Caesar sent his whole cavalry force into the territory of the rebellious Euberones, giving their Roman officer instructions 'to see if he could gain any advantage by travelling quickly and striking at a favourable opportunity'.[23] Arriving before any news of their approach, they very nearly succeeded in capturing the rebel chieftain Ambiorix in his own home.

The Gauls excelled in these operations, which called upon the same skills as the low-level raiding that was the mainstay of intertribal warfare. Formal battles were rare in these campaigns and such fights as occurred with enemy horsemen tell us relatively little about the auxiliaries' actual combat skills. Caesar, who could assume a certain level of technical knowledge of such things in his contemporary readership, doesn't describe them in great detail, a tendency encouraged by the fact that his cavalry were usually fighting against identical opponents (his auxiliaries had to bare their right shoulders in battle to distinguish themselves from the foe). More instructive are the encounters they had with less similar opponents.

When Caesar made his first raid into Britain in 55 BC, bad weather in the Channel forced the ships bearing his cavalry to return to the Continent. Those carrying the infantry completed the crossing, but horses make a far less stable cargo unless carried in specially designed ships divided internally into numerous narrow horse boxes, a fact which the Athenians had realized as early as the Peloponnesian War but which Caesar seems to have overlooked in his haste on this occasion. Caesar was therefore forced to continue the operation without cavalry support. The very limited achievements of this first expedition are usually attributed to the fact that further storms damaged more of the Roman fleet, threatening to cut Caesar off from Gaul over the winter, but it was his own weakness in cavalry that prevented him from achieving more while his ships were being repaired.

Even before the Romans were off their ships, the British superiority in mounted troops was causing difficulties. The idea, still to be found repeated in print, that the Britons had no cavalry before the Roman conquest (supposedly relying entirely on chariots due to their undersized ponies) is laughable. Caesar's own account describes how the natives opposed the landing by sending forward 'their cavalry and a number of the chariots which they are accustomed to use in warfare', while the infantry deployed behind.[24]

It is not surprising that the Roman soldiers, faced with leaping into deep water from high-sided transports while encumbered with armour and attacked by British cavalry and chariots galloping into the surf to hurl javelins at them, 'did not show the same alacrity and enthusiasm as they usually did'. Caesar ordered his shallower warships to run themselves aground on the beach on the right flank, the looming ships apparently frightening the Britons, or more probably their horses. The British were then driven back some way with a barrage from the catapults, slingers and archers on the ships' decks and the legionaries reluctantly resumed their attempt to land.

> Both sides fought hard. But as the Romans could not keep their ranks or get a firm foothold or follow their proper standards, and men from different ships fell in under the first standard they came across, great confusion resulted. The enemy knew all the shallows, and when they saw from the beach small parties of soldiers disembarking one by one, they galloped up and attacked them at a disadvantage, surrounding them with superior numbers, while others would throw javelins at the right flank [their unshielded side] of a whole group.[25]

Caught at such a disadvantage, it is a testament to the discipline and training of these veteran troops that they eventually got themselves into some sort of order and drove off the Britons, although no pursuit was possible without their own cavalry. It seems also that British cavalry were more lightly equipped than the continental Celts, or at least less inclined to shock action, relying more on javelin throwing. A decent force of shock cavalry should have made Caesar's troops pay much more dearly in this situation. On a subsequent occasion the Seventh legion was encircled and attacked by British horsemen and chariots while gathering crops. The Gauls had stopped using chariots in war centuries before, so they were a novelty to Caesar and he accordingly described their tactics in detail:

> First, they drive about in all directions and throw their weapons and generally break the ranks of the enemy with the very dread of their horses and the noise of their wheels; and when they have worked themselves in between the troops of horse [who were presumably also attacking with their javelins], leap from their chariots and engage on foot. The charioteers in the meantime withdraw some little distance from the battle, and so place themselves with the chariots that, if their masters are overpowered by the number of the enemy, they may have a ready retreat to their own troops. Thus they display in battle the speed of horse, the firmness of infantry; and by daily practice and exercise attain such expertness that they are accustomed, even on a declining and steep place to check their horses at full speed, and manage and turn them in an instant and run along the pole, and

stand on the yoke, and thence betake themselves with the greatest celerity to their chariots again.[26]

Caesar, alerted by the clouds of dust thrown up, arrived in the nick of time with reinforcements to find 'our men being dismayed by the novelty of this mode of battle'. The enemy backed off to regroup but Caesar, who relates with marvellous understatement that he deemed the situation 'unfavourable for provoking the enemy', meekly withdrew his whole force to their camp.

Emboldened, the British gathered 'a large force of infantry and cavalry', and presumably chariots, and marched on Caesar's camp a few days later.[27] Caesar was unsure about emerging to give battle, seeing that even if he beat them his own shortage of cavalry would allow the enemy to escape. Apparently what tipped the scales in favour of fighting in the open was the arrival of a mere thirty Gallic cavalry that had finally made the crossing. In the event the legions, fighting with the safety of the fortifications at their backs, easily overawed and routed the enemy. As soon as his storm-damaged ships were sufficiently repaired, Caesar was happy to return to the Continent, consoling himself with British promises of hostages and payments, although these went almost completely unfulfilled.

When Caesar prepared to return to Britain the following year, he gathered 'the cavalry of the whole of Gaul, four thousand in number'.[28] This was not in fact the full cavalry strength Gaul was capable of, as later events would demonstrate, but contingents representing all the tribes. Half of these, and three legions, he left with his most trusted lieutenant. The remaining two thousand embarked in specially constructed transports, designed to be both more seaworthy and capable of rapid unloading in case he faced another contested landing. Caesar also took five legions, some twenty to twenty-five thousand men, the cavalry representing a similar portion of the total force as in armies raised under the old citizen militia system.

This time the landing was unopposed, a few prisoners brought in by patrols revealing that their compatriots had been overawed by the size of the fleet, some eight hundred ships in total, and had 'concealed themselves on the higher points'. Leaving three hundred cavalry and a strong force of infantry to protect the ships and camp, Caesar made a rapid night march to where the main concentration of the enemy was reported. At dawn the two forces were in sight of each other and the British sent their cavalry and chariots 'to annoy our men and give battle'.

These were repulsed by Caesar's cavalry, whereupon the whole British force retreated to a strongly fortified position in dense woodland. This was stormed by the Roman infantry later that day with fierce fighting, but the fleeing enemy could not be pursued due to the late hour.[29]

The strategic pursuit was further delayed when Caesar learnt that much of his fleet had again been wrecked by gales in the Channel. But this was not to be a rerun of the previous expedition with the Romans penned defensively on the coast and Caesar resumed the offensive as soon as he had set the repair of his fleet in motion. This in spite of news that many of the British tribes had this time united temporarily to oppose him, sending large numbers of warriors, including many horsemen and chariots, to serve under the command of Cassivellaunus, a chieftain of great experience. The only strategic factor that had changed in favour of a Roman advance since the previous year was the presence of the auxiliary cavalry.

When British mounted troops attempted to attack the Romans on the march, they were met by the Gallic cavalry. It was 'a fierce encounter', writes Caesar, 'but our men had the best of it everywhere and drove them into the woods and hills, killing a good many'.[30] Some casualties were sustained when the Gauls repeated the old mistake of pursuing too eagerly, no doubt being counter-attacked once their formation was lost and their horses blown, but the march continued.

Later that day the Romans were once more attacked at the vulnerable time when most of the legionnaires were busy fortifying the day's camp. British cavalry and chariots swept out of the surrounding trees and attacked the outposts. More and more reinforcements had to be drawn from the defences and sent out to join the fight. Caesar again describes the difficulty that his men, both infantry and cavalry, had in dealing with the bewildering and highly flexible tactics of the enemy chariots: rapid attacks and feigned retreats to draw off a few pursuers who were then assaulted by the charioteers dismounting to fight as infantry. In addition, chariot wheels were apparently very noisy, and their squealing may well have upset horses not accustomed to them.

The British cavalry were also a tricky proposition, refining the usual elusive hit and run tactics of light cavalry with a clear appreciation of the value of mutually supporting units and tactical reserves.

In engaging their cavalry our men were not much better off: their tactics were such that the danger was exactly the same for pursuer and pursued. A further difficulty was that they never fought in very close order, but in very open formation, and had reserves posted here and there; in this way the various groups covered one another's retreat and fresh troops replaced those who were tired.[31]

Frustrating as such tactics were, they lacked sufficient hitting power to defeat well-organized and well-led troops fighting in the security of close formation, and the attack was eventually beaten off. The British then attempted to attack Roman troops while they were out on a foraging mission, as they had done the previous year with some success. Caesar had sent out three legions, protected by all his cavalry. The legions stood up to the assault well, but the fight was only concluded when the cavalry struck a really telling blow:

> The cavalry ... made a charge that sent the natives flying headlong. A great many were killed and the rest given no chance of rallying or making a stand or jumping from their chariots. This rout caused the immediate dispersal of the forces that had assembled from various tribes to Cassivellaunus' aid, and the Britons never again joined battle with their whole strength.[32]

Cassivellaunus retreated to his own territory with Caesar hot on his heels and tried to defend the only ford across the River Thames, but his demoralized troops fled in the face of an impetuous attack across the shallows led by Caesar's cavalry with the infantry in close support. Cassivellaunus now gave up all hope of defeating the Romans in the open and decided instead to wear them down by means of a guerrilla campaign. Disbanding most of his forces, he retained only some four thousand charioteers (Caesar might mean two thousand chariots with two men to each, still a very impressive force). With these he shadowed the Roman column as it marched through his territory, wreaking punitive destruction as it went. Making good use of his local knowledge of woodland paths, he launched 'formidable attacks' on any Roman cavalry detachments that strayed too far afield. This forced Caesar to keep the cavalry close to the main column and 'let the enemy off with such devastation and burning as could be done under the protection of the legionaries'; but these were essentially nuisance tactics and couldn't do enough damage to prevent Caesar reaching Cassivellaunus' main stronghold, which the legions stormed in short order. Cassivellaunus was still at large but sent an envoy to ask for terms of surrender. Caesar, anxious to return to the Continent before winter closed in, set an annual tribute and took hostages as a guarantee, before returning to the coast and withdrawing his whole force.[33]

The encounters between the Gallic cavalry and Germanic opponents make an even more interesting case study. In particular they throw an interesting light on the subject of saddles. It is only with Caesar's Gallic cavalry that we can finally discuss with safety the use of the famous Celtic 'horned saddle'. Such saddles are first represented on the Gundeström Cauldron (although even this is open to interpretation), which is usually assigned a late second century or early first century BC dating, and more clearly on a relief of a battle between Gauls and Romans found near Provence. Many clear examples were later depicted on the first century AD tombstones of auxiliary cavalrymen in Roman service.

Constructed of leather over a wood and horn frame, this type of saddle has a pair of rigid, slightly curved 'horns' at the front, and another pair at the back, which hold the rider's seat in place. In addition to generally improved security against unseating by sudden changes of direction or speed by the horse, these helped the effective use of the rider's weapons. The rear horns are held to have special significance in allowing a successful charge with a lance to connect without the rider being driven back over his horse's rump by the 'equal and opposite reaction' of his lance striking its target. The front horns also offer lateral stability because the rider could use his knees tucked under them to shift his weight to either side or could even lean far over to take a swing with a sword, giving him greater reach. Reconstructions of such saddles have performed impressively in tests, although it should by now be clear that riders had been managing lance and sword effectively enough for centuries before their introduction.[34]

Such technological advances were no doubt a welcome aid to those who used them, but those tempted to attribute the horned saddle with the same decisive revolutionary status long-enjoyed by the stirrup should beware. One might expect that the combination of the long-famed Celtic prowess as mounted warriors with this new state-of-the-art military equipment (to which add spurs, superior ironwork in their weapons and armour and, at first, larger horses) would have proved unstoppable, yet it is the German cavalry who really stand out in Caesar's accounts and we are specifically told they did not have the advantage of saddles. Indeed, Caesar makes clear that the Germans positively scorned such aids as a sign of weakness: 'In their eyes it is the height of effeminacy and shame to use a saddle, and they do not hesitate to engage the largest force of cavalry riding saddled horses, however small their own numbers may be.'[35]

The first relevant encounter occurred in 58 BC. Shortly after Caesar's victory over the Helvetii, in which his cavalry had made a poor impression, many Gallic tribes sent envoys seeking Roman friendship and protection. During an earlier war between rival groupings of Gallic tribes, one side had hired a large group of mercenaries from the Germanic tribes across the Rhine. These mercenaries, finding fertile Gaul to their liking and seeing an opportunity in the war-weariness of their hosts, decided to seize a slice of it for themselves and invited more German warriors over to share in the enterprise. By 58 BC many of the Gallic tribes were exhausted by their efforts to contain the Germans and so now sought Caesar's aid, the Aedui in particular relating that most of their noble cavalry had perished. Caesar, quick to seize an opportunity for further glory and to ensure the submission of his new clients, agreed to help. It was Ariovistus, the leader of these Germans, whom he went to meet with his improvised guard of infantrymen mounted on horses, but the ensuing negotiations broke down and a test of arms was required.

As the two armies faced each other for several days, sizing each other up for the coming battle, the cavalry regularly skirmished in the space between their two camps. Caesar's four thousand Gauls were heavily outnumbered and may also have been discomfited by the German practice of integrating light infantry with their cavalry.

> The Germans were trained in the use of a special battle technique. They had a force of six thousand cavalry, each of whom had selected from the whole army, for his personal protection, one infantryman of outstanding courage and speed of foot. These accompanied the cavalry in battle and acted as a support for them to fall back upon. In a critical situation they ran to the rescue and surrounded any cavalryman who had been unhorsed by a severe wound. They acquired such agility by practice, that in a long advance or a quick retreat they could hang on to the horses' manes and keep pace with them.[36]

Caesar reports this tactic as something novel, but his descriptions of later fights demonstrate that some Gallic cavalry were familiar with the practice, and he would employ it himself in the Civil War. Of course, similar methods had been employed by various people over the centuries, notably the Numidians but also the Romans themselves at Capua in the Second Punic War. If it seemed novel to Caesar, this merely highlights a simple fact of ancient warfare: although some tactical treatises existed along with the memoirs of various generals, the absence of systematic officer training meant that successive generations largely learnt to deal with each tactical situation by direct experience. Caesar is silent as to who had the better of these skirmishes, but that in itself probably indicates that his Gauls failed to excel themselves.

When Caesar finally forced a pitched battle upon the Germans, his cavalry were clearly held in reserve, for at a crucial point of the battle it was 'young Publius Crassus, who was in charge of the cavalry', who spotted that the Roman left was in danger of being turned and ordered up the third line of infantry. Caesar explains that he was able to do so 'because he was better able to move around and see what was happening than those in the fighting line'. The fact that the cavalry themselves were not sent in at this point may indicate that the German horsemen were still hovering nearby, necessitating that the Roman cavalry mass be kept intact and ready to counter them. The German cavalry are not in fact mentioned at all in Caesar's account and it may simply be that cavalry played such a small role because of unsuitable terrain, Caesar having advanced close to the German camp, which was sited 'at the foot of a mountain'. When the Germans were defeated and the survivors scattered in flight towards the Rhine, Caesar unleashed his cavalry in pursuit and he himself rode in the chase. A few managed to swim the river and Ariovistus himself escaped by boat. 'All the rest', claims Caesar, 'were hunted down and killed by our cavalry.'[37]

In 55 BC two German tribes, the Usipetes and Tenctheri, migrated into Gaul. They scored an early success when their cavalry demonstrated the great stamina of their shaggy little mounts by making what would normally have been a three-day march in one night. The Gallic Menapii were taken by surprise and slaughtered. Caesar, having gathered his auxiliary cavalry, brought his army close to the enemy while simultaneously engaging them in negotiations. Caesar claims that he gave specific orders to his cavalry vanguard not to provoke the enemy and only to act in self-defence, as a truce was theoretically in force while envoys shuttled back and forth. Caesar suspected the Germans were playing for time as the bulk of their cavalry, that is their noblemen and leaders, were absent in search of forage and plunder, although it is quite possible he himself already intended to launch a pre-emptive attack.

Although not more than eight hundred German horsemen were present, as soon as they caught sight of Caesar's cavalry they charged and 'soon threw them into disorder' – all five thousand of them. The Celts did not break immediately, 'but in their turn, made a stand' and a sharp fight ensued in which the Germans, 'overthrowing a great many

of our men, put the rest to flight'.[38] It is true that many Germans dismounted to fight once they found themselves in the midst of the Celtic
host, even employing the decidedly underhand tactic of stabbing horses
in the belly, but this needn't indicate that their lack of saddles rendered
them too unstable for true mounted combat, which they engaged in
on other occasions. The lesson of this incident is that decisive leadership, initiative and offensive spirit are often more important factors in
cavalry warfare than technological ones, however useful.

Following this débâcle, Caesar realized that to delay giving battle
again would only allow the rest of the German cavalry to return and
that he must act quickly. When German envoys again approached the
next morning, Caesar had them arrested and led his whole army on a
rapid march towards the enemy, with the infantry marching in three
parallel columns that could readily be turned into the customary triple
battle line. His cavalry, having again lost their commander's trust,
were relegated to bringing up the rear 'because he thought it had been
demoralized by its recent defeat'.[39] The Germans were surprised in
their camp and offered only a brief and uncoordinated resistance to the
Roman infantry before they scattered in desperate flight; only then were
Caesar's cavalry unleashed in pursuit.

In 53 BC, when Caesar declared the territory of the rebellious
Euberones open to plundering by all neighbouring tribes, the Sugam-
bri, a German tribe, sent two thousand horsemen across the Rhine to
get their share. Some of their Euberone prisoners persuaded them that
richer pickings were to be had by attacking a Roman outpost where
Caesar had left a large part of his stores guarded by one legion and two
hundred auxiliary cavalry. The Germans appeared shortly after the
garrison commander had reluctantly allowed five cohorts (theoretically
around 2500 men but probably understrength) and the cavalry to venture out to gather supplies and let the animals graze. Although many of
the merchants encamped outside the walls were cut down, the Sugam-
bri's initial dash for the open gate was narrowly thwarted by the cohort
on guard, so they turned their attention to attacking the returning
foraging party. The five cohorts of Roman infantry consisted mainly of
inexperienced troops, but contained a small contingent of veterans who
led a bold dash through the enemy. This allowed the bulk of the force,
including most of the Gallic cavalry, to reach the safety of the walls, but
left two cohorts to be cut to pieces by the German horsemen.

By the time the great Gallic rebellion of 52 BC broke out, Caesar
had his own force of four hundred German cavalry, in addition to his

Gallic auxiliaries, some of whom were now of doubtful loyalty. The rebel leader, Vercingetorix of the Arverni, had forged a powerful alliance of many tribes and demanded troops from each, 'paying particular attention to the cavalry arm'.[40] The two main forces first approached each other when Caesar was besieging Noviodunum, a town belonging to the Bituriges. The town was just about to surrender when the cavalry, forming the vanguard of Vercingetorix's army, appeared on the horizon. Caesar sent out his Gallic cavalry to engage them but these, being identical to the enemy but far fewer in numbers, quickly got into difficulties. Caesar now sent in his four hundred German riders, whom he had held back as a reserve, and 'their charge overpowered the enemy, who were put to flight and fell back with heavy loss on their main body'.[41] The town surrendered.

Vercingetorix now persuaded his followers to adopt a scorched earth strategy to deprive the Roman army of supplies rather than facing it in open battle or being tied down to sieges. The Bituriges and neighbouring tribes burnt the villages and crops in Caesar's path. Vercingetorix took personal command of all the cavalry which he used to inflict heavy casualties on Roman foraging parties. In these actions the rebel horsemen were joined by 'the light-armed infantry who regularly fought among the cavalry', showing that this was not a uniquely German trick.[42] Although this strategy imposed severe privations upon the Roman forces, it failed to prevent the siege and capture of the Bituriges' main town, Avaricum, which they had refused to abandon.

When Caesar carried the war into Arverni territory, he suffered his one serious reverse outside of Gergovia. Vercingetorix again kept his main force encamped outside the town's own defences and harassed the besiegers. In a further development of the combination of cavalry with close light infantry support, which had probably largely been provided by javelinmen on earlier occasions, he summoned all the bowmen that could be found, 'and almost daily the cavalry were sent into action with archers dispersed amongst their ranks'.[43] Although gathering supplies was again made diffucult, Caesar's troops could move between their various siege positions in relative safety thanks to a double row of twelve-foot-wide trenches. Caesar's decision to withdraw was largely based on the wavering loyalty among the Aedui, who had been the most favoured of his Gallic allies. They provided a sizeable portion of the auxiliary cavalry, while their territory contained Caesar's main supply depots and bordered the province of Transalpine Gaul, which in turn guarded the roads to Italy.

The first open act of revolt by the Aedui was a massacre of the Roman garrison and merchants in one of their towns to which Caesar had sent much of his treasury, stores of grain and, most interestingly, 'numbers of horses he had bought in Italy and Spain for use in the war'.[44] That such a measure was necessary suggests that he could no longer get enough horses in Gaul. Although Spanish horses were perhaps the most prized in the western Mediterranean, the larger Gallic horses were also well thought of and it would have been easier for Caesar to rely on local supplies if these had been available in sufficient numbers.

With many of his normal recruiting grounds in rebellion, Caesar's inferiority in cavalry was temporarily more pronounced than ever. To address this situation, Caesar sent for cavalry from the German tribes on the far side of the Rhine. Although some of these tribes may have made vague acknowledgements of Roman superiority after Caesar's brief but uneventful shows of force across the Rhine in 54 and 53 BC, those that answered the summons probably came for regular pay and the promise of plunder. The horsemen brought with them their attendant light infantrymen, suggesting they were intending to fight in their normal manner, but Caesar decided their horses 'were unsuitable for the service required of them'.[45] Instead he mounted them on horses, presumably mainly of Gallic stock, requisitioned from officers and time-expired volunteers among the auxiliary cavalry. Caesar does not tell us how many Germans were recruited this way; but if they were all remounted this way, they surely cannot have been many. Perhaps this was his intention for the Spanish and Italian horses stolen by the Aedui. Caesar does not say whether these horses were handed over with their saddles, but given the German attitude to these devices it seems unlikely that they would have taken this as anything other than an insult.

For his part, Vercingetorix told those tribes under him that he could make do with the infantry he already had, but demanded more cavalry until he had amassed some fifteen thousand. He convinced the assembled chieftains that the hour of victory was at hand if they would just make one concerted cavalry attack on the Roman army as it marched encumbered with a large baggage train. 'As for their cavalry', he is supposed to have boasted, 'not a man of them will dare even stir outside the column.'[46] His horsemen responded by swearing an oath not to allow any man who had not ridden through the enemy column twice to return to his home or family.

On the day of the attack Vercingetorix divided his cavalry into three sections, the first was to attack the head of the column to force it to halt, while the others attacked from either side. On their approach Caesar also divided his cavalry into three and sent them out to meet the enemy, while the infantry formed a hollow square with the baggage in the middle. Cavalry fights raged for some time on all sides. Whenever he saw a unit being driven back Caesar ordered detachments of legionary infantry to go out and form up behind them, 'which hindered the enemy's pursuit and encouraged the cavalry by the assurance of support'. The hard-pressed unit could then rally behind the infantry before returning to the fray. It was the German cavalry, possibly with their own light infantry in support even though they are not mentioned, who made the breakthrough.

> At length the German horse gained the top of some rising ground on the right, dislodged some of the enemy, and chased them with heavy loss to a river where Vercingetorix's infantry was posted. At this the rest of his cavalry fled, afraid of being surrounded, and were cut down in numbers all over the field.[47]

'The Gauls', Caesar goes on to explain, 'were terrified by the defeat of their cavalry, the arm on which they placed the greatest reliance.' As a direct result Vercingetorix despaired of gaining a victory in the open field and led his whole army into Alesia, the strongly fortified capital of the Arverni. This played right into Roman hands and Caesar began encircling the hilltop town with ten miles of siege works. Outside of this circumvallation (defences facing the town) he constructed a line of contravallation (defences facing outward) some fourteen miles long, to protect his besieging troops from attack from behind. The Roman army were deployed in the space between the two rings, forming what has been called 'a tactical doughnut', with Alesia in the middle.[48]

While the fieldworks were still being constructed, the rebel cavalry made a sortie and was met by Caesar's Gallic cavalry in a three-mile stretch of level ground between the works and the town. The fight went on for some time before the more numerous rebels started to gain the upper hand. Once more Caesar had kept his German cavalry back as a reserve for the crucial moment; when these were committed, the enemy was quickly routed. Too many of the fugitives tried to get through the narrow entrances at once, soon blocking them with a confused mass of frightened men and horses that were easy prey for the Germans who had followed hard behind. Many men were killed while others scrambled across the outer ditch, abandoning their horses to be captured by the Germans.

Vercingetorix now decided to send all his cavalry away, knowing they would be next to useless in the siege once the Roman ring of fortifications was closed and impossible to feed in any case. They broke out by night with instructions to hasten to their various tribes and return with all available manpower to rescue Alesia and the rebellion. Many of the tribes responded and a massive force, estimated at an incredible quarter of a million men by Caesar, was soon lumbering toward the besieged town. But only eight thousand cavalry returned with the relieving force, easily outnumbering Caesar's, but little more than half the earlier rebel strength in this arm. Although many may have ridden home from Alesia and stayed put, this low turnout, for what was clearly a critical point of the rebellion, is probably evidence of very severe losses sustained in the earlier defeats. Even so, when the vast host finally arrived in view of the outer Roman defences and deployed their cavalry in a show of strength, the massed squadrons stretched for three miles.

The defenders inside Alesia, allegedly driven by hunger to consider cannibalism, began to form up outside their walls, preparing to make a do or die assault on the inner Roman defences when the rebels attacked from outside. Caesar sent his own cavalry out from his defences to meet the enemy on the plain, no doubt attempting to buy time for the legions to prepare for the inevitable onslaught, but also for the psychological purpose of meeting their challenge aggressively.

> The plain was visible from all the camps on the surrounding hilltops and the whole army was intently watching to see the result of the engagement. The Gauls had placed archers here and there among their cavalry, to support them if they had to give ground and to help them meet our cavalry charges. These took a number of our men by surprise and forced them to retire wounded from the battle. Feeling confident that their cavalry was winning, since it was obvious that our force was heavily outnumbered, the Gauls on every side – both the besieged and the relieving force – encouraged them with shouts and yells. As the action was taking place in full view of everyone, so that no gallant exploit and no act of cowardice could pass unnoticed, the thirst for glory and the fear of disgrace was an incentive to both sides. They had fought from midday till near sunset and the issue was still in doubt, when the Germans massed all their squadrons at one point, charged the Gauls, and hurled them back. When their cavalry broke and fled, the archers were surrounded and killed. The rest of our horsemen advanced from other points, pursued the fugitives right up to their camp,

and gave them no chance of rallying. At this the Gauls who had come out of the town went back in, bitterly disappointed and now almost despairing of success.[49]

Valuable time had been bought, but the danger was far from over. The Gauls spent the next day preparing vast numbers of fascines (bundles of wood for filling ditches), ladders and grappling hooks. Leaving their camps around midnight, when Caesar's cavalry would be less effective, they launched an all-out assault on the outer ring, rapidly filling sections of the ditches and pressing on to attempt to scale the palisades. Alerted by shouting and trumpet calls, Vercingetorix and his men attacked simultaneously from the inside. This first assault failed after desperate fighting and was called off at dawn, but another the following afternoon eventually succeeded in driving the Roman defenders back from the wall and breaking it down.

Caesar, alerted of this dire peril by Labienus, his subordinate commanding that section, now took bold and decisive action. He hurried to the threatened point with part of his cavalry, riding round the arc of safe ground between the two walls, with four cohorts of infantry withdrawn from the nearest redoubt following as best they could. Meanwhile he had ordered the rest of the cavalry to leave the safety of the defences, exiting by a section not currently under attack and riding round the outside to take the attackers in the rear.

Caesar arrived at the crucial sector just as the Gauls prepared to hurl themselves on the new Roman fighting line Labienus had cobbled together inside the breach in a last effort to contain the penetration. By a stroke of fortune or timing, the audacious flanking move also appeared right on cue.

> The enemy knew that he was coming by the scarlet cloak which he always wore in action to mark his identity; and when they saw the cavalry squadrons and cohorts following him down the slopes, which were plainly visible from the heights on which they stood, they joined battle. Both sides raised a cheer, which was answered by the men on the rampart and all along the entrenchments. The Romans dropped their spears and fought with their swords. Suddenly the Gauls saw the cavalry in their rear and fresh cohorts coming up in front. They broke and fled, but found their retreat cut off by the cavalry and were mown down ... and only a few men of all the large army got back unhurt to their camp.[50]

Vercingetorix surrendered next day, ending the great rebellion. Although there were further rebellions in the winter of 52/51 BC, these were rapidly stamped out, with Caesar's cavalry again playing a prominent part. Those Celtic cavalry that had remained loyal to Caesar throughout the conquest and pacification of Gaul, and the Germans added later, were now a very experienced corps of veterans, with immense confidence in both themselves and their commander, and a fearsome reputation.

In the meantime, while under the hand of a far less able commander, some of them had been involved in one of the most spectacular Roman defeats of all time. Caesar's long uninterrupted command in Gaul had only been possible because of his political alliance with the enormously wealthy Marcus Crassus and Pompey the Great. This First Triumvirate, as it is known, combined their influence to play fast and loose with the republican constitution, taking their pick of magistracies and military commands. By 53 BC Crassus was jealous of Caesar's military reputation and, having secured a consulship (Pompey took the other) and having been allocated Syria as his province, he determined on a war against the Parthians, who had carved an empire from the wreckage of Mesopotamia as Seleucid power collapsed. Crassus' son, Publius, had been serving with Caesar and 'had received a number of decorations for his gallantry in war'.[51] Caesar released him to join his father and sent with him one thousand veteran Celtic cavalry.

Once his son had arrived, Crassus crossed the Euphrates at Zeugma and advanced along the far bank, intending to advance to the key city of Seleucia via Carrhae, one of several towns in which he had installed a garrison during an earlier preparatory incursion. He had seven legions of Roman infantry, around four thousand light infantry, Publius' Gallic horsemen and nearly three thousand other cavalry, most of which were probably from Syria or other eastern provinces. King Artavasdes of Armenia, a Roman client, joined him with six thousand cavalry and promised to provide a further ten thousand armoured cavalry if Crassus would approach Parthia via his own kingdom. Despite his own strong cavalry, Artavasdes was well aware of Parthian superiority in this arm and suggested that the mountainous country of Armenia offered a safer route. Arrogantly, Crassus rejected this sound advice and let Artavasdes ride back to Armenia, where he was soon to be too occupied by Parthian attacks to come to Crassus' aid. Crassus also rejected advice to stay close to the river where he would have had ample fresh water and protection from encirclement, instead allowing a treacherous local guide to lead his army far into an area with 'deep sand underfoot, a level plain with no trees and no water'.

After several days, scouts galloped in with news that the Parthians were approaching in great strength. Crassus immediately deployed for battle but was indecisive about what formation to adopt. He first extended his line as far as possible, dividing the cavalry between the wings, but then realized this left his line dangerously thin without doing anything to prevent an outflanking manoeuvre, as there were no natural obstacles to anchor a flank on. He then opted instead for a hollow square, the classic defence against a force with cavalry superiority in open terrain. He also allocated a squadron of cavalry to each infantry cohort, 'so that no part of the line might be without the support of cavalry, and the whole force could advance with equal protection'. In this formation he continued to advance, reaching a stream, the Balissus, when the day was already well advanced. Most officers advised waiting here for the enemy but Crassus 'was carried away by the eagerness of his son and of the cavalry who were with him and who were all in favour of pressing on and engaging the enemy'. Crassus resumed the advance before all the infantry had even had a chance to drink.[52]

Finally the Romans came in view of the enemy. The Parthians were originally a Scythian people who had moved in off the southern steppes and their military methods reflected that. The force was entirely mounted and consisted of two distinct, specialized types of troops. The majority were unarmoured archers, armed with powerful composite bows. They even still 'wore their hair long in the Scythian fashion and bunched up over their foreheads so as to make themselves appear more formidable'. The remainder, the nobles and their personal retinues, were armoured from head to toe, typically in a long coat of scale armour or chain mail, complete with sleeves and hand protection, and helmets sometimes also completed with a veil of chain mail. The horses too were protected with what Plutarch calls 'plates of bronze and steel'; actually housings of scale mail, some perhaps with alternate bronze and steel rows, producing a very striking effect.[53] Each carried a long heavy lance, or *kontos*.

Initially their armour was concealed by their cloaks, perhaps in part to protect them from the full effect of the blazing sun; and, as they were also in a deep column which concealed their true numbers from view, Crassus was apparently unimpressed. But then with an ominous rumble of kettle-drums the horsemen fanned out on to either side and the cataphracts cast back their cloaks, their armour 'blazing like fire' under the desert sun.

According to Plutarch the cataphracts launched a charge but turned back 'when they saw the depth of the wall of shields with which they were confronted and how steadfastly and firmly the men were standing'. If the Roman infantry had shown signs of wavering the charge would no doubt have been pressed home, but the move may always have been intended as a feint followed by a feigned flight, the classic steppe warriors' trick. Even as the attackers withdrew, 'giving the impression that they were breaking their ranks and losing all cohesion', the rest of the Parthians 'actually succeeded in surrounding the hollow square before the Romans realized what was happening'.[54]

The unprotected mounts of the Parthian horse archers were vulnerable to missiles, so Crassus ordered his light infantry outside the square to drive off the assailants, but they ran into such a storm of Parthian arrows that they were quickly driven back into the centre of the square in panic, seeking shelter behind the more heavily armoured legionaries. Now the Parthian horse archers began simply riding up in groups and loosing off volley after volley of arrows. At close range the arrows from their composite bows could punch through armour and the legions started to suffer a steady flow of casualties, the Parthians making 'no attempt at accurate marksmanship, since the Romans were so closely crowded together that it was impossible to miss'.[55] Plutarch speaks of shafts pinning shields to hands and feet to the ground, while many exacerbated their wounds by trying to pull the barbed arrowheads from their bodies.[56]

It is unclear where the Roman cavalry were at this stage. They too may have been withdrawn inside the square, or it may be the cavalry that Plutarch is referring to when he describes Roman efforts to come to close quarters failing in the face of another classic steppe tactic – for Plutarch says the Parthian light cavalry 'shot as they fled'. This was the famous 'Parthian shot' (corrupted in modern speech into 'parting shot'), the horsemen turning to shoot behind them, most often to their rear left, as they galloped out of reach of a charge. For some time the bulk of the Roman force simply stood and soaked up this punishment, waiting for the Parthians to run out of arrows. But when it became evident that their quivers were being replenished from a train of baggage camels, Crassus attempted to regain the initiative by ordering his son to sally out from the square, the attacks being most intense at the point where he was stationed.

Publius duly led out a task force of 1300 cavalry, one thousand of which were his Gauls, accompanied by five hundred archers and eight cohorts (around four thousand men before casualties) of heavy infantry.

The Parthian horse archers appeared to turn and flee before them, no doubt loosing a few Parthian shots as they did so, and Publius gave chase, the infantry running behind to keep up. Once they had led him a considerable distance from the main Roman force, the 'fleeing' Parthian horse archers peeled off to either side to reveal the cataphracts formed up in a solid mass directly ahead. Realizing he had been lured into a trap, Publius halted while his infantry caught up. Meanwhile more horse archers, along with those who had appeared panic-stricken moments before, rode round the flanks and rear and began shooting again. The plight of the trapped Romans was grim. They soon glimpsed the enemy horsemen only as fleeting shapes through an almost impenetrable curtain of sand and dust thrown up by their myriad hooves, while arrows whistled out of the gloom and pierced shields, mail, flesh and bone.

As the casualties mounted, Publius decided to charge with his cavalry at the cataphracts, a target he might finally be able to get to grips with. His Gallic veterans spurred their horses straight at the cataphracts, who responded with a counter charge. In the resultant combat, Publius' men found themselves at a severe disadvantage. Their spears had a shorter reach than the Parthian lances, which was a severe handicap in the initial clash, and many of the leading ranks lost their horses, 'through driving them onto the long spears'.[57] The shorter weapons may have been handier in the vicious mêlée that followed, but they were also relatively light and could not easily penetrate a cataphract's armour. Although Celtic helmets gave good cranial and neck protection, the open faces were vulnerable to the thrust of a long lance; and even if all the veteran Celts were by now wearing mail shirts, which is uncertain, their unprotected hands, arms and thighs were particularly vulnerable to the cuts of the long slashing swords that both sides carried as back-up weapons (some Parthians also probably using maces and axes).

Despite their disadvantages, and being outnumbered on top of everything else, the Gauls fought back fiercely. Some resorted to grabbing the enemy lances with their hands, grappling with the cataphracts, 'clumsy with all their weight of armour', and unhorsing them.[58] The Parthians would have been using saddles with a raised front (pommel) and rear (cantle) by this stage, but the outward curving horns of the Celtic saddle would have been useful for such grappling, the rider bracing his knees under the front pair. Those that had lost their mounts in the charge, and others dismounting voluntarily when immobilized by the press, crawled under the bellies of the big Parthian horses and stabbed them in the belly, bringing them down screaming in a tangle of frenziedly kicking legs or causing them to rear and trample indiscriminately.

They may have inflicted considerable casualties on the Parthians, but the Gauls suffered more heavily themselves before fighting their way back to their infantry, suffering casualties every step of the way. Publius himself sustained multiple wounds. Reunited, the survivors made their way to a sand dune and formed a defensive circle, the cavalry leaving their horses in the centre with the wounded while they took their place in the perimeter of locked shields. Still the casualties mounted and Publius, ignoring pleas to try to save himself, died by his own sword, apparently enlisting his servant's assistance as his sword hand was already pierced by an arrow. Many of his officers also committed suicide. Still the survivors fought on until the Parthians, eager to complete their victory before nightfall, grew impatient. The cataphracts charged up the slope 'and rode them down with their long spears'.[59] Only five hundred were taken prisoner.

Meanwhile the main Roman army had enjoyed something of a reprieve as virtually the whole Parthian force had ridden off to deal with Publius' force. Crassus redeployed the legions in line on some rising ground and waited for his son to return, only starting to move again when a messenger from Publius galloped up with the news that he was lost unless immediate support arrived. The Romans had not got far before a cloud of dust and a rumble of kettle drums announced the return of the enemy, headed by the demoralizing sight of a rider with Publius' head stuck on the point of his lance.

The Parthian light cavalry again rode around the flanks while the cataphracts launched repeated frontal attacks. The Romans, driven 'closer and closer together' to resist the charges of the cataphracts, formed a dense, passive target for the horse archers. The contribution of the armoured cavalry to this effective tactical combination has been underestimated by modern summaries, for the Romans were not kept on the back foot merely by a *latent* threat of shock action. The cataphracts' charges were not mere feints, some at least were pressed home and shattered attempted counter-attacks by Crassus' remaining cavalry, which 'did little damage and soon died'. The cataphracts, whose own horses were well protected, may well have deliberately targeted the Roman horses, 'since the spears used by the Parthians against the horses were heavily weighted with steel and made great mortal wounds'. Plutarch surely exaggerates when he goes on to describe them 'often having enough impetus to transfix two men at once', but this does suggest he was also describing their use against infantry. The Parthian system was a highly effective tactical combination of firepower and shock action.[60]

Somehow, the Romans held on until nightfall forced the Parthians to withdraw, managing to reach the Roman outpost at Carrhae by leaving their unburied dead and at least four thousand seriously wounded on the blood-soaked sands. Declining to stand a siege in Carrhae, the remnants of Crassus' army left the town the following night, splitting into several bodies. Crassus again allowed the main body to be misled by a local guide and was still in the area at dawn, although his second in command had made his own way to safety with five hundred cavalry, probably most of those who had survived. Overhauled by the Parthians, Crassus was soon forced to halt again. A separate force of five thousand abandoned a strong defensive position to come to his aid but only succeeded in also getting themselves trapped. Eventually, after being enticed into a parley under a temporary truce, Crassus and his remaining senior officers were killed. The rest of his army either surrendered or were hunted down as they scattered in flight. An entirely mounted force had killed an estimated twenty thousand Roman soldiers and taken another ten thousand prisoner.

Returning our attention to the west, by 49 BC Caesar had conquered all of Gaul, and some chieftains across the Channel and the Rhine acknowledged his authority. The other surviving triumvir, Pompey, along with many other senators, feared his ambition and power. Pompey backed the senate's demand that Caesar lay down his command and disband his armies. In late December, Caesar responded by marching south with his men still under arms. Crossing the Rubicon river, which marked the legal boundary of his province, with the famous comment 'the die is cast', he effectively declared civil war. The reputation of his fierce barbarian horsemen preceded him, causing a panic in Rome, 'for there were reports that Caesar was on his way and his cavalry with him, and would arrive at any minute'.[61]

In fact Caesar had launched his riskiest gamble yet with only one legion and three hundred cavalry, although further reinforcements caught up with him later, including another three hundred cavalry supplied by the king of Noricum (roughly modern Slovenia). As he swept through northern Italy, towns and garrisons came over to him with very little resistance. At Rome, the consul Lentulus emptied the treasury reserve and fled southwards. Pompey, who had been boasting that he only needed to stamp his foot to raise legions of veterans all over Italy, now decided that the capital was indefensible and followed Lentulus southwards, along with much of the senate. For a while it looked like the senatorial forces might make a stand at Capua, but they soon continued on to the port of Brundisium where Pompey was preparing a fleet to carry his senatorial supporters and the forces so far gathered into exile. Caesar arrived at Brundisium too late to prevent the evacuation to Greece.

From Caesar's account, the complete extinction of the old military traditions of the equestrian order appears evident from the desperate measures resorted to by the senatorial leaders to raise a cavalry force. While at Capua, Lentulus apparently formed an ad hoc cavalry guard by freeing slave gladiators belonging to Caesar himself and providing them with horses, although he later took advice and had them disarmed and dispersed for safety among the slave gangs of Campania. As for Pompey, around Brundisium 'he issued weapons to the slaves and shepherds, from whom he made up about three hundred cavalry'.[62] Yet when Plutarch describes the Pompeian forces mustered for the decisive battle at Pharsalus, the following year, he says 'As for the cavalry, it was the flower of Rome and of Italy, 7000 men, well born, rich and full of spirit'.[63] It is generally believed that the equestrian class as a whole stayed neutral in the civil war, hedging their bets against further purges in the style of Marius or Sulla, but it is easy to see that Caesar had a political motive for playing down the level of opposition he faced from the equestrian class.

However many Italian troops he took with him, Pompey's evacuation robbed Caesar of quick total victory, although it did deliver Rome and Italy into his hands almost without a fight. Pompey's plan was to buy time to gather and bring to bear the resources of the eastern provinces, where he still had a powerful powerbase of clients. Lack of available shipping prevented Caesar following immediately and keeping up the pressure. After installing his own senate at Rome and declaring himself dictator, he made good use of the time while a fleet was readied, marching through Gaul to the Spanish provinces to secure his rear lest 'auxiliaries and cavalry be raised there and harry Italy and Gaul in his absence'.[64]

For the Spanish campaign Caesar was heavily outnumbered in infantry, perhaps by two to one, but for once had an advantage in cavalry. The force Caesar sent on ahead under Gaius Fabius included 'about three thousand cavalry, whom he had had with him in all his previous campaigns, and a similar number [also] from Gaul whom he himself had collected by summoning individually all the noblest and bravest members of the Gallic tribes'. He soon joined the force himself with a further 'nine hundred cavalry whom he had kept as a personal body-guard', probably the Germans. For their part the enemy could field five thousand horsemen drawn from both Spanish provinces, Iberians, Celtiberians and Lusitanians with a tradition of excellence and greater experience of Spanish conditions and terrain. Although the numerical disparity was considerable, the fact that most of Caesar's men had long and successful experience under his command was probably as great a factor in the complete ascendancy they achieved in this campaign.[65]

Initially there was a cautious stand-off as the two armies faced each other around Ilerda. As thousands of horses quickly devoured all the grazing in the immediate vicinity, both sides attempted to use their cavalry and light forces to disrupt the other's attempts to bring in suf-ficient supplies from an ever-widening area. Caesar's had by far the greater share of success in the frequent clashes that resulted. On one occasion the Pompeian cavalry attempted to ambush a wagon train, but the accompanying Gallic cavalry, although surprised, 'lost no time in forming up and engaging in battle'.[66] Although greatly outnumbered, they held their own while the rest of the column was moved to a strong position on high ground, then skilfully disengaged with only light losses when the enemy legions hove into view. On another occasion a foraging party, returning with captured cattle, completely turned the tables on the Spanish infantry sent out to retrieve the livestock, isolating and annihilating an entire cohort before returning with no losses. This occasion, which required a rapid division of forces and redeployment (one part remaining with the cattle), followed by prompt execution of an improvised plan in the face of the enemy, speaks highly of the level of experience and discipline Caesar's veteran horsemen had acquired.

Such was the ascendancy gained by Caesar's cavalry that the enemy became afraid that they would be prevented completely from foraging or receiving supplies 'because of Caesar's great cavalry strength'.

> The enemy had been shaken by the bravery of our cavalry, and now made their forays with less freedom and confidence ... and if they had the least setback or saw our cavalry in the distance they would drop their loads in their tracks and flee.[67]

When the Pompeians were finally forced to shift position, this brought no respite from Caesar's cavalry, who were able to harass them mercilessly. Although the cavalry were unable to inflict decisive

damage, they repeatedly forced the enemy infantry to turn about and
form up to repel their attacks. They imposed such delay on them that
Caesar was able to march his legions right around the enemy force and
form up across their path in battle formation, forcing them to reverse
direction and head away from the mountain passes they had hoped to
reach in order to shake off Caesar's cavalry.

Completely overawed, the Pompeian cavalry offered no protection;
not even when four whole cohorts of Spanish light infantry, dispatched
to seize a commanding height, were caught in the open by Caesarian
cavalry and butchered to a man in full view of both armies. The psychological dominance established by Caesar's horsemen was complete:

> They did have a large number of cavalry; but so far were these from being
> any help to them that they actually had to be taken into the middle of the
> column for protection, since they had completely lost their nerve as a result
> of earlier skirmishes; and none of them could leave the line of march with-
> out being picked off by Caesar's cavalry.[68]

With plummeting morale and a steadily increasing flow of desertions,
the Pompeian army was soon so immobilized that Caesar's legions were
able to hem them in with earthworks. Four days later the Pompeians
completely ran out of fodder for the cavalry horses (all other animals
having already been slaughtered), as well as water and corn for the men,
and were forced to surrender.

While Caesar had been securing Spain, one of his generals, Curio,
had first seized Sicily and then crossed to North Africa, with two
legions and five hundred cavalry to wrest control from the Pompeian
governor, Varus. Curio's horsemen, most probably Gauls, swept all
before them in a string of victories around Utica. Twice they routed the
enemy's main force with no help from the legions, bottling Varus up in
the city, to which Curio laid siege. The Numidian cavalry opposed to
them proved completely unable to withstand their charges, even when
supported with light infantry, and were given no respite to get into their
usual hit and run tactics. But Curio eventually asked too much of both
horses and riders.

Curio joined battle with a major relief force of both cavalry and
infantry sent by King Juba of Mauretania, even though only two
hundred of his own cavalry were present. Even these were exhausted
following a long night march and an earlier fight in which they had surprised and destroyed the African cavalry of the Mauretanian vanguard.
Significantly the Mauretanian cavalry was reinforced on this occasion

by two thousand Spanish and Gallic mercenary horsemen, whom King Juba 'was accustomed to keep by him as a bodyguard'. Curio's weary squadrons did their best, but it was not enough.

> Wherever they attacked the enemy line [they] did, indeed, force the enemy to give ground, but they were unable to pursue them far or spur their horses strongly. The enemy cavalry on the other hand, began to outflank our line on both sides and trample our men down from behind.[69]

Curio died fighting, surrounded by the enemy cavalry; most of his own cavalry and all the infantry of two legions perished with him.

Having returned to Italy briefly to secure his control there, Caesar was finally ready to move against Pompey directly. He concentrated a force of twelve legions and 'all the cavalry' at Brundisium, but could still only find enough shipping for fifteen thousand infantry and five hundred cavalry. Embarking with just these, he was fortunate to evade the patrolling naval squadrons of the enemy and landed at Palaeste in Epirus. Caesar was hampered throughout the ensuing campaign by Pompey's vast cavalry superiority and his command of the seas, which prevented adequate reinforcements of any sort reaching him from Italy, although Marcus Antonius did eventually get through with four legions and eight hundred cavalry.

Caesar first tried to negate Pompey's cavalry advantage by corralling him against the coast near Dyrrhachium with fortifications, aiming 'to prevent Pompey from getting fodder and making his cavalry ineffective'. This almost succeeded, Pompey stubbornly maintaining his position until the shortage of fodder forced his men to slaughter all the other animals except the cavalry horses, which they resorted to feeding 'with leaves stripped from the trees and with the tender roots of reeds'. With his horses 'wasted with hunger', Pompey changed his strategy and attempted a breakout, which was partially successful. Caesar, himself running short of supplies, was then forced to abandon the siege and march inland after bungling a counter-attack. Pompey then unleashed his cavalry in pursuit, but Caesar's outnumbered horsemen, perhaps in part because they were better fed, saw them off easily enough and the pursuit was abandoned. Various manoeuvres followed involving detachments under various subordinates of both sides, but eventually the two armies concentrated and faced each other for battle near Pharsalus in Thessaly. Pompey had about forty-seven thousand infantry and seven thousand cavalry, while Caesar had twenty-two thousand infantry and approximately one thousand cavalry.[70]

Pompey's cavalry were drawn from several eastern provinces and allies. The breakdown Caesar gives of the latter demonstrates the range of equestrian resources now available to Rome: 600 Galatians, 500 Cappadocians, 500 Thracians, 200 'of outstanding valour' from Macedonia, 300 from Gallograecia, 500 from Egypt and 200 mounted archers from Syria. This was not by any means the full strength of these regions but a representative collection of token forces supplied by those local rulers indebted to Pompey. Most of the balance Caesar accounts for as mercenaries, some more Macedonians, Thessalians and 'other peoples and states'. Plutarch was clearly wrong to think the whole seven thousand consisted of 'the flower of Rome and Italy', but Caesar's apparently meticulous count may deliberately gloss over the presence of a substantial number of the equestrian class embodied as squadrons of citizen cavalry to defend the Republican constitution. Some may have joined Pompey's exodus from Italy while others may have been expatriate citizens from colonies all around the Mediterranean. We cannot be sure of their number. The only Italian cavalry whose presence Caesar admits to in the enemy ranks are the eight hundred he disparages as gathered from Pompey's 'own slaves and herdsmen'.[71] Yet a pro-Caesarian source says that three thousand men of equestrian status were still among the Pompeian forces at the later battle of Munda and, although it is not clearly stated that they fought as cavalry, it seems unlikely that such a large number would all have been dispersed as officers to other troops.[72]

Another contingent among the enemy ranks whose presence may have caused Caesar some embarrassment were the Celtic and German horsemen led by Labienus, formerly Caesar's most trusted lieutenant. It was Labienus who had commanded in newly conquered Gaul during Caesar's British adventures, and he it was who held the breach just long enough at Alesia, but he had refused to join Caesar in his march on Rome and had gone over to the enemy, taking some of his veterans with him. Now at Pharsalus he commanded Pompey's cavalry.

During the customary several days of threat and counter-threat before the battle, which must surely decide who would be master of Rome, both commanders frequently sent out their cavalry forces to test the other's resolve. Caesar reinforced his outnumbered cavalry with light infantry, hurriedly trained to cooperate closely in amongst the squadrons. Here Caesar was clearly drawing on his experiences in Gaul. For his German horsemen, at least, this was merely a return to what had been their normal mode of operation before Caesar had turned them into his reserve shock force. 'The result', claims Caesar, 'was that one thousand cavalry were able, even though on rather open ground, to venture to withstand the attack of seven thousand Pompeians, when necessary, without being greatly dismayed by their numbers.'[73] These were only the cautious preliminaries, however, and the Pompeians remained convinced that it was their cavalry superiority that would prove the decisive factor, even though they also had a two to one advantage in infantry. Labienus allegedly boasted that he would win the battle with the cavalry alone by enveloping Caesar's flank, without their own legions having to be risked at all. Pompey himself, although almost sixty years old, provided the troops with 'a most encouraging and inspiring sight' with his daily riding exercises, 'drawing his sword with no trouble at all while his horse was at full gallop and putting it back with perfect ease in its sheath'.[74]

On the day of battle, both armies formed up with one flank of their infantry line resting on the Enipeus, 'a stream with steep banks'. The open end of Caesar's infantry line, his right, was entrusted to the veteran Tenth Legion. The legions of each side were drawn up side by side, with each one formed into the traditional three lines. On the open flank each posted their whole cavalry force, Caesar's again interspersed with squads of javelinmen while Pompey supported his with large numbers of archers and slingers. As they deployed, Caesar soon realised that the much longer line of the opposing cavalry would allow them easily to outflank his own line and made a last-minute adjustment. Withdrawing one cohort from the third line of each legion, he formed them in line someway to the rear of his own cavalry, the bulk of the horses and the dust of their deployment shielding this development from the eyes of Pompey and Labienus. Plutarch, believing the enemy horsemen were all inexperienced young aristocrats, the resurrected citizen cavalry, has it that Caesar instructed his legionaries to use their javelins as spears and thrust at the faces of the horsemen, telling them that 'these handsome young fellows, behaving as though they were in some kind of pageant ... will run away to save their good looks'.[75]

The battle opened with an advance by the Pompeian cavalry and their supporting archers, the latter presumably halting as soon as they were in effective bowshot to unleash a preparatory barrage upon Caesar's cavalry. Labienus then led the cavalry forward in a massed charge, which quickly drove Caesar's cavalry back. The interspersed skirmishers, who had performed well in the tentative skirmishes over previous days, were evidently not able to deter an all-out charge and must have suffered heavily as their cavalry fell back. While some squadrons kept up the pressure on Caesar's horsemen, most began to re-form and re-deploy in a line facing at a right angle to their original line of attack, ready to charge upon the exposed right flank and rear of the Tenth Legion and roll up Caesar's infantry line, which was now hotly engaged in hand to hand combat.

Labienus must still have been unaware of Caesar's fourth line, unsurprisingly amid the dust and excitement of the charge, because as he reorganized his squadrons for what should have been the *coup de grâce*, he exposed their own flank and presented an open target. Caesar's specially deployed force, who may have been ordered to crouch on one knee while waiting in the traditional manner of the Roman reserve line, rose up and charged the Pompeian cavalry, thrusting for the faces of those they reached. Caught side on and at a virtual standstill, Pompey's cavalry had no chance. Many horses would have fled away from the sudden appearance of a wall of men rushing out of the dust, even if their riders hadn't turned their heads. Labienus could not halt their flight and the whole lot streamed back the way they had come, now exposing their light infantry to slaughter.

Seeing that the arm on which he depended most for victory had failed him, Pompey fled. Caesar's reserve left off the pursuit and began swinging inwards to roll up the Pompeian infantry line. Abandoned and outmanoeuvred, Pompey's men soon threw down their weapons and ran. A large body of the survivors were surrounded on a hill and surrendered next morning. By then Pompey was well on his way on a journey by horse and boat that eventually led him to Egypt, where he was promptly murdered in an attempt to curry favour with Caesar, who was in hot pursuit.

Pompey's death removed the central figure in the resistance to Caesar's seizure of absolute power, but there was still hard fighting ahead to secure his grip on the whole Roman world. Pompeian forces, including Labienus, rallied around Pompey's two sons in Libya while Caesar was embroiled in Egypt's internal strife caused by a disputed succession among the remnants of the Ptolemaic dynasty. Caesar spent most of his six months in Egypt besieged in a quarter of Alexandria, the cavalry having little part to play in confused street fighting. Open operations were restored when reinforcements under Mithridates of Pergamum, a bastard son of Mithridates IV of Pontus, approached. Leaving Alexandria by sea, Caesar managed to link up with Mithridates at Pelusium before the Egyptian king could bring his superior forces against him.

The Egyptian forces then fled in the face of an assault crossing of a branch of the Nile delta led by the German cavalry. King Ptolemy XII drowned while trying to escape by boat and his sister Cleopatra was soon installed as a puppet ruler.

Before he could turn his attention to mopping up the Pompeian diehards, Caesar had first to dash back to Asia Minor, where another son of Mithridates had taken the opportunity to rebel in an attempt to regain his ancestral Pontic kingdom. At the battle of Zela, Caesar easily crushed Pharnabazus, whose generalship seems to suggest that tactical ineptitude may be hereditary. It was here that Caesar uttered his famous laconic remark: '*veni, vidi, vici*' (I came, I saw, I conquered).

Finally able to turn his attention back to the main task, Caesar landed once more in Africa. Having sailed in winter weather that scattered his fleet, he arrived with only three thousand infantry and 150 cavalry. As so often before, the invading army had to contend with masses of Numidian and Moorish cavalry provided by King Juba, but in an early clash 'an incredible thing happened; less than thirty Gallic cavalry beat off two thousand Moorish cavalry'.[76] Even so, this was a tough campaign for Caesar's cavalry, who were greatly outnumbered and faced with such difficulties of supply that they were at one point reduced to feeding the horses on seaweed.

At the battle of Ruspina, by which time reinforcements had brought Caesar's strength up to thirty cohorts of infantry and 400 cavalry, Labienus deployed Numidian cavalry in such dense masses that from a distance Caesar mistook them for infantry formations. Although his own cavalry was initially unable to prevent the legions being surrounded and forced to fight with the cohorts arrayed back to back, they did cooperate with the infantry in disciplined counter-attacks that eventually forced the enemy to retire with heavy losses. The hard-won victory could not be fully exploited, however, because 'Caesar's cavalrymen found that their horses were worn out as a result of recent sea sickness, thirst, fatigue, wounds and fighting against the odds, and lacked the speed to keep up a steady pursuit of the enemy'.[77]

On a later occasion near the same town, a squadron of Caesar's Spanish cavalry, supported by light infantry, were attacked by Labienus with Numidian horsemen and his loyal and experienced Gallic and German squadrons. Caesar sent his own cavalry out and managed to approach the enemy flank under cover of a large fortified farm building. Charging downhill into the enemy rear, they instantly put the Numidians to flight, but Labienus' Germans and Celts attempted to fight back and were all cut down. In the aftermath, the bodies of German and Celtic troopers, 'remarkable for size and comeliness, now lay hacked and limp all over the plain'.[78] Africa was finally secured by a resounding victory at Thapsus, where the Pompeian forces were routed by their own war elephants panicking and rampaging through their battle line.

Pompey's sons escaped to Spain and again provided a focus for Pompeian diehards, but Caesar soon followed. The Pompeian cavalry, mainly locally raised Spanish, did score some initial successes in minor engagements but the civil war was finally brought to an end by Caesar's victory in the pitched battle at Munda. Caesar deployed some eight thousand cavalry. Although their full impact may have been blunted by the refusal of the Pompeians to leave their commanding position on high ground, they played a vital part. When the Tenth Legion drove back their left wing, the enemy attempted to shift a legion from their right to bolster that flank, but an attack by the Caesarian cavalry put them under such pressure that they were pinned in place, leading to the collapse of the Pompeian line. Labienus was among the dead. Pompey's sons escaped, but the elder was hunted down and killed soon after, while the younger turned to a life of piracy. Those that survived the pursuit took refuge in Munda but surrendered after being surrounded by a rampart made from the bodies of their fallen comrades, topped by their severed heads on spears. Our main source for the battle is *The Spanish War* by an anonymous author thought to be one of Caesar's own officers and an eyewitness. What are we to make of his statement that the heaped enemy corpses included those of 'about three thousand Roman equestrians, some from Rome and some from the province'?[79] Although we cannot be absolutely sure they had served in their traditional role as cavalry, it is certainly possible. If so, the last of the citizen cavalry lay wrecked upon the grave of the old Republican order.

Munda ended the last serious chance that the conservative forces might prevent Caesar seizing absolute power. Caesar, having already announced that the post of dictator, traditionally an emergency measure for six months at a time, was to be his for life, was assassinated in 44 BC by senators fearing that he sought to be proclaimed a god or, worse still, a king. But this only resulted in another civil war, from which Caesar's adoptive son and heir, Gaius Octavius, eventually emerged with absolute sole power, albeit cloaked in the thinnest veil of respect for a redundant senate. Initially he allied himself with Mark Antony, Caesar's loyal master of horse to hunt down his father's killers and their supporters. The last, Cassius and Brutus, were defeated in 42 BC at Philippi, where twenty thousand cavalry (none of them Italian) formed fully twenty per cent of their total force; Octavius and Antony fielded thirteen thousand horsemen, around fourteen per cent of their total array. After a period of shared rule, Octavian turned on Antony, defeated him in the naval battle of Actium, and seized absolute sole power, effectively becoming Rome's first emperor.

7

Imperial Rome

Upon establishing himself as sole ruler of the Roman world, Augustus set about a thorough rationalization of Rome's armies. These reforms, achieved in stages, created the fully professional force befitting a stable, centralized empire, the instrument that would carry Rome's frontiers to their furthest extent and secure the golden age of the 'Pax Romana' for those within. As the army continued to evolve, cavalry played an increasingly important role.

After the battle of Actium, at which he defeated Mark Antony, Augustus found himself in supreme command of sixty legions, but immediately reduced these to twenty-eight. In making this drastic cut he was balancing the requirements of defence (and expansion) of the empire against the financial burden and the risk of further coups by overpowerful generals. The legions continued to be supported by large numbers of auxiliaries, both infantry and cavalry, but these were now thoroughly reorganized. Under the Republic, auxiliaries had traditionally been mustered on a short-term, ad hoc basis for a specific campaign or war, before being disbanded again. Under the Empire the auxiliaries were full-time professional units permanently embodied, although this was probably only a regularization of a trend towards keeping them in the field for increased periods during the tumultuous events of the first century BC. It is thought that the total number of auxiliaries roughly equalled that of the legions, that is between 120,000 and 140,000 men.[1] What proportion of Rome's total forces was cavalry is not definitely known, but is generally estimated at around ten per cent.

Augustus' reforms were intended to create a two-tier system that would allow the army to act not only as a war-making machine but also as a vehicle for the full 'Romanization' of its diverse subjects. Entry to the legions was only open to those in possession of full citizenship. The auxiliary regiments, on the other hand, offered non-citizens the prospect of citizenship upon their discharge, which usually followed completion of twenty-five years' service. In the meantime the recruits received regular food and pay, as well as security and military training, while simultaneously being disciplined into obedient servants of the emperor and taught Latin. Whereas auxiliaries in the Republican period had often served under their own chieftains, they were now placed under Roman officers. In the case of cavalry units this was a *praefectus equitum*, who would usually be a citizen of equestrian status.[2] Despite the famously harsh Roman discipline, the package on offer attracted many individual recruits from beyond the frontier, who were accepted and turned to the service of the Empire.

In practice the neat citizen/non-citizen distinction between legions and auxiliaries was progressively diluted. Although the legions remained the exclusive preserve of citizens, even if local recruiting officers bent the rules by granting citizenship on entry, an increasing number of citizens could also be found serving as auxiliaries. The citizenship granted to retiring auxiliary veterans was hereditary, so many sons of auxiliaries could theoretically have served in the legions, but many chose to serve with their father's units in whose camps they had probably grown up. Individual auxiliaries, or whole units, could be prematurely awarded citizenship while still serving as a reward for outstanding valour in battle. Furthermore, especially in times of local hardship, there were citizens who might volunteer to serve with the local auxiliary regiment rather than the legions. In addition, after the disastrous loss of three legions and their accompanying auxiliaries to an ambush by Germanic tribesman in the Teutoburg forest in AD 9, several units were hurriedly created from citizens but organized as auxiliaries rather than legions, which were more expensive and less flexible than the smaller auxiliary units.

We need not concern ourselves with the development of the legions, which remained essentially heavy infantry, except to note that they regained the integral cavalry component they had lost early in the first century BC. Initially the legionary cavalry (*equites legionis*) were only 160 men for each legion and presumably intended only to provide it with a reconnaissance and patrolling capacity, as well as with messengers in battle, but would later be much enhanced. There was also a mounted component to the Praetorian Guard, the emperor's elite guard stationed in Rome, but it is among the auxiliary units that the bulk of the cavalry were to be found.

Auxiliary horsemen were organized into two basic kinds of unit: purely cavalry or mixed cavalry and infantry. A unit composed entirely of cavalry was called an *ala* (plural *alae*),[3] literally a 'wing', while a mixed unit was known as a *cohors equitata*. Both types came in two sizes, designated either *quingenaria* or *milliaria*, meaning five hundred or a thousand strong, respectively; but these were nominal labels only.

Each *ala* was subdivided into *turmae*, equating to the squadrons of a modern regiment. Each *turma* seems to have consisted of thirty-two men, including a *decurio*, a *duplicarius* (double-pay man) and a *sesquiplicarius* (one-and-a-half-pay man). While the *decurio* exercised overall command, the other two can be thought of as junior *decurions*, each officer having direct control over a section of nine ordinary troopers. A standard-bearer and trumpeter completed the complement and, by allowing the effective transmission of orders, played a vital role in battlefield command and control. An *ala quingenaria* contained sixteen such turmae, a full strength of 512 men, while an *ala milliaria* had twenty-four turmae making a total of 768 men – considerably fewer than the designation suggests but still a potent force.

The composition of the mixed *cohors equitata*, introduced early in the first century AD, is a little less clear but it is likely that standard *quingenaria* cohorts consisted of four *turmae* of cavalry and six centuries of infantry. If the centuries actually only contained approximately eighty men each, as was the case in the legions and auxiliary infantry cohorts in this period, this would give each *cohors equitata* a strength of 128 horsemen and about 480 foot soldiers. The actual numbers recorded on three surviving strength returns tie in well with this nominal cavalry strength but record much lower totals for the infantry. This small sample, all three coming from Egypt, may relate to under-strength units and should remind us that there must have been much variation from the theoretical model across the empire and over time. The historian Josephus, an eyewitness to the Jewish revolt of AD 66–70, claims the Roman forces gathered by the future emperor Vespasian included thirteen cohorts, each consisting of six hundred infantry and 120 cavalry. Josephus, one of the rebellious Jews who later switched sides, may have made the easy mistake of assuming a 'century' actually meant one hundred men, but as he came to observe the Roman army at close hand we might expect him to know better. Another explanation is that these units were padded out with new recruits for this major crisis, beyond the standard strength, it being much easier rapidly to equip and give rudimentary training to infantrymen than horsemen. When *milliaria*-sized mixed regiments were raised these had eight *turmae* of cavalry and ten centuries, meaning a total of 256 cavalry and around eight hundred infantry, a very useful combined arms force.

The logic behind the *cohors equitata* may have been to encourage the kind of closely integrated combined arms tactics the Romans had encountered in use by certain German tribes, although there are no historical sources that make it clear whether this was the case or if they fought separately. As auxiliaries were usually posted around the frontiers of the empire, where they did most of the routine patrolling, the mixed regiments may simply have been a way of providing a garrison suitable for a wide range of tasks and circumstances without the administrative expense of raising two units.

The titles of units, as preserved in inscriptions, hold interesting clues about their origins and combat record. Take, for example, a unit based at Stanwix on Hadrian's Wall: Ala Augustum Gallorum Petriana milliaria civium Romanorum bis torquata. 'Augustum' tells us this cavalry ala was raised by Augustus; 'Gallorum' that it was recruited initially in Gaul, although most units were then kept up to strength by local recruiting in the area in which they were stationed. 'Petriana' probably refers to the original commanding officer and 'milliaria' tells us this was one of the larger units. 'Civium Romanorum' designates it as one of those proud units that had been awarded the citizenship en masse for outstanding performance in battle, although subsequent recruits would largely be drawn from non-citizens. 'Torquata' denotes the granting of the torc, another traditional reward for exemplary courage, which may have been represented on the unit's shields by a laurel wreath design. The designation 'bis torquata' means this unit received this distinction not once but twice, and was therefore a very distinguished unit.

Although there were always some specialist light cavalry units, many equipped with bows and lacking armour, the vast majority of *alae* and *cohortes equitatae* were well equipped for close combat, while remaining adaptable for a wide variety of general duties, including reconnaissance. Armaments were made either in imperial arsenals (*fabricae*) or under contract with local smiths, and in both cases relied on the skills of local craftsmen and resources, so variations in style and technique across the empire were inevitable. Such variations notwithstanding, there was probably considerable uniformity within each unit, at least at the start of a campaign. Thanks to the numerous surviving reliefs on gravestones (*stelae*) it is possible to describe the arms and equipment of the 'typical' cavalry trooper of the first century AD. Celtic influence was much in evidence.

Most wore short-sleeved shirts of chain mail (*lorica hamata*) with reinforcements on the shoulders, but extending not far below the groin to afford ease of movement at the hips. Some wore armour of similar pattern but rendered in scale mail (*lorica squamata*), probably more common initially among units raised in the eastern provinces where this type of armour had its ancient origins. Beneath their armour, close-fitting breeches were worn to save the legs from chafing. Ending just below the knees, these might be of fabric or supple leather, which would give the seat some additional grip on the saddle. The wearing of any type of trousers had traditionally been considered an uncouth barbarian habit not fit for civilized men, these short *bracae* originating in southern Gaul.

Helmets also continued to develop from those adapted from the Celtic 'Coolus' type under the Republic. The cavalry variants diverged from the infantry in that the back of the bowl, which was beaten from a single sheet of iron, extended further down the back of the neck before turning out to form the ledge of the neck guard. This offered excellent protection against blows to the back of the neck, perhaps from the backhanded slash of a passing rider. The cheek-pieces also evolved to completely cover the ears. These, like the shoulder reinforcements, were valuable features for a horseman finding himself in a confused cavalry mêlée where blows could come from all directions and where he was likely to be cut about the head and shoulders. In the second century reinforcing strips were added to the crown and to the brow where it formed a small peak.

Another style of helmet found from the first century onwards has a close-fitting iron bowl, usually decorated with embossed stylizations of human hair, or occasionally real hair, again extending to cover the back of the neck. Attached to these are iron masks with realistic human features, completely covering the wearer's face, except for the eyeholes. Early examples are usually dismissed as ceremonial pieces reserved for parades or as 'sports helmets' worn only for demonstrations of the *hippika gymnasia* cavalry exercises. There is no good reason, however, to assume they were not worn in battle, where the eerily impassive masks might have had an unnerving effect on an unfamiliar foe. A fine example was recovered from the site of the battle of the Teutoberg Forest, where three Roman legions and their supporting auxiliaries were ambushed and slaughtered by German tribesmen in AD 9. They may well have been limited to standard bearers or officers at this early date but were certainly used by troopers in later specialist shock units.

Shields were also carried, usually oval, sometimes an elongated hexagon, but always flat, again on the Gallic and German model, rather than the semi-cylindrical type of the legionary infantry, for easier handling on horseback. The flat shape also allowed it to be slung, when not in use, from one of the horns of the saddle; the Celtic saddle now was certainly predominant and probably universal.

Primary offensive armament still consisted of a thrusting spear (*hasta*) with a socketed iron head of various patterns at one end and the other end capped with an iron cone to form a spike. Grave stelae seem to show a short spear perhaps only six feet in length, which may be due to space restrictions upon the sculptor, but a surviving example preserved in boggy ground is ten feet long and elsewhere a group of shafts ranging from seven to nine feet have been recovered. The cavalry spear was probably sturdy but light enough to be a good multipurpose weapon, capable of being used in either under-arm or over-arm style in close combat, or even thrown at short range, but lighter weapons specifically designed for throwing as javelins were also, on occasion, carried in addition. Josephus says each Roman horseman carried a quiver, presumably hanging from the saddle, containing 'three or more broad-headed javelins'.[4]

Josephus describes these cavalry in action in a passage which clearly suggests a combination of shock and missile action:

> For, once their front ranks were broken by the cavalry, a rout ensued, and, the fugitives falling foul of those in their rear who were pressing forward to the wall, they became their own enemies, until at length the whole body, succumbing to the cavalry charges, were dispersed throughout the plain. This was extensive and wholly adapted to cavalry manoeuvres, a circumstance that materially assisted the Romans and caused great carnage among the Jews. For the cavalry headed off and turned the fugitives, broke through the crowds huddled together in flight, slaughtering them in masses, and in whatever direction parties of them fled, the Romans closed in and, galloping round them, found them an easy mark for their javelins.[5]

The chosen style of sword, the *spatha*, usually had a pommel and hilt much like that of the famous Roman *gladius*, but the far greater length made it more akin to the Celtic tradition. With a double-edged blade usually over 30 inches long, sometimes much longer, the *spatha* offered a horseman good reach and was primarily intended for cutting, although thrusting was also viable with the sharp tapering of the last few inches forming a triangular point.

With his horned saddle, breeches, chain mail and long sword, the 'Roman' trooper of the early imperial period looked much like a traditional Celtic nobleman, and that is exactly what a great many of them were. But whereas tribal armies generally could only field a small core of cavalry so well equipped, the Roman army contained regiment after regiment of them.

Under the early emperors, the period known as the principate, Rome's forces were spread as garrisons around newly conquered and frontier provinces. The auxiliaries tended to be stationed on the borders, providing the front line of defence and shouldering the burden of the routine patrolling, while the legions tended to be stationed further back where they acted as a local reserve and also as a deterrent to civil unrest or rebellion by the conquered population. There were no large concentrated field armies to act as strategic reserves, partly to minimize expense and partly because such a force might tempt the provincial governor in charge of it to march on Rome and seize power. When a major campaign was required, units would be gathered from the frontiers of several provinces.

For some of these campaigns we can get a good idea of the make-up of the Roman forces and the role of the cavalry within them. Josephus claims that the army Vespasian led against the Jewish Revolt totalled sixty thousand. His detailed breakdown includes six cavalry *alae* (perhaps three thousand horsemen), thirteen of the mixed *cohortes equitatae* with 120 horsemen each (1560 horsemen who may have been brigaded together) and eight thousand cavalry provided by four client kingdoms, half of them Arab light cavalry. Even without adding the small mounted component integrated with each of Vespasian's three legions, the cavalry therefore totalled around 8500, roughly fourteen per cent of the total.

For his initial invasion of Britain in AD 43, Aulus Plautius is believed to have commanded forty thousand infantry and five thousand cavalry (eleven per cent), although this is not entirely certain. More reliably, Tacitus describes the force with which his father-in-law Agricola, pressing deep into what is now Scotland, faced approximately thirty thousand Caledonian tribesmen at Mons Graupius in AD 84. His force of approximately twenty-one thousand men consisted of two legions plus eight thousand auxiliary infantry and three thousand auxiliary cavalry, the cavalry again accounting for fourteen per cent of the total. On this occasion the legions played little part in the fighting, being deliberately kept in reserve close to their camp because 'the victory would be vastly more glorious if it cost no Roman [meaning citizen] blood'.

Agricola formed his auxiliaries into a conventional battle line, with the infantry in the centre and cavalry posted on either flank, but with four *alae* of the cavalry held back as a first tactical reserve. Although these units may not have been at their full strength, which would have meant two of the three thousand cavalry present, Agricola was clearly keeping a large proportion of the cavalry in hand to await developments and this was to prove vital. The two armies faced each other across a valley floor, the front line of the enemy being on level ground but the masses behind seeming 'to mount up the sloping hillside in close-packed tiers'. The British deployment was covered by 'the noisy manoeuvring of the charioteers' who then almost certainly retired to the flanks when all was ready. When Agricola realized how numerous the enemy were, and how much the longer their line was, he ordered his own line to spread out, either by reducing the number of ranks in each unit or by leaving greater gaps between each formation. Even though his own line now looked dangerously thin everywhere, and still vulnerable on its flanks, he decided not to bring up the legions.

The battle opened with a sustained but indecisive exchange of missiles before Agricola ordered some of his most experienced troops to close in with the sword. These soon began to make headway, driving their immediate opponents back off the plain and up the slopes. The rest of the auxiliaries now joined in a general advance. By this time, Tacitus tells us with irritating lack of detail, the auxiliary cavalry had already defeated the enemy chariots on the plain and now charged into the infantry battle. Although 'their first onslaught was terrifying', they were unable to make a quick breakthrough due to the 'solid ranks of the enemy and the roughness of the ground', instead becoming dangerously entangled in a static brawl and in places making things more difficult for their own infantry as terrified horses 'came plunging into the ranks from the side or in head on collision'.

The Caledonian forces on the higher slopes which had not yet been engaged now began to sweep down and round one of the flanks to envelop the Roman auxiliaries from the rear, scenting victory. Agricola now committed his reserve cavalry, who charged the onrushing tribesmen 'and turned their spirited charge into a rout'. The reserve, possibly joined by any of the front-line cavalry who had extricated themselves from their predicament, now rode round the rear of those enemies still resisting on the slopes and charged in upon their rear. This unexpected turn of events broke the Caledonian resistance. All the surviving cavalry now led a ruthless and effective pursuit.

> The open plain now presented a grim, awe-inspiring spectacle. Our horse-men kept pursuing them, wounding some, making prisoners of others, and then killing them as new enemies appeared ... Equipment, bodies and mangled limbs lay all around on the bloodstained earth.[6]

Some of the fugitives, reaching the cover of wooded ground, made a stand and inflicted some casualties on the boldest horsemen. But once they had re-formed, and with the help of some light infantry ordered up by Agricola to form a cordon, the cavalry gave them no respite even here. Some troopers dismounted and entered the densest thickets to flush them out into the clearings where other horsemen again took up the chase.

The invasion of Britain was the only major campaign of conquest undertaken in the first century after the Teutoburg disaster effectively halted expansionist ambitions across the Rhine. But at the very begin-ning of the second century Trajan launched two major offensives across the Danube against the Dacians. Although very little evidence for these important campaigns has survived, a single sentence of Trajan's own account and a few vague pages in Dio Cassius, modern scholarship has painstakingly reconstructed the order of battle at his disposal through the use of epigraphic evidence. The campaigns are also recorded visu-ally on Trajan's column. These reliefs, all 670 feet of them spiralling up the one hundred feet high column and containing more than 2500 figures, form the only full narrative of the course of the Dacian Wars. The fifty-four carved panels at the Tropaium Traiani at Adamklissi, in what was Dacian territory, are also believed to relate to the first Dacian War, or certainly to a period very close to it. Seven of the panels are devoted to cavalry actions.

Assuming all the units that are thought to have been used in Dacia were at full strength rather than merely represented by detachments (known as vexillations),[7] Trajan's force consisted of around 112,000 men, of whom around 12,500, or 11 per cent were cavalry. The bulk of these horsemen, 9500 men, were incorporated in sixteen *alae*, three of which were of the enlarged *milliaria* type. A further 1500 were provided by the mounted components of eight *cohortes equitatae*, four of these being *milliaria*, and the same number again by the legionary cavalry of thirteen legions, which could be brigaded together for use in battle. The unit names of the *alae* involved neatly illustrate the diverse origins of 'Roman' cavalry, including Spaniards, Gauls and at least one unit from Britain.

Among Trajan's cavalry regiments we also find the *Ala Ulpia contariorum milliara civia Romanorum*. While the title 'Ulpia' tells us this was a unit raised by Trajan himself (his full name being Marcus Ulpius Traianus), the designation 'contariorum' tells us that these riders were armed with the *contus*. 'Contus' is the Latin version of the Greek word *kontos*, which literally means a barge pole but was used euphemistically for exceptionally long spears. Although Trajan's unit is the first example of a unit specifically designated as specialist *contarii* (contus-bearers), Josephus describes Vespasian's cavalry carrying a *kontos* as well their quiver of javelins a few decades earlier, although this could just be an imprecise usage of the word.

Throughout the first century and after, Rome was intermittently at war on her eastern frontier with the Parthians, whose heavy cavalry were also still using the long lance which Plutarch also calls a *kontos*, and which he describes skewering two men at once at the battle of Carrhae in 53 BC. The Romans, however, seem to have adopted the *contus* from the Sarmatians following increasingly troublesome contact along the Danube frontier in the second half of the first century AD, and the weapon was sometimes specifically called the *contus Sarmaticus*. In the *Ars Tactica*, a training manual for cavalry written around AD 125, Arrian lists the types employed by the Romans and refers to the *contarii* as those who charge the enemy ranks and drive them off with their lances 'like the Alans and Sarmatians'.[8] Indeed, many of the troopers in the Roman units were probably themselves Sarmatians attracted by the regular pay and certainty of Roman army life.

Although many Sarmatian warriors, true to their steppe nomad background, also carried bows, their chief tactic was a mass shock charge with the *contus*. One of the earliest descriptions of the Sarmatians in action is Tacitus' account of their meeting with Parthian cavalry in AD 35. The Parthians, intending to rely on missile fire and probably expecting their foes to do the same, fanned out into open order to give themselves room to shoot. 'But the Sarmatian horsemen on the other side instead of shooting back, their bows being inferior in range, charged with lance and sword.' The Parthians, to their credit, were not instantly broken by this charge, Tacitus speaking of 'successive advances and retreats', which suggests groups breaking off, regrouping and charging again; but the Persians eventually broke after the battle degenerated into a close-packed tussle in which men 'shoved and heaved at one another'.

For the Romans the trouble with the Sarmatians began in the early spring of AD 69, when nine thousand of them launched their first major raid across the Danube into the Roman province of Moesia, which they plundered. On their return they were confronted by a Roman legion close to the bank of the river, which was swampy due to the spring thaw. Thanks to the poor going and the loot they were carrying, the Sarmatians were unable to deliver their trademark charge. Robbed of their mobility and impetus, they were forced into a close fight in which, Tacitus explains, they could not make use of their long lances. He adds that the 'leaders and most distinguished persons' who were unhorsed had difficulty rising due to the weight of their armour. Although the Sarmatians were defeated with heavy loss, Tacitus makes it clear that the Romans had been lucky on this occasion and says that 'when they charge in squadrons, hardly any formation can stand against them'.[9]

Judging from surviving representations from the Sarmatian-dominated Bosporus region north of the Black Sea, the *contus Sarmaticus* was approximately twelve feet long. It appears to have been used in a very different way to the similarly long lances of Alexander's Companions. Various representations of Sarmatian, Persian and late Roman horsemen almost always show the lance being gripped in both hands, either alongside the horse's neck, or diagonally across the rider's body so that the butt end was to his right rear and the business end passed the horse's left ear. The development of this technique was undoubtedly encouraged by the widespread use of saddles which supported the lower back and held the rider's bottom in place against the recoil of impact, as did the Celtic/Roman 'horned' saddle. But the two-handed grip may also have been necessary due to the fact that the *contus*, unlike the Macedonian lance, is never depicted with the counterbalancing second head; and, although the evidence admits no certainty, the shaft may not have been tapered. The tapering and counterbalance, it will be remembered, had allowed Macedonian lancers to wield their weapons one-handed, gripped at the point of balance about one third of the way from the butt end.

Tapered or not, the *contus* was clearly a heavy and unwieldy weapon, perhaps thicker and more robust than its earlier counterpart. The two-handed method may have allowed a much more forceful blow to be delivered in the initial charge, compared to the one-handed Macedonian technique, but it would have been impractical in the ensuing melee and even if it had not been broken would have been best abandoned in favour of the sword. One source suggests the Sarmatians themselves made the shafts of fir wood, which presumably had the advantage of being locally available to them; but as fir could shatter into long splinters that would be a danger to man and horse alike, Roman copies may have been made of ash or some other suitable wood. As secondary weapons they favoured very long, straight sabres, with blades sometimes in excess of forty inches. These must have been used one-handed on horseback, although Tacitus describes Sarmatians wielding them in both hands once unhorsed, due to their 'excessive length'.

The two-handed method of using the contus meant a shield could not be used effectively at the same time, but it is likely that wicker and leather shields were often carried slung, ready for use with the sword. The wealthiest Sarmatians were well armoured with iron helmets and body armour, usually a long coat of scale that came to mid thigh. This scale armour could be made either of iron or bronze scales, split horn or horse hooves. Bizarre as it may seem, hoof must have been a very efficient protective material, light but tough and flexible and freely available to a nation of horse herders, if laborious to prepare. The geographer Pausanius spoke highly of Sarmatian ingenuity in this matter:

> They collect hooves and clean them out and split them down to make them like snake scales – you will not go far wrong if you think of this hoof-work like the notches of a pine cone. They bore holes in these scales and sew them with horse and cattle-hair to make breastplates no less good-looking than Greek ones, and no weaker; they stand up to striking and shooting from close range.[10]

Such scale coats are shown in detail among the captured weapons on the pediment of Trajan's Column, along with another type of similar cut but made of broad horizontal bands fastening down the front, possibly of rawhide. Some of the wealthiest Sarmatians would have worn chain mail, this becoming increasingly common through the second century AD and into the third. Chain mail, although harder to make than scale, and so more expensive, was more flexible and better ventilated. Helmets were typically conical and made up of four triangular sections fixed to an iron framework. Those on Trajan's Column and a graffito from the Bosporus region seem to have had a flap protecting the neck, again covered in scales. Roman *contarii* units were probably equipped with the usual helmet and chain mail or scale shirt, with shields slung from the horns of the saddle while the contus was in use.

A small proportion of Sarmatian lancers also had armour for their horses. Several panels of Trajan's column show the cavalry provided by the Dacians' allies, the Roxolani, one of the tribal groups of which the Sarmatians consisted.[11] They are depicted with both riders and horses covered in scale armour, although the actual design of the horse armour is impossible, probably due to the sculptor trying to depict something that had only been described to him. In reality it would have taken the form of a housing protecting the horse's chest flanks and rump and probably hanging just below the level of the belly; this was probably most often of scale, or perhaps lamellar construction (where elongated rectangular 'lames' rather than scales are laced together in rows), and maybe later of chain mail. This would be in keeping with eastern horse armour under the Parthians and the Sassanid Persian dynasty that replaced them, and also appears to be the style depicted on a first century AD Bosporan gravestone, the only other definite representation of horse armour from the Sarmatians' territory. Those on the column, which is a propaganda piece, are depicted being defeated and chased off by less completely armoured Roman cavalry, but there is no reason to doubt that such troops, though few in number, could have provided a formidable cutting edge to the Sarmatian charge. The first century poet Valerius Flaccus vividly conjures up the menacing prospect of such an attack:

> A fierce band of Sarmatians came thronging with savage yells; stiff are their lorica [body armours] with supple chains; and such too the coverings of their steeds; but stretching out over the horse's head and shoulders the fir wood shaft, firmly resting on their knees, casts a long shadow upon the enemy's field, and forces its way with all the might of both warrior and steed.[12]

Additional psychological impact may have been added by the type of standard carried by the Sarmatians and their Dacian allies. Known to the Romans as a *draco*, this consisted of a gaping dragon's head in metal with a long, brightly coloured windsock body. When carried by a horse-man moving at speed, the dragon appeared to writhe as the windsock streamed out behind and the rush of air funnelled through the mouth emitted an unearthly moaning. To judge from modern replicas, it was not unlike the sirens fitted to the German Ju–87 Stuka dive-bomber in the Second World War as a deliberate and effective psychological weapon. The demoralizing effect of this banshee wail on inexperienced soldiers (or horses) in a more superstitious age can only be guessed at. The *draco* was widely adopted by Roman units, probably starting with the *contarius* units, the bearer of such a standard being known as a *draconarius*.

The respect engendered by the Sarmatian lancers not only prompted the Romans to adopt the *contus* for some of their own cavalry but also forced the development of special tactics to withstand their charge. Under Trajan's successor Hadrian (117–138 AD), the province of Cappadocia was threatened by the Alans, the last of the major Sarmatian subgroups to migrate westward into the Black Sea region. Fortunately for Hadrian, he appointed as governor of Cappadocia Flavius Arrianus Xenophon, better known as Arrian, the famous biographer of Alexander the Great and author of the *Ars Tactica*.

Arrian's operational orders for the expected battle survive and are known as *Acies contra Alanos* (The Formation against the Alans). He instructed that the army be drawn up with the legionary heavy infantry in the centre formed eight ranks deep, with auxiliary archers immediately behind them. Auxiliary infantry cohorts were to hold high ground anchoring either end of the infantry line. Most of the cavalry would be deployed to guard both flanks, with the more heavily armed units in front and the mounted archers sheltering a suitable distance behind to fire over them. Selected units were also to be retained close to Arrian himself as a reserve.

A Sarmatian attack on the centre was ideally to be broken up by a deluge of missiles, accompanied by as loud a war cry as possible to increase the chance of panicking the enemy horses, but the first few ranks of the legionary infantry were instructed to retain their characteristic heavy javelins (*pila*) to use as stabbing spears in case the enemy kept coming. The first rank was to level their weapons 'in order that when the enemy comes near them, they can thrust the iron points of the spears at the breasts of the horses in particular'; but if the rows of lethal tips did not deter them then the legionaries had to be ready to withstand the shock of impact as hundreds of lances, each propelled by the momentum of a galloping horse, struck them:

> If they do close in though, the first three ranks should lock their shields and press their shoulders [against them] and receive the charge as strongly as possible in the most closely ordered formation bound together in the strongest manner. The fourth rank will throw their javelins overhead and the first rank will stab at them and their horses with their spears without pause.[13]

What Arrian was recommending for the infantry was an abandonment of the legion's usual flexible order, developed over five or six hundred years, in favour of a return to the ancient phalanx.

If some or all of the Sarmatians attempted to circle round the flanks instead of (or perhaps after) attempting a frontal charge on the centre, Arrian foresaw that they were likely temporarily to expose their own flank as they manoeuvred across his front. If such an opportunity arose, the Roman cavalry were to instantly seize it and counter-attack. 'In that case', he wrote to make clear that they should close quickly to engage the enemy by shock action, 'the cavalrymen must not attack with a missile shower but with swords and axes.'

Arrian is the only author of this period to mention axes being carried by the Roman cavalry, and if some of his units carried them as a side-arm in preference to swords it may have been a local peculiarity. The weapon he had in mind may have been the ice-pick-like *sagaris*, which already had a very ancient pedigree in the east. In the *Ars Tactica*, Arrian refers to an 'axe with spikes set all round', perhaps meaning a mace of some kind. In the middle ages, maces were particularly valued for use against armoured opponents.

At first reading Arrian appears to contradict himself with regard to the Alans' armour. The legionary infantry are instructed to 'put the rider out of action with the spear stuck in their heavy body armour', yet he clearly expects his cavalry to have the advantage once they have got into close combat due to the Sarmatians (whom he calls Scythians) 'being lightly armed and having unprotected horses'. This merely confirms that while the best-equipped riders would be expected to lead an all out assault on the centre, most of the enemy were less well equipped, despite their predilection for shock action. Furthermore, the lack of shields enforced by the use of the *contus* could indeed make them relatively vulnerable in an exchange of sword blows.

Once the attack was repulsed, as Arrian expected it to be whether it fell on the flanks or the centre, half the cavalry were to launch an immediate pursuit, while the remaining half were to follow 'in perfect formation and not in hot pursuit'. In the event that the enemy proved to be completely routed, these supporting squadrons could take over with fresher horses from the leading pursuers to maintain the pressure, but they should also act as a precaution against the enemy turning to counter-attack their pursuers or luring them into an ambush. This shows Arrian's grasp of some of the most enduring principles of cavalry warfare, the retention of a fresh reserve and the dangers of pursuing too rashly. He could have written the following extract from this early twentieth century British cavalry manual:

> The actual pursuit of an enemy in disorder and in full flight can only be kept up by men also in loose order and at full gallop. In such a state pursuing cavalry are at the mercy of any fresh hostile body that may appear. They must, therefore, be followed as closely as possible by formed bodies which have been retained in hand or rallied.[14]

Unfortunately, we do not know if Arrian ever had to put his plans to the test; all we know of the subsequent operations is that the invaders were repelled or deterred. The historian Cassius Dio says the Alans withdrew after being persuaded by the gifts of the Persian king, whose lands were also threatened, 'and frightened by Flavius Arrianus the governor of Cappadocia'.[15]

In his *Ars Tactica*, Arrian's survey of Roman cavalry types is first divided into 'unarmoured' and 'armoured' types. These are relative terms, however, as the vast bulk of the cavalry are lumped together in the unarmoured category alongside the specialist light cavalry units, 'who do not come to close but discharge their weapons at a distance', even though their standard defensive equipment is given as 'broad oval shields, an iron helmet, an interlocked corselet and small greaves'. Interestingly even some of those units supposedly specialized as skirmishers are trained to 'first discharge their weapons and then join battle with the enemy, either retaining one of their spears or using a *spatha*'. The label of 'armoured cavalry' Arrian reserves for that part of the cavalry which 'comprises both armoured horsemen and armoured horses, the former wearing corselets of scale-armour, linen or horn, together with thigh guards, and the horses covers for their sides (*parapleuridia*) and chamfrons'.

What Arrian is describing are cataphracts, which may have been a new addition to the Roman arsenal as the first evidence for a specific Roman regiment of this type, *Ala I Gallorum et Pannonium catafractata*, also dates to Hadrian's reign. Again it is Josephus who suggests the possibility that they were adopted earlier. In his eyewitness account of the siege of Jotopata in 68 BC, Vespasian selected some of his cavalry to dismount and form up in three ranks to lead the final assault on foot, 'covered with armour on every side and lances [*kontoi*] in their hands'. This they did, successfully storming the breached walls, despite the defenders' use of heated olive oil poured from the walls 'still hissing from the heat of the fire', which got under the armour of some and 'fed upon their flesh like the flame itself'.[16] The only perceived advantage that could have justified asking these cavalry to fight dismounted in this way is if they were considerably more heavily armoured than the plentiful specialist heavy infantry to hand. If this is so then they may well have been cataphracts, although there remains the possibility that they were supplied by one of the allied kings, not a regular Roman unit.

Although cataphract regiments, whenever they were actually introduced, were armed with the *contus*, what distinguished them from the units of *contarii* was their heavier armour, which made them even more specialized for a shock role. Although we have seen that a small proportion of Sarmatian cavalry rode armoured horses, it is likely that the strong force of *cataphracts* employed by the Parthians provided the main inspiration and model for the addition of these units to the Roman array.

Eastern cataphracts can be seen in action on the rock bas-reliefs at Firzubad. They depict the coup by which the Parthian rulers of Persia were overthrown and replaced with a native dynasty, the Sassanids. The riders depicted at Firzubad are depicted on very powerfully built horses, presumably the famous Nesean breed, charging one another with such impact that lances are shattered and some of the horses bowled over. Ammianus Marcellinus describes the awesome sight of massed Persian squadrons threatening the Roman retreat from Ctesiphon in AD 363. Although he was writing at a much later date than that at which the reliefs were made, there doesn't seem to have been significant change.

> About dawn an immense host of Persians appeared with Merena, the master of the horse, two of the king's sons and many other grandees. All their troops were clad in mail; their bodies were covered with plates so closely fitting that the stiff joints of the armour conformed to the articulation of the limbs beneath, and representations of human faces were so skilfully fitted to their heads that the whole man was clothed in metal scales. The only spots where a weapon could lodge were the tiny holes left for the eyes and nostrils, which allowed some degree of vision and a scanty supply of air. Those of them who were to fight with pikes [sic] stood so still that they might have been fixed to the spot by metal ties.[17]

Ammianus' description of the riders in Roman cataphract regiments is very similar, suggesting they were close copies of the Persian originals:

> At intervals were mailed cavalrymen, the so-called ironclads [sic], wearing

masks and equipped with cuirasses and belts of steel they seemed more
like statues polished by the hands of Praxiteles than living men. Their
limbs were entirely covered by a garment of thin circular plates fitted to
the curves of the body, and so cunningly articulated that it adapted itself
to every movement the wearer needed to make.[18]

The masks bring to mind the helmets referred to earlier, often
referred to as 'parade helmets', which were shaped in the likeness of
a human face. A graffito from Dura Europos appears to show a rider
(who could be either a Roman or a Parthian) with a tall conical helmet
and a chain mail veil (the medieval term would be an aventail), which
may have been a better-ventilated alternative. His body is protected by
what looks like a composite of scale and lamellar armour made up of
much larger rectangular plates. His limbs are protected by articulated
defences made up of segmented bands (probably what Ammianus
was trying to describe as 'thin circular plates'). As we have seen, such
defences had certainly been worn by Seleucid cataphracts in the second
century BC, and may well have been observed on Persian cavalry by
Xenophon as far back as the fourth century BC.

The horse in the graffito has a scale housing, evidence supported by
actual examples also recovered from Dura Europos. Ammianus says of
the Persian heavy cavalry that 'all their horses were protected by housings of leather', and the horse armour in the Firzubad reliefs could be
leather or a thick fabric like felt, with metal ornaments attached. A later
Sassanid relief shows another option, a horse with chain mail head and
neck protection and a chain mail apron that protects its chest, shoulders and front legs but leaves its rear quarters uncovered. This probably
represents a compromise between the dangers of overheating and
protection from an enemy to the front. Roman chamfrons have been
unearthed in many areas, including at Newsteads on Hadrian's Wall.
Made either of a single piece of moulded leather, or of three connected
metal plates, these curved round to protect the sides as well as the front
of the horse's face, with perforated guards covering the eyes.

Another term associated with the heavily armoured cavalry is 'clibanarius', apparently from a Persian word for an oven or furnace, which
must have seemed most apt under the Mediterranean or Persian sun.
It is sometimes anachronistically translated as 'ironclad'. Although
probably starting as a nickname for cataphracts, some of the evidence
suggests that *clibanarius* seems to have gained a specific and distinct
technical meaning. To add to the confusion, a unit could be referred

to as *cataphractus clibanarius*. Some scholars have suggested that *clibanarii* carried bows as well as the lance (as did most of the Persian horsemen) or that one had full horse armour and the other only the frontal half armour. It has also been suggested that the distinction was not one of equipment but of tactical use and training with *clibanarii* being trained to cooperate closely with light horse archers. By this way of thinking, a unit trained in both might operate as *cataphracti* on one occasion or *clibanarii* on another.[19]

In addition to the variety of types in service, the main impression of the Roman cavalry that Arrian gives his reader is of a highly disciplined force, rigorously trained through constant practice. In cavalry tactics, as in so many fields, the Romans were the beneficiaries of centuries of development among many peoples, both their conquered subjects and those still beyond their borders. The eclectic range of formations and manoeuvres that the empire's regiments were expected to master included the Celtic toloutegon, the Cantabrian gallop, the Thessalian rhombus, and of course the wedge, so valuable for cutting through enemy formations in shock action, which the Macedonians had learnt from the Thracians and Scythians.

By Hadrian's reign, when the cataphract was finally adopted by the Roman army, the Roman Empire had reached its high watermark. As well as annexing Dacia (roughly modern Rumania), Trajan had campaigned in the east, capturing the Parthian capital at Ctesiphon and carrying the Empire's borders to their greatest territorial extent. After that Rome was increasingly on the defensive. In Britain of course, this retrenchment was clearly embodied in the construction of Hadrian's Wall and the other frontiers also gradually ossified into fixed defensive systems.

On the Danube, Hadrian began paying subsidies to the Roxolani and awarded citizenship to their king, Rasparagus, but other Sarmatian groups remained a major threat, despite a significant victory by the Emperor Marcus Aurelius in the winter of AD 173/174. Once more the Sarmatian dependence upon the headlong charge proved their undoing in a battle fought upon the frozen River Danube. It seems incredible that any cavalry force would willingly give battle on ice, yet, remarkably, the historian Cassius Dio claims that the Iazyge raiders, who had been retreating with their loot, actually halted on the river and waited for the Romans, expecting to have the advantage 'as their horses had been trained to run safely even over a surface of this kind'.

When the Romans came up the Sarmatians tried to employ exactly the tactics Arrian had prepared to face, with some dashing straight at the Roman centre while others attempted to envelop both flanks. The Romans, however, did not panic and 'drew together in a compact body'; possibly a square with the cavalry in the centre since they are not mentioned in the ensuing fight. The Sarmatian assault failed to break the Roman infantry, many of the men having thrown down their shields for the front ranks to stand upon for firmer footing. The Iazyges did manage to drive their horses into the waiting lines but many mounts lost their footing and went down 'since the barbarians, by reason of their momentum could no longer keep from slipping'. Those piling in from behind became embroiled in a vicious struggle in which many were bodily hauled from their horses 'so that but few escaped out of a large force'.

Marcus Aurelius adopted the soubriquet 'Sarmaticus' as a result of this victory and, after further campaigning, was able to negotiate a favourable peace two years later. The terms of this settlement illustrate how the Romans, although not expanding territorially, still sought to incorporate the manpower of defeated enemies. As a result of this defeat, the Iazyges returned some one hundred thousand captives taken in raids over the years, and also undertook to furnish eight thousand cavalry for service with the Roman army, of whom 5500 were sent to Britain.[20] The peace lasted for a generation, but a new threat was already emerging in the region.

The Goths are believed to have migrated southwards through central Europe, arriving in the Southern Ukraine in the early third century, encroaching on the land of the remaining Iazyges, who resumed their raiding of Roman lands in the early 220s. The Goths are believed to have had few horses when they began their migration, but once they had access to the herds of their new nomadic neighbours they assimilated the arts of horsemanship and mounted warfare with remarkable rapidity, so that Isidore of Seville wrote of them: 'in the skills of fighting they are quite distinguished, ... and in battle they attack not only on horseback but also on foot; nevertheless they rely more on the swift running of their horses'.[21] Procopius confirmed that the Gothic cavalry came to specialize in shock action when he wrote 'the horsemen are accustomed to use only spears and swords, while the bowmen enter the battle on foot'.[22] They soon took up the favourite local pastime of raiding Roman property and became the main threat on the Danubian front.

Such tribal movements and general restlessness among the barbarians beyond the Rhine and Danube created mounting pressure on the

Roman defences, contributing to what is now called the Third Century Crisis. A more important factor at this stage was the reinvigoration of the Persian threat when a rebellion by the native aristocracy, led by a regional magnate called Sassan and then by his son Ardashir, overthrew their Parthian overlords. Ironically it was the success of the Roman Emperor Septimus Severus in AD 195 that had fatally weakened the already-declining Parthian Arsacid dynasty, creating the conditions for revolt. Ardashir became the first 'Sassanid' king in AD 224, and in AD 226 revived the ancient title King of Kings, which no Persian had claimed since Alexander's defeat of Darius III. The Sassanid rulers proved much more efficient at harnessing the military and economic resources of the region than the Parthians had been and, for the first time since the final defeat of Mithridates, the Romans were confronted with a rival power that could field large and well-equipped armies capable of sustained efforts across the full spectrum of military operations.

Militarily the Sassanids continued the Parthians' heavy dependence on the combination of cataphracts (and clibanarii) and light horse archers, adding a powerful force of war elephants obtained from India and an efficient siege train for good measure. Large numbers of infantry could also be raised but the traditional Persian weakness in this arm still applied and their quality was definitely inferior to the average Roman legion. The lack of good infantry was never solved, and in one of their last battles against the Islamic invasions in the seventh century, the Sassanid commanders had so little faith in their infantry levies that they were chained together in long lines to stop them running away. It was always their cavalry in which the Sassanids put their faith.

Under the able leadership of Ardashir I, Sassanid armies invaded Rome's eastern provinces, capturing the strategic cities of Carrhae, Nisibis and Hatra in the late 230s and early 240s. The burgeoning Persian threat coincided with, and contributed to, a period of intense political instability and recurrent civil war in the Roman Empire. A simple statistic illustrates this vividly: between AD 226 and 379 the Persians had only eight kings, while the Romans got through some thirty-five recognized emperors, many of them killed by their own troops. In addition there were numerous pretenders, rebels and would-be usurpers. Such internal turmoil inevitably hindered a timely and coherent response to external threats.

By the time Rome launched the first major counter-attack the Sassanid crown had passed to Ardashir's son, Sapor I (240–272). An expedition led in person by Emperor Gordian III was defeated at the battle of Misiche in 244, Gordian himself dying soon after, probably from wounds sustained in the battle. His hastily appointed successor, Philip, was defeated in turn and forced to sign a humiliating peace deal which included acknowledgement of Persia's conquests and a large cash payment. In AD 252–53 Sapor captured much of Roman Syria, including the capital, Antioch. In 260, the Emperor Valerian attempted to settle matters face to face with Sapor only to be taken prisoner during the negotiations. He remained a captive for the rest of his life, even being forced to help the Persian king into his saddle by kneeling before him and acting as a human mounting-block. Nor did the humiliation end with his death, for Sapor had him stuffed as a trophy.

The squandering of military resources and efforts in repeated bouts of civil war not only weakened the response to the Persian threat but also encouraged other enemies. Every time an emperor was murdered, killed in battle or, more rarely, died of natural causes, various claimants gathered their forces to argue their case with armed force. The resultant stripping of the frontier garrisons did not go unnoticed by barbarian eyes across the Rhine and Danube.

On the Danube frontier barbarian pressure mounted through the 230s and 240s and was becoming relentless by mid-century, with the Goths in particular raiding into Lower Moesia but also by sea into Asia Minor. Attacks by the Germanic Carpi were repulsed from the province of Dacia in 245–47, but in 250 they attacked again just as the Goths invaded Moesia. The Emperor Decius was twice defeated in battle against the Goths, the second time leading to his death, and his successor, Gallus, was forced to offer them easy peace terms. By the early 260s, the Romans had been forced to accept the permanent loss of the provinces beyond the Danube, undoing all of Trajan's hard-won Dacian conquests. The abandonment of the *Agri Decumantes*, the defensive system spanning the gap between the Rhine and Danube, opened the Alpine routes through Raetia (modern Switzerland). It was largely the Gothic threat to Western Asia that prompted Valerian to seek his fateful meeting with Sapor, hoping to establish a stable peace that would free some of the precious military resources constantly tied down in the east by the Persian threat in order to bolster the overstretched defences closer to Rome. The Gothic menace reached as far as southern Greece and in 268 they launched their biggest assault yet in conjunction with the Heruli. Storming through the Balkans they reached and sacked Athens.

Attacks across the Rhine into Gaul had also escalated from occasional raiding to a serious problem by mid century. Most of this is attributed by our sources to the Alemanni, a name which literally means 'all of them', itself an indicator of the increasing tendency of the Germanic tribes to cooperate in larger confederations to better prey upon their Romanized neighbours. The dozens of tribes along the Rhine known to Julius Caesar and the early emperors had now been incorporated into a much smaller number of major groupings, of which the most important were the Franks, Suebi, Vandals and Alemanni. Exploiting the weaknesses created by Gothic success along the Danube, the Vandals attacked Pannonia (modern Hungary) while the Alemanni seized Raetia, putting Italy itself within reach of their raids.

These multiple threats would have been serious enough even if the Roman response had been a unified one, but it wasn't. Instead the competing demands of the various fronts only exacerbated internal division and prevented an efficient concerted marshalling of the empire's still massive resources. After Valerian's capture, just as it seemed Roman fortunes must be at their nadir, the legions based on the Rhine, understandably believing their troubles should be the top priority, took drastic action. They proclaimed one of their own officers, Postumus, as emperor, the first of a string of usurpers, not recognized by the senate at Rome, who would rule Britain, Spain and Gaul as the so-called 'Gallic Empire', levying its taxes and, generally successfully, defending the Rhine frontier. Postumus and those who replaced him were not secessionists or rebels throwing off Roman dominion, but local leaders doing what the central authorities were failing to do.

An even more serious weakening of the unity of the empire developed in the east where the defence of the provinces was increasingly left in the hands of the client ruler of Palmyra. Although he acknowledged the authority of Rome and led the resistance against Sassanid encroachments and Gothic raiding in the capacity of *Corrector Totius Orientis* (Supervisor of the Whole East) bestowed upon him by the Emperor, Odenathus was virtual ruler of a large and valuable swathe of the empire, stretching from the Black Sea to the borders of Egypt. When he died in 267, or thereabouts, his widow Zenobia soon threw off any pretence of subordination to Rome. Claiming descent from Cleopatra, she proclaimed her young son Vallabathus as emperor, and, acting as his regent, seized Egypt in addition to the lands already held. The African provinces were the breadbasket of the empire, providing the cheap grain that was a vital ingredient in the famous 'bread and circuses' recipe for the obedience of the Roman mob. Now Egypt was gone and endemic raiding by nomads operating out of the desert fringe plagued the other African provinces.

Despite this string of disasters the Roman Empire survived the third century pretty much intact. Although some of the threats were managed with a combination of diplomacy and financial payments to hostile tribes that amounted to little more than protection money, the key ingredient of recovery was the army's continued ability to win victories in the field, this in turn being made possible by the willingness to adapt. At Naissus, the Emperor Gallienus inflicted a severe defeat upon the Goths who had recently sacked Athens, although conspiracy forced him to return to Italy, where he was killed before he could finish the job. The following year, 269, the Emperor Claudius II gained a more decisive victory over the Goths, earning himself the soubriquet 'Gothicus'. Some of the defeated warriors were incorporated into the Roman forces, while the rest were pushed back over the Danube where they posed a relatively minor nuisance for a century or so. In 270 Aurelian defeated the Vandals in Pannonia and then, in the following year, thwarted a major Alemanni incursion into Italy before turning east to deal with Zenobia in 272.

While a trusted general invaded Egypt by sea, Aurelian crossed the Hellespont into Asia Minor with the main force. Most of the communities abandoned Zenobia's cause, especially after the one city that actively resisted was stormed but spared a massacre at the last moment. But as he approached Antioch, the regional capital, along the valley of the Orontes river, Aurelian found the self-styled Queen of the East waiting on the same bank, blocking the way with a powerful force that may have consisted entirely of cavalry and certainly included large numbers of cataphracts.

Unfortunately we do not even know how large Aurelian's own army was, or what proportion of it was cavalry, but Zosimus suggests it was the quality of the Palmyran cavalry, not their numbers, that concerned Aurelian and it was upon his own cavalry that he intended to rely to counter them. All of which suggests that his own cavalry force was substantial. So impressed was the emperor by the massed formations of Zenobia's cataphracts that he didn't wish to risk his infantry having to face their charge.

> But observing that the Palmyrene cavalry placed great confidence in their armour, which was very strong and secure, and that they were much better horsemen than his soldiers, he planted his infantry by themselves on

the other side of the Orontes. He charged his own cavalry not to engage immediately with the vigorous cavalry of the Palmyrenians, but to wait for their attack, and then, pretending to fly, to continue so doing until they had wearied both the men and their horses through excess of heat and the weight of their armour; so that they could pursue them no longer.[23]

This plan, the classic feigned flight manoeuvre, has led many to conclude that Aurelian must have employed only specialist light cavalry. He is known to have had some regiments of Dalmatian light cavalry, who are thought to have been unarmoured apart from small round shields and with light javelins or darts as their primary armament. But it is very likely that most of his cavalry were of the usual type with thrusting spear and spatha, probably in addition to javelins, and protected by a larger shield, metal body armour and helmet. They may even have included units of *contarii*, in fact anything other than cataphracts. To make the emperor's plan work they had only to be able to outrun the armoured horses of Zenobia's troops. As noted earlier, most Roman cavalry were thoroughly trained in a wide range of techniques, including both evasive manoeuvres and close combat. On this occasion they do not even appear to have been required to make the repeated hit and run missile attacks that were the speciality of true skirmishing cavalry, just a single sustained withdrawal until the moment was right for shock action. Victory was clinched by a well-timed assault that caught the Palmyrans as their own charge ran out of impetus on blown horses.

> As soon as the cavalry of the emperor saw their enemy tired, and that their horses were scarcely able to stand under them, or themselves to move, they drew up the reins of their horses, and, wheeling round, charged them and trod them underfoot as they fell from their horses. By which means the slaughter was promiscuous, some falling by the sword, and others by their own and their enemies' horses.[24]

Zenobia abandoned Antioch but soon offered battle again at Emessa. Both armies had been reinforced, Zenobia's apparently to a strength of seventy thousand, considerably outnumbering the Romans, although we do not know how many men Aurelian had. Despite their losses at the Orontes, Zenobia still relied chiefly upon her heavy cavalry, which still outnumbered Aurelian's horsemen. In addition to the Dalmatians, the Romans certainly now included North African Mauretani, who were definitely light-armed cavalry, but also Pannonian and Moesian units that were probably of heavier type. Recruited in the Danube frontier provinces, the latter units probably held large numbers of troopers of Sarmatian or Gothic origin, raised on the ethos of the charge.

The Romans were drawn up in conventional style with the cavalry on the flanks of the infantry, with orders to repeat their previous tactics. When it came, however, the Palmyran charge was better timed, or the Roman feigned flight was bungled, so that the cataphracts were able to catch their opponents. Their superior armament enabled them to defeat the shaken Roman cavalry easily in close combat, to the extent that Zosimus says 'most of them fell', but the Palmyran formations inevitably became disorganized in the process. Before they could regroup and reform, perhaps even while the mounted fight still raged, some of the Roman infantry turned about and attacked them in the rear. The clubs and staves of a Palestinian contingent proved particularly effective in bludgeoning and crushing horses and riders alike, despite their armour. The Palmyrans broke and attempted to flee, leaving the field 'filled with dead men and horses, whilst those few who could escape took refuge in the city'.

Zenobia was captured shortly after and paraded in Aurelian's triumphal procession, although she was, unusually, allowed to live, ending her days in Rome as the wife of a senator. Having settled accounts with Palmyra, Aurelian returned to Europe and marched against the unlicensed franchise that was the Gallic Empire. By then, Postumus was long dead and his successors had experienced much less success in keeping Franks, Alemmani and the like out of Gaul and Saxons from Britain. In the face of this display of legitimate imperial strength, the latest incumbent, Tetricus, surrendered without any serious resistance, allowing Aurelian to take the title of Restorer of the World. In 295 Galerius soundly defeated the Persian general Narses, restoring some equilibrium to the eastern frontier and ending the crisis where it had begun.

Intense stress had wrought significant changes upon the structure of the empire. When he defeated the Persians, Galerius was not the only legitimate emperor. In 285 Diocletian had become emperor through a coup. He took a great step towards ending the spiral of usurpation and disputed successions through a clever four-way power-sharing arrangement now known as the tetrarchy. Appointing his potential rival, Galerius, as his co-emperor, they each took the traditional title Augustus along with responsibility for half the empire. Each then appointed a deputy, bestowing upon him the title of Caesar and marking him out as his successor. There were precedents for multiple emperors from the second century, Marcus Aurelius sharing power with his adoptive brother, but it was the simultaneous demands upon opposite extremes of the empire after the rise of the Sassanids that hammered home the truth that a single emperor could not campaign in more than one place at a time. Diocletian's system was merely a development of a well-established practice, as there had been multiple emperors, mutually recognized ones rather than usurpers, for most of the third century.

The tetrarchic system did not last long after the unprecedented retirement of Diocletian and his latest fellow Augustus in 305. It was destroyed by Constantine, who had successively killed off all his colleagues by 325 and continued to reign supreme until his death in 337, although he did grant three of his sons the junior title of Caesar. Upon his death his three sons all took the title Augustus and multiple emperors again became the norm. Although for practical purposes these imperial colleagues tended to allocate geographical spheres of action, each held authority throughout all the provinces and were partners in running an empire that was still a single entity. Eventually, in AD 395, the empire was formally and permanently split into two distinct entities, the eastern empire being governed from Constantinople.

The third century crisis had also forced great changes upon the Roman army, a process of adaptation that continued throughout the fourth century to meet the threats that continued on all fronts. Some of the stages in the process cannot be clearly followed and there is much debate over the order and speed at which changes occurred, and which Emperors can be credited with which reforms, but the main outlines can be identified. Our best evidence for the composition and structure of the army of the late empire comes from the *Notitia Dignitatum*, an official roster of units comprising the various commands. It is thought to have been compiled around the time of the final division of the empire, by which time the transformation was more or less complete.

The most significant thing about the later Roman army is that it had become much larger. When Septimius Severus had defeated the Parthians in AD 195, Rome's forces are believed to have totalled somewhere in the region of 340,000 men. By the accession of Diocletian, in AD 285, the army numbered 389,704 men, according to John the Lydian, the precision of the figure giving us some confidence that he had access to official records now lost to us even though he did not write until the sixth century. As crises multiplied, the rapid expansion of the regular army could only be paid for by harsh measures, including the debasement of the currency and heavier taxation – an increasing proportion of which had to be paid in kind with clothing, food and fodder to supply the armies directly. Conscription was also reintroduced, although the theoretical liability of every citizen for military service had never officially been abolished. These were bitter pills for the empire's inhabitants to swallow but Diocletian and his colleagues were prepared to enforce them and the expansion accelerated dramatically, leaving contemporary chroniclers to complain about the expense despite the obvious dangers assailing the frontiers. The figures Zosimus gives for the forces available to each tetrarch in AD 312 add up to 581,000.

Despite the return to conscription, an increasing amount of this manpower was drawn from the very 'barbarians' who made it necessary. From the third century onwards the Roman army had increasingly been fleshed out by recruiting from barbarian tribes. With conscription deeply unpopular, it made sense to draw on these tribal societies, many of which had a strong warrior ethic, simultaneously reducing the number of restless and hungry warriors beyond the frontier while providing tough recruits for Rome. Typically, large groups of these men were recruited as a condition of the peace terms imposed after a Roman victory.

As the army expanded, the proportion and importance of cavalry within it also increased. They were required to counter the powerful mounted forces of the Persians, Sarmatians and Goths. Even on the Rhine where the enemy were largely infantry-based, mobility was still at a premium to regain the initiative against scattered raiding parties. Gallienus, emperor from 253 to 268, is generally credited with a major development when he assembled up to thirty thousand cavalry, usually based around Mediolanum (Milan), to form the empire's first real central reserve. Here they were strategically placed to defend Italy against attack via the Alpine passes, or to reinforce either Gaul or the Balkan front. Gallienus is also usually credited with the massive increase in the legionary cavalry contingents that seems to have taken place, each legion now having 726 horsemen, the equivalent of a full regiment, permanently attached. A further boost came when Aurelian incorporated the forces of the defeated Zenobia, which included a high proportion of cataphracts and horse archers. Diocletian created new mounted guard units called *scholae*, which replaced the mainly infantry Praetorian Guard, the latter being finally abolished by Constantine around AD 312 after the battle of the Milvian Bridge.

Although all these developments may be seen as significant for the role of cavalry, it seems that the great increase in their total numbers didn't occur until the fourth century. Zosimus' breakdown of the tetrarchs' forces only included 51,000 cavalry. This is very close to the estimate for the auxiliary cavalry of the second century AD derived from epigraphic and textual references to named units.[25] If we accept Zosimus' figures as they stand, the cavalry formed only eight per cent of total forces in the early fourth century. Even if we add in an estimated fifteen thousand cavalry for the mounted contingents of the *cohortes equitatae*, on the assumption that Zosimus counted these units among the infantry, it still only brings the cavalry up to eleven per cent of the total. It is perhaps not surprising that the massive increment of additional manpower mobilized in the late third century consisted of hastily conscripted infantry. With the depths of the crisis weathered and long-term structural reforms having taken root, the emperors of the fourth century oversaw a massive shift in emphasis towards cavalry.

The change can be clearly seen in the *Notitia Dignitatum*, where a high proportion of the units listed are cavalry, the old *alae* and *cohortes equitatae* appearing alongside new formations, the *scholae* of Imperial guards, *vexillationes* and *cunei* (literally 'wedges' which is suggestive of a shock role). Problems with regard to the size of the units listed make firm totals based on this source controversial, but one of the lower estimates puts the total forces at 514,500 men, which would mean an overall decline due partly to losses; but of these 165,500, an impressive thirty two per cent, were cavalry. The same calculation gives a higher proportion of cavalry for the eastern half of the empire, some forty per cent, than for the west, where it was around twenty per cent. The higher proportion in the east is understandable in view of the nature of the Sassanid threat and in certain areas cavalry was actually in the majority. The Ducate of Mesopotamia was protected by 3000 infantry and 6500 cavalry (68.4 per cent); the Ducate of Osrhoene by 3000 infantry and 7500 cavalry (71.4 per cent); both of these being territories regularly disputed by the Persians. The ducate of Scythia along the Danube was garrisoned entirely by cavalry, around 3500 of them in seven *cunei*. It must be reiterated that such precise figures can only be arrived at using a degree of speculation about unit sizes, but the fact that roughly one third of the units listed were cavalry is suggestive enough.

Gallienus' cavalry reserve can be seen as the beginning of a major shift in strategy that evolved in response to the crisis. Simultaneous threats meant the old strategy of spreading the entire force in a cordon around the perimeter was no longer viable, since a field army could only be gathered to meet a major invasion or launch a counteroffensive by dangerously weakening the line elsewhere. By the fourth century a large part of the army was still posted as garrisons along the frontier, but mobile field armies were held in readiness at strategic points on the road network, often deep behind each front, ready to counter any major threat.*

In the *Notitia Dignitatum*, units are listed as belonging either to the frontier forces (*limitanei*), or to the field armies (*comitatenses*), the latter enjoying higher status. This distinction had replaced the old one between citizen legions and non-citizen auxiliaries, which had been rendered obsolete at a stroke when Roman citizenship had been extended to all free male inhabitants of the empire in AD. 212. Cavalry seem to have formed a higher proportion of the lower-status *limitanei* (some fifty per cent), than of the *comitatenses* (around twenty per cent), but we should be careful of drawing any inference about the value of cavalry in general from this. First, their use as border troops reflects their extreme usefulness in the type of work required there for patrolling and chasing down raiding parties or bands of illegal immigrants. Secondly, notwithstanding the existence of an edict of AD 372 that recruits not meeting the height requirement for field armies should be

---

*It is not unusual for books to make a link between the need to move cavalry rapidly by road with the invention of the horseshoe, either suggesting the Romans introduced them for this purpose or remarking that their unshod horses must have suffered from the use of such roads. The truth of the matter is that the Romans did not have horseshoes as such, despite some attempts to date their invention much earlier than the archaeological evidence allows. What they did have was the so-called hipposandal, which basically consisted of an iron sole laced onto the foot. This would have fallen off at anything more than a walk and was almost certainly used only as an emergency measure to protect the foot when moving an already injured horse. But it is probably a good thing for Roman horses that they did not have true horseshoes, and not merely because they tend to skid on hard surfaces. There is a growing body of opinion among modern horse-owners and veterinarians (although still opposed by the tradition-bound majority) that horseshoes are detrimental to horses' feet. In shod horses, the part of the foot known as the frog is underdeveloped and so cannot play the vital shock-absorbing role assigned it by millions of years of evolution, nor can the hoof wall splay out slightly as it should on contact with the ground. On a hard road surface, the concussive effects upon a horse's foot and legs when walking with shoes are three times greater than trotting without them. According to this school of thought, horseshoes, a medieval invention, have done little but harm.

enlisted into the *limitanei*, few modern scholars view the frontier forces as the next to worthless rabble they have sometimes been portrayed as. Indeed, in particularly troubled stretches of the frontier, and there were plenty of them in the fourth century, the *limitanei* must have had more combat experience than most troops in the field armies. Furthermore, when field armies mobilized to repel an attack, or launch a pre-emptive or punitive strike into the *barbaricum*, as the world beyond the borders was known, they took *limitanei* troops under command. On occasion these ended up being permanently transferred and recategorized as *pseudocomitatenses*. Finally, it should be noted that even the twenty per cent cavalry content of field armies represents a massive increase in emphasis for the Romans. It is a much higher proportion than Alexander's Macedonian armies used or even Hannibal's Carthaginians, both accepted as great proponents of cavalry warfare.

It is interesting to note the attitude of Flavius Renatus Vegetius, who wrote a famous military manual, *De Rei Militari* for the emperor around 385. Vegetius' aim was to show how Rome's fortunes could be restored by learning from the military methods of the past. Yet, while he decried the woeful slipping of standards and discipline in the infantry of his own time, he decided the ancients had little to teach Rome's much improved cavalry:

> Many instructions might be given with regard to the cavalry. But as this branch of the service has been brought to perfection since the ancient writers and considerable improvements have been made to their drills and manoeuvres, their arms, and the quality and management of their horses, nothing can be collected from their works. Our present mode of discipline is sufficient.[26]

He also specifically contrasts the tendency for the cavalry to become better equipped and armoured while the infantry became less so.

> But the method of the ancients is no longer followed. For though, after the example of the Goths, the Alans and the Huns, we have made some improvements in the arms of cavalry, yet it is plain the infantry are entirely defenceless. From the foundation of the city till the reign of the Emperor Gratian, the foot wore cuirasses and helmets. But negligence and sloth having by degrees introduced a total relaxation of discipline, the soldiers began to think their armour too heavy, as they seldom put it on.[27]

We can see the army of the fourth century in action in the campaigns of Julian the Apostate. In 357, he offered battle near Strasbourg

to an unusually large Alemanni force, said to number some thirty-five
thousand, which had crossed the Rhine and wrought serious devastation under the leadership of Chnodomar. With a force of only thirteen
thousand men, Julian was outnumbered nearly three to one. We know
his cavalry included the two specialist extremes of horse archers and
cataphracts, but not how many of each.

Julian drew all his cavalry up on his right flank and our source for
the battle, Ammianus Marcellinus, says the enemy responded by placing all their cavalry opposite their Roman counterparts. In fact the
Germans may have deployed first since it transpires that Chnodomar
had covered his own right by digging trenches, within which troops lay
in ambush. This would explain why Julian put no cavalry on his left,
either because he observed that all the German horse were opposite his
right, or because he already knew of the trenches (he had captured a
German scout). Whether they deployed first or not, the German horsemen were arrayed with infantry interspersed among them. Ammianus
explained this as a defensive measure that acknowledged the man-for-
man superiority of the Roman cataphracts in combat with less well
protected horsemen:

> They knew that for all his skill a mounted warrior meeting one of our
> cuirassiers [a common modern translation of *cataphracti*], and using one
> hand to hold his reins and shield and the other to brandish his spear, could
> inflict no harm on an opponent dressed in mail, whereas in the heat of the
> fight, when a man is occupied solely with the danger that stares him in the
> face, someone on foot, creeping along unnoticed close to the ground, can
> stab a horse in the flank, bringing his rider headlong to the ground, and
> finish him off without difficulty.[28]

Of course we know this mixing of infantry and cavalry was an age-
old trick of the German tribes, one that Julius Caesar had emulated
with mixed success. At least some of the Roman cavalry, perhaps the
majority, seem to have been armed with the traditional array rather
than as cataphracts, for when the Germans rushed upon them 'with
horrible grinding of teeth and more than their usual fury', they
defended themselves by 'protecting their heads with their shields, and
trying to strike fear into the foe with drawn swords or the deadly javelins that they brandished'. The Roman cavalry seem to have been caught
out by the speed of the German attack and to have received it at the halt,
inevitably being thrown into some confusion. As they tried to regroup,
they were assisted by the nearest infantry holding firm on their flank,

but suddenly a panic broke out and the Roman cavalry 'unexpectedly gave way in disorder'.

Ammianus says the panic was started when the commander of the cataphracts was wounded and another of their comrades, presumably also wounded, slumped over the neck of his horse, which promptly collapsed under the weight of his armour. While the wounding of their commander might alone have been enough to trigger a panic in troops already in a bad situation, the collapse of the horse may be a clue that they had been fighting for some time and were becoming exhausted. Detractors of the cataphracts regularly cite the incident as evidence of their unsuitability for battle. It is incontestable that cataphracts, like all highly specialized weapon systems, had vulnerabilities and required careful handling, but it is to their credit that they began to rally when they ran into the reserve infantry line and then returned to the fray when harangued by Julian, helping to turn the tide for a famous Roman victory.

It was Persian cataphracts that were largely responsible for Julian's eventual downfall. By 363 Julian was sole emperor (he had merely been Caesar to Constantius' Augustus at Strasbourg) and felt sufficiently secure in the west to attack Persia. Julian made good initial progress, having the better of a number of hard-fought engagements in which the Persian cataphracts and elephants proved the most dangerous opponents, forcing them to retreat to Ctesiphon. Determined to press his advantage, the emperor burnt his fleet of supply and transport boats on the Tigris to free the troops required to defend them. Julian then allowed himself to be duped into marching away from the river in a manner tragically reminiscent of Crassus before the battle of Carrhae, four centuries previously. The Romans were cautiously crossing a plain bounded by hills when the Persians attacked.

Aware that Persian scouts were observing from the vantage point of the hills, Julian's forces were moving in a defensive formation, their main battle line protected by strong vanguard, rearguard and flanking forces. The earlier engagements had already demonstrated the wisdom of such measures. Ammianus Marcellinus, who was an eyewitness, writes of 'the Persian horse, whose daring in open country inspires unspeakable dread in all peoples'. Julian was riding with the vanguard when he received news that the rearguard had been engaged by the enemy and was in trouble. No sooner had he set off for the rear, not bothering even to don his body armour, than he learnt that the vanguard was now also under attack. He duly rushed back to address this threat also, only to hear that a force of Persian cataphracts, supported by elephants, had overwhelmed his left flank guard and was pressing in on the centre, throwing the Roman forces into confusion. Julian rushed from one trouble spot to another, organizing resistance. Roman light infantry succeeded in driving off the elephants after hamstringing several of them, but the situation was so desperate that Julian himself entered the fighting. Although the Persians began to retire, the emperor's bodyguard were scattered in the confusion and were unable to prevent Julian being mortally wounded in the liver by a Persian cavalry spear.[29]

Following Julian's death the Roman army was forced into a desperate retreat, harassed all the way by the Persian cavalry, some of whom even managed once to fight their way in through the gates of the Roman marching camp. A humiliating peace soon followed in which territory and large sums of money were handed over. Yet, despite this disaster and another succession dispute arising from Julian's death, the Romans felt strong enough by the 370s to launch another major expedition against the Persians. While operations were already under way in the east, however, a crisis arose on the Danube that was to prove one of the major turning points in the history of the empire.

In 376, the Thervingi, one of the two largest Gothic groups, began to gather on the north bank of the Danube. This was no raiding party, nor even an army, but a whole people on the move, with women, children and wagons full of all their moveable possessions. They came not to fight but to seek permission to cross into the Roman Empire to settle, promising in return to provide troops when called upon. They were fleeing from the Huns, an agglomeration of nomadic groups who had suddenly embarked on a major westward drive, the latest episode in a decades-long migration that had brought them from the borders of China and which would eventually bring them to what we know as the Hungarian plain. They had already shattered the Alans and other Sarmatian groups, driving those fragments they did not absorb westward into the Goths. The Gothic Greuthungi had tried to defend their territories by building lines of fortifications but had been defeated by a surprise Hun attack and were now also abandoning their land. The Thervingi had therefore decided to seek the protection of the Roman Empire.

The Emperor Valens, responsible for the east, including the lower Danube, while his nephew and co-Emperor, Gratian, ran the west, was already committed to war against Persia. He decided to turn a problem into an opportunity and ordered the Goths to be admitted, with the intention of recruiting their warriors as *foederati* for use against Persia. There was nothing radically new in this, the only novelty of Valens' decision being that these Goths had not been recently defeated by Rome as well as the sheer number of them. His plan to settle them within the empire and recruit from them was sound but mismanaged. The local Roman authorities kept the Thervingi lingering on the banks of the Danube and treated them abysmally, tricking them out of money and goods and then demanding slaves in return for provisions. When they were joined by their kinsmen of the Greuthungi, who infiltrated across the river without permission, their discontent boiled towards open revolt, which was finally triggered by a botched Roman attempt to kill or imprison their leader, Fritigern, at a feast. The Goths destroyed the local Roman forces, partly re-equipping with their weapons, and embarked upon a sustained rampage across Thrace. They were joined by considerable numbers of Goths who had been settled in Adrianople many years previously, and who now feared attack by angry locals.

Valens sent two subordinates to deal with the situation in AD 377, but these were defeated and it was not until the summer of AD 378 that the emperor himself was able to lead an army to confront them. Reaching Adrianople, he was informed that the main enemy host was nearby and, incorrectly, that it numbered only ten thousand warriors. Infuriatingly, our main source, Ammianus Marcellinus, does not tell us how many men Valens had with him but it was a well balanced force 'made up of various elements', and 'not to be despised, seeing that it contained a large number of veterans'. The report of the enemy strength made most of Valens' officers so confident of 'a victory which in their opinion was already as good as won', that it is probably safe to assume that the Romans believed they enjoyed a significant numerical advantage. Modern estimates have tended to accept a figure of sixty thousand, but more recently this has been revised downwards to nearer fifteen thousand. The master of horse advised the emperor to wait for the reinforcements expected to arrive from the west with Gratian, his nephew and co-emperor (a position he nominally shared with his infant brother Valentinian II). Gratian had been delayed by an opportunist Alemmanic raid which had forced him to turn back to secure the Rhine, but the head of his household troops had arrived to say that he had been victorious and would arrive soon. Buoyed by the general mood of confidence and envious of the success of his nephew, Valens overruled this lone voice of caution and decided to attack.

At dawn on 9 August AD 378, Valens led his army out to find the enemy in light order, all their impedimenta being left under guard at Adrianople. After marching eight miles across rough country, they came in view of the Goths' encampment, their wagons drawn into a defensive circle. The Romans began to deploy from marching column into battle formation, the cavalry and light infantry of the vanguard forming the right wing, the main body of infantry forming up on their left to become the centre, and then more cavalry and supporting light infantry of the rearguard, which had furthest to travel, forming the left wing. The Goths were alerted and raised 'wild and doleful yells', and, although Ammianus never actually says they deployed, it is likely that most of them streamed out to form up in front of their wagons, anxious to keep the Romans away from the families sheltering within.

The Roman centre and left were still marching up to their positions when Gothic envoys approached. Fritigern had sent low-ranking messengers whom Valens refused to deal with and sent back. Valens was probably happy to spin things out while his army deployed, but Fritigern had an even greater need to play for time as the Gothic cavalry were some distance away, probably finding fresh pasture for their horses. Presumably riders were sent to fetch them the moment the Romans were spotted.

Fritigern, by means of another messenger, offered to come in person to negotiate with Valens, but only once a suitable high-ranking Roman had been given as a hostage as security. Gratian's representative, Richomer, volunteered for this and was setting out for the Gothic lines when all hell broke loose. Some archers and a unit of *scutarii* heavy cavalry took it upon themselves to attack the enemy in breach of the truce.

Now, the disaster that was shortly to befall the Romans is generally assumed to have been caused by a surprise attack by the returning Gothic cavalry striking the rear of the Roman army as it was already engaged in attacking the main Gothic position. It is not entirely clear, however, that Ammianus' description of the events set in motion by the renegade Roman attack necessarily supports this interpretation:

> He [Richomer] was on his way to the enemy's rampart with evidence of his rank and birth, when the archers and *scutarii* commanded by Cassio and the Iberian Bacurius impulsively launched a hot attack and engaged the enemy. Their retreat was as cowardly as their advance had been rash, a most inauspicious start to the battle. This untimely proceeding not only thwarted the errand of Richomer, who was forbidden to go at all, but also

brought on an attack by the Gothic cavalry under Alatheus and Syphrax, who had now arrived supported by a party of Alans.[30]

It sounds as if the archers and *scutarii* attacked the main Gothic position and were repulsed and/or fled before the Gothic cavalry launched their attack. Maybe something has been lost in translation, but 'who had now arrived' is not the same as 'who now arrived'. It may be that the Goths had moved into position while the diplomatic charade was being played out and only attacked when the renegade Romans were in retreat. In any case, there is nothing to suggest that the rest of the Roman line was yet involved and the right wing at least must have been fully deployed by the time the Gothic and Alan cavalry launched their counter-attack. It was a hot, dry August day and Ammianus went on to make great dramatic play of the choking and blinding clouds of dust, so the approach of thousands of horsemen would have been visible for miles. It is unlikely then that the opening charge of the Gothic cavalry was a complete surprise, although this is a controversial interpretation. What Ammianus leaves us in no doubt about is the effectiveness of that attack when it came: 'They shot forward like a thunderbolt from the sky and routed with great slaughter all who came within their reach.'[31]

It seems probable that it was the Roman right wing that bore the brunt of this initial charge and was driven back. Even this is not certain, but as Ammianus specifically says the left wing cavalry initially made the greatest progress until they found themselves deserted by the other cavalry it seems logical. The Roman cavalry briefly rallied 'with shouts of mutual encouragement' as the main lines advanced to engage, but they suffered numerous casualties from Gothic arrows and javelins and 'became disheartened', which may mean they took off again. If some did stay they must have been caught up in the vicious and confused clash as the two armies collided all along the line and the fighting became general. The arrival of the Gothic cavalry meant that the Romans were now heavily outnumbered.

The Roman left-wing cavalry almost cut their way through as far as the wagons before becoming isolated and overwhelmed by numbers. Unless the Gothic cavalry upon their arrival had already had time to divide themselves between both flanks of their infantry line, these Romans must have been fighting against Fritigern's infantry. Ammianus makes it clear that the right-wing cavalry had already fled before those on the left wing 'abandoned by the other cavalry and under pressure of numbers, gave way and collapsed like a broken dam'.

With both flanks stripped of their protecting horsemen, the Roman infantry of the centre were quickly surrounded and herded together, along with remnants of their defeated cavalry, into a confused mass. Their ranks were so disordered and pressed together that they could not effectively wield their weapons as the 'barbarians poured on in huge columns, trampling down horse and man'. Great clouds of choking dust obscured their view of the cavalry, which hovered upon their flanks long enough to soften them up with showers of javelins hurled into the unmissable target before closing in to come to sword and axe strokes. The situation was like that experienced by the legions of Paullus and Varro at Cannae, nearly six centuries before and the result was much the same. Many of Valens' army may have been of 'barbarian' origin, but they knew how to die like Romans.

> Our men were too close-packed to have any hope of escape; so they resolved to die like heroes, faced the enemy's swords, and struck back at their assailants. On both sides helmets and armour were split in pieces by blows from the battle-axe ... In this mutual slaughter so many were laid low that the field was covered with the bodies of the slain, while the groans of the dying and severely wounded filled all who heard them with abject fear ... Most had had their spears shattered in the constant collisions, so they made do with their swords and plunged into the dense masses of the foe, regardless of their lives and aware that there was no hope of escape. The ground was so drenched with blood that they slipped and fell, but they strained every nerve to sell their lives dearly ... In the end when the whole field was one dark pool of blood and they could see nothing but heaps of slain wherever they turned their eyes, they trampled without scruple the lifeless corpses.[32]

This brave, but ultimately futile, resistance went on for a considerable time, the midsummer afternoon sun adding to the torment of the troops below before the Roman line finally 'gave way under the overpowering pressure of the barbarians, and as a last resort our men took to their heels'. A ruthless pursuit followed as Gothic cavalry hunted down the fugitives. Valens was deserted by his bodyguard and then his senior officers. The emperor's body was never found but Ammianus recorded the rumour that he was wounded and carried by his few remaining attendants to a nearby cottage, which the Goths promptly burnt down, only one occupant escaping to tell the tale. When nightfall forced an end to the chase, two thirds of Valens' men were dead.

The role of the Gothic cavalry in this defeat, which Ammianus says was the most disastrous for Rome since Cannae, can have done nothing to discourage the continuing shift in emphasis towards the mounted arm. Of the twenty-nine units on the *Notitia Dignitatum* that appear to have been raised in the aftermath of Adrianople, no less than twenty were cavalry; but this was certainly the continuation, although perhaps accelerated, of an established trend. J. F. C. Fuller included Adrianople in his classic *Decisive Battles of the Western World*, and is largely responsible for the belief, which has proved surprisingly resilient, that Adrianople represented a tactical revolution: the decisive defeat of the Roman infantry by Germanic cavalry. In the light of what has already been shown about the nature of ancient cavalry, there is little about the cavalry's part in the battle that can be described as revolutionary. The old idea that the traditional Roman way of war held little place for cavalry was a fallacy.

Defeat at Adrianople was not in itself the end of the Roman Empire, but is often seen as the beginning of the end. It did mark the beginning of a period of sustained crisis that saw the piecemeal dismantling of the empire, but it was not so much a knockout blow as one of the first incisions in an agonizing death of a thousand cuts. It is a tribute to the continued potency of Roman arms that this slow demise took another hundred years.

After Valens' death, the surviving emperor, Gratian, appointed one of his generals, Theodosius, to be his co-emperor in the east, which probably seemed something of a poisoned chalice. He gamely continued the war but in 382 was forced to grant the Goths a peace treaty in which they were given the land to settle that they had been seeking. Although nominally imperial subjects, they were to have almost complete autonomy under their own rulers as long as they agreed to defend the frontier against further enemies and to provide men to serve in the emperor's armies when requested. The granting of this *foederate* status, which the Goths had won by force of arms, set a dangerous precedent.

In the short term the settlement offered a breathing space for the empire to recover and brace itself to face the next external crisis, but internal developments ensured the imperial response was divided. Gratian and his younger brother Valentinian III were both killed by usurpers, in 383 and 392 respectively, the perpetrators in each case being defeated and killed in turn by Theodosius, who then reigned as sole emperor until his death in 395, upon which the empire was divided into two distinct entities between his two sons. Honorius, aged ten, inherited the western empire, while the eastern empire went to Arcadius,

aged seventeen, with his capital at Constantinople. Each realm soon
have its hands full with its own problems and, with rare exceptions,
faced them alone. Indeed, there was increasing tension between the two,
at times coming close to open warfare.

Encouraged by the example of the Goths, and with the Huns continuing to encroach on their own territory, the other Germanic tribes
redoubled their efforts and increasingly raised their ambitions from hit
and run raids for plunder to permanent settlement of the more developed imperial lands. Although each group followed their own agenda,
these often coincided, whether by deliberate cooperation or force of cir-
cumstance, overstretching the imperial defences. The most severe blow
fell on the last day of 406, when large numbers of Vandals, Suevi, and
Alans all crossed the frozen upper Rhine with their families in tow and
moved into Gaul searching for new lands to settle, safely away from the
Huns who were now masters of the Hungarian plain and still extending their dominion. In a separate invasion the Burgundians carved an
enclave for themselves close to the Rhine, but over the course of three
or four years the others fought their way into Spain, which they divided
up between them and settled down.

Although the number of fighting men which each of these peoples
could field was not great, the defences of the western empire were
simply overstretched. The west's share of the units on the *Notitia Dignitatum* probably amounted to between 200,000 and 250,000 men.
But with garrisons to provide from Hadrian's Wall in the north to the
fringes of the Sahara Desert in the south, not more than a third of these,
say seventy or eighty thousand, were allocated to the field forces of the
comitatenses, theoretically available for mobile operations elsewhere.
Even these could certainly not all be gathered in one place, and even
more certainly could not be everywhere at once in sufficient force. And
this is without taking into account losses from actual casualties, desertions and those forces that were still holding out but were isolated by
the Germanic advance, most of whom would eventually melt away into
the civilian population once it became clear that no pay, provisions or
reinforcements were going to arrive. In the fifth century, a Roman general had done well if he could scrape together much more than fifteen
or twenty thousand men for a major campaign.

Because those parts of the surviving copy of the *Notitia Dignitatum*
which relate to the western empire were updated until around 420, we
can get some idea of the attrition suffered in these years of warfare.
By that date, the west's field armies contained 181 units, an apparent

increase from around 160 in 395. But, of these, ninety-seven had been
raised since 395, while another sixty-five were frontier troops re-graded
as *pseudocomitatenses* to fill the gaps. That means only nineteen of
the original field army had survived intact since 395. This does not
mean all the others had been wiped out, but many of the new units
consisted of the combined remnants of others, padded out with new
recruits. With this kind of turnover of manpower, the standard of training for new recruits before being committed to action was inevitably
compromised and vulnerable and inexperienced troops suffer higher
casualties and desertions. True, those who survive long enough gain
valuable combat experience and become veterans, but constant drafts
of fresh, half-trained conscripts have to be rushed in to replace those
who do not.

In order to maintain any kind of grip on the situation, the western
emperor, or rather those who ruled on his behalf, could find no better
option than to try to reach a compromise with the invaders, offering the
same kind of deal they had made with the Visigoths. They were allowed
to settle and farm the land they had occupied anyway, with virtual
autonomy and their own leaders, although they remained nominally
part of the empire. In return they were to protect those lands from
further invasion and to provide contingents of troops to fight alongside
the imperial armies when required. These troops served under their
own leaders, with their own weapons and equipment, a good proportion of them being the nobles who were effectively full-time warriors
and in most tribes fought as cavalry. Several large enclaves of immigrant Germans were thus established within the tattered remnants of
the old frontiers, Franks in north-eastern Gaul, Burgundians in the
south-east. The Goths ended up in possession of much of Aquitaine in
the south-west.

The original arrangement between the Romans and the Goths of
382 had not lasted long. The Goths were reluctant to be used in Roman
civil wars and dissatisfaction with their situation was exacerbated when
Theodosius defeated a usurper by sending his expendable Gothic *foederati* into a costly frontal assault on a strong defensive position. When
Theodosius was replaced by his young sons, the bulk of the Greuthungi
and Thervingi elected as their joint leader (and later king) a young
nobleman, Alaric. Under Alaric's leadership they soon merged to form
the Visigoths ('wise' Goths) and alternated between open rebellion and
uneasy alliance with first one emperor and then the other. In 401 Alaric
invaded Italy for the first time but he was defeated by Honorius' general,

Stilicho (himself the son of an Italian mother and a cavalry officer of Vandal origin). Yet when the mass invasions of 406/7 occurred, Stilicho was in the process of planning to use Alaric's troops to attack the eastern empire. In 410 the Visigoths shocked the whole empire by sacking Rome, the first time the city had fallen to a foreign enemy since the Gallic invasion nearly eight hundred years before. Alaric died of disease shortly after and the Visigoths left Italy and headed west across Gaul to settle in Aquitaine. Despite everything their *foederate* status was again recognized in 425.

A few years later, Aetius, the latest general to wield effective power on behalf of a weak western emperor, used these Visigothic allies against the Sueves, Vandals and Alans in Spain. This was effective in the short term but the real result was to give most of Spain to the Visigoths and to prompt the Vandals (who had absorbed most of the surviving Alans) to cross over to North Africa where they seized the western empire's most important remaining provinces. The Vandals, now holding the important grain supply routes to Italy, were granted *foederate* status, but this was mere imperial face-saving.

Roman armies continued to win battles throughout this period, but losses were increasingly difficult to replace. As each chunk of territory was ceded to immigrant communities, these lands ceased to contribute to the central treasury, so there was less money for the raising and equipping of regular units. The population base available for conscription also shrunk, not only because territories were physically beyond the control of imperial representatives, but because the average Roman townsman would take increasingly desperate measures, such as cutting off his thumbs, to avoid army life which was more dangerous than ever and likely to end in violent death or isolation in some outpost with no pay in return. The regular forces therefore dwindled, regardless of actual success or failure in battle, encouraging ever-greater reliance on barbarian *foederati*. The 'Roman army' with which Aetius fought and defeated Attila the Hun at the battle of the Catalaunian Plain in 451, which proved to be the last great battle of the Roman west, consisted largely of Visigothic, Alannic and Frankish allies serving under their own kings.

It had been the movement of groups of Huns into central Europe that had indirectly caused the progressive dismantling of the western empire by prompting the great tribal migrations, but the Huns were still fragmented into many groups and what little direct threat they posed was the problem of the eastern emperor. Indeed, Hun mercenaries were often used by both emperors. Their raids gradually eroded the defences along the lower Danube and even prompted massive additions to the fortifications of Constantinople itself from 412 onwards, but it was not until they were unified into a single empire that the Huns became, briefly, a true regional superpower. Attila's uncle, Ruaga, had already done much to unite the various groups of Huns in the subjection of numerous tribes such as the Sciritans and the remaining fragments of the Goths and Sarmatians. Ruaga died some time around 433, leaving Attila and his brother Bleda as joint heirs. Attila killed Bleda and became sole ruler of an empire that soon stretched from the Baltic to the Black Sea, and routinely bullied the eastern emperor for ever-larger payments of gold. But in the spring of 451 Attila launched a massive invasion of Gaul. 'Suddenly', wrote one provincial aristocrat, 'the barbarian world, rent by a mighty upheaval, poured the whole north into Gaul'.[33]

The Huns themselves fought as horse archers in classic steppe nomad style. Lightly armoured, they relied chiefly on their mobility and fire-power to hurt an enemy from a distance. Their mounts, which they rode with wooden framed saddles, perhaps much like Mongol saddles, were thought small and ugly by the empire's standards, but were surprisingly fast and incredibly tough with great stamina. Roman observers rated only the Alans as their equals in cavalry warfare. The Huns used a type of composite bow, thought to be larger and more powerful than most others then in use. The bow was asymmetric, the lower 'limb' being shorter than the upper, facilitating movement to either side of the horse's neck and thus allowing a bigger bow to be handled easily on horseback. But when the situation allowed, or required it, they also engaged in hand-to-hand combat with particular ferocity, using an array of swords and lassos. Ammianus sums up their traditional tactics:

> When they join battle they advance in packs, uttering their various war cries. Being lightly equipped and very sudden in their movements they can deliberately scatter and gallop about at random, inflicting tremendous slaughter ... At close quarters they fight without regard for their lives, and while their opponents are guarding against sword-thrusts they catch their limbs in lassos of twisted cloth which make it impossible for them to ride or walk.[34]

Like the 'Roman' army it faced, the force with which Attila stormed across Gaul in 451 was a polyglot one, containing large numbers of subject peoples. Significant among these were the Ostrogothic and

Alan contingents, the wealthier members of which would have constituted units of heavier cavalry, but there would also have been large
numbers of infantry and even a siege train. After years of amassing
Roman gold through fair means and foul, many of the wealthier Huns
may themselves have been sporting the best protective armour money
could buy.

Attila's army appears to have advanced in several columns across a
wide front, with many key cities such as Metz and Trier falling, while
others were bypassed. By June, the invaders had concentrated to besiege
Orleans. The city was home to a sizeable enclave of Alans who had been
settled there and Attila hoped to pressure their king, Sangiban, into
coming over to his side. However, Aetius had wasted no time gathering
what Roman forces he could and calling in the federated allies. Most
crucially he managed to persuade the Visigothic king, Theoderic, that
his best interests were served by joining against this terrible common
enemy. The Visigoths therefore came out in force to settle scores with
the Huns who had driven their grandfathers out of central Europe.
The approach of Aetius' army forced Attila to abandon the siege or
face being trapped against the walls of Orleans with no room for manoeuvre. He retreated eastwards, with Aetius dogging his steps, until he
came to the Catalaunian Plain, somewhere in the Champagne region of
France, and turned at bay.

Our best source for the battle comes from the Gothic historian, Jordanes, but his account is vague on vital points. As usual, we are reduced
to educated guesswork about the numbers involved. The ancient estimates of Attila's army range from three to five hundred thousand,
which are considered impossible; but even if we follow a common rule
of thumb and knock a nought off the end, this would have been a formidable host for this period. We have just as little real evidence for the
size of Aetius' forces, Jordanes using the same vague phrases such as 'a
countless host' to describe the Visigothic contingent. But, as Jordanes
says that Aetius 'had assembled warriors from everywhere to meet them
[the Huns] on equal terms', it seems they were roughly evenly matched
and if Attila had possessed a large numerical advantage he might not
have abandoned the siege of Orleans. Both armies probably contained
in the region of fifty thousand men.

It was a contingent of Franks that first caught up with the enemy,
running into Attila's Gepid subjects by night. Both groups suffered
heavy losses before disengaging, although Jordanes' claim of fifteen
thousand dead seems excessive for a chance encounter of detachments

by night. If he hadn't been before, Aetius was now aware that Attila was making a stand. The next morning he deployed, he himself commanding the left wing with his Roman troops. The right wing was entrusted to Theoderic and his Visigoths. Sandwiched between the two were Sangiban and his Alans 'in whose loyalty they had little confidence', and probably the lesser *foederati* contingents such as the Franks and Burgundians. Attila, by contrast, took station in the centre surrounded by 'his bravest followers', probably consisting chiefly of Huns. On either wing he deployed 'the innumerable peoples of the diverse tribes, which he had subjected to his sway', with the Ostrogoths under their king Valamir on the left, facing off against their distant kinsmen the Visigoths. It was late in the afternoon before both armies were ready to fight, Attila apparently being happy to wait so that he might continue his retreat under cover of darkness if things went wrong.

The battlefield, which was soon to become 'the threshing floor of countless races', was largely open plain but there was a ridge of high ground which both sides identified as crucial, although it is unclear exactly where this lay in relation to the starting points of the two armies. Attila's opening move was to send part of his army to seize the ridge, but they were too late. Roman forces under Aetius and Theoderic's eldest son, Thorismund, with some Visigothic cavalry, beat them to it 'and through this advantage of position easily routed the Huns as they came up'. As Aetius' Romans and Theoderic's Visigoths had initially deployed at opposite ends of the line, it is possible that the bulk of Aetius' army had been manoeuvred up onto the high ground, which must have been a very extensive feature. It is perhaps more likely that the ridge lay on the right flank and that Aetius, seeing the need to secure the heights first, had led a detachment across to that wing, with Thorismund's horsemen either being collected en route or sent up the hill on the initiative of his father, Theoderic.

The Huns' first attack was thrown back from the hill. Attila then ordered a general assault, which he led himself with the promise to his army that 'I shall hurl the first spear at the foe. If any can stand at rest while Attila fights, he is a dead man'. There is no hint in Jordanes' account of the Huns making use of their firepower or traditional loose-order manoeuvring in the ensuing combat that soon sprawled across the slopes and the plain below.

And although the situation was itself fearful, yet the presence of their king dispelled anxiety and hesitation. Hand to hand they clashed in battle, and the fight grew fierce, confused, monstrous, unrelenting; a fight whose like no ancient time has ever recorded. There such deeds were done that a brave man who missed this marvellous spectacle could not hope to see anything so wonderful all his life long.[35]

In this broiling fight King Theoderic fell by the banks of a brook already swollen and flowing red with the blood of the slain. Jordanes records conflicting traditions regarding his death; he either fell from his horse and was trampled by those following behind or was struck down by the spear of an Ostrogoth. The two of course are not mutually exclusive, the blow from a spear knocking him from his saddle. His immediate entourage may have died with him, as his sons were later puzzled by his absence in the aftermath of battle, or it may simply be that the confusion of battle was so great that his fall went unnoticed. But whether they knew of their king's fate or not, the Visigoths soon gained a measure of vengeance: 'Then the Visigoths, separating from the Alani [Alans], fell upon the horde of the Huns and nearly slew Attila. But he prudently took flight and straightway shut himself and his companions within the barriers of his camp, which he had fortified with wagons.'[36]

This decisive charge, launched late in the day as the light was already failing, may have been the work of the main body of the Visigoths on the plain, or Thorismund's cavalry detachment on the hill. In either case the battle was settled by the inability of the Hun contingent to stand up to the shock action of the heavier Visigothic cavalry. The gathering darkness allowed much of Attila's army to flee or join their overlord in the relative safety of the camp, although clashes between elements of both armies continued for some time. Disorientated in the darkness, Thorismund and his men almost rode right into the Hun encampment and had to fight for their lives. As the Visigothic prince was 'fighting bravely, someone hit him in the head and dragged him from his horse'. Fortunately, he was rescued by his men and carried off to safety. Elsewhere Aetius also became lost and isolated, wandering for some time in the midst of retreating enemy troops before eventually reaching the safety of the Visigothic camp 'and passed the remainder of the night in the protection of their shields'.

When dawn broke over the scene of carnage, what remained of Attila's army prepared to defend their wagons against the renewed attack they were sure must come. Attila was so convinced the end was nigh that he had a pyre built from saddles, preparing to throw himself into the flames when defeat was imminent to deprive his enemies of the satisfaction of killing or capturing him. For their part, the Visigoths were keen to oblige and finish the Huns once and for all, particularly once their king's death became clear. But Aetius had his eye on the long game and decided it was better to allow the Huns to escape in the hope of using them as a counterbalance to Visigothic power. He persuaded Thorismund that his best interests were served by immediately leading his men home, where five brothers would soon be vying to fill his father's royal shoes. So, Attila was allowed to escape and withdraw back to his central European lair, his reputation for invincibility shattered. The very next year he attacked Italy, aiming straight for Rome but, probably harassed by Aetius' troops, he was soon forced to retreat again by supply problems. Before he could threaten the empire again he died an ignominious death, choking to death on a nosebleed while lying in a drunken stupor on the night of his latest wedding. With no clear heir to Attila, the Hun empire promptly collapsed.

The Western Roman Empire did not long survive Attila's. The Emperor Valentinian III murdered its greatest defender, Aetius, jealous and suspicious of his power, only to be assassinated himself in March of 455. In June of that year Rome was sacked again, this time by a Vandal army arriving from North Africa by sea. A confusing series of weak puppet emperors followed as Rome once more consumed itself in internal wrangling while real imperial power dwindled to just Italy itself, and even this was subject to Vandal piracy. The last of these emperors, Augustulus Romulus (a name mockingly redolent with glorious associations), was deposed by his own mercenary Ostrogothic guards on 4 September 476. They proclaimed their leader, Odoacer, not emperor but king, raising him upon a shield according to Germanic custom. The imperial regalia was sent to the emperor of the east in Constantinople. Nine hundred and eighty six years after Rome had thrown off its last foreign king, it had another. By this time Gaul was already divided among Franks, Burgundians and Visigoths; Spain between Visigoths and Sueves; North Africa was in the hands of the Vandals; and Britain had long since been abandoned to the mercies of Angles, Saxons and Jutes.

The deposition of Augustulus Romulus provides a convenient end to the epic story of the Roman Empire, although, of course, it was only the western portion that had fallen. The eastern Empire continued for another thousand years, still considering themselves Romans although we know it as the Byzantine Empire (after Constantinople's original name). The Byzantine army continued to adapt and develop to meet emerging threats just as the Roman army had, marrying traditional discipline and professionalism to an acceptance of new weapons and equipment. While large infantry forces were still maintained, the importance of cavalry continued to grow. By the time the Emperor Maurice wrote (or commissioned) the military manual known as the *Strategikon*, sometime between 592 and 610, he seems to assume that cavalry were the dominant arm.

The manual goes into great detail about the cavalry formations, equipment and the tactics to be used, followed by a shorter section on deploying cavalry and infantry, but there is no corresponding section dedicated to the infantry.

> Having discussed the principles of organizing and commanding cavalry, without which, we so believe, it is impossible to confront the enemy with any degree of safety, we must now treat of the tactics and characteristics of each race which may cause trouble to our state.[37]

For major battles and most campaigns infantry would of course be present and usually in the majority, but they were clearly now thought of as a supporting arm for the cavalry.

The cavalry itself had continued to develop along the two divergent specialist lines. While bow-armed light cavalry were employed in large numbers, this is how the *Strategikon* says troops should be equipped, presumably describing the standard type:

> They should have hooded coats of mail reaching to their ankles, which can be caught up by thongs and rings, along with carrying cases [for the mail]; helmets with small plumes on top, bows suited to the strength of each man and not above it, more in fact on the weaker side, cases broad enough so that when necessary they can fit the strung bows into them, with spare bow strings in their saddle bags; quivers with covers holding about thirty or forty arrows, in their baldrics small files and awls; cavalry lances with leather thongs in the middle of the shaft [for carrying looped over the shoulder] and with pennons; swords; round-neck pieces of the Avar type with linen fringes outside and wool inside. Young foreigners unskilled with the bow should have lances and shields ... The horses, especially of officers and the other special troops, in particular those in the front ranks of the battle line, should have protective pieces of iron armour about their heads and breastplates of iron or felt, or else breast and neck coverings such as the Avars use.[38]

Ideally, then, the dominant arm and main striking force of Byzantine armies was to be equipped as far as possible as cataphracts or clibanarii, although in its details it was now more influenced by the Avars, the latest nomadic enemy to drift westwards across the steppe. With lance, sword and heavy armour for both rider and horse, the Byzantine troopers were well equipped for close combat. They and their horses were too heavily encumbered to sustain evasive open-order skirmishing tactics, but by carrying bow and arrows in addition to their other armament, such cavalry could provide their own missile barrage to soften up the enemy for decisive shock action. They stood at the pinnacle of one and a half millennia of evolution in cavalry warfare.

8

The Medieval Knight

The preceding chapters have tried to demonstrate that ancient cavalry was capable of a full range of battlefield roles including shock action, which often proved decisive. By the fall of the Western Roman Empire, conventionally taken as the end of the ancient period, a sophisticated art of cavalry warfare was already drawing on many centuries of development and horsemen had been indulging in shock action for well over a thousand years. So what are we now to make of the surprisingly persistent theory that mounted shock combat was an invention of the middle ages and constituted a 'revolutionary new way of doing battle'?[1]

Around AD 730 the de facto ruler of the Franks, Charles Martel, started to confiscate land from the church and redistributed it to his supporters on the condition that they equip and prepare themselves to do military service when summoned. This is often seen as the beginning of feudalism, the pattern of landholding and social relations that defined the European middle ages. Because these Frankish landowners were required to fulfil their obligations equipped as heavy cavalry they were effectively the prototypes of the medieval knight.

Martel's efforts to raise an effective cavalry force have been seen as particularly significant due to a belief that the Franks, along with the Saxons, had previously been notable among the invaders of the Roman Empire for their complete reliance upon infantry. When, in 732, Martel's Franks halted an invading Islamic army at the battle of Poitiers (also called the battle of Tours), it seems they did so on foot. Unfortunately the sources for the battle are disappointing in the extreme. The strategic setting is clear enough. A large Muslim army under Abd-er-Rahman had crossed the Pyrenees, advanced to the River Garonne, where they easily defeated the local forces of the count of Aquitaine, then continued their advance in the direction of Tours. They had sacked Tours, or were about to, and were pillaging all the surrounding territories when they were confronted by Charles and a large Frankish army. But when it comes to the actual fighting, the best-known source has only this to say:

For almost seven days the two armies watched one another, waiting anx-
iously the moment for joining the struggle. Finally they made ready for
combat. And in the shock of battle the men of the North seemed like a sea
that cannot be moved. Firmly they stood, one close to another, forming as
it were a bulwark of ice; and with great blows of their swords they hewed
down the Arabs. Drawn up in a band around their chief, the people of
the Austrasians [the Franks], carried all before them. Their tireless hands
drove their swords down to the breasts [of the foe]. At last night sundered
the combatants.[2]

It is this 'bulwark of ice' metaphor that has ever since conjured up
the image of a steadfast infantry shield wall. The other relevant western
source, the chronicle of St Denis is even more vague, adding only the
improbable estimate that Charles slew three hundred thousand of the
enemy for a loss of only fifteen hundred men of his own. That and the
fact that this is where Charles won the sobriquet of Martel or hammer,
'for as a hammer of iron, of steel, and every other metal, even so he
dashed and smote in the battle all of his enemies'.[3] Fortunately there is
also an Arab chronicle. Understandably, this portrays the encounter as
a much closer-run thing, stretching into a second day of fighting:

Near the River Owar [Loire], the two great hosts of the two languages and
the two creeds were set in array against each other. The hearts of Abderrahman, his captains and his men were filled with wrath and pride, and
they were first to begin the fight. The Moslem horsemen dashed fierce and
frequent forward against the battalions of the Franks, who resisted man-
fully, and many fell dead on either side, until the going down of the sun.
Night parted the two armies: but in the grey of the morning the Moslems
returned to the battle. Their cavaliers had soon hewn their way into the
centre of the Christian host. But many of the Moslems were fearful for the
safety of the spoils which they had stored in their tents, and a false cry
arose in their ranks that some of the enemy were plundering the camp;
whereupon several squadrons of the Moslem horsemen rode off to protect
their tents. But it seemed as if they fled; and all the host was troubled. And
while Abderrahman strove to check their tumult, and to lead them back
to battle, the warriors of the Franks came around him, and he was pierced
through with many spears, so that he died. Then all the host fled before the
enemy, and many died in the flight.[4]

Between them the sources seem to justify the generally accepted
view of a doughty shield wall of Franks stoically resisting the repeated

cavalry charges. The morale of the Arabs eventually broke, probably as much due to heavy casualties as genuine fears for their camp, but perhaps not before they had in places penetrated the Frankish line. There is no mention of Frankish cavalry.

A mere seventy years later, Martel's grandson Charles the Great (better known as Charlemagne) is believed to have had as many as thirty-five thousand heavily armed cavalrymen available to him, although these would never all have been called up at once. By then the Frankish domain encompassed all of France, the Low Countries and most of Germany, over half of Italy and a part of northern Spain, with varying degrees of control also being exercised in the Balkans and central Europe. The *scarae* (hence the modern word squadrons) of heavy cavalry are deemed to have played a prominent, even dominant, part in these conquests. Glimpses of them in action can be gleaned from the inadequate chronicles of the period, such as this entry in the *Annales Regni Francorum* for the year 782: 'Each individual seized his weapons and charged with as much speed as he could muster, just as fast as his horse would carry him, upon the place where the Saxons were drawn up in battle array.'[5]

The archaeological record shows us that just a little before Martel initiated this transformation, stirrups began to be added to the other weapons deposited in Frankish warrior graves. This coincidence of new technology, reform and subsequent Frankish dominance did not go unnoticed by twentieth-century historians. The arrival of the stirrup in Western Europe has become central to the myth of the medieval invention of shock cavalry and great claims have been made for this simple device, such as the following:

> The entire middle ages was built on a few bits of leather and metal. For without the stirrup, the medieval lancer, to which the entire economic system was dedicated, would not have constituted a fully credible weapons system.[6]

Thus has the stirrup been credited with causing not only a seismic shift in military tactics, but also a social revolution in the form of the development of feudalism. Although a few military writers had previously noted the stirrup as a militarily useful invention, the link between the stirrup, feudalism and the rise of the medieval knight was really developed and popularized by an American writer, Lynn White Jr ... in the 1960s. White was a 'technical determinist', a member of a school of thought that seeks to explain historical development in terms of technological leaps. This agenda is quite clear from the title of the work in which his stirrup theory first saw the light of day: *Medieval Technology and Social Change.*[7] From this standpoint it seemed clear that it was the availability of the stirrup that convinced Charles Martel that it was worth the effort to turn a nation of foot soldiers into horsemen. Successful as the Franks had been at establishing themselves in the anarchic world of post-Roman Europe, their rulers simply did not possess the centralized financial and bureaucratic resources to pay and equip a standing army; even less so one of expensively equipped cavalry. The only way to subsidize an adequate supply of horsemen was to give warriors land upon which to exploit tenants and raise horses, and the biggest land-owning organization, then as now, was the church.

Taking land from the church was not something to be done lightly, as the Franks had long since converted to orthodox Christianity and religion was an important prop to royal authority. Martel himself was careful to get papal backing for the coup in 737 by which he deposed the king whom he had served as mayor of the palace. His son, Pepin III, was crowned by Pope Boniface in 751 (completing the replacement of the Merovingian dynasty with the Carolingian) and his grandson, Charlemagne, who ruled from 768 to 814 and led the revamped Frankish armies to their greatest string of conquests, later enjoyed the title of Holy Roman Emperor bestowed upon him by Pope Leo III. If cavalry could only be had at the cost of risking excommunication, then why bother?

By the early eighth century the Franks had already proved by far the most successful of the invaders that had fastened upon what had been the western Roman Empire and already dominated the lion's share, simply using their traditional armies. Obviously the stirrup's credibility as a motive for major political change depends upon it having had real military significance. White believed that the stirrup revolutionized warfare by making mounted shock combat viable for the first time, and thus gave Charles Martel a new option worth pursuing despite the cost and political effort involved. According to White, he summoned the Frankish cavalry into being specifically to take advantage of the 'revolutionary new way of doing battle' presented by the stirrup. The fundamental flaw in this argument is that cavalry had been effectively employed in a shock role, alongside other tactics, by diverse nations for more than a millennium before the adoption of the stirrup. We shall examine the stirrup's contribution to horseback fighting in more detail shortly, but first we must address the question of the stirrup's origins, for one of the many problems with the whole theory is that early medieval warriors were far less instantly impressed with it than modern historians have been.

When one looks for the evidence for the spread of stirrups, it is striking how little there is, and how long it is between their first appearance and the point at which we can be confident that they were in general use. Even making allowances for the general paucity of sources for most things relating to the early medieval 'dark ages', we might hope for more of a historical footprint if it was a truly decisive innovation.

The existence of rudimentary leather or rope stirrups has been proposed by various writers, and attributed to various cultures, but hard evidence is in decidedly short supply. Although perishable materials would not easily survive in the archaeological record, some firm literary or artistic evidence would seem a reasonable prerequisite for accepting such theories. Carvings from the Deccan plateau in central India do show horsemen riding with their big toe in a leather or rope loop from as early as the second century BC.[8] This would have helped to keep the rider's feet in a good riding position, but it would be difficult and uncomfortable to put much body weight on just the big toe with the loop tightening round it, so would not have been half as useful as a true stirrup. Besides, there is no evidence that the toe loop spread beyond India, perhaps not least because it could not be used with closed-toe shoes or boots.

Stirrups as we know them originated in or near China. They are represented on statuettes dated to around AD 300, and the earliest literary reference is in the memoirs of a Chinese general dating to AD 477.[9] They may have been a Chinese invention and it is sometimes suggested that they were a way for the sedentary Chinese to narrow the skill gap between their regular cavalry and the natural horsemanship of the nomadic steppe peoples that constantly threatened their northern borders. Many experts now believe that innovations in equestrian equipment are more likely to have originated among the nomads. If a new piece of horse tack introduced into the volatile horse-dominated world beyond China's northern border had really conferred some massive inherent advantage in mounted combat, we might expect it to have spread across the Eurasian grassland like lightning, galvanizing all horse warriors along the way. Instead it appears to have taken several centuries.

The Huns did not have stirrups. In a fine demonstration of the way in which the exaggeration of the stirrup's significance still colours popular writing and common perception, the most recent biographer of Attila asserts his belief that the Huns must have had stirrups in the fourth century, apparently on the basis that he could not believe they were such famously good horsemen without them. Yet this same author admits that there is no literary or archaeological evidence to support his supposition.[10] The Avars seem to have brought stirrups across the steppe, the first examples in the west appearing in Avar graves of the late sixth century, in what is now Hungary. The Avars were a nomadic people, of either Turkic or Mongolian stock, who arrived on the southern steppes in the second half of the sixth century and carved an empire centred on the Hungarian Plain that was eventually destroyed by the Franks under Charlemagne in 796.

The earliest written evidence for the arrival of stirrups in the west is in the *Strategikon*, where they are listed amongst the equipment each trooper should have. As we have seen, this tactical manual, written at the cusp of the sixth and seventh centuries, reveals how the Byzantine armies were increasingly focused on heavy cavalry tactics and were strongly influenced by Avar equipment. On the face of it this could seem to support the idea of the stirrup's importance for mounted shock combat, but we have already seen that the Byzantines were merely continuing a trend started centuries before.

Byzantium's arch-enemies, the Sassanid Persians, had begun to introduce the stirrup into their powerful cavalry arm by the middle of the seventh century, to judge by the depiction upon a late Sassanian silver plate now located in the Hermitage Museum, St Petersburg.[11] Whatever assistance it gave was not enough to prevent that empire's defeat, completed by 651 by the religiously inspired fervour of the armies that had burst forth from Arabia in the 630s. These early Muslim armies made relatively little use of cavalry, large numbers of camels being used instead to provide a high degree of strategic mobility. Horsemen did play a significant part at the second battle of the Yarmuk River in August 636, where a major victory over the Byzantines was sealed by the Islamic cavalry charging with a fortuitous (divinely sent, the faithful would argue) sandstorm at their backs. But as they went on to convert virtually all of the Middle and Near East at the point of the sword, and then to overrun the length of North Africa, cavalry became increasingly important to them.

The Arabs themselves did not adopt iron stirrups until 694, on the order of the general Al Muhallab, by which time their most dramatic conquests had already been made, but some ambiguous evidence of a much later chronicler may suggest they had already been using wooden ones which repeatedly broke in combat.[12]

Although there is a general stereotype of Muslim cavalry as lightly equipped, through the eighth and ninth centuries they often fielded larger numbers of armoured cavalry than their Byzantine foes. Once Turkish elements were absorbed, they also fielded large numbers of light horse archers, but among the Arabs themselves there was always a greater emphasis on long lances. These were about twelve feet long and made of cane and, although they were weaker than western types, they were also more easily managed. Muslim tactics were often modelled on Byzantine methods, stressing the coordination of the different arms, the infantry acting as a solid defensive base from which the cavalry could launch repeated controlled charges.

Although it is true there is a broad coincidence of timing between the Arab adoption of stirrups and the increasing weight and number of their cavalry, we should not assume any causal link. It is much more probable that the determining factor was the securing of an adequate supply of horses. Horses were such a scarce and valuable resource in Arabia that during the early conquests they were led on the march and only mounted immediately before going into battle. Once they had completed the destruction of the Sassanids at the battle of Qaddasiya in 636, the caliph's force gained access to the famous equine resources of Persia. North Africa too had long been renowned for its horses, and it was under Muslim rule that the tough, enduring barb was crossed with the more refined and spirited eastern types to produce the famous Arab breed. In 711, Islamic forces crossed the straits of Gibraltar and began the rapid conquest of Spain, taking control of another of the most ancient centres of horse-breeding excellence (and bringing the Frankish domain within raiding distance).

The same expansion that brought more and better horses within reach also brought contact with the stirrup. It may be that the Arabs, whose collective experience of horses was initially limited by their scarcity, had more to gain from using stirrups than did others. One of the very few scraps of written evidence comes from an Arab source, Al Jahiz (d. 868), who passed on the opinion that 'stirrups are among the best trappings of war for both the lancer who wields his spear and he who brandishes his sword'.[13] Of course the Arabs themselves soon became only one of many components of Islamic armies as conquered peoples were converted and recruited, and its adoption among some of their subjects was slow and uneven. Most Berber cavalry, heirs to the Numidian tradition of supreme horsemanship, were apparently still riding bareback in the ninth century, and many Syrian Mirdasid tribesmen were still doing so in AD 1030 when they helped defeat a Byzantine force. They have a reputation in the written sources as 'daring bare-back riders' and 'dare devil riders'.[14]

Some Franks, as far as we can tell, may have begun using stirrups about the same time as the Arabs, that is in the late seventh century. But as they first appear in graves in East Prussia and Lithuania, on the eastern fringe of the Frankish domain, it seems most likely they came directly from the Avars. This means the stirrup had taken about a century to travel the few hundred miles from where they first appear in Avar graves in Hungary.

Were the Franks just slow on the uptake because of their complete unfamiliarity with mounted warfare? This would certainly be an over-simplification, for the idea that they made no use of cavalry before the Carolingian period seems to be a fallacy. It is widely accepted that wealthy Franks of the Merovingian period rode horses on campaign, but commonly assumed that they dismounted to fight as infantry. Yet the *Notitia Dignitatum* listed cavalry units recruited among the Franks. Literary clues include a passage in Gregory of Tours' sixth-century *History of the Franks*, describing how the Thuringians dug concealed pits and 'many of the Frankish cavalry rushed headlong into these ditches'.[15] A sixth-century Frankish plaque depicts a horseman charging with a stout lance held in the two-handed grip used by Sarmatian tribesmen and Roman or Persian cataphracts in shock charges.[16] This is not to say that the impoverishment of the post-Roman world had not reduced the number of Merovingian Franks who could afford to raise or buy horses. This may well have caused a decline in the use of cavalry prior to Martel's time.

Even if early Frankish use of cavalry has often been overlooked, the timing of the stirrup's arrival in Francia might, on the face of it, fit well enough with the idea of a significant reform and increase in cavalry under Charles Martel. But if they really were decisive military assets we might expect them to have become a cherished part of every mounted warrior's equipment very rapidly, but this doesn't seem to have been the case. Of over seven hundred Frankish warrior graves identified from the late seventh to the ninth century, that is those containing other military accoutrements, less than two per cent contain stirrups.[17] So we may accept that stirrups were known to some Franks in the early eighth century, but the archaeological record gives no reason to believe that their use had yet become general, or even common, a century later.

Pictorial evidence seems to suggest an even later date for the generalized use of the stirrup. The earliest western European representations of horsemen using the stirrup are in the St Gallen Psalter, dated to the second half of the ninth century at the earliest. White argued that the late appearance of stirrups in manuscripts was due to the ignorance of the monks responsible for them, yet they faithfully reproduce other details of military equipment, including 'winged' spears which White claimed were specifically linked to the use of shock cavalry. Furthermore, the St Gallen Psalter shows some horsemen with stirrups and some without. Its illustrator was clearly aware of their existence but chose not to show them as universal, even though he gave the horsemen uniform spears, shields and helmets. The Utrecht Psalter, dated to about 830, shows no stirrups in its battle scenes. Depictions of stirrupless cavalry can be found even from the tenth century, suggesting they were either still not general or not considered particularly significant. We might also note that the only existing equestrian statue of Charlemagne, whose stirrup-equipped cavalry supposedly conquered most of western Europe, depicts him without stirrups.

Contemporary European written sources are silent on the arrival of this wonder weapon. One place we might have expected to find a mention is in Charlemagne's revision of the laws of the Salian Franks, which gives a detailed list of the compensation values of horses, weapons and equipment.[18] Although bridles and saddles are listed, stirrups are not mentioned. Perhaps they were included with the saddle, but the inclusion of such minor items as sheaths, listed separately from swords, might lead us to expect that stirrups would also get a separate mention if they were considered essential.

What few clues there are in the surviving literature suggest that mounting without the aid of stirrups remained the norm well into the ninth century. Notker's biography of Charlemagne tells of a newly appointed bishop eschewing the mounting-block provided for him, preferring to vault into the saddle. Charlemagne then demanded the bishop's company on campaign where this ability would come in useful. Around 856, Rabanus Maurus, the bishop of Mainz, produced a new edition of Vegetius' late Roman manual, *De Re Militari*. He specifically stated in the preface that he had included only those parts relevant to current practice, including this description of training recruits to mount and dismount:

> The recruits at first try to mount unarmed, then they mount carrying shields and finally very large pole weapons. And this practice was so thorough that

they were forced to learn how to jump on and off their horses not only from the right but from the left and from the rear, and in addition they learnt to jump on and off their horses even with an unsheathed sword ... indeed the exercise of jumping [on and off one's horse] has flourished greatly among the Frankish people.[19]

With stirrups, mounting a horse, even with spear and shield, requires no special training, as the author can attest from personal experience. Clearly training was still necessary in Maurus' time because most Frankish horsemen might be called upon to mount quickly, armed and ready, without stirrups.

The stirrup was almost certainly known in Frankish lands in the early eighth century, but the evidence seems to suggest that it only came into general use there much later, probably in the second half of the ninth century. It follows from this that stirrups, whatever else they were responsible for, were not behind Charles Martel's proto-feudal land reforms nor the success and importance of Charlemagne's cavalry in his many conquests. The increased use of cavalry by the Franks was not prompted by the arrival of a new technology, it was the continuation of an existing trend, accelerated by Charles Martel's land reforms.

Although academics now reject the direct link between the stirrup and the development of feudal institutions, White's underlying assumption that stirrups were essential for shock combat still has a powerful grip. Stirrups after all did become ubiquitous and the western knight was indeed a formidable force in medieval warfare. The Byzantine princess and historian Anna Comnena famously wrote in the eleventh century that the charge of European knights was irresistible and could drill right through the walls of Babylon.[20] So it is time now to look at exactly what it is that stirrups are meant to have offered and also at what the medieval knight could do that the ancient horseman could not.

Stirrups are simple in the extreme, each consisting of a metal footrest which usually closes the base of an arch by which it is suspended by a strap from the saddle, one being attached to either side. When the rider places one foot in each stirrup, he or she can put his weight on one foot or the other to adjust his balance in the saddle, or even stand up in them. There is no doubt that they make it easier to retain or regain one's balance, particularly at a trot, and would be particularly valuable during fast turns and unexpected manoeuvres such as inevitably occur in a fast-moving cavalry action; but the extent to which horsemen who had never learnt to depend upon them were restricted in their movements or confidence has been grossly exaggerated.

It has been said that ancient horsemen were handicapped because they had to rely on leg contact and their sense of balance to maintain their seat. Anyone who has endured a riding lesson (in the United Kingdom at least, Americans and others ride differently) will know that this is precisely what one is supposed to do even when riding with stirrups. The toes only rest lightly in the stirrup, helping to keep the desired leg position, but leg pressure and good posture should do most of the work of signalling the horse, balancing and taking one's weight when raising oneself from the saddle in rising trot or over jumps. Routinely relying on the stirrups to balance, though an easy habit to slip into, leads to poor posture and is heartily discouraged. Significantly, modern European cavalry, though equipped with stirrups, were trained to ride without, precisely to prevent an overdependence upon them which might have led to poor riding habits and potential disaster should the trooper lose his stirrup (that is to say his foot slipping out) in action. Medieval knights rode differently of course; with very long stirrups and a straight-legged posture which was largely forced upon them by the increasingly high saddles used. Interestingly, this posture fits that recommended by Xenophon because it allows one 'to put more power into ... delivering a blow from horseback'. It was not a medieval innovation.

By offering a firmer platform, it is argued, the use of stirrups greatly increased the effectiveness and confidence with which horsemen could use close-combat weapons. White had argued that before stirrups the horseman was 'much restricted in his methods of fighting. He was primarily a rapidly mobile bowman and hurler of javelins'.[21] Supposedly only the added stability afforded by stirrups allowed cavalry to trade effective blows with the enemy at close quarters. This of course is unsustainable in the light of the evidence advanced for earlier periods.

The weapons historically used by horsemen for close combat can be divided into two categories. First, one-handed cutting or concussive weapons, predominantly swords but also axes and maces. Secondly, shafted thrusting or stabbing weapons; that is spears of various description which, when used from horseback, can be generically termed lances. Advocates of the stirrup's revolutionary status have claimed that the use of both categories of weapons was ineffectual before its introduction.

Carolingian cavalry carried long, double-edged swords, tapering elegantly to a point but primarily designed for cutting. The general trend through the middle ages was for blades to become longer, and the quillons which protected the hand also became longer as well as straighter to give the crucifix shape befitting the defining emblem of a Christian knight. Now, others have argued that 'with a long, heavy sword but without stirrups your slashing horseman ... had only to miss to find himself on the ground'.[22] Stirrups can certainly provide useful lateral stability, and in particular a horseman fighting against infantry can, by standing in his stirrups, get more of his weight over a downward blow and can more easily reach an opponent to his front left, although this remained a vulnerable spot and his rear left even more so. But practical experiments and conversations with experienced re-enactors and stuntmen show that a stirrupless rider can deliver an effective sword stroke without loss of balance.[23]

Such reconstructive research can give useful insights but is of secondary importance to compelling literary evidence we have already seen for the aggressive use of swords by ancient cavalry. The reader might recall Xenophon opening the cut-versus-thrust debate with a recommendation for the *kopis*. This weapon was certainly shorter than medieval swords, but very blade heavy and designed only for brutal slashing blows with plenty of shoulder behind them. Indeed it was probably such a sword with which Alexander the Great's helmet was cleft at the River Granicus and with which, a few moments later, his Companion Cleitus the Black severed the arm of the Persian Spithridates. And who can forget the horror of later Macedonians at the terrible mutilation, 'the necks completely cut through, internal organs exposed', wrought by the hacking of Roman cavalry with their Spanish swords in 200 BC? The Celts, among the most famed horsemen of antiquity, favoured slashing swords at least as long and less well balanced than the more tapered Carolingian patterns. The Romans crossed this with their Spanish swords to produce the *spatha*, over three feet long, carried by their cavalry at the height of their Empire. Sarmatian swords could have blades in excess of forty inches and certain stylistic features are likely to have directly influenced medieval Germanic types. What the Greek poet Archilochus called 'the grievous work of the sword' was well known to ancient horsemen.

But it is the lance that is considered the weapon *par excellence* of shock cavalry. White explains why he believed stirrups revolutionized its use:

Before the invention of the stirrup it was wielded at the end of the arm

THE MEDIEVAL KNIGHT 315

and the blow was delivered with the strength of the shoulder and biceps. The stirrup made possible – although it did not demand – a vastly more effective mode of attack: now the rider could lay his lance at the rest, held between the upper arm and the body, and make at his foe, delivering the blow not with his muscles but with the combined weight of himself and his charging stallion.

The stirrup, by giving lateral support in addition to the front and back support offered by pommel and cantle, effectively welded horse and rider into a single fighting unit capable of a violence without precedent ... The stirrup thus replaced human energy with animal power, and immediately increased the warrior's ability to damage his enemy.[24]

So awesome was the power of this new method, allegedly, that it called for the development of a new weapon. The early Carolingian cavalry carried a lance some eight to ten feet long, with projections or 'wings' below the head designed to prevent the head penetrating too far into a victim's body to be retrieved easily in battle. Despite the fact that they had been known earlier and were also carried by Frankish infantrymen, White asserted:

their novel design is intelligible in terms of the new style of mounted shock combat with lance at rest [couched under the arm] ... an unstirruped rider ... could seldom have impaled an adversary so deeply that his weapon would get stuck ... The generalization of the wing-spear in itself is evidence that under Charles Martel and his sons the meaning of the stirrup for shock combat was being realized.[25]

It is accepted that there is no firm evidence for ancient riders making use of 'couching', as this technique of tucking the lance under the armpit is known, although at least one depiction of a Sarmatian-influenced Bosporan cavalryman might be tentatively claimed as such. But we have already seen that ancient cavalry made effective enough use of their lances across the centuries, using three other techniques which it might be useful briefly to recap. First, the most common across the whole period covered was the overarm method, with thumb to the rear, which Xenophon recommended for use 'against adversaries in front or behind or to either side of you'. Most Greek and Roman cavalry used this approach.

Secondly, we have the method with which Alexander the Great is depicted skewering a Persian on the Issus Mosaic, the lance held underarm in one hand with thumb forward, but slightly away from the body rather than couched. It was Alexander's Macedonian cavalry, above all, who proved that this method was a formidable one.* Then of course there is the two-handed grip used by Sarmatian tribes and by those Roman, Parthian and Persian troops who also used the heavy *kontos* or *contus*. This was probably the technique used by those Parthians at Carrhae that Plutarch describes impaling two Roman infantrymen at a time, as well as horses and riders. The same technique can be seen tumbling men and horses amid the splintering of shafts on the Firzubad rock carvings.

The *kontos*, or 'barge pole', which the poet said 'casts a long shadow upon the enemy field', was an inherently unwieldy weapon occupying both of the rider's hands and would never have gained acceptance by riders who were anything less than very secure and confident in their ability. Much the same might be said of the long lances that the Macedonian Companions put to such devastating effect, although these were at least sufficiently well-balanced to be wielded in one hand. And we might also do well to remember the perennial problem the ancients faced of lances being shattered upon the enemy by the force of their blows, requiring Greek, Macedonian and Roman weapons to have a spike or a second head on the butt end. The sound of splintering shafts must have been as much a part of the cacophony of ancient battles as of any medieval fracas.

The one technique that was not well tried and widely established before the arrival of the stirrup was that of couching, wherein the shaft of the lance is tucked under the armpit. As a result many writers have associated couching closely with the advent of the stirrup, so that the two things seem essentially and inextricably linked and couching is presented as the decisive contribution of that invention to the conduct of cavalry warfare, at the very heart of the supposed military revolution.

*The author's own tentative, not to mention painful, experiment showed that the blow is not delivered with the rider's strength alone (although of course infantry spearmen did enough slaughter in this manner) and that even with a light, blunt shaft (a broomstick as it happens), sufficient of the horse's impetus can be imparted through a shield to knock a standing man over. The author wishes to thank Catherine and Chloe Wildish, Maria Chittenden, Merlin and Midnight Express for their help on 20 February 1998. Others have since conducted more scientific tests with replica lances against dummies, and these have been referred to earlier: Peter Connolly, 'Experiments with the *Sarissa* – the Macedonian Pike and Cavalry Lance: A Functional View', *Journal of Roman Military Equipment Studies*, 11 (2000), pp.79–88.

There is little room for doubt that a couched lance does indeed transmit more of the charging horse's momentum than any of the other three modes of attack, although it is unfortunate that nobody has, to our knowledge, been able to measure scientifically just how much more. This method completed the neat causal chain of White's theory: the stirrup allowed couching of the lance; couching of the lance made mounted shock combat vastly more effective; and efforts to secure a supply of this new improved cavalry led to major social and political reform. Besides the evidence already presented to show that mounted shock combat was already far more effective and widespread than this theory allows, there are other problems.

There is an increasing realization among historians that it is an over-simplification to lay all the credit for the development of the new tactic at the door of the stirrup. The reader may have noticed in the quotation above that even White slipped in a mention of the pommel and cantle of the saddle, and most other authors tip a passing nod in this direction. Indeed, the practical experience of re-enactors of medieval jousting confirms that the raised saddle plays a bigger part in transmitting the momentum of the horse to the target via the lance and in preventing the lancer being driven off the back of his horse by the impact. The stirrups are very useful when the rider pushes down and forward against them, forcing his back tight against the cantle so that there is less give at the moment of impact. Bracing himself in this way helps the rider maintain balance and deliver a more solid blow by preventing any of the impact being absorbed by the rider's backside sliding in the saddle. It also reduces the likelihood of receiving a painful blow in the lower back from the cantle.

The practitioners consulted on this matter were generally agreed that while stirrups were very desirable for jousting, a good saddle was essential. One purist however, the only one incidentally who was interested in horsemanship across the ages, would not concede that either was absolutely essential.[26] Saddles had of course been developing for centuries before the stirrup arrived and continued to do so throughout the middle ages, with a general tendency in the west towards ever-higher pommels and cantles, which were also increasingly shaped to curve around the rider's pelvis. From this perspective, the couching of the lance, if it is technologically driven at all, is to be seen in the context of this gradual evolution, and the stirrup is clearly revealed as a useful accessory to the saddle, not the other way round as some would have us believe. Of course we must recall that heavy cavalry predates even the saddle with pommel and cantle. Furthermore, in Julius Caesar's campaigns, the German cavalry derided saddles as effeminate and continued to outclass the Gallic cavalry that used them. The type of saddle shown on the St Gallen Psalter is thought to be essentially similar to late Roman saddles, the four horns having evolved into continuous pommel and cantle, and not at all dissimilar to the Portuguese saddles favoured by some modern re-enactors of jousting.[27]

A more fundamental problem with the whole stirrup-couching-feudalism chain is that there is no good evidence for widespread couching of the lance before the late eleventh century, one of the first clear depictions of it being in the Bayeux Tapestry's scenes of the battle of Hastings in 1066, some four centuries after the stirrups 'revolutionary' arrival in western Europe and well after the feudal system was established throughout the former Frankish empire (which had by then fragmented). Contemporary manuscripts depict the Carolingian cavalry with their winged spears using the overarm method, and the same is true of the majority of the Norman and French knights on the Bayeux Tapestry, the very same technique shown in use by those first Assyrian lancers.

None of this is intended to suggest that stirrups were worthless. They made it safer and more comfortable for mounted combatants to do those things they had been doing for centuries. The added stability they offered was particularly useful in offsetting the topheaviness of a rider's defensive equipment, his armour and shield. The added stability simplified the old dilemma of balance versus protection in favour of the latter. It would have made it easier for a warrior to learn to ride in armour, enabling him to enter battle with the best protection he could afford with more confidence in his safety, and confidence is an essential ingredient in martial prowess and mounted combat in particular.

The early Carolingian cavalry were clad in a short-sleeved waist-length garment, the byrnie or brunia, most often made of metal scales but sometimes of the more expensive chain mail, and wore distinctive open-faced iron helmets with a brim that turned up to a slight peak at the front. The wealthiest may have worn lamellar greaves on their shins. In addition they were well protected by large circular shields with a metal framework and a pronounced, often spiked, iron boss covering the central handgrip. The total level of protection was no better than that offered by the equipment that had been worn by the bulk of imperial Roman cavalry regiments, the rider's face in particular actually being much more vulnerable, and was much inferior to that enjoyed by cataphracts or *clibanarii*, whose limbs were also encased.

By the time of the battle of Hastings, the byrnie had been replaced by the much longer hauberk, most often of chain mail, which protected the thighs and arms. The face was now better protected by a conical helmet with a nose guard, or nasal, worn with a chain mail hood, or coif, that gave excellent protection to the neck and ears. The round shield had evolved into the longer, so-called kite-shaped type (possibly influenced by Muslim types), usually supported by a shoulder strap. It was more bulky but gave nearly complete cover to a rider's vulnerable left-hand side where it was difficult for him to effectively bring his weapon to bear. Even so, it was not until the twelfth century, with the reintroduction of full chain mail protection from toe to fingertips and fully enclosed helmet, that the medieval knight gained the same level of protection as the eerily masked cataphracts of the ancient world who were said to appear like polished statues.

The wearing of heavy armour and armour is pertinent to one of the functions of the stirrup which is often overlooked or underrated, that of easing the task of mounting. Indeed, there is one interesting line of inquiry which suggests that this, not enhanced combat capability, was at least initially seen as its defining function. In the *Strategikon*, the first literary evidence for the stirrup west of China, the term used is *skala*, literally a step or ladder. In its Chinese birthplace the relevant word is composed of *ma* (horse) and *den* (to mount). Our English 'stirrup' is derived from the Saxon *stigan* (to climb) and *rap* (rope), while its German name, *steigbugel*, translates as 'stephanger'. Although the value of this function should not be underestimated, especially for a heavily armed warrior, it hardly seems the basis for a reputation as an epoch-making development.

One thing that certainly did not change between the ancient and medieval period was the vast expense of equipping and maintaining a mounted force. What this meant to a warrior in a Europe where the monetary economy took centuries to recover from the collapse of the Western Roman Empire is shown by an interesting ninth-century document listing various items of equipment evaluated against the value of a cow. A helmet would set you back six cows, sword and scabbard seven cows, greaves six cows, and a spear and shield two cows. For a further twelve cows you could protect yourself with a byrnie and a horse would cost you the same again.[28] The more labour required to produce an item, the greater the cost. By the eleventh century, the

longer hauberk, consisting of some 25,000 steel rings, has been estimated to have cost roughly the equivalent of the annual income of a
fair-sized village. The sophisticated pattern-welded long sword took
over two hundred hours of skilled labour to produce and would have
cost at least as much and the cost of warhorses had at least kept pace.[29]
It is reckoned that a knight had to spend about a year's income to equip
himself with the essentials of his trade, but for a particularly well-bred
warhorse the sky was the limit.

The horses themselves did become bigger through the middle ages,
but there was not as dramatic or rapid a shift as is often supposed.
Under the late Roman Empire, the average size of mounts in most cavalry units had probably been somewhere between fourteen and fifteen
hands, although smaller types would have been found amongst the specialist light cavalry units, just as larger ones would have been reserved
for the cataphracts. The loss of the resources and bureaucracy of the
Western Roman Empire almost certainly brought a decline in systematic selective breeding for some time after, but there is archaeological
evidence that nobles were breeding for greater size again by the ninth
century. Even so, the mounts of eleventh century Norman knights
still probably averaged between 14.2 and 15 hands high. The horses so
famously portrayed on the Bayeux Tapestry look compact and sturdy
enough, but not tall.

Of course height alone is not all, or even primarily, what was sought
by either Roman or medieval breeders. Speed, endurance, weight-bearing capacity and a suitable temperament were also required. Norman
horses were probably akin to the stocky modern Frisian, or the similar British Fell and Dales breeds. Frisian horses were already listed as
among the best all-round cavalry horses by the Roman writer Vegetius.[30] It was not until the late middle ages that the greatly increased
weight of armour for rider and horse led to some horses being specially
bred for weight-bearing alone, creating the massive *destrier* or great
horse, which most people imagine being lumbering monsters like
modern shire horses. Even then, most knights probably still rode something more akin to a heavy hunter type, not much above 16 hands and,
although muscular, still proportioned well enough to be quite agile.

More powerful horses, high saddles, stirrups and heavy lances tucked
under the arm (and later supported by a bracket built into their armour)
all meant that the medieval knight very probably could deliver a charge
with more physical impact than the ancient horseman. Of course this
can have had little effect on determining the outcome of combats with

other heavy cavalry, since if they were similarly equipped any potential effect would be cancelled out. Furthermore, whatever the load-bearing capacity of the *destrier* and the stability offered by higher saddles and stirrups did to improve methods of attack was at least offset, eventually, by a corresponding increase in the technology of defensive armament. When knights fought other knights it must often have been a less lethal affair than the clashes we have seen between ancient squadrons.

When fighting against light cavalry, such as the Turkish horse archers encountered during the Crusades, the armoured medieval knights experienced the same difficulties in coming to grips with them as the ancient Macedonians did with Scythian horsemen or the Romans against Numidians or Parthians. Indeed, as they became heavier and less agile in the late middle ages they would have found this problem ever more severe. On the other hand, the light horsemen could not gain a rapid decision over the armoured horseman and could not stand their ground if kept under pressure, requiring plenty of space and time if they were to achieve a decisive result.

The deciding factors in cavalry fights remained the same as they had always been. Numbers of course were important when all else was equal, but the smaller side often won if they had greater cohesion, determination and offensive spirit. The timing of the charge could be crucial and the decisive leadership required to seize a fleeting opportunity remained at a premium, along with the discipline to regroup and launch another attack if required, though few in the middle ages could match Alexander's Companions in these things, and none surpassed them. If the initial charge did not win a fight, it remained true that the side with the last reserve in good order would probably win. The dynamics of cavalry versus cavalry combat had not altered in any appreciable way.

Those that wish to assert the relative inferiority of early cavalry often point to those occasions when they dismounted to fight. Medieval knights also often dismounted to fight among the infantry and for the same reasons. Sometimes it could be because the tactical situation made the holding of a particular fixed position a priority or because the terrain made mounted action disadvantageous. Often it was because the accompanying infantry (who were still usually in the majority in medieval battles) required the morale bolstering of having their social superiors literally standing shoulder to shoulder with them. The decision of the English knights to dismount and fight among the infantry at Crecy, Poitiers and Agincourt (many of the opposing French doing likewise at the latter two), to name only the most famous examples, did not indicate a lack of skill in mounted fighting any more than similar decisions by the Roman nobles who fought on foot to save the young Republic at Lake Regillus in 496 BC and several other battles did.

This leaves the question of cavalry versus infantry, and for this we have the perfect case study in the most famous medieval battle of all. The battle of Hastings in 1066 has often been seen as the coming of age of the feudal knight – not its apogee, that was still some distance in the future – but the point at which many see the elements of the 'revolutionary new way of doing battle' as essentially in place. The fact that Harold's Saxons fought on foot has earned it a place in many minds as the symbolic victory of the 'new' medieval shock cavalry over the 'obsolete' infantry phalanx. Whereas the Muslim horsemen at Poitiers in 761 had broken upon the rock of the Frankish infantry, at Hastings, the Saxon shield wall was broken and trampled by the Norman knights; surely proof positive that the full effects of the stirrup-instigated revolution had matured (a mere five hundred years after the Avars brought stirrups across the steppe). That fateful day of 14 October 1066 therefore provides an appropriate landmark from which to complete this brief survey of just how far the fundamentals of cavalry warfare had by then been transformed.

Duke William of Normandy, having filled a fleet of ships 'with mighty horses and valiant men',[31] landed unopposed at Pevensey on the Sussex coast on 29 September 1066 while King Harold of England was occupied defeating a Norwegian invasion attempt in Yorkshire. William soon moved the bulk of his force to Hastings, rapidly fortifying his base and began sending troops out to forage and pillage the surrounding area. This not only brought in stocks of vital fodder, it also issued a challenge to Harold by demonstrating his inability to protect his subjects, even here in an area which was his traditional family power-erbase and where he held many of the estates directly. In this manner William hoped to draw Harold to him for a decisive battle, rather than risk a long ambush-prone march through hostile territory, away from the coast where his fleet provided communication with Normandy and a route of reinforcement or retreat.

Harold answered the challenge. He probably heard of William's landing while he was still in York setting things in order after his victory at Stamford Bridge (26 September). Despite the casualties and inevitable fatigue that battle had cost his army, he immediately marched the 190 miles south to London with the core of his army. Or rather he rode. For although the Saxons would fight on foot at Hastings, the English nobility and their armed retainers, like nobility everywhere the horse was known, rode to war. It is increasingly accepted that Anglo-Saxon forces did at times fight mounted when the situation favoured it, as their long experience of harrying Viking raiders often did, but we cannot dispute that they placed a much stronger reliance on infantry tactics. Saxon armies were built around the bands of full-time warriors, or huscarles, maintained by each noble household, including the king's own. To these were added the local levies, or *fyrd*. Harold left whatever remained of his local levies in the north, not least because they could not have kept up with the pace. When he reached London, he delayed for several days, sending out the order for the southern shires to muster their forces and gather at the appointed spot. Rejecting advice to wait for all his forces to gather, he once more set off southwards at speed, no doubt hoping to surprise William as he had the Norwegians at Stamford Bridge.

On the morning of 14 October, William, warned by his scouts of the enemy's approach, led his army north to seize the initiative. Several of the earliest sources say it was Harold who was surprised when the Normans found him nine miles north of Hastings. He was either still hurrying south or halted at the place appointed for the rendezvous of the local troops, probably the 'hoary apple tree' mentioned by one version of the Anglo-Saxon Chronicle.[32] Either way, Harold still did not have his full strength but, finding himself in a strong defensive position, decided to stand and fight. He deployed his army at the top of a hill, named in one source as Senlac Hill, with a forest behind him through which his army had just marched along the road from London. Strong arguments have been put forward in recent years that this was actually Caldbec Hill, not Battle Hill where Battle Abbey now stands, traditionally believed to have been built to mark the exact site of Harold's last stand.[33]

All Harold's nobles and their retinues who had arrived on horseback dismounted, presumably sending their horses back with grooms to be tethered among the trees. One French source, the poem known as the *Carmen de Hastingae Proelio*, saw this as evidence of the Saxons' backwardness; being a 'race ignorant of war', the poet sneers, 'the English scorn the solace of horses and trusting in their strength they stand fast on foot'. But regardless of the truth about Saxon familiarity with mounted warfare, the decision to dismount, far from showing ignorance of war, shows Harold's grasp of the tactical use of terrain. Whichever hill he actually planted the dragon banner of Wessex on, it appears to have presented a steep slope to the enemy in front, while his rear was protected from encirclement by the forest. The *Carmen* itself adds that 'the ground was untilled because of its roughness'.[34] Not great cavalry country then, but an ideal position for a static defence by infantry.

Once dismounted, the huscarles, the most experienced and best-equipped men, were mostly clustered in the centre around Harold on the highest point of the hill, but he also 'strengthened both his wings with noble men'.[35] Some of the huscarles then were placed among the militia massed on either flank, probably forming the front rank because of their better armour and, perhaps more importantly, offering leadership by example and stiffening the resolve of the lesser men. The huscarles wore mail coats, helmets and shields essentially identical to those worn by the Normans. Saxon spears and swords were also similar, but some also carried the famous long-handled Danish axe, which could be unwieldy but was also potentially devastating in expert hands. There were only a very few archers among the English ranks, represented by a solitary figure on the Bayeux Tapestry. Although archers had featured in other Saxon battles, including the recent victory at Stamford Bridge, they were perhaps not a speciality of the southern counties.

The Saxon infantry formed up in the very close order usually referred to as a shield wall, which several sources liken to a forest. Our most reliable source, William of Poitiers' *Gesta Willelmi ducis Normannorum et regis Anglorum*, says 'their extraordinarily tight formation meant that those killed hardly had room to fall'.[36] What William's army faced then was an infantry phalanx drawn up on high rough ground, the oldest response in the book against an army superior in cavalry.

The numbers present on each side are impossible to glean from the sources. The pro-Norman sources naturally exaggerate the numerical superiority of the enemy to magnify the achievement of overcoming them (and excuse the difficulty with which this was achieved), while Saxon sources emphasize the fact that Harold's army was not yet fully assembled, admitting also that many deserted him at the approach of the Normans. Many well-educated guesses, and much detailed academic research into the resources theoretically available to each leader, have resulted in a broad consensus that both armies were probably somewhere between five and ten thousand strong and that Harold's may well have been the larger but not necessarily by very much. Of William's force, the cavalry would certainly have been less numerous than the infantry, perhaps only two thousand and probably not more than three thousand strong.

William's army was a more balanced combined arms force and his deployment was accordingly more sophisticated. 'He advanced with his troops in the following highly advantageous order,' explains William of Poitiers:

> In the vanguard he placed infantry armed with bows and crossbows; behind them were also infantry, but more steady and equipped with hauberks [presumed to be spearmen with shields, though they hardly feature in the written accounts of the fighting and are not identifiable on the Bayeux Tapestry]; in the rear the cavalry squadrons, in the midst of which he took his place with the elite. From this position he could command the whole army by voice and gesture.[37]

From the *Carmen* we learn in addition that the Normans themselves were in the centre, while their French and Flemish allies held the right wing and the Breton contingent the left.[38] All was in place by the third hour of the day, about nine o'clock, and with a blaring of trumpets William's army began a steady, disciplined advance and 'in no way frightened by the difficulty of the place, began slowly to climb the steep slope'.

According to the *Carmen*, as the advance continued a Norman knight named Taillefer rode ahead and capered about to taunt the enemy, and an unnamed Saxon accepted the challenge and came forward to engage in the kind of single combat that had been common in early Roman battles. As soon as this English champion drew near, Taillefer easily rode him down with his lance, then dismounted to decapitate him with his sword before brandishing his head as a trophy.[39] Although the *Carmen* is considered to be highly suspect as a source by many due to its uncertain date of composition and the fact that it is a poem rather than straight history, there is nothing inherently implausible about the scene which is strikingly similar to many in ancient literature (probably consciously so on the poet's part); and there is certainly nothing surprising about the easy triumph of a horseman over a foot soldier on a one to one basis, neither at this period nor for the greater part of two millennia before.

When they came within range, the Norman archers and crossbowmen unleashed a heavy barrage of missiles upon the enemy lines in an attempt to soften them up and create gaps in their ranks for a close assault to exploit; 'provoking the English and causing wounds and death with their missiles'.[40] The archers would have delivered the greater number of shafts, but the crossbow bolts had the greater penetrating power. The anonymous author of the *Carmen* exclaims that 'against crossbow bolts, shields are of no avail!' and tells us that while the archers 'transfixed bodies with their shafts', the crossbowmen 'destroyed the shields as if by a hailstorm, shattered them by countless bows'.[41]

The Saxons replied as best they could with their few archers but also with thrown spears, their elevated position helping them carry further and apparently also with crude clubs of stones tied to sticks, presumably prepared in advance by the poorer militia lacking spears. William of Poitiers refers to the English response as a 'deadly hail'. He also refers to the English fighting back with 'the most lethal of axes', presumably meaning the long Danish axes which would never have been thrown; this is one of the few clues that the Norman armoured infantry soon came to close quarters and traded blows. They made little headway against the tight-knit shield wall and were soon in trouble, so that Duke William was forced to commit his cavalry. William of Poitiers says 'the mounted warriors came to the rescue and those who had been in the rear found themselves in front', which might suggest that some of the Norman infantry pulled back and allowed the cavalry to pass through to the attack before once more moving up again in support.

'Disdaining to fight from a distance', the *Gesta Willelmi* continues, 'they rode into battle using their swords'.[42] On the Bayeux Tapestry, the horsemen are shown galloping in through a shower of javelins and hurled clubs. Most wield their lances overhead in that ancient technique, some may even be throwing them as though they too were mere 'hurlers of javelins' of the type denigrated by White. Only one or two figures in the leading ranks use the new technique of couching their lances under their arm as they attempt to batter a gap in the line of English shields, now bristling with embedded arrows and bolts. A fierce fight raged for some time (which no doubt seemed longer to those involved than it actually was). The *Carmen* says the English 'met missile with missile, sword-stroke with sword-stroke'.[43] The *Gesta Willelmi* says that in addition to superior numbers, the Saxons had the advantage of 'their weapons of attack, which penetrated without difficulty shields and other pieces of armour', which must mean the great axes were being put to good effect as the other weapons were common to both sides. The same source also notes that their position also favoured the English who 'did not have to march to the attack, but remained tightly grouped', suggesting that William's formations were becoming ragged as they laboured up the steep and rough incline.[44] The relevant scene on the Tapestry has the succinct caption 'Here French and English died together'.

For all the slightly bigger horses, high saddles, stirrups and new techniques available to the Norman knights, these had not changed the timeless fact that cavalry charging uphill against determined infantry in close order have the odds stacked against them. Despite all the pre-paratory softening up by the missile troops and armoured infantry, the English line held and the first attack of the Norman knights failed. Indeed, much of William's line now turned tail. In the *Gesta Willelmi*, William of Poitiers has it that the rout was started by the infantry, who were clearly still involved in the mêlée, and the Breton cavalry on the left wing, who were 'frightened by such ferocity', the panic spreading until 'almost the whole of the duke's army yielded'. He does add in mitigation that they thought Duke William himself had fallen, a clear indication that the Normans in the centre were also having a hard time of it.[45] A fair portion of the Saxon army, particularly the less experienced levies, not unreasonably thought they had the day won and streamed down the slope after the fleeing foe.

Duke William, seeing his men being chased off, rode into their path, shouting at them to turn and fight. He is clearly depicted on the Tapestry lifting his helmet back by the nasal so they could see he was alive and well. The cavalry, which must have easily been outdistan-cing its pursuers, rallied and counter-attacked. Those Saxons who had rushed forward in pursuit and lost their formation, and who may now have been on more even ground, proved easy meat to the returning horsemen. 'As the meek sheep fall before the ravening lion', waxes the *Carmen*, 'so the accursed rabble went down, fated to die.'[46] That cavalry could by shock action easily destroy infantry caught moving in disorder on open ground was no new development. We have seen numerous examples earlier, but one need only think of the Megarians, Phliasians and others carved up by the Boeotian cavalry at Plataea in 479 BC.

Those Saxons that survived fled back up the hill to where the main body had remained but the triumphant horsemen were hot on their heels and immediately launched into another assault. This time they managed to break into the shield wall in several places, perhaps exploit-ing gaps created as fugitive Saxons were readmitted. Once penetrated by cavalry, we would normally expect the collapse of a phalanx to follow shortly after, yet somehow the Saxons clung on and fought back hard, containing the penetrations. The horsemen were becoming dangerously bogged down and those who had broken in to the enemy ranks were at great risk of being cut off, surrounded and killed; some probably were. Those horsemen that could again broke off the fight and rode away.

According to the *Gesta Willelmi*, this second retreat was intentional from the start, a deliberate trick to lure more of the enemy to break formation in pursuit, for 'they remembered how, a little earlier, flight had led to the succes they desired'. Once more a good number of the Saxons fell for it:

> As before, several thousands were bold enough to rush forward, as if on wings, to pursue those who they took to be fleeing, when the Normans suddenly turned their horses' heads, stopped them [the Saxons] in their tracks, crushed them completely and massacred them down to the last man.[47]

Some writers have questioned whether the Norman cavalry was yet sophisticated enough to carry out such a manoeuvre, but there is no reason to doubt it. For we have seen that the feigned flight to draw an enemy out of position and formation so that they can then be rapidly defeated by shock action is one of the oldest tricks in the book, with a pedigree of many centuries. Examples that spring readily to mind are the destruction of Spartan peltasts by Olynthian cavalry in 381 BC and Aurelian's victory over Zenobia's cataphracts in AD 272. True, this is a tactic most closely associated with light cavalry, but medieval knights and their horses had not yet become as unwieldy as they would become in the late middle ages (although even this is often exaggerated) and were certainly agile and disciplined enough to outmanoeuvre infantry.

Though weakened, the remaining core of the Saxon army still stood firm on the hill, the shield wall repaired, and was clearly going to prove a tough nut to crack. The ancient sources, even the pro-Norman ones, are full of admiration for the resilience of Harold's men, one likening his army to a great boar at bay. William now brought his archers back into play to thoroughly soften the enemy up. The Saxons, with few archers of their own, had no effective answer to this and faced a similar dilemma to that experienced by the Romans at Carrhae in 53 BC. They dared not leave their position to chase off the lightly armed archers for fear of again leaving themselves vulnerable to the cavalry. Forced by fear of the cavalry to stand their ground in close order, they surrendered all initiative and made a dense, static target for the enemy arrows. It seems that William now subjected the Saxons to showers of missiles interspersed with controlled cavalry charges to exploit the resultant confusion, demoralization and gaps in the ranks:

> Then an unusual kind of combat ensued, one side attacking in bursts and in a variety of movements, the other rooted in the ground, putting up with the assault. The English weakened, and, as if they admitted their wrongdoing

by the defeat itself, now undertook their punishment. The Normans shot arrows, wounded and transfixed men; the dead, as they fell, moved more than the living. Even the lightly wounded could not escape, but perished under the dense heap of their companions.[48]

Despite the punishment they were soaking up from the archers, the Saxons still put up a stout fight against the cavalry. Even with infantry support, dislodging disciplined heavy infantry from a hilltop was always risky for cavalry, as Alexander the Great had found against the mercenary hoplites at the Granicus in 334 BC, where his horse took a sword in the ribs. William had two or three animals killed under him in these attacks. Each time he had to defend himself vigorously on foot until he could find a new mount (on the first occasion he did this by grabbing one of his French soldiers, who refused his call for aid, by the nasal of his helmet and hauling him from his saddle). Each time he apparently avenged his horse by slaying its killer, starting, according to the *Carmen*, with Harold's brother Gyrth, whom he hewed limb from limb.[49] The Bayeux Tapestry, on the other hand, shows both Gyrth and Leofwine, Harold's other brother, being killed by mounted warriors. Gyrth receives a couched lance in the face but looks as if he is burying his own spear in his assailant's throat at the same instant. Leofwine's last seconds are depicted as he stands defiantly in the path of a charging squadron, feet planted wide and axe raised for one last swing. The sources agree that the fighting went on all afternoon, and 'continued amid a welter of carnage and slaughter until nightfall' as one puts it, but the cavalry must have rested their horses between attacks, possibly exchanging them for fresh animals held at the rear.[50]

This proper application of combined arms tactics steadily wore the Saxons down, until, just as the light was fading, a decisive breakthrough was made. Harold was hit in the eye and grievously wounded; the most famous scene on the Bayeux Tapestry shows him gripping the long shaft to yank it out. The exhausted, dispirited remnants of his army began to waver and some started to run for the safety of the forest. The Norman cavalry, again inspired by the example of William still leading in person like some latter-day Alexander, charged in and cut down Harold and those that remained clustered round his banner. With Gyrth and Leofwine already dead, the English were leaderless and soon all that remained was a scattering flock of fleeing fugitives. The Norman cavalry pursued hard and cut them down relentlessly wherever they could.

A band of Saxons, reaching the relative safety of a ravine or ditch (or series of ditches), which later became known as the Malfosse, turned and made a stand. Some of the French under Eustace of Boulogne thought better of tackling these desperate men in failing light and rough terrain, and decided to call off the pursuit. But William refused to relent and ordered a final onslaught, although Eustace was severely wounded (perhaps by a javelin) while the duke was still haranguing him. In the final charge of the day, this last knot of resistance was broken, but only after 'some of the most famous Norman warriors fell, because the difficulty of the lie of the land meant that they could not show their usual courage'.[51]

Nothing that happened at Hastings would have surprised the Athenian horsemen that Xenophon wrote for or Alexander's Companions (although Alexander might have wondered what took the Normans so long), nor Hannibal's polyglot squadrons or Caesar's Gallic and German cavalry (though the latter might have mocked the knights' need for elaborate saddles as effeminate). Cavalry, of course, continued to develop and change in its technical details throughout the middle ages and beyond, but the fundamental relationships governing its use had been established centuries before on the bloodsoaked battlefields of the ancient world.

Notes

Notes to Chapter 1: Origins

1. Herodotus, *The Histories*, translated by Aubrey de Selincourt, edited by John M. Marincola (London, 1972), i, c.78.
2. Stephen Budiansky, *The Nature of Horses* (London, 1997), pp. 42–47.
3. A. Azzaroli, *An Early History of Horsemanship* (Leiden, 1985) pages 6–7.
4. The height of horses is measured in hands and inches, a hand being four inches, and usually expressed as so many 'hh' or 'hands high' (thus 12.2hh equals 12 hands and 2 inch). The measurement is taken from the withers, the juncture of neck and back, to the ground.
5. Sir Walter Galbey, Bart, *Small Horses in Warfare* (London, 1900), p.3.
6. Ibid., p.14.
7. Ibid., p.16.
8. Ann Hyland, *The Horse in the Ancient World* (Stroud, 2003), p.11.
9. A. Azzaroli, *Early History of Horsemanship* (Leiden, 1985), p.11.
10. Stephen Budiansky, *The Nature of Horses* (London, 1998), chapter 2.
11. This is still perpetuated in recent works. See Elwyn Hartley Edwards, *The Encyclopaedia of the Horse* (London, 1994), chapter 1.
12. Hyland, *The Horse in the Ancient World*, pp. 13–14.
13. Further east, the chariot reached China by about 1500 BC, while much of India had come under the influence of the Aryans by 1000 BC, as described in the epic poetry of the Rig Veda.
14. Ann Hyland, *The Horse in the Ancient World* (Stroud, 2003), p.17.
15. Xenophon, *Anabasis*, translated by Rex Warner (London, 1949) iii, c.3.
16. Quoted in Ian Fletcher, *Galloping at Everything* (Staplehurst, 1999), p.130.
17. Ibid.
18. Quoted in H. Saggs, *The Might That Was Assyria* (London, 1984), p.197.
19. Nigel Stillman and Nigel Tallis, *Armies of the Ancient Near East* (Worthing, 1987).
20. Ann Hyland, *The Horse in the Ancient World*, p.90.

21. Quoted in Holger Herwig et al., *Cassell's World History of Warfare* (London, 2003), p. 27.

22. Ibid.

23. M. Horace Hayes, *The Student's Manual of Tactics* (London, 1884), p. 26.

24. Jeremiah, 50:41–42.

25. Herodotus, *Histories*, i, c. 103.

26. Herodotus, *Histories*, i, c. 214.

27. Herodotus, *Histories*, iv, c. 128.

28. Asclepiodotus, *Tactics*, translated by W. A. and C. H. Oldfather (London and New York, 1923), c. 7, line 3.

29. Herodotus, *Histories*, i, c. 215.

Notes to Chapter 2: Classical Greece

1. Xenophon, *Anabasis*, translated by Rex Warner (London, 1949), iii, c. 2.

2. I. G. Spence, *The Cavalry of Classical Greece* (Oxford, 1996), pp. 277–79.

3. Diodorus Siculus, *Universal History*, translated by C. Bradford Welles (London and Cambridge, Massachusetts, 1963), xv, c. 31.

4. Even in Sparta, with its dual monarchy, equality before the law was absolute and the actions of the two kings were severely constrained by the five elected magistrates (*ephors*), the council of elders (*Gerousia*) and the assembly of citizens.

5. Thucydides, *History of the Peloponnesian War*, translated by Rex Warner (London, 1972), vi, c. 12.

6. J. E. Lendon, *Warriors & Ghosts* (New Haven, 2006) is a fascinating study of this aspect.

7. Late sixth century BC, Attic black-figure vase in Martin von Wagner Museum.

8. Leslie J. Worley, *Hippeis* (Boulder, Colorado, 1994), p. 26.

9. Thucydides, *Peloponnesian War*, iv, c. 55.

10. Herodotus, *The Histories*, translated by Aubrey de Selincourt, edited by John M. Marincola (London, 1972), v, c. 63.

11. Herodotus, *Histories*, viii, c. 28.

12. Thucydides, *Peloponnesian War*, ii, c. 100.

13. Peter Connolly, *Greece and Rome at War* (London, 1983), p. 58.

14. Xenophon, *On Horsemanship*, translated by Robin Waterfield (London, 1997), c. 12, lines 5–7.

15. Xenophon, *On Horsemanship*, c. 12, line 8.

16. Xenophon, *Hellenica*, translated by Rex Warner (London, 1966), iii, c. 4, line 14.

17. E.g. Attic red figure vase from Melos, *c.*400–390 BC, now in the Musée du Louvre, Paris (S1677).

18. Xenophon, *On Horsemanship*, c.12, line 11.

19. D.H.Gordon, 'Swords, Rapiers and Horsemen', *Antiquity*, 37 (1953), p.75.

20. I.G.Spence, *The Cavalry of Classical Greece*, p.20.

21. The Marquess of Anglesey, *A History of the British Cavalry*, iii, *1872–98* (London, 1982), p.370.

22. V.D.Hanson, *The Wars of the Ancient Greeks* (London, 1999), p.59; based on archaeological evidence.

23. Xenophon, *On Horsemanship*, c.12, line 9.

24. Xenophon. *On Horsemanship*, c.6, lines 13–15.

25. Ibid., c.2, line 5.

26. Ibid., c.9, lines 11–12.

27. Ibid., c.8, lines 1–2.

28. Xenophon, *Hellenica*, vi, c.4, lines 10–11.

29. Xenophon, *Agesilaus*, translated by Robin Waterfield (London, 1997), iii, c.4, line 16.

30. Xenophon, *The Cavalry Commander*, translated by Robin Waterfield (London, 1997), c.1, line 7.

31. Xenophon, *Cavalry Commander*, c.2, lines 3–5.

32. Xenophon, *Cavalry Commander*, c.2, line 5.

33. William Tomkinson, *The Diary of a Cavalry Officer, 1809–15* (Staplehurst, 1999), p.280.

34. Herodotus, *Histories*, v, c.63.

35. Herodotus, *Histories*, ix, c.68.

36. Herodotus, *Histories*, ix, c.69.

37. Thucydides, *Peloponnesian War*, v, c.73.

38. Ibid., vi, c.70.

39. Ibid., vi, c.101.

40. Ibid., iv, c.48.

41. Ibid., c.4, line 44.

42. Ibid., iv, c.96.

43. Ibid., iv, c.96.

44. Ibid., iv, c.96.

45. Ibid., vii, c.5.

46. Ibid., c. vii, c.6.

47. Xenophon, *Hellenica*, vi, c.5, line 14.

48. Thucydides, *Peloponnesian War*, ii, c.79.

49. Ibid., vi, c.67: 'half of the army was drawn up in advance, eight deep; the other half was in a hollow square, also eight deep'.

50. Xenophon, *Anabasis*, translated by Rex Warner (London, 1949), iii, c.3.
51. Xenophon, *Agesilaus*, c.32.
52. Thucydides, *Peloponnesian War*, vi, c.66.
53. Ibid., iv, c.44.
54. Ibid., iv, c.10.
55. Xenophon, *Hellenica*, iii, c.4, line 14.
56. Xenophon, *Agesilaus*, c.32.
57. Xenophon, *Hellenica*, iv, c.3, vv. 4–9.
58. Xenophon, *Hellenica*, iv, c.2, line 16 (Nemea), and iv, c.3, line 15 (Coronea).
59. Ibid., iv, c.2, line 19.
60. Xenophon, *Hellenica*, vii, c.5, line 19.
61. Xenophon, *Hellenica*, v, c.2, lines 40–42.
62. See, for instance, Ernest and Trevor Dupuy's analysis of Gaugamela in *The Collins Encyclopedia of Military History: From 3500 BC to the Present Day* (London, 1993), p.55. Others have cited the battle of Kadesh in 1294 as the first instance, but here the Egyptians were attacked while strung out on the march and the forces that saved the day appeared fortuitously, as they had been marching up the road anyway.
63. Thucydides, *Peloponnesian War*, vi, c.67.
64. Thucydides, *Peloponnesian War*, ii, c.56.
65. Ibid., iii, c.1.
66. Ibid., vii, c.4.
67. Xenophon, *Hellenica*, iv, c.5, line 16.
68. Xenophon, *Hellenica*, v, c.3.
69. Ibid., v, c.4, line 54.
70. Ibid., v, c.4, lines 43–44.
71. Xenophon, *Hellenica*, iv, c.5, line 14.
72. Thucydides, *Peloponnesian War*, v, c.57.
73. Plutarch, *Pelopidas*, translated by Ian Scott-Kilvert (London, 1973), c.2.
74. Plutarch, *Pelopidas*, c.17.
75. Diodorus, *Universal History*, xv, c.6.
76. Ibid.
77. Ibid.
78. Xenophon, *Hellenica*, vi, c.4, line 12.
79. Plutarch, *Pelopidas*, c.23.
80. Xenophon, *Hellenica*, vi, c.4, line 13.
81. Plutarch, *Pelopidas*, c.32.
82. Diodorus, *Universal History*, xv, c.10.
83. Ibid., c.10.

84. Xenophon, *Hellenica*, vii, c.5, line 23.

85. Ibid., line 22.

86. Ibid., line 23.

87. Ibid.

88. Diodorus, *Universal History*, xv, c.10.

89. Ibid.

90. Xenophon. *Hellenica*, vii, c.5, line 24.

91. Diodorus, *Universal History*, xv, c.10 (my italics).

92. Xenophon, *Hellenica*, vii, c.5, line 25 (my italics).

Notes to Chapter 3: The Macedonians

1. For example, John Keegan in *A History of Warfare* (London, 1993), thinks it 'risky', at p.286, to accept the existence of true heavy cavalry in the ancient world on the basis of their lack of saddles and stirrups – yet, at pp.259–62, he attributes Alexander's success to his dynamic actions at the head of 'his own shock force' of armoured heavy cavalry.

2. As demonstrated in the Thracian invasion of 428 BC. Thucydides, *History of the Peloponnesian War*, translated by Rex Warner (London, 1954), i, c.100.

3. Diodorus Siculus, *Universal History*, translated by G.Booth (London, 1814), xvi, c.1.

4. Diodorus, *Universal History*, xvi, c.14.

5. Asclepiodotus, *Tactics*, translated by W.A. and C.H.Oldfather (London and New York, 1923), c.7, verse 3.

6. Arrian, *Ars Tactica*, c.16, verse 7, quoted in Michael M.Sage, *Warfare in Ancient Greece: A Sourcebook* (London and New York, 1996), p.176.

7. Minor M.Markle, 'The Macedonian Sarissa, Spear and Related Armor', in *American Journal of Archaeology*, 81(1977), pp.323–39.

8. Z.Grbasic and V.Vuksic, *A History of Cavalry* (Oxford, 1989), pp.20–21. Interestingly this was apparently adopted by the hussars to counter the bigger horses and heavier armour of their opponents, a situation which would be faced in some instances by Alexander's cavalry in Asia and may already have been faced by Philip against Scythian noble cavalry.

9. Peter Connolly, 'Experiments with the Sarissa – the Macedonian Pike and Cavalry Lance: a functional view', in *Journal of Roman Military Equipment Studies*, 11 (2000), pp.79–88.

10. Alexander himself seems to have swapped his composite linen and metal cuirass, depicted in the Issus Mosaic, for a thickly quilted Persian one

captured at Issus. Plutarch, *Alexander*, translated by Ian Scott-Kilvert (London, 1973), c.32.

11. According to the calculation of Peter Green, *Alexander of Macedon, 356–323* (Berkeley and Los Angeles, 1991) p.43.

12. Quintus Curtius Rufus, *The History of Alexander*, vi, c.5, lines 18–21.

13. Ibid., vii, c.1, lines 32–34.

14. Ibid., viii, c.12, line 16.

15. Herodotus, *The Histories*, translated by Aubrey de Selincourt, edited by John M.Marincola (London, 1972), vii, c.40.

16. Herodotus, vii, c.196.

17. Remains from the Achaemenid period suggesting a height of sixteen hands are cited by A. Azzaroli, *An Early History of Horsemanship* (Leiden, 1985), p.177, and still accepted by Ann Hyland, *The Horse in the Ancient World* (Stroud, 2003), p.30. The Nisaean's stocky build is attested by Persian friezes and bas-reliefs.

18. Diodorus, xvii, c.110, says they were reduced from 160,000 to 60,000; Arrian, *Anabasis*, vii, c.13 gives 150,000 and 50,000.

19. Hyland, *The Horse in the Ancient World*, pp.30–31.

20. For the modern Akhal-Teke see Elwyn Hartley Edwards, *The Encyclopaedia of the Horse* (London, 1994), pp.74–75.

21. Hyland, *The Horse in the Ancient World* (Stroud, 2003) p.23.

22. Hartley Edwards, *The Encyclopaedia of the Horse*, pp.55–56; R.Ernest Dupuy and Trevor N.Dupuy, *The Collins Encyclopaedia of Military History*, 4th edition (London & New York), 1993.

23. Hyland, *The Horse in the Ancient World*, p.29.

24. Arrian, *Anabasis Alexandri*, translated by Aubrey de Selincourt under the title *The Campaigns of Alexander*, edited by J.R.Hamilton (London, 1971), iv, c.5.

25. Arrian, *Anabasis Alexandri*, iii, c.8.

26. Len Deighton, *Blitzkrieg* (London, 1996), p.148.

27. Fragments attest to more than two dozen now-lost accounts of Alexander written between his death and the work of Diodorus.

28. Eugene N.Borza in his preface to Ulrich Wilken, *Alexander the Great*, translated by G.C.Richards (New York and London, 1967), p.xxvi.

29. Plutarch, *Alexander*, c.1.

30. These figures are based on the thorough analysis of N.G.L.Hammond, although he states definite unit strengths with more confidence than the evidence warrants. See N.G.L.Hammond, *The Genius of Alexander* (London, 1997), p.66.

31. Arrian, *Anabasis Alexandri*, i, c.13.
32. Ibid., c.15.
33. Ibid., c.15.
34. Ibid.
35. N.G.L.Hammond and F.W.Walbank, *A History of Macedonia*, iii, *336–167 BC* (Oxford, 1988), pp.68–69.
36. Ibid., pp.48–50 and passim.
37. Plutarch, *Alexander*, c.16.
38. The figures are Arrian's which I have followed Hammond in accepting due to the likelihood that they come directly from the king's journal. Plutarch's figures differ only slightly. Diodorus' figures are much higher but all his figures and most of the narrative for this battle are unreliable.
39. Plutarch, *Alexander*, c.18. Plutarch himself admits that Aristobulus gave a different version in which Alexander simply took out the yoke pin and slid the pole out. As Aristobulus may have been an eyewitness, this may be correct; in any case the allegorical effect is much the same.
40. Arrian, *Anabasis Alexandri*, ii, c.7.
41. Ibid.
42. Nick Sekunda, 'The Persians', in John Hackett (ed.), *Warfare in the Ancient World* (London, 1989), p.99. Alexander later experimented with a hybrid phalanx with some ranks equipped as archers.
43. Arrian, *Anabasis Alexandri*, ii, c.8.
44. Ibid., ii, c.10.
45. Ibid., ii, c.11.
46. According to Quintus Curtius Rufus, *History of Alexander*, iii, c.2, both horses and riders 'were weighed down by their rows of armour-plating'.
47. Ibid.
48. Arrian, *Anabasis Alexandri*, ii, c.11
49. Ibid., c.10.
50. Ibid., c.10.
51. Ibid., c.11.
52. Ibid., c.11.
53. Diodorus, *Universal History*, xvii, c.5.
54. Quintus Curtius Rufus, *History of Alexander*, iv, c.9, line 3.
55. Ibid., line 4.
56. Ibid., line 9.
57. Xenophon, *Anabasis*, translated by Rex Warner under the title *The Persian Expedition* (London, 1949), i, c.8; at Cunaxa, allegedly, only one man was slightly hurt by the chariots.

58. Xenophon, *Hellenica*, translated by Rex Warner (London, 1966), iv, c.1, lines 17–19.

59. Arrian, *Anabasis*, iii, c.11. If the Persian infantry guard retained their traditional ornamented spears, this may be a further clue that the new longer spears were intended for the cavalry.

60. Ibid. I have followed Arrian's account here, not least because the centre was the traditional position for the Persian king in battle. Quintus Curtius Rufus, *History of Alexander*, iv, c.14, line 5, has Darius leading the fight from the left flank surrounded by men selected from his infantry and cavalry.

61. Arrian, *Anabasis*, iii, c.16. Darius escaped with the 'Bactrians that he had kept posted by him in the fight'. It is possibly a reference to these Bactrians that made Curtius think that Darius was on the left with Bessus' main Bactrian contingent.

62. As the Agrianians had demonstrated at Granicus, even lightly armed infantrymen moving among cavalry that were already bogged down in a static fight with other horsemen could do a lot of damage.

63. Arrian, *Anabasis Alexandri*, iii, c.13.

64. Ibid.

65. Quintus Curtius Rufus, *History of Alexander*, iv, c.15, line 16.

66. Ibid., line 4.

67. Arrian, *Anabasis Alexandri*, iii, c.13

68. Ibid., c.14.

69. Plutarch, *Alexander*, c.33.

70. Arrian, *Anabasis Alexandri*, iii, c.14.

71. Quintus Curtius Rufus, *History of Alexander*, iv, c.15, line 24.

72. Arrian, *Anabasis Alexandri*, iii, c.14.

73. Arrian, *Anabasis Alexandri*, iii, c.15.

74. Quintus Curtius Rufus, *History of Alexander*, iv, c.16, line 23.

75. Arrian, *Anabasis Alexandri*, iii, c.15.

76. Arrian, *Anabasis Alexandri*, iv, c.4.

77. Arrian, *Anabasis Alexandri*, iv, c.4, and Quintus Curtius Rufus, *History of Alexander*, vii, c.9, line 15.

78. Quintus Curtius Rufus, *History of Alexander*, vii, c.9, line 17.

79. Ibid., c.13, lines 8–9.

80. Arrian, *Anabasis Alexandri*, v, c.11.

81. Arrian, *Anabasis Alexandri*, v, c.14.

82. Quintus Curtius Rufus, *History of Alexander*, viii, c.14, lines 2–3.

83. Arrian, *Anabasis*, v, c.15.

84. Infantry: Diodorus Siculus, *Universal History*, xvii, c.10, says 50,000;

Arrian, *Anabasis Alexandri*, v, c.15, and Quintus Curtius Rufus, *History of Alexander*, viii, c.13, line 6, agree on 30,000; Plutarch, *Alexander*, c.62, says 20,000. Cavalry and Chariots: Arrian 4000 cavalry and 300 chariots; Quintus Curtius also has 300 chariots and mentions 4000 cavalry, although in the advanced force; Diodorus says 'above 3000 cavalry' and 'above 1000 chariots', so 4000 horse-borne troops in total. Plutarch gives 2000 cavalry.

85. Arrian, *Anabasis Alexandri*, v, c.15.
86. Quintus Curtius Rufus, *History of Alexander*, viii, c.14, line 19.
87. Diodorus Siculus, *Universal History*, xvii, c.10; Quintus Curtius Rufus, viii, c.14, line 13.
88. Plutarch, *Alexander*, c.60.
89. Arrian, *Anabasis Alexandri*, v, c.16.
90. Quintus Curtius Rufus, *History of Alexander*, viii, c.14, line 14.
91. Arrian, *Anabasis Alexandri*, v, c.17.
92. Ibid.
93. Diodorus, *Universal History*, xvii, c.10.
94. Quintus Curtius Rufus, *History of Alexander*, viii, c.14, lines 18–19.
95. Arrian, *Anabasis Alexandri*, v, c.17.
96. Diodorus Siculus, *Universal History*, xvii, c.10.
97. Arrian, *Anabasis Alexandri*, v, c.17.
98. Quintus Curtius Rufus, *History of Alexander*, viii, c.14, lines 26–28.
99. Diodorus, *Universal History*, xvii, c.10, and Quintus Curtius Rufus, *History of Alexander*, viii, c.14, line 19.
100. Eight hours according to Plutarch, *Alexander*, c.60; 'till late in the day', according to Quintus Curtius Rufus, *History of Alexander*, viii, c.14, line 28.
101. Arrian, *Anabasis Alexandri*, v, c.18.
102. M.H.Hayes, *The Student's Tactical Manual* (London, 1884), p.26.

Notes to Chapter 4: The Successors

1. Diodorus Siculus, *Universal History*, translated by G.Booth (London, 1814), xviii, c.2.
2. Prior to the battle of Issus, Antigonus had defeated a series of Persian attacks aimed at cutting Alexander's lines of communication as he marched south into Syria.
3. The Antigonid dynasty's grip on the Macedonian throne was interrupted only by a brief spell when Pyrrhus of Epirus seized power.
4. Diodorus Siculus, *Universal History*, xix, c.6.

5. Ibid.

6. Ibid., xix, c.2.

7. Ibid.

8. Ibid. Eumenes wanted to resume the battle the next day, but the Argyraspids betrayed him and handed him over to Antigonus in return for their baggage, which had been captured by a light cavalry detachment while the battle was still raging.

9. Plutarch, *Demetrius*, translated by Ian Scott-Kilvert (London, 1973), c.29.

10. Diodorus, *Universal History*, xix, c.6.

11. Plutarch, *Pyrrhus*, translated by Ian Scott-Kilvert (London, 1973), c.30.

12. Diodorus Siculus, *Universal History*, xviii, c.3.

13. Xenophon, *On Horsemanship*, c.12, verse 9.

14. Ian Heath, *Armies of the Macedonian and Punic Wars* (Worthing, 1982), p.117. As Ian Heath pointed out, 'illustrations of Hellenistic cavalry with the long spear are quite numerous, and so are illustrations of cavalry with shields; it is not likely to be coincidence that the two are never seen together'.

15. Mostly these were mercenaries equipped in 'Tarantine' style, rather than men actually from Taras.

16. Livy, *The History of Rome*, translated by Henry Bettenson (London, 1976), xxxi, c.35.

17. Ibid., c.33.

18. See Mielczarek, M., *Cataphracti and Clibanrii* (Lodz, 1993), plate 15, p.133.

19. Flexible horse armour covering the horse's body would be a 'trapper', 'housing' or 'barding'; the Pergamum piece might equate to a 'half-trapper'.

20. Quintus Curtius Rufus, *The History of Alexander*, translated by John Yardley (London, 1984), iv, c.9, line 3.

21. Livy, *History of Rome*, xxxvii, c.40.

22. Livy, *History of Rome*, xxxvii, c.41.

23. Ibid.

24. Ibid., c.42.

25. Ibid.

26. See, for example, Lynn White Jr., *Medieval Technology and Social Change* (Oxford, 1962), p.9, where it is suggested that a charge of cataphracts would amount to 'general suicide'.

Notes to Chapter 5: Early Rome

1. John Warry, *Warfare in the Classical World* (London, 1980), p. 109.
2. By the Roman dating system this was year 1 AUC, *ab urbe condita*, from the founding of the city.
3. Members and former members of the senate formed the senatorial class at the pinnacle of Roman society, but they started their careers as equestrians, so they can be considered an elite subset of that class.
4. The question is not beyond doubt, Polybius saying in one place that 200 cavalry was the norm, only expanding to 300 in emergencies. Livy contradicts his own earlier statement by describing the cavalry being expanded from 200 to 300 before Cannae. All Polybius' other descriptions of legionary organization assume 300 cavalry and this fits more easily with their internal organization. Compare Polybius, *Histories*, i, c. 16; iii, c. 109; vi, c. 20; and Livy, *History of Rome*, viii, c. 7; and xxii, c. 36.
5. Plutarch, *Corolianus*, c. 14.
6. Livy, *History of Rome*, iv, c. 20.
7. Livy, *History of Rome*, viii, c. 7.
8. Robert L. O'Connell, *Of Arms and Men* (New York and Oxford, 1989), p. 74.
9. Livy, *History of Rome*, ii, c. 20.
10. Livy, *History of Rome*, vii, c. 8.
11. Michel Feugère, *Weapons of the Romans*, translated by David G. Smith (Stroud, 2002), p. 83.
12. Polybius, *Histories*, vi, c. 25.
13. Livy, *History of Rome*, v, c. 38.
14. Plutarch, *Marcellus*, c. 6.
15. Livy, *History of Rome*, x, c. 26.
16. Ibid.
17. Livy, *History of Rome*, x. c. 28
18. Ibid.
19. Plutarch, *Pyrrhus*, c. 16.
20. Ibid.
21. Ibid.
22. Plutarch, *Pyrrhus*, c. 17.
23. Plutarch, *Pyrrhus*, c. 21.
24. Polybius, *Histories*, ii, cc. 22–23.
25. Polybius, *Histories*, ii, c. 28.
26. Polybius, *Histories*, ii, c. 30.
27. Plutarch, *Marcellus*, ch. 6.

28. Plutarch, *Marcellus*, ch.7.

29. Ibid.

30. Polybius, *Histories*, ii, c.34.

31. Plutarch, *Marcellus*, ch.7.

32. Polybius, *Histories*, i, c.34.

33. Appian, *Roman History*, translated by Horace White (London and New York, 1899), vii, c.9.

34. Polybius, *Histories*, iii, c.45.

35. The Roman subjugation of Celtic north Italy had been more or less completed in the years following the victory at Clastidium, but the establishment of colonies along the Po, at Placentia and Cremona, had driven the Boii and Insubres to take up arms again shortly before Hannibal's arrival.

36. Polybius, *Histories*, iii, c.65. Livy states that he was following the 'greater number of historians' in stating that Scipio's own son, also called Publius, led the rescue, but acknowledges a divergent tradition. *History of Rome*, xxi, c.46.

37. Polybius, *Histories*, iii, c.72.

38. Polybius, *Histories*, iii, c.74; Livy, *History of Rome*, xxi, cc.54–56.

39. The surviving accounts of Livy and Polybius tally very well. Livy specifically says his was based on that of Quintus Fabius Pictor, 'a contemporary witness of these events' who may even have been with the cavalry. Polybius, closer in time than Livy, probably had other contemporary sources in addition to Pictor, and may even have spoken to aged survivors of the battle.

40. Polybius, *Histories*, iii, cc.87–88.

41. Polybius, *Histories*, iii, c.101.

42. Polybius, *Histories*, iii, c.116.

43. Livy, *History of Rome*, xxii, c.47.

44. Livy, *History of Rome*, xxii, c.47; Polybius, *Histories*, iii, c.114.

45. Polybius, *Histories*, iii, c.115.

46. Gregory Daly, *Cannae* (London and New York, 2002), p.75.

47. Livy, *History of Rome*, xxii, c.47.

48. Livy, *History of Rome*, xxii, c.38. This oath had apparently been common among the men previously but this was the first time it had been made compulsory and officially administered.

49. Polybius, *Histories*, iii, c.117. The emphasis is mine.

50. Livy, *History of Rome*, xxv, c.19.

51. Livy, *History of Rome*, xxvi, c.4.

52. Appian, *Roman History*, vii, c.30.

53. Livy, *History of Rome*, xxiii, c.26.

54. Livy, *History of Rome*, xxiii, c. 29. Livy relates that there were five hundred Moorish cavalry present whose normal practice was to lead a spare horse into battle and, when the first tired, leap 'like circus riders, fully armed onto the back of the fresh one'. On this occasion they were forced to flee with the rest.
55. This was the same Publius Scipio who had encountered Hannibal's troops on the Rhône, Ticinus and Trebbia.
56. Livy, *History of Rome*, xxv, c. 34.
57. Polybius, *Histories*, x, cc. 38–39. The battle itself offered little chance for cavalry action, the Romans attacking the Carthaginians in their camp on a fortified plateau.
58. Livy, *History of Rome*, xxviii, c. 13.
59. Livy, *History of Rome*, xxviii, c. 14.
60. Livy, *History of Rome*, xxviii, c. 15.
61. Polybius, *Histories*, xv, c. 12.
62. Polybius, *Histories*, xv, c. 14.

Notes to Chapter 6: Later Republican Rome

1. Livy, *History of Rome*, xxxi, c. 33. See Chapter 4 above.
2. Ibid., c. 34.
3. Ibid., c. 35. See Chapter 4 above.
4. Livy, *History of Rome*, xxxvii, cc. 39–44.
5. Appian, *Roman History*, vi, c. 11.
6. Ibid., c. 12.
7. Mcipsa died in 118 BC, bequeathing his kingdom to Jugurtha and to his two natural sons Hiempsal and Adherbal. Jugurtha had Hiempsal killed but Adherbal fled to Rome, whereupon the Roman senate forced Jugurtha to accept an equal division with Adherbal, an uneasy arrangement lasting until 112 BC.
8. Sallust, *Jugurthine War*, c. 48.
9. Ibid., c. 45.
10. Ibid., c. 98.
11. Plutarch, *Marius*, cc. 25–27.
12. This force had been led by Arcathias, another of Mithridates' many sons, but he died shortly after his promising success, so Archelaus' authority to take his troops under command was undisputed.
13. Plutarch, *Pompey*, c. 6.
14. Ibid., c. 7.
15. Plutarch, *Sulla*, c. 29.

16. Ibid., c. 29.

17. Adrian Goldsworthy, *In the Name of Rome* (London, 2003), pp. 142–45.

18. Plutarch, *Pompey*, c. 17.

19. Ibid., c. 32; Appian, *Mithridates*, cc. 99–101.

20. Julius Caesar, *The Gallic Wars*, translated by S. A. Handford, revised by J. F. Gardiner (London, 1982), i, c. 42.

21. Ibid., ii, c. 11.

22. Ibid., ii, c. 27.

23. Ibid., vi, c. 29.

24. Ibid., iv, c. 24.

25. Ibid., iv, c. 26.

26. Ibid., iv, c. 33.

27. Ibid., iv, c. 34.

28. Ibid., v, cc. 1–8.

29. Ibid., v, c. 9.

30. Ibid., v, c. 15.

31. Ibid., v, c. 16.

32. Ibid., v, c. 17.

33. Ibid., v, cc. 18–23.

34. See, in particular, Ann Hyland, *Training the Roman Cavalry* (London, 1993), ch. 5.

35. Caesar, *The Gallic Wars*, iv, c. 2.

36. Ibid., i, c. 48.

37. Ibid., i, cc. 48–53.

38. Ibid., iv, c. 12.

39. Ibid., iv, c. 13.

40. Ibid., vii, c. 4.

41. Ibid., vii, c. 13.

42. Ibid., vii, c. 18.

43. Ibid., vii, c. 36.

44. Ibid., vii, c. 55.

45. Ibid., vii, c. 65.

46. Ibid., vii, c. 66.

47. Ibid., vii, c. 67.

48. Professor P. A. G. Sabin in lectures at the Department of War Studies, King's College, London, 1996.

49. Caesar, *Gallic Wars*, vii, c. 80.

50. Ibid., vii, c. 88.

51. Plutarch, *Crassus*, c. 17, translated by Rex Warner in *The Fall of the Roman Republic* (London, 1972).

52. Ibid., c. 23.
53. Ibid., c. 24.
54. Ibid., c. 24.
55. Ibid., c. 24.
56. Ibid., c. 25.
57. Ibid., c. 25.
58. Ibid., c. 25.
59. Ibid., c. 25.
60. Ibid., c. 27.
61. Julius Caesar, *The Civil War*, translated by J. F. Gardner (London, 1967), i, c. 14.
62. Ibid., i, c. 24.
63. Plutarch, *Pompey*, translated by Rex Warner, in *The Fall of the Roman Republic* (London, 1972), c. 64.
64. Caesar, *Civil War*, i, c. 29.
65. Ibid., i. cc. 38–41.
66. Ibid., i, c. 57.
67. Ibid., i, c. 59.
68. Ibid., i, c. 79.
69. Ibid., ii, c. 41.
70. Ibid., iii, cc. 43–81.
71. Ibid., iii, c. 4.
72. Anonymous, *The Spanish War*, c. 31, translated by J. F. Gardner and published with Caesar's *Civil War* (London, 1967).
73. Caesar, *Civil War*, iii, c. 84.
74. Plutarch, *Pompey*, c. 64.
75. Ibid., c. 69.
76. Anonymous, *The African War*, c. 6, translated by J. F. Gardner and published with Caesar's *Civil War* (London, 1967).
77. Ibid., c. 18.
78. Ibid., cc. 40–41.
79. Anon., *The Spanish War*, ii, c. 31.

Notes to Chapter 7: Imperial Rome

1. Largely on the basis of Tacitus' comment that the auxiliary forces were 'scarcely inferior' in number to the legions, but broadly supported by estimates based on epigraphic evidence.
2. Equestrian status was still gained by a wealth qualification but was divorced from the traditional obligation of mounted service. Although

some equestrians still pursued a military career, they were to be found as officers of either infantry or cavalry.

3. Confusingly, under the early and middle Republic, *ala* originally referred to the whole contingent of allies that accompanied the legions, comprising both cavalry and infantry, because these had formed the wings of the army, being stationed on each flank of the citizen legions.

4. Josephus, *The Jewish War*, iii, c.92.

5. Josephus, *The Jewish War*, iii, c.2.

6. Tacitus, *Agricola*, c.37.

7. After the square vexillum standard such detachments carried.

8. Arrian, 'Ars Tactica', translated in Ann Hyland, *Training the Roman Cavalry From Arrian's Ars Tactica* (London, 1993), p.70.

9. Tacitus, *Histories*, i, c.79.

10. Pausanius, i, c.21, quoted in R.Brzezinski and M.Mielczarek, *The Sarmatians* (Oxford, 2002), p.20.

11. Another, the Iazyges, adopted a pro-Roman stance during the Dacian wars and may have offered active assistance, providing Trajan with some irregular troops. It was under Trajan's reign that the practice became established of supplementing the regular legions and auxiliaries by hiring 'barbarian' troops en bloc along the empire's borders. Such irregular troops, known as *symacharii* or *feoderates* were not organized or equipped along Roman lines but fought in their native style.

12. Valerius Flaccus, *Argonautica*, vi, 233 quoted in Brzezinski and Mielczarek, *The Sarmatians*, p.18.

13. Arrian, *Acies contra Alanos*.

14. *Cavalry Training* (War office, 1904), p.32.

15. Quoted in Ann Hyland, *Training the Roman Cavalry*, p.5.

16. Josephus, *The Jewish War*, iii, cc.24–28.

17. Ammianus Marcellinus, *Histories*, trans Wallace Hadrill, published as *The Later Roman Empire* (London, 1986), xxv, c.1, v. 5.

18. Ammianus Marcellinus, *Histories*, xvi, c.10.

19. For a discussion of the issue see Mariusz Mielczarek, *Cataphracti and Clibanarii* (Lodz, 1993), passim.

20. Some see a tantalizing link between this and the historical basis for the legend of King Arthur. The Sarmatians would have been horsemen, some at least clad in shining mail (though not uniquely so among Britannia's garrison) and fighting under a dragon standard (although again not uniquely, for *draco* standards were widely used by the late Roman army). Add to this that Sarmatian religious beliefs, true to their Scythian roots, included the veneration of an ancient sword plunged in the ground, and

connections are tempting indeed. A Sarmatian unit was still based in Lancashire in the third century and there is archaeological evidence for their presence around AD 400, just before the official Roman abandonment of Britain. At one point they were even commanded by one Lucius *Artorius* Castus. See R. Brzezinski and M. Mielczarek, *The Sarmatians* (Oxford, 2002), pp. 40–41.

21. Isidore of Seville, *History of the Goths*, c. 70.

22. Procopius, quoted in Ann Hyland, *The Medieval Warhorse from Byzantium to the Crusades* (Stroud, 1996), p. 25.

23. Zosimus, *New History* (London, 1814), i, c. 45.

24. Ibid.

25. G. L. Cheeseman, *The Auxilia of the Roman Army* (1914), *passim*.

26. Flavius Renatus Vegetius, *De Re Militari*, iii.

27. Ibid., i.

28. Ammianus Marcellinus, *Histories*, xvi, c. 12.

29. Ibid., xxv, c. 3.

30. Ibid., xxxi, c. 12.

31. Ibid., xxxi, c. 12.

32. Ibid., xxxi, c. 13.

33. Sidonius Apollinarius, quoted in Peter Heather, *The Fall of the Roman Empire* (London, 2005), p. 335.

34. Ammianus Marcellinus, *Histories*, xxxi, c. 2.

35. Jordanes, *Getica*, translated by C. C. Mierow (Princeton, 1908), c. xl, 207.

36. Jordanes, *Getica*, c. xl, 211.

37. Maurice, *Strategikon*, translated by George T. Dennis, (Philadelphia, 1984), introduction to book xi.

38. Maurice, *Strategikon*, i. c. 2.

Notes to Chapter 8: *The Medieval Knight*

1. Lynn White Jr, *Medieval Technology and Social Change* (Oxford, 1962), p. 2.

2. From the chronicle of Isidore of Beja, quoted in William Stearns Davis, ed., *Readings in Ancient History: Illustrative Extracts from the Sources*, ii, *Rome and the West* (Boston, 1913), p. 364.

3. Chronicle of St Denis, quoted in Davis, *Readings in Ancient History*, ii, p. 364.

4. Anonymous Arab Chronicler, quoted in Davis, *Readings in Ancient History*, ii, p. 362.

5. *Annales Regni Francorum* (revised), s.a. 782, in P. D. King, *Charlemagne: Translated Sources* (Kendal, 1987), p. 117.
6. Robert L. O'Connell, *Of Arms and Men: A History of War, Weapons and Aggression* (New York and Oxford, 1989), p. 85.
7. Lynn White Jr, *Medieval Technology and Social Change* (Oxford, 1962), drawing on Heinrich Brunner, 'Der Reiterdienst und die Anfange des Lehnwesens', *Zeitschrift der Savigny-Stiftung für Rechtsgeschichte, Germanische Abteilung*, 8, (1887).
8. Ann Hyland, *The Horse in the Ancient World* (Stroud, 2003), p. 54.
9. Ann Hyland, *The Medieval Warhorse: From Byzantium to the Crusades* (Stroud, 1994), p. 11.
10. John Man, *Attila* (London, 2005) pp. 53–56.
11. Hyland, *The Medieval Warhorse*, p. 11.
12. Ibid., p. 45.
13. Ibid., p. 45.
14. David Nicolle, *The Armies of Islam, 7–11th Centuries* (London, 1982) pp. 14 and 17.
15. Gregory of Tours, *Historiae Francorum*, iii, c. 7.
16. Reproduced in D. Quammen, 'The Ineffable Union of Horse and Man', *Military History Quarterly*, 1, no. 2 (Winter 1989).
17. Bernard Bachrach, 'Charles Martel, Shock combat, the stirrup and feudalism', *Armies and Politics in the Early Medieval West* (Aldershot, 1993), p. 54.
18. Ibid., p. 61.
19. Quoted in R. H. C. Davis, *Medieval Warhorse: Origin, Development and Redevelopment* (London, 1989) pp. 14–15.
20. Anna Comnena, *Alexiad* (Harmondsworth, 1969), pp. 163–5 and 416.
21. White, *Medieval Technology*, p. 1.
22. D. H. Gordon, 'Swords, Rapiers and Horsemen', *Antiquity*, 37 (1953), p. 75.
23. The author's own experiments and exercises observed at The Medieval Tournament School on 15 March 1998 – including eight stirrupless riders cantering in two concentric circles, in opposite directions, striking repeated blows upon shields with various practice weapons.
24. White, *Medieval Technology*, p. 2.
25. Ibid., p. 27.
26. My thanks to Russell Chalk and Heath Pye for sharing their jousting experience in telephone conversations with the author; Janet Rodgers and Roger 'Faris' Collins and their students at the Medieval Tournament School for my visit on 15 March 1998, and Faris again for subsequent phone calls.

27. Opinion on St Gallen Psalter, Ann Hyland, *Medieval Warhorse*, p.7. Portugese saddle viewed by courtesy of Janet Rodgers of the Medieval Tournament School.

28. Ian Heath, *Armies of the Dark Ages, 600–1066* (Worthing, 1980), p.89.

29. Andrew Ayton, 'Arms, Armour and Warhorses', in *Medieval Warfare: A History*, edited by Maurice Keen (Oxford, 1999), pp.187–88.

30. Hyland, *The Medieval Warhorse*, pp.3, 67, 86.

31. William of Jumièges, *Gesta Normannorum Ducum*, translated in Stephen Morillo, ed., *The Battle of Hastings: Sources and Interpretations* (Woodbridge, 1996), p.18.

32. The Anglo-Saxon Chronicle, 'D', entry for 1066, in Morillo, *Battle of Hastings: Sources*, p.24.

33. For a superbly clear and concise presentation of the arguments see Jim Bradbury, *The Battle of Hastings* (Stroud, 1996), pp.168–178. Bradbury favours Caldbec Hill.

34. *Carmen de Hastingae Proelio*, in Morillo, *Battle of Hastings: Sources*, p.46.

35. Ibid.

36. William of Poitiers, *Gesta Willelmi ducis Normannorum et regis Anglorum*, in Morillo (ed.), *Battle of Hastings: Sources*, p.13.

37. Ibid., p.12.

38. *Carmen*, in Morillo, *Battle of Hastings: Sources*, p.47.

39. Ibid., p.47.

40. William of Poitiers, *Gesta Willelmi*, in Morillo, *Battle of Hastings: Sources*, p.12.

41. *Carmen*, in Morillo, *Battle of Hastings: Sources*, p.47.

42. William of Poitiers, *Gesta Willelmi*, in Morillo, *Battle of Hastings: Sources*, pp.12–13.

43. *Carmen*, in Morillo, *Battle of Hastings: Sources*, p.47.

44. William of Poitiers, *Gesta Willelmi*, in Morillo, *Battle of Hastings: Sources*, p.13.

45. Ibid., p.13.

46. *Carmen*, in Morillo, *Battle of Hastings: Sources*, p.48.

47. William of Poitierrs, *Gesta Willelmi*, in Morillo, *Battle of Hastings: Sources*, p.14. Note that the author of the *Carmen* has it that the first retreat had been deliberate, at least on the part of the French contingent (he is thought to have been French himself), and that this second retreat was the genuine panic which William rallied with bared head. For our purpose the exact sequence of event matters little; both agree that the first two cavalry attacks ended in flight, one induced by fear, the other controlled.

48. William of Poiters, *Gesta Willelmi*, in Morillo, *Battle of Hastings: Sources*, p.14.
49. *Carmen*, in Morillo, *Battle of Hastings: Sources*, p. 49.
50. William of Jumièges, *Gesta Normannorum*, p.18.
51. William of Poitiers, *Gesta Willelmi*, in Morillo, *Battle of Hastings: Sources*, p.15.

Glossary

Ala: Literally meaning a 'wing', this originally referred to the contingents of troops, both infantry and cavalry, sent to fight for the Romans by their allies. By the early Imperial period it denoted an auxiliary unit entirely of cavalry.

Brunia or byrnie: Short sleeved, waist-length shirt of scale or chain mail.

Caetra: A small round shield carried by some Iberian and Celtiberian warriors, both infantry and cavalry.

Cantle: The rearmost part of a saddle, which rises behind the rider's seat.

Cardiophylax: A simple rectangular or circular metal plate strapped to the chest worn in early Italian armies, offering much less protection than a cuirass or chainmail shirt, but far cheaper and lighter than either.

Cataphract: A type of very heavy lancer with both rider and horse well-protected by armour. The name is first used in relation to Seleucid cavalry of the early second century BC.

Chamfron: A piece of armour protecting a horse's face. This is a medieval term.

Clibanarius: A Persian term, usually translated as 'oven-wearer'. It probably originated as a nick name for cataphracts but in later Roman usage seems to have been a designation for certain units.

Cohors Equitata: A mixed unit of cavalry and infantry introduced under the early Roman Empire.

Companions: Macedonian heavy cavalry drawn predominantly from the native aristocracy with a sprinkling of foreigners admitted on merit.

Contarii: Roman cavalry armed with the contus in imitation of Sarmatian warriors (see kontos, below).

Coif: A chain mail hood.

Couching: the technique of using a lance by tucking the shaft under the armpit and holding tight against the body. It was developed in the Middle Ages.

Cuirass: Rigid upper body armour, comprising a breastplate and, usually, a back plate. Cuirasses are still worn for ceremonial duty by the Household Cavalry.

Decuria: Subdivision of a Roman turma (see below), nominally of ten men.

Decurio: Commander of a decuria. The senior decurio in each turma also commanded that turma.

Dekas (plural dekades): A tactical subdivision of a phyle or other unit, nominally of ten men and forming one file in normal formation.

Dekadarchos: Commander of a dekas.

Destrier: A large very muscular type of warhorse bred in the late middle ages.

Doru: Generic Greek word for a thrusting spear, as apposed to one thrown as a javelin. The most common type in the Classical period was about eight feet long with an iron blade and a spike, or *saurator* (literally a 'lizarder'), on the butt end.

Draco: A standard in the form of a beast with a gaping mouth and a long windsock-like body which emitted an eerie wailing when moving at speed. Of barbarian, probably Sarmatian, origin, it was adopted by Roman units and born by a *draconarius*.

Equestrian: Roman citizens exceeding a certain level of wealth formed the equestrian class (ordo equestris). Until the first century BC this social status, second only to that of senators, carried the obligation (and privelege) of performing military service as cavalrymen (equites), rather than as footsoldiers.

Equites: Latin for horsemen.

Equites legionis: The cavalry contingent attached to each legion.

Extraordinarii: Troops selected from republican Rome's Italian allies, amounting to one third of the cavalry and one fifth of the infantry contingents provided. They formed the vanguard and rearguard on the march and, probably, a reserve under the general's direct control in battle.

Falcata: A recurved sword used by Iberian warriors, similar to the Greek kopis but with a less exaggerated curve and a useful point allowing both cut and thrust.

Fyrd: That part of Anglo-Saxon armies made up of a general levy of the populace.

Girpisu: A helmet in the language of Mitanni.

Greaves: Shin guards.

Hand: The unit of measurement of the height of horses, equal to four inches. A horse's height in hands is measured from the withers, at the base of the mane where the neck joins the shoulder, to the floor.

Hauberk: A long shirt of chain mail.

Hipparch: A Greek cavalry commander. In Athens in the fourth century BC two hipparchs were appointed each year.

Hipparchia: The cavalry commanded by a hipparch.

Hippeus: A horseman in ancient Greece. Only the wealthiest could afford to serve as cavalry so the word carried huge social significance.

Hoplite: A Greek heavy infantryman armed with a spear and protected by a distinctive large round shield and varying degrees of armour.

Huscarles: Full time Saxon warriors forming the core of Anglo-Saxon armies.

Hypaspists: Literally 'shield carriers'. The elite Macedonian infantry guard, which Alexander deployed on the right of the phalanx, next to the Companion cavalry.

Ila: Macedonian cavalry unit. Each ila of Alexander's Companions was a little over two hundred strong, except the Ile Basilike (Royal Squadron), which was three hundred strong.

Kardakes: A corps of Persian heavy infantry, probably intended to provide a home-grown equivalent to the Greek hoplite. They were fielded by Darius at the battle of Issus where they were destroyed by Alexander's Companions.

Katoiki: The Seleucid equivalent of klerouchoi.

Kleros: A plot of farm land given in return for military service under the Ptolemaic kings of Egypt.

Klerouchoi: Troops serving in return for the grant of a kleros.

Kontos: (latin form contus): A long, heavy lance usually wielded in both hands. The Romans may have adopted it from Sarmatian tribesmen and sometimes called it the *contus Sarmaticus*.

Kopis: A recurved sword, similar in general shape to the Gurkha kukri, designed for slashing and hacking, recommended for horsemen by Xenophon.

Lamellar armour: Armour made up of strips of metal laced to each other and to a fabric or leather backing.

Latifundia: Large industrial farms run by slave labour.

Lochos: A subdivision of an ila.

Machaira: Literally 'chopper'; an alternative name for the kopis.

Magister Equitum: Master of Horse. Deputy appointed by a Roman dictator. Although the name suggests this office originally had some special responsibility for the cavalry, in the period for which good sources exist both the dictator and the magister equitum could command any type of troops.

Milliaria: Designation applied to an ala or cohors equitata to denote that it was the larger of two unit sizes (the other being quingenaria). An ala milliaria contained twenty-four turmae, theoretically 768 horsemen. A cohors equitata milliaria probably contained 256 cavalry in eight turmae and approximately eight hundred infantry.

Milu: In Mitanni, armour for the horse's neck made from thick felt or hair.

Ouragos: In a Greek formation, the man appointed to the rear place in a file. Often chosen from among the oldest and most experienced men to stop those in front from running away.

Optio: Junior Roman officer appointed by a decurio to be his deputy.

Paides Basilikoi: Royal Pages. Under Philip and Alexander, the sons of Macedonian nobles served their king as pages, simultaneously being educated and trained for service as Companions and acting as guarantees of their fathers' loyalty.

Parma Equestris: Circular Roman cavalry shield.

Peltast: A type of light infantry, recruited from or modelled on Thracian warriors. They were better equipped than psiloi but more lightly equipped and in more flexible formation than hoplites. Usually armed with javelins and a light shield, the latter originally being the traditional crescent-shaped Thracian *pelta*.

Pommel: The front part of a saddle which rises, to varying degrees, in front of the rider.

Parashshamu: In Mitanni, a protective horse blanket made from thick felt or hair.

Pempadarchos: Leader of five men in Xenophon's recommended formation.

Peytral: A medieval term for armour for the horse's chest.

Phalangite: Member of a phalanx, particularly a Macedonian or Hellenistic pike phalanx rather than one of traditional Greek hoplites.

Phalanx: A dense formation of infantry, particularly spearmen such as hoplites or Hellenistic pikemen. The word literally means a roller. It was very difficult to penetrate frontally, especially for cavalry, but could be clumsy and was vulnerable if attacked in flank or rear.

Phylarch: The commander of one phyle of cavalry.

Phyle: A 'tribe' or administrative division of Athens, of which there were ten. In the scheme described by Xenophon each phyle was to provide one hundred horsemen who would serve together as a tactical unit, which may also be called a phyle.

Praefectus Equitum: Roman officer in command of auxiliary cavalry.

Prodromoi: Literally 'front runners'. A term used by Xenophon to mean riders sent to scout ahead of a cavalry unit, but under Alexander denoting specialist light cavalry units, who seem also to be known as Sarissophoroi.

Psiloi: The very lightly armed infantry drawn from the poorest citizens of Greek states.

Pteruges: Flexible strips of leather or thick fabric hanging from the lower edge of a cuirass to protect the groin and upper thighs.

Quingenaria: Designation applied to ala and cohors equitata indicating that the unit was of the smaller, more common size (as opposed to units designated as milliaria). Such an ala contained just over five hundred men in sixteen turmae, while a cohors equitata so designated probably contained 128 horsemen in four turmae and between four and five hundred infantry.

Sariam: In Mitanni, a coat of scale armour worn by chariot crews.

Sarissa: The long pike used by the Macedonian phalanx from Philip II's reign, and some specialist units of cavalry (the Sarissophoroi) during Alexander's reign, at which time the sarissa was probably around fifteen feet long, although a shorter cavalry version is often assumed. Sarissae used by later phalanxes could exceed twenty feet.

Sarissophoroi: A unit of Macedonian cavalry equipped with the sarissa.

Scara: (pl. scarae) A tactical unit of cavalry in Frankish armies of the Carolingian period. It is the word from which 'squadron' derives.

Sagaris: A battleaxe, often with a pick-like head for punching through armour.

Scutum: Long oval or, later, rectangular body shield used by Roman infantry.

Spatha: Long straight sword used by Roman cavalry.

Spolia Opima: The ultimate honour achievable by a Roman for individual prowess, awarded for killing an enemy king or chieftain in single combat and stripping him of his armour. Only granted three times, it conferred the right to hang the captured armour in the temple of Jupiter.

Tarantine: A type of light cavalry equipped with large shield and javelins, modelled upon those of the city of Taras in Italy.

Triarii: Heavy infantry consisting of older veterans, forming the last of three main lines in the traditional Roman battle formation.

Triplex Acies: The traditional battle formation of the Roman legion, consisting of three lines of heavy infantry.

Turma: Basic tactical unit of Roman cavalry, usually about thirty men.

Velites: Roman javelin-armed light infantry skirmishers.

Wedge: A triangular formation of cavalry designed to allow rapid changes of direction and the delivery of a concentrated charge to break into or through enemy formations. It was believed to have been invented by the Scythians or Thracians but was most famously used by the Macedonian cavalry.

Xiphos: Greek name for a straight thrusting sword.

Xyston: Macedonian and Hellenistic cavalry lance, probably about 12 feet long with a secondary head on the butt of a tapered shaft to improve its balance, allowing it to be wielded in one hand.

Index